THE DOW STORY

THE DOW STORY

The History of the Dow Chemical Company

BY DON WHITEHEAD

McGRAW-HILL BOOK COMPANY

New York   St. Louis   San Francisco   Auckland
Bogotá   Hamburg   Johannesburg   London   Madrid
Mexico   Montreal   New Delhi   Panama   Paris
São Paulo   Singapore   Sydney   Tokyo   Toronto

THE DOW STORY: The History of the Dow Chemical Company

Copyright © 1968 by McGraw-Hill, Inc. All Rights Reserved.
Printed in the United States of America. No part of this
publication may be reproduced, stored in a retrieval system, or
transmitted, in any form or by any means, electronic, mechanical,
photocopying, recording, or otherwise, without the prior written
permission of the publisher.

2 3 4 5 6 7 8 9 DOC DOC 8 9 8 7 6 5 4 3

ISBN 0-07-069948-8

Library of Congress Cataloging in Publication Data
Whitehead, Don, 1908-1981
  The Dow Story.

  Reprint. Originally published: New York: McGraw-Hill,
1968.
  Includes index.
  1. Dow Chemical Company — History. 2. Dow, Herbert
Henry, 1866-1930. 3. Chemical industry — United States —
History. I. Title.
HD9651.9.D6W45 1983   338.7'66'00973   83-19959

AUTHOR'S NOTE

Gathering material for this volume involved several months of research that included many interviews, sorting through private papers and business correspondence, delving into the files of The Dow Chemical Company, and visiting company plants and offices in the United States and Canada. Many people gave generously of their time. Most especially I wish to acknowledge the help of Miss Ruth Perry, secretary of former president, Leland I. Doan, and custodian of the archives. Others who contributed much were Earl W. Bennett, A. P. Beutel, Leland I. Doan, E. N. Brandt, and the staff at Midland's Grace A. Dow Memorial Library. Not the least of those to whom I am indebted is my wife, Marie—researcher, critic and editor-at-home.

D. W.

Concord, Tenn.,
Winter, 1968.

To Ned and Jeannette

Contents

Author's Note — v

INTRODUCTION — 1

PART ONE *1890-1913* — 15

PART TWO *1914-1930* — 77

PART THREE *1931-1949* — 126

PART FOUR *1950-1968* — 230

Index — 283

Introduction

This is the story of a man and his family, the small Michigan town in which they lived and loved, and the great company they built with the help of a remarkable supporting cast. It is the story of a young man's dream that was shaped into a chemical empire girdling the globe—a dream that influenced the course of this country's history in war and altered the living habits of hundreds of millions of people in peacetime. That dream is still unfolding after three-quarters of a century and it seemingly has no end, only a progression of discovery and surprise.

The man was Herbert Henry Dow. The town is Midland, which sits in the palm of the mitten-shaped Lower Peninsula of Michigan. The company is The Dow Chemical Company—now one of the giants of the chemical industry, but once a struggling concern whose officers were so cash-poor they were forced to talk their neighbors into accepting stock for credit with which to pay the operating expenses and personal household bills. Those who accepted the stock reluctantly and with misgivings—and held onto it—became rich.

Discovery! That is the key word in this saga of a business which had its beginning shortly before the turn of the century. It was started in the then remote, stump-covered, derelict country abandoned by the loggers after they had stripped the land of its towering stands of white cork pine. The discovery of how to extract and blend chemical elements from Michigan's vast underground brine deposits (later from the sea itself) and convert them into useful products for man was the foundation on which the company was built. And discovery remains the solid base on which the company has grown in a world where the demand for chemicals—chemicals for the manufacture or preparation of medicines, food, synthetic rubber, metals, plastics, lubricants, synthetic fibers, and scores of other products—has steadily increased.

Herbert Dow made his first important discovery in a laboratory at

Cleveland's old Case School of Applied Science (now Western Reserve University). Laboratory and engineering discoveries through the years explain in large part the company's growth from a small, struggling concern to a world-wide organization doing more than $1,000,000,000 worth of business annually.

They called him "Crazy Dow" when he first came to Midland from Cleveland in 1890. He was twenty-four years old, fresh out of school, and so embarrassed by his own youth that he grew a mustache and later a beard to make himself look older. He was a stockily built young man with a thick chest, dark hair, heavy eyebrows overhanging light blue-gray eyes, and a manner that verged on cockiness. He loved to argue and to play chess. Most of the townspeople regarded him at first with amused tolerance. Many were antagonistic and suspicious of the stranger. Few believed one so young could make a success of his crazy scheme to extract bromine (and later chlorine) from salt water by using electricity. It just didn't make sense that a young fellow barely old enough to grow a beard could compete with established Ohio Valley producers or successfully challenge the powerful German syndicate which dominated the world market for the bromides used in photography and in medicines.

It didn't make much sense to anyone except Herbert Dow and a few investors in Cleveland and Midland who were willing to gamble on his secret process for extracting bromine cheaply from brine. And even the faith of Dow's backers—with a few exceptions—was so shallow that they were ready to run at the first sign of trouble. There had been one failure which young Dow explained away by saying his process hadn't been sufficiently developed. At another point Herbert Dow found himself eased out of the management of the company he had created. For a time others controlled the patents and processes he had developed. This happened when the "money men" in Cleveland became jittery over his enthusiasms for further experiments and expansion. They wanted quick profits, not promises of dazzling successes in the future. They almost crushed the young man's dreams before the dreams could take form. They would have crushed them, too, except for the streak of stubborness that ran through Herbert Dow like a seam of New England granite.

"Crazy Dow." That's what they were still calling him (behind his back) one summer day some months after The Dow Chemical Company was formed in 1897. On that day the train from Flint deposited a most unlikely female visitor on the platform of the Midland railroad station. She was a tall, full-bosomed woman with keen blue eyes. Her faded dress looked as though it was five or six seasons old and had been slept in, which it had. She carried a few belongings in a ragged cloth bag tied with strings. In one hand was an umbrella. Her hat was a battered relic of an earlier style. She hardly looked to be a woman worth more than $100,000,000 and bearer of the title: "The richest woman in the world." But she was precisely that. She was Hetty Green, a genius at making money and perhaps the most despised woman in the United States according to newspaper accounts of the time. Her greed and miserliness were renowned.

No one in Midland, for a time, knew the identity of the stranger who trudged from the railroad station down the dusty main street, past the row of rowdy saloons, to a boarding house. She kept her business to herself. The fact was that she had left her $15-a-month flat in the slums of Hoboken and had come to Michigan to check on reports that thieves were robbing her of timber she owned in the Lower Peninsula. Some say she had bought the timberlands from Civil War veterans who had received land from the federal government as a bonus for their war service.

At any rate, Hetty was past sixty years of age when she came to Midland, but she was still a formidable looking woman. No doubt she enjoyed the anonymity, being able to walk the streets unrecognized with no reporters about to hound her and report her every move in the newspapers as they had for years in New York. As for what anyone thought of her odd attire, Hetty was unconcerned.

During her brief stay in Midland, she stopped one day in W. L. Baker's general store on Main Street to buy lunch. In her Wall Street office, she generally satisfied her noonday hunger with a bowl of cold oatmeal which she carried from her flat in a paper sack. But this time she purchased ten cents worth of cheese and crackers. As she munched on the dry cheese and crackers, she looked through the doorway and saw Herbert Dow drive down Main Street in a buggy drawn by a high-stepping horse. He sat stiff-backed in the seat, looking neither to the right nor to the left. He probably was returning to the plant at the end of Main Street where several new wooden buildings were under construction for the manufacture of bleach—a product derived from chlorine, found in the brine pumped from deep wells. The bleach was used in large quantities by the paper industry.

"Who is that man?" Hetty asked.

"That's Crazy Dow," a bystander said, laughing. He explained that Dow was general manager and chief stockholder of a small chemical company that bore his name. And then the gossip began: It wasn't much of a company (so they said) and everyone in town knew they were having a hard time at the "bleach works" to make a go of it. They were always having small explosions in the plant from which the curious were barred. Everybody also knew that only a short time before Herbert Dow hadn't had two nickels he could call his own to rub together. A lot of people couldn't understand why the pretty school teacher, Grace Ball, the daughter of an old Midland family, had married Dow only two years after his arrival in town. The two of them had thought they were being so secretive in their courtship, sending notes back and forth to each other from the plant to the school and from the school to the plant. It was plain to anyone with eyes in his head that the boy who pedaled his bicycle so furiously up and down Main Street was carrying love notes. Folks agreed it was a wonder the boy ever got any studying done.

But in sifting through the gossip, Hetty learned also that several Midlanders had enough faith in the young chemist-inventor to buy stock in his enterprise. In fact, one of the investors was the proprietor of the general store where Hetty was eating her cheese and crackers. His customers were always kidding him about being a stockholder in Crazy Dow's venture and asking him when he was going to sell his stock—that is, if he could find anyone to buy it.

No one, not even her bookkeeper or her husband, ever knew how Hetty Green determined when an investment was attractive. All anyone ever knew, even after her death in 1915, was that she had a genius for buying stocks and properties that almost invariably ballooned in value. There is no record that she ever met Herbert Dow and talked to him. The oldtimers in Midland only remember her sitting in the general store, eating cheese and crackers, and asking questions about Crazy Dow.

But apparently she liked what she saw of Herbert Dow in the brief glimpse she had of him, and she liked what she heard about him and his business. At any rate, she decided Dow wasn't as crazy as most of the townspeople thought. After returning to Hoboken she bought one hundred shares of Dow stock which at her death became a part of the estate of her son, Colonel E. H. R. Green. At his death in 1936 the stock had multiplied through stock splits the purchase of subscription rights, and options to more than six thousand shares worth $766,339.25. It would have pleased Hetty mightily to have known that her snap judgment of a man and his company had been so handsomely vindicated.

Very likely Hetty Green's enemies on Wall Street—men whom she had bested and humiliated in financial deals for years—would have snickered had they known she had gambled even a dab of her money on the success of a Michigan backwoods chemical company managed by an unknown who looked like a young General U. S. Grant. Indeed, it even seems preposterous today to think that a small concern isolated from the population centers and money markets of the country had any worthwhile future. Its only transportation links with the outside world were rutted roads and a single rail line. Its managers were scarcely more than upstarts not long out of the college classroom. They were not widely traveled or experienced in the ways of big business. In sophisticated industrial circles, they would have been rated as little more than country bumpkins in the fields of finance, management, manufacturing, engineering, and selling on any large scale.

And yet despite all the deficiencies of location and experience—and often because of them—The Dow Chemical Company survived and grew. Herbert Dow, even as a young man, clearly saw the importance and rewards of mass production and mechanization. Many of his colleagues never quite understood that he was thinking in terms of world markets and world competition rather than in terms of a safe, sheltered, limited market with risk held to a minimum. Often they were appalled when they glimpsed the breadth of his ambitions. Appalled and even frightened. It is interesting that Herbert Dow and Henry Ford, laboring only 125 miles distant from each other but never having met, should have developed at the same time such similar viewpoints on the benefits of mass production and mechanization to manufacturer and consumer alike.

Herbert Dow drew around him in those early days a team of tough, inventive, inquisitive young minds who were to make a great deal of chemical history. They were not men widely known outside Midland.

They were too young to have established reputations. There were names such as Griswold, Bennett, Barstow, Strosacker, and Putnam. Later these earliest pioneers would be joined by other men of unusual talent—Beutel, Collings, Veazsey, Grebe, Hirschkind, Hale, Britton, Boundy, Ballman, Gerstacker, and Branch among others.

Through the years, they beat the British United Alkali bleach trust when that group tried to drive them out of the bleach market. They won with no help from the outside. They took on the powerful German bromine syndicate, the Deutsche Bromkonvention, whose representative traveled all the way from Germany to St. Louis to issue an ultimatum to Dow: drop all exports of bromides to Europe or be destroyed. They went to war with the Germans on their own home grounds and broke grip on the world bromine market. It could only have been a day of triumph for young Herbert Dow when he traveled to London and sat in the Savoy Hotel to hear his German competitors sue for peace.

Dow and his band of helpers came through the money panic of 1907 battered but intact. They pushed on to help establish an American chemical industry which made the nation independent of foreign chemical producers who had ruled the chemical world for years.

They helped break the German monopoly on the manufacture of dyes. When all others in the United States had given up the costly and unprofitable production of magnesium metal, they persisted on the faith that one day there would be a need for the tough, light metal. That need came dramatically in the early days of World War II when the federal government urgently called for the production of hundreds of millions of pounds of magnesium. The metal was essential in the building of lighter, faster war planes which could fight the German and the Japanese air forces at least on even terms. The emergency was met with tons to spare and Dow was the leader in the field.

Herbert Dow died in 1930. But his elder son, Willard, and the men trained in the Dow workshop carried on. They went to the sea to get bromine needed for anti-knock gasoline. They went to the sea again for magnesium and other chemicals which were there in limitless quantity. And the sea remains a Comstock lode for Dow. The knowledge they had gained in working with the Michigan brine was the knowledge required to "mine the sea" of its treasures.

They found in the laboratory the chemical substances known as styrene and butadiene which became essential ingredients in the making of synthetic rubber—and they shared their secrets and their know-how with competitors to whip the World War II crisis of a shortage in tires. The Japanese armies had overrun the rubber plantations of the Far East. The Allied armies needed tires for their vehicles as did the civilian population at home. Styrene and butadiene played a vital part in overcoming the shortage.

They developed a process to squeeze millions of tons of oil from the earth in fields where production was dropping. They found better and cheaper ways to take the valuable elements from brine and to combine them with other chemicals to produce new products useful in industry and in homes. They found a method for making iodine which helped break the Chilean iodine monopoly and forced the price down from $5 a pound to 81 cents a pound.

They discovered ways to make plastic materials which could be used where wood, metal, cardboard, and paper had been used before. With each passing year they discovered more and more new chemical products derived primarily from brine and from oil. From Midland, the company expanded its operations from coast to coast in the United States and then into forty-two other countries around the globe.

One wonders how it was that a company conceived in what was then a Michigan backwoods town could become one of the world leaders in the manufacture and distribution of chemicals and chemical products. There are many answers to the question, not just one.

Discovery in the laboratory was the first answer. Imaginative management was another. Technical engineering know-how of a high caliber was another. The growing worldwide industrial hunger for chemicals was yet another. And still another was pure luck—a factor that cannot be sneered at in business any more than in a horse race, where the unknown hazards can never be found in a form chart.

Luck entered the picture when Herbert Dow decided to set up his plant in Midland. He knew there was brine in plentiful quantities beneath the crust of the earth. For years men had been pumping salt water in the Saginaw Valley and evaporating it to make salt. Michigan in the late 1800's was the leading salt-producing state in the nation. But what Herbert Dow couldn't know at the time was that he had located his first plant over the center of an almost inexhaustible prehistoric sea of brine. The salt water was trapped in the porous rock formations far below the earth's surface.

This sea of brine was his raw material waiting to be processed. It cost him nothing except the expense of pumping it. The earth was his storage tank to be drawn on any time he chose. The Michigan brine was rich in bromides, and in calcium, magnesium, and sodium chlorides. And with his revolutionary process (using electricity to separate the bromine and chlorine from the brine, along with an ingenious "blowing out" process to be described later) his early manufacturing costs were lower than his competitors realized. And Dow knew it.

It is not possible to separate the story of The Dow Chemical Company from the story of the Dow family because one is so intimately intertwined with the other. Neither is it possible to separate the story from the town of Midland nor to ignore the long procession of talented men who helped build the company. They were all a part of the adventure in the building of a strong American chemical industry free from domination by European cartels.

In the early days, these men worked, played, and planned together with small-town, first-name intimacy that would not have been possible in a larger city. While their wives gathered after dinner in one room, the men gathered in another to swap stories and discuss possible solutions to business problems. Managers were not isolated from engineers and chemists and foremen and workers. Herbert Dow could be found in the plant checking on operations more often than he could be found in his office. They had not yet heard of the problem of "communication" because it was no problem. They were in communication at work and at play.

Dow often got into violent arguments with his engineers and plant managers over how a chemical problem should be approached, how a piece of equipment should be constructed, or whether bricks or wood should be used as a building material. He almost invariably lined up on the side of economy because the lean, cash-short early years had forced him to be cost conscious. And yet he was ready to take long risks when he was convinced the results would show a profit.

One of the early employees recalled, "Dow would get his engineer, Tom Griswold, Jr., and his production manager, E. O. Barstow, in his office and they would go at it. You could hear them all over the lot shouting at each other and pounding the table. Just when it sounded as though they were going to have a fist fight, Dow would start singing,

'Old Black Joe.' The others would join in. When they came out of the office you'd never suspect there had been a harsh word. A decision had been reached and the matter was closed. I guess Dow always started singing when he knew he was wrong."

Such a free and easy association at all levels is no longer possible as the company has grown in size. And yet many of the attitudes and practices of the past curiously remain in the present, such as the vigorous airing of clashing viewpoints. It has always been that way and no one has given any serious thought to changing it. There is a relaxed and informal air about the Dow headquarters even today that is reminiscent of the older days of Herbert Dow.

The outsider who spends some time at the Dow headquarters in Midland has the strange feeling that this could not possibly be the center of a billion dollar enterprise. There is no sense of rush apparent. The executive offices are neither expansive nor expensively plush nor isolated in a remote penthouse sanctuary. There are no batteries of receptionists and layers of secretaries standing guard in the outer offices of the decision-makers. The executives often have their lunch in the headquarters cafeteria and wait their turn in line along with the lower echelon workers; there is no executive dining room. Such holdovers from the past may be inefficient—but no one at Dow seems to think so.

For many years, until 1956, executives, office workers, and factory workers alike were required to punch a time clock when they came to work and when they departed. In the old days Herbert Dow would lurk around the clock room to pounce on anyone—even a company officer—who was late. He felt they were being paid for eight hours' work and they should give the full eight hours if they had the company's best interests at heart.

One day a visiting businessman watched in amazement as Earl Bennett, then the company's treasurer and a member of the board of directors, dutifully punched the time clock on arrival at the plant.

"Why are you, the treasurer of this company, punching a time clock?" the visitor asked.

Bennett looked at the man, surprised that he should ask such a question. "Because I want to get paid," he replied.

It is tempting to play with the idea that the location of a huge business and its headquarters in a small town has a subtle influence on the decision-making processes of the company's officers. People are more aware of each other as individuals in a small town—more conscious of one another's problems, ambitions, capabilities, and limitations. Decisions are not made in long-distance remoteness from the actual manufacturing process and from the people who must carry out the decisions.

In Midland, the homes and golf courses are hardly more than a ten-minute drive from the factory gates for most executives and employees. From thirty to sixty minutes away are woodlands, lakes, trout streams, and—for those who seek it—total solitude. The location that once was dubious because of its remoteness is no longer remote because of planes, telephones, and teletypes. But it now has the appeal of offering executives and other employees escape from the pressures of the big city, the long hours of commuting, and the tensions of living in a crowded place. Children have the freedom to roam the outdoors. Life goes at a more leisurely and relaxed pace.

On the other side of the coin, those who seek anonymity after working hours and who wish to build a wall between their business lives and their private lives find the small town a difficult place. Such walls are not easy to build in a small town. The town's life is not a separate thing from the life of the company. One impinges on the other in many ways. One has a responsibility to the other as Herbert Dow discovered early in his career.

It is something of an oddity that while The Dow Chemical Company has grown mightily, the top management has never seriously considered moving the headquarters from Midland to New York or Detroit or Chicago or any of the industrial and financial centers of the country more easily accessible by air. Being off the beaten path has had its advantages. The most important of these, during the formative years, was a deliberate and often stubborn policy of independent research and development. It seemed that Herbert Dow and his son, Willard, were fearful that if too much attention was given to what competitors were doing, Dow would become an imitator and not an innovator. They wanted each product and service to be better than anything on the market if the Dow name was to be involved.

As a typical illustration, one day a group of researchers went to Willard Dow in the 1930's for money to launch a new product. They laid their case before him, and then the spokesman said; "This is going to work, Willard. This is the way Du Pont is doing it."

Willard said: "If you can't figure out a way to do it better than Du Pont, we are not going to do it."

Perhaps sentiment had something to do with the company's being content to remain in Midland. Through the years the name Midland has become synonymous with the name Dow. Herbert Dow was content to stay in Midland and his children and grandchildren have kept their roots there, too. It is reasonable to assume that Midland will continue as the nerve center of the company's wide-flung operations—although the Dow family today controls only about 12.4 percent of some 30,000,000 shares of common stock outstanding.

The story of the company falls into four clearly defined periods, the first span covering twenty-three years and the other roughly twenty years each. Those periods went about like this:

1890—1913 After six years of struggle and frustration, Herbert Dow persuaded a group of Cleveland businessmen to back him in a fresh start. He organized The Dow Chemical Company and gathered around him a strong team of young men, most of them graduates of the Case School of Applied Science. They had no ready-made blueprints for building a chemical plant because the chemical industry itself was in its infancy in this country. They made their own blueprints for electric cells, machinery, equipment, and buildings. They learned by trial and error. Yet the company survived two price wars, first with the British and then with the Germans, and a Wall Street money panic that jolted the economy of the entire nation.

1914—1930 Britain's blockade of German shipping in World War I and the Germans' submarine warfare abruptly shut off the supplies of chemicals on which American industry had largely depended for years. After the war, Congress approved tariffs to protect the infant chemical industry and avoid further dependence on foreign producers. Dow pushed into the field of magnesium metal production and fabrication even though there was little demand for the metal. His men developed a process for making phenol—the raw material for a long line of plastics and other products—that gave the company world leadership in the manufacture of phenol. Dow became the supplier of an essential chemical used in the Ethyl Corporation's anti-knock gasoline. Then, just as the Great Depression of the 1930's came, Herbert Dow died in the Mayo Clinic at Rochester, Minnesota, and his elder son, Willard, became president of the Dow Chemical Company.

1931–1949 The nation was in the agony of the Great Depression when Willard Dow took over as president; and yet, in the midst of social turmoil and economic chaos, the company expanded rapidly. Except for two years, 1932 and 1933, Midland scarcely felt the shocks of the economic upheaval. It was known as "the town that never had a depression." New products came onto the market so rapidly that no one knew what some of them could be used for. Dow went to the sea to get bromine, magnesium metal, and other chemicals. Dow was chosen by the Canadian government to help solve the rubber shortage. The British came to Dow to set up a plant for producing magnesium metal. Dow turned over to the United States government its secrets for making styrene and butadiene when a war-time crash program was launched to make synthetic rubber. Dow expanded virtually all of its operations and plants to meet the war needs after the Japanese attack on Pearl Harbor. Through all this era of tremendous discovery and development, Willard Dow held a tight one-man control over the decision-making for the company. But when the war ended, Dow Chemical had become much too large and complex for one-man control. As fate would have it Willard Dow died in 1949 as the company was on the threshold of an almost unbelievable expansion. The presidency fell to Leland I. "Lee" Doan, a tall, urbane, much-traveled man who had married Herbert Dow's daughter, Ruth. He stepped up to the presidency from the office of director of sales.

1950–1968 Lee Doan brought to Dow's presidency for the first time a broad-based concept of management in which major decisions were made through a consensus of top executives. Dow had outgrown the old one-man management methods and Doan realized it. He placed greater emphasis on sales and market research. Younger men were drawn into the management circle to consult with the graybeards who had done so much to build the company. In the postwar adjustments, the demand for chemicals and for chemical product know-how skyrocketed. Businessmen from abroad came knocking on Dow's Midland door asking for help in building chemical plants. They came from Japan and South America and England and Europe and India. At first, Dow was reluctant to move into the foreign field. Their thinking had been concentrated on the domestic market so intently that no one in the upper echelons had taken the time to step back and survey the world scene. But the pressures and opportunities literally shoved Dow into the overseas markets. The company had made a strong start in this direction by 1962 when Lee Doan resigned from the presidency and his son, Herbert Dow "Ted" Doan, then only forty, was chosen as his successor. This lean, dark-haired, intense young man led a quiet revolution in the company. The first major move he made was to centralize the controls of management which had gradually been dispersed in the rush of postwar expansion. Much of the decision-making power in Dow had drifted into the hands of division production managers. Ted Doan quietly centered control in a team composed of himself, Cart Gerstacker, the brilliant young chairman of the board, and Ben Branch, a hard-driving vice president who had risen from the Dow production ranks. Young Doan shifted the power structure without a crippling inner fight. The older men who had ruled their domains with such force and strength for so many years accepted the logic of the situation. Doan led the company even further into developing partnerships with producers in foreign countries. He moved strongly toward the direct-to-consumer market, building with products such as Saran Wrap, agricultural chemicals, textiles, and household cleansers bearing the Dow trademark. In the six years after he took office, sales rose from $890,639,000 to more than $1,400,000,000. The changing of the guard marked the beginning of a new era as the company moved toward the final quarter of its first century.

The leadership in Dow has moved from grandfather to grandson as the years have passed. But the shadow of the grandfather is still there because it was he who shaped the basic thinking which gave the company its form and direction. That is why the story of today must go back to the story of yesterday for a picture of how a small-town company became one of the world's largest chemical complexes.

* * *

On a hot summer day in 1924, a six-year-old boy emerged from the big, rambling, two-story Victorian house shaded by tall trees a short walk from downtown Midland. He wandered across the lawn into a garden of flowers and shrubs and grassy vistas where anyone with any imagination could see elves and fairies dancing in the shadows. He crossed an arched stone bridge over a quiet pool covered with lily pads. He walked on to the apple orchard. The apples were just beginning to form on the branches and were too bitter for eating. But the trees were fine for climbing.

For a time the boy surveyed the world through the leaves from his perch in a gnarled tree. Then he wandered back to the garden and lay down beneath a pine tree to watch the cloud masses march across the blue Michigan sky.

Soon a grayhaired man came from the house and he, too, turned to the garden. Herbert Dow liked to walk in the garden and the orchard he had created from sandy, brush-covered acres. He saw the boy—his grandson, Lee A. Doan—lying beneath the pine tree. He walked over and lay down beside him and together they watched the clouds.

Finally, the grandfather said, "What do you see in the clouds?"

The boy said, "I see a dragon. Look! There is his head and there is his tail and there are his legs."

The man said, "I see a dog. Over there. Look quickly before it changes into something else."

"I see a castle," the boy said.

"I see a horse."

For a long time they lay side by side, watching a sky filled with animals and castles and weird creatures that magically changed their shapes as the clouds drifted by. Then they got up and walked together back to the big house.

That is the way Lee A. Doan—they call him "Young Lee" to distinguish him from his father—remembers his grandfather best. Not as a scientist or an inventor or a captain of industry, but as a man who could take time out to lie beneath a pine tree and watch the clouds.

Almost everyone who knew Herbert Dow remembers him in a different way. But the one thing on which they all agree is that he had a mind which was forever seeking ways to do things differently and better. "If we can't do it better than the others—why do it?" was one of his favorite remarks in rejecting an approach to mediocrity.

He was an adventurer and a discoverer. And the story of the company he launched is one of the amazing success stories of American industry.

PART ONE   *1890-1913*

Chapter One

In the old city of Prague in the sixteenth century, the chemists, alchemists, astrologers, and artists found a protector and patron in the mad Roman emperor Rudolph II. Like many others before him, he clung to the centuries-old belief that base metals could be turned into gold through alchemy. It was an idea hinged on the theory that any solid could be changed into another solid under the proper conditions. All one had to do was to find the right conditions.

One narrow street behind Rudolph's castle became known as Alchemists' Row. Men who dabbled in the mysteries of chemical reactions had their laboratories equipped with apparatus which, except for the modified forms, is still in use today. There were furnaces, stills, flasks, beakers, and water baths common to the most modern laboratory. Some of the alchemists were true artisans, using chemical reactions in search of knowledge as they worked with iron, copper, lead, mercury, and other materials. But among their ranks, too, were charlatans merely practicing fraud on the gullible as they held out the promise of vast riches once they had perfected their alleged methods of transmitting base metal to gold.

Rudolph was not alone among the monarchs of his period in encouraging the alchemists to pursue the search even though other kings before them had tried and failed. In the fifteenth century, King Henry VI of England had approved the organization of a company to make gold despite Parliament's disapproval of "alchemists' gold." And Charles VII of France had his court alchemist produce "gold" which to his embarrassment later had to be redeemed with the real thing taken from his treasury.

Royalty found it amusing and exciting to invite their friends and guests to demonstrations of gold-making. The court alchemist would be ordered to be ready for an evening of entertainment. And then the royal party would arrive at the laboratory where fires burned beneath bubbling pots and shadows flickered on smoke-blackened walls. Mumbling strange words and making mystic signs over his molten brew, the alchemist would stir the cauldron while an assistant made the fire blaze with his bellows. Perhaps there was a dramatic flash as a powder was added to the brew. Perhaps something was dropped into the pot as the guests' eyes were blinded momentarily by the flash. Perhaps something came from a long sleeve or from a hollow stirring rod. At any rate, flakes of gold were lifted from the pot to be passed around and examined by the wondering and amazed guests. Almost everyone agreed the alchemist was a fellow with powers that promised much.

But not all the frauds succeeded. Sometimes the tricksters were caught in their sleight-of-hand and had to flee for their lives. The less lucky found themselves on a scaffold with a rope around their necks, to be hanged as an example of what happens to those who toy with the credibility of a monarch.

But despite all the fraud and mumbo jumbo, advances were made in chemistry, which has been described as "the science that deals with the nature of and the changes in the composition of matter." Slowly the horizon of knowledge was expanded in science to the confirmation of the theory that all elements are composed of atoms, and then the revelation that atoms have their own substructures. Tremendous strides were made in the later part of the nineteenth century and the early part of the twentieth century leading to a greater understanding of the structure and behavior of chemical elements and compounds.

In seeking to give his students early in this century a broad understanding of the meaning of research, Professor Ira Remson of Johns Hopkins University would say to his classes: "Suppose you are in a wilderness in a pitchblack night. You can see nothing and you know nothing. Then you light a candle. Immediately there is a small circle of light in the darkness. Within this circle you can see. Now, suppose you light a kerosene lamp. You have a larger circle of light and you can see more. But at the same time that you have made your circle larger, you have also made your surrounding perimeter of darkness (the unknown) larger. Now, suppose you light an arc lamp. You have a circle yards in diameter which is lighted—and you also have a vastly greater perimeter of unknown darkness outside the circle of light. Let no research man be proud of having made this somewhat greater light—for as knowledge increases so does the border of the unknown."

This "border of the unknown" was expanding rapidly when Herbert Dow entered Case School of Applied Science in 1884 as a young man of eighteen. At this time, German scientists had taken the lead in applying scientific knowledge to the manufacture of chemical products. William Perkin, an Englishman, had discovered the first aniline dye in

1856 and its manufacture had become an important industry in England and France. But gradually the dye-making center shifted to Germany as huge factories were built and improved processes designed. From the dye factories also came drugs and chemicals which were useful in other fields of manufacture. They produced synthetically many compounds which previously they had been forced to import from other parts of the world.

The Germans also developed a system of using teams of scientists in industrial research, and it became the pattern to be followed in other countries around the world. The scientists employed by industry were closely allied with the scientists in German universities. And thus Germany in the latter part of the last century became the most important center for industrial research in the world—with virtual control of the world chemical markets.

Young Dow, of course, could not know when he entered Case as a student that within a very few years he would be singled out as a target by members of this powerful German combine. Indeed, none could foresee that the time was coming when the German domination of the chemical world would be shattered by a torrent of events leading the United States into its first world war.

Dow's only assets of note when he became a freshman at Case were a strong body and an inquiring mind. He had hoped to become an architect but there wasn't enough money in the family till to finance his study away from home. So when he was offered a scholarship at Case, he accepted it, even though Case offered no course in architecture. He was not a "good student" in the orthodox sense of the phrase. He was argumentative in the classroom, prone to dispute conclusions, and more interested in asking questions than listening to a set lecture.

But he was fortunate that Case had a small but brilliant faculty willing to hear the students out and to guide them in their work. Among Dow's teachers were Albert Michelson, who would later win a Nobel Prize for physics; Edward Morley of Cleveland's Western Reserve University, who occasionally taught at Case; Charles F. Mabery, who was a pioneer in petroleum chemistry and in electric furnace development; and John E. Stockwell, who later would win wide recognition as an astronomer.

Dow grew up in a period of ferment and discovery and invention in the United States—not only in chemistry but in other fields. He was thirteen years old when Thomas A. Edison invented an incandescent electric light. Two years earlier, hydroelectric power had been generated at Niagara Falls—and Nicola Tesla had discovered the rotating magnetic field which made long-distance power transmission possible. He was twenty when Germany's Benz invented an internal combustion engine using gasoline and installed it in an automobile. Electricity was being used commercially for the first time and its use in chemical processes was exciting the imagination of men in many countries. New industries were being developed around coal, oil, and steel. Railroads were pushing out to new frontiers and world commerce was expanding. The industrial revolution that had started in England had jumped the Atlantic and was gaining momentum in the United States. The excitement of discovery was everywhere.

As a boy in Cleveland, Dow had made some interesting discoveries of his own. One day he realized that the hens with nests on one side of the barn were laying more eggs than the hens in another part of the barn. It was a mystery that needed investigating.

The "Case of the Industrious Hens" had its beginning when the Dows' cow had a calf. The arrival of the calf required the building of an addition to the barn—and a new chicken coop was installed near the cow's stall. The flock of chickens was divided, part of them going into the new coop and the others remaining in their old quarters. This division of the flock in itself obviously had no influence on the egg-laying abilities of hens. And yet the hens in the new coop were doing a better production job than the hens in the old part of the barn.

Dow found the solution to the mystery in the working habits of the family's hired hand. This fellow was an elderly farmer who came to the barn before dawn each day to milk the cow and do other chores about the place. The first thing he did on arrival was to light lamps near the cow's stall in order to do the milking. The lights and the banging of buckets awakened the hens near the stall but did not disturb the hens sleeping in the old, darkened part of the barn. The awakened hens got off their roosts and went about their daily chores much earlier than the hens in the other part of the barn. They also laid more eggs. Deduction: lights in a hen house shortened the sleeping hours of the hens and resulted in more eggs.

From egg production, Dow turned to the incubation of eggs by mechanical means. He read a story in Youth's Companion that ostriches in Australia laid a good many eggs but few of the eggs got incubated because mama and papa ostriches were not very good about sitting on the eggs long enough to hatch them. However, an Australian had solved this problem by devising a crude incubator to relieve the parent birds of any responsibility.

Dow figured if an incubator would work for ostrich eggs, it also would work for hen eggs. So he set to work to build one. The greatest difficulty was in finding a means to keep the temperature inside the incubator automatically at a constant level. It wasn't an easy problem for a boy to solve. He made and discarded thirty-nine devices before, on the fortieth try, he succeeded in making one that worked. Then he went into the business of building and selling incubators. No one knows how word got as far as the West Coast that young Dow was building incubators, but a California rancher bought one for $100. He had a brisk sale for a time—then came disillusion. He discovered some of his customers were buying his incubators, copying them, and taking his market away from him.

Calling a halt to the manufacture of the incubators, he decided to sell an incubator kit. He offered, for a modest fee, the blueprints for a make-it-yourself incubator. But the market was limited in the Cleveland area and soon young Dow was busy on other ventures.

"Herbert," an uncle said one day in exasperation, "it would take six men to keep up with all your ideas."

"I'll get the six men," Herbert said. "But they won't be enough."

Part of Herbert Dow's inventiveness and inquisitiveness no doubt can be traced to his father, Joseph Dow, who built one of the first steam turbines in the United States (the turbine was used for a time in U. S. Navy torpedoes). The father was a master mechanic with an inventive turn of mind and no doubt in a later era would have been called a mechanical engineer. He often discussed mechanical problems with his son, even when the son was a mere boy.

Joseph Dow was a descendant of an old New England family. The first Dow to reach the American shores was Henry Dow who arrived in Massachusetts from England in 1637. He later settled in New Hampshire and that was where the family remained for many years. Joseph was born in New Hampshire and he lived there until 1865. Indirectly, the end of the Civil War brought a sudden change in Joseph Dow's fortunes. After the war an industrial slump hit New England. Joseph Dow left New Hampshire with his pregnant wife for a job in Belleville, Ontario, Canada. He went there to oversee the operation of a sewing machine factory and it was there that Herbert Henry Dow was born on February 26, 1866.

Apparently the Belleville job didn't work out satisfactorily for after a few months Joseph brought his family to Derby, Connecticut. Then they moved to Cleveland where Joseph Dow was master mechanic for the Chisholm Steel Shovel Works. It was in Cleveland that Joseph Dow developed his turbine, which had a speed of some 30,000 revolutions a minute—quite a spectacular achievement for the times. But as so often happens, others had the same idea and obtained the first patents.

At Case, young Dow divided his interests between chemistry and mechanical problems. One of his best friends was A. W. Smith, who was in the class ahead of him. Often they would discuss the future.

Once Smith said, "Herbert, what are you going to do when you get out of school?"

"I don't know," Herbert said. "But I'd rather work for myself for $3,000 a year than to work for someone else and make $10,000."

During his senior year, Dow's primary interest was a study of the heating efficiency of various fuels. The subject of his thesis was "The Chemical Uses of Fuel in Boilers." In gathering material for the thesis, he made a trip to an oil well near Cleveland to get a sample of natural gas for laboratory analysis. The gas that gushed from the well along with the crude oil brought to the surface a good deal of brine. The brine had no value to the oil men and in fact was a nuisance. Often in drilling for oil and gas they found salt water.

The well driller helped Dow get a sample of the gas and then he called young Dow's attention to the brine and asked him to taste it. Dow tasted a few drops and made a wry face.

"Bitter, isn't it?" the driller said with a grin.

"It certainly is," Dow agreed.

"Now why would that brine be so bitter?" the driller asked.

"I don't know," Dow said, "but I'd like to find out."

He got a bottle and filled it with the brine which he carried back to the laboratory along with the sample of gas. In analyzing the brine he found it had an unusually high content of lithium and bromine, which explained the exceptional bitterness. But Dow didn't stop there. A little simple arithmetic showed him that there was about three dollars worth of lithium in a barrel of brine plus a few cents worth of bromine. With crude petroleum selling for one dollar a barrel, the brine coming from the well theoretically was worth more than the oil. But the market for lithium was a very small one while there was at times a good market for bromine.

This was when Dow began studying ways to get the bromine from the brine as cheaply as possible. He saw that the pennies in bromine offered a better opportunity than the dollars in lithium. The bromine manufacturers in Ohio and Michigan at the time actually were more interested in the production of salt from the brine because there was a more stable market. Bromine was a by-product produced if and when the market justified it, the chief buyers being pharmaceutical houses and firms selling photographic supplies. Bromine was an important ingredient in patent medicines and in the development of films. Most of it was imported from Germany and Germany dictated the prices.

The making of salt was a simple process. The brine was pumped from the ground into vats and heated until evaporation caused the salt to crystallize. The liquid that did not fully evaporate was the "bittern" or mother liquor which contained bromine. If an operator wished to obtain bromine as well as salt, he took the mother liquor, added a few necessary chemicals to free the bromine, and heated the batch until the bromine came off with the steam. Two or three pounds of bromine could be obtained from each ton of brine.

Both processes, to be profitable, required cheap fuel. And cheap fuel was available in many areas from the waste wood that accumulated around sawmills. But the giant stands of trees in Michigan and Ohio were disappearing by the time Dow began his bromine studies. He knew that one day the sawmills would no longer be a reliable source of fuel as the forests disappeared. He also realized the methods used to release bromine from the brine were crudely inefficient and wasteful of both time and energy. Surely, he reasoned, a better and cheaper way could be found to produce bromine on a continuous basis, without heat, rather than in batch-lots requiring heat. It was an idea that pushed everything else into the background of his mind.

After his graduation from Case in 1888, Dow got a job teaching chemistry at the Huron Street Hospital College in Cleveland. There he had a small laboratory and an assistant, a few dollars each month to cover living expenses, and time in which to pursue the bromine problem. During the winter of 1888–89, he found in his laboratory that bromine could be produced from cold brine if certain chemicals were added to the brine and then a current of air was passed through the solution onto wet scrap iron. The moisture that collected on the iron and dripped into a container as ferric bromine—laden held a high bromide percentage of commercial-quality bromine. He called the procedure a "blowing-out process" and for many years this basic idea was one of the keys to the success of the Dow operation.

Dow was so firmly convinced that his idea was sound that in the spring of 1889 he began looking for capital to build and operate a plant. The amazing thing was that the beardless, twenty-three year old could find anyone willing to gamble his money on a process tested only in a laboratory. But he was a persuasive talker. He found three men who were willing to put up a few hundred dollars—if Dow would do the work. They were Joseph P. Smith, a Cleveland egg merchant, and Jacob Miller and J. A. Linville of the Buckeye Mower and Reaper Company of Canton, Ohio. A partnership was formed and Dow jauntily set forth to seek his fortune in what the partners rather grandly named The Canton Chemical Company.

Dow set up his plant in Canton where he was able to lease a brine well. It wasn't precisely a plant. It was a shed. The choosing of this particular well was his first mistake because even the best pumps of the day could hardly handle the load of pumping brine from a depth of 3,000 feet—and Dow couldn't afford a new pump. Nevertheless, he set to work, building an apparatus inside his wooden—shed factory that might have been designed by Rube Goldberg. He conceived the idea of having the treated brine drip onto panels of burlap sacking stretched across a wooden trough. Air was blown over and up through the soaked sacking. The air carried the brownish-red bromine vapor into a tower where there was a mesh-like collection of wet scrap iron. The bromine-laden liquid gathered on the iron and dripped into carboys.

Through the summer and fall, there were such notations in Dow's notebooks as: "Pump rod broke. Got Mr. Ritz to weld it. Only about 4 gal. of bromide were made last night and not more than one or two today. Bromine blows through badly. Broke up the iron some but still it works poorly.... Finished putting in rods and began pumping about 2 p.m. Mr. Smith worked all day and began again at 12 midnight. Mr. Platt worked all day and until 12 at night.... Sold to C. A. & Co. 2 carboys.... Smith worked scant 8½ hrs. Platt worked 12 hrs. Pump began to throw water about 5 p.m.... Pump broke at about 8 a.m... I have been to Cleveland and got the patent matter fixed and paid $15 for same...."

Through the cold, dreary winter months of December and January, Dow struggled to keep the little plant running, often working fifteen to twenty hours a day. The partners sold sixty-three carboys of bromine at $3.10 each, but expenses continued to outrun income. During these weeks, Dow somehow found time to sketch his thoughts on such matters as "How to make an instrument for measuring the intensity of a magnetic field," "How to make a telephone receiver," and "How to make a solar engine." But the most important sketch of all was the diagram dated December 16, 1889. The notes beside the drawing said: "To make a cell for the decomposition of bromides. Have the plates horizontal and sealed into the sides of wooden boxes for cells."

Already Herbert Dow was thinking of a method to liberate bromine from brine by using an electric current along with the blowing-out process. He was not the first to think of electrolysis in chemical production—but the cell he devised was unique in its simplicity and design and eventually it would be the workhorse that would bring Dow fame and fortune.

Having electricity as a servant in factory and home was something new and exciting at the time. Relatively few people had any understanding of how and why electricity worked. Electric lights were not even installed in the White House until after President Benjamin Harrison became Chief Executive in March, 1889—roughly the same time that Dow was rounding up money to begin the Canton operation. Both President Harrison and his wife, Caroline, were afraid of the mysterious power of electricity, so much so that neither at first would touch the electric switches. A White House employee turned on the lights in the halls and parlors in the evening, and they burned until he arrived the following morning and turned them off. The Harrisons' bedrooms remained dark until the President and his wife overcame their fear of the electric switches and were reasonably sure they weren't going to be electrocuted.

It was a remarkable period of transition from the old century to the new. Mechanization was growing in industry. The horseless carriage was being readied for its appearance. The railroads were pushing on to new frontiers. The move from farm to city was underway. The Morgans and Rockefellers and Vanderbilts and Astors and Harrimans were high on the list of great names in the financial world. Across the country young unknowns were starting small businesses that would grow into commercial giants and very often success grew out of the ashes of failure.

Herbert Dow was one of the young unknowns. His struggle to improve the production of bromine solely by the blowing-out process ended in failure. The partnership could not stand the financial strain. And on Wednesday, February 5, 1890, Herbert Dow wrote the last entry in his Canton notebook: "Quit work at Canton...." The partnership was dissolved.

The failure could have been a shattering blow. But it wasn't. Dow was by no means crushed. In fact, there are indications that he turned his back on Canton in an optimistic mood, determined to raise more money to start another chemical plant. At least he had proved what he started out to prove. He had proved he could produce bromine without heat. His process worked, even if it worked poorly. And he was certain that with improvements, it would work well.

Dow wasted no time brooding over his Canton experience. Soon after returning to Cleveland he marshalled his facts and arguments and took them to an old family friend, J. H. Osborn, a sewing machine manufacturer and later an executive of the National Carbon Company. No one knows how Dow did it, but he convinced Osborn that despite the Canton failure, he knew how to produce bromine cheaply by using electricity with his blowing-out process.

He already had picked the location for the new plant. It would be at Midland, Michigan, about 125 miles north of Detroit. Midland was his choice because in analyzing brine samples two years earlier at Case he had found the Midland brine to be richer in bromine than the brines of Ohio and other states east of the Mississippi River. Also the Michigan brine lay closer to the earth's surface than the Canton brine and would be cheaper to pump.

Osborn agreed to make small but regular payments to Dow until he could get the Midland plant on a profitable basis. The partnership arrangement seems to have been that Osborn would furnish the starting capital while Dow would supply the muscle, management, and chemical and engineering know-how. The older man acted on faith alone—faith in the young man's enthusiasm for an untried process and faith in the young man's character. It was a gamble.

Chapter Two

A hot August sun beat down on the dusty, listless Main Street of Midland in 1890 when twenty-four year old Herbert Dow stepped from the stifling heat of the railroad coach that had brought him on the last leg of his journey from Cleveland. He carried a battered suitcase in his hand and a head full of plans for starting another chemical plant. In his pocket were $100 in cash and a bank draft for $275. On his upper lip was the beginning of what would be in another few months a luxuriant, dark brown handlebar mustache. He fancied it made him look more mature, more of a man of the world qualified to talk business and finance with older men.

His youthful looks bothered young Dow. He had said to his mother some months earlier, "I wish I looked older." His mother had smiled and said, "Time will take care of that, Herbert. Don't be impatient." But he was not one to wait patiently for time to give him an older appearance. He began to grow the mustache which later would become a full-fledged beard.

There was no one to greet Dow when he stepped onto the platform of the railroad station. He was a stranger. Once, while at Case, he had visited Midland briefly to get a sample of its brine. But he had made no friends and he hardly expected to see a familiar face at the railroad station. He brushed the cinders from his jacket and the dust from his polished shoes. Then he headed for the Larkin Hotel on Main Street.

Midland's Main Street wasn't exactly a scene to impress a stranger, inspire civic pride among the town's two thousand inhabitants, or fan a flame of hope for better days. The battered board sidewalks were scarred by the caulks of loggers' boots. A dilapidated wagon rolled down the street, drawn by a dispirited horse and a cow hitched together in harness. The cedar blocks that had once paved the streets in Midland's lumbering heyday had long before sunk beneath the mud now turned to dust. Occasionally a drunk wandered into or out of the swinging doors of one of the fourteen saloons standing elbow-to-elbow on the sleazy north side of the street. A woman was not a lady if seen too often on the wrong side of Main Street.

At night, Saloon Row threw off its lethargy and became more lively. The sound of music came from tinny pianos and men crowded to the bars to talk of the days when Midland had been the center of an exciting, boisterous, money-making logging industry.

The golden era for Midland had begun in the 1850's after timber cruisers had discovered the majestic stands of white pine in Central Michigan's Saginaw Valley. The trees towered to cloud-brushing heights of 185 feet. Their trunks were from 4 to 7 feet in diameter at the butts, encased with a dark gray bark. They rose with only a slight tapering of the trunks, giant pillars with scarcely a knot or a flaw for three-quarters of their length. The branches with their needles of dark green formed a canopy for mile after mile. The forest floor was a soft carpet of fallen needles strewn with pine cones, and free of underbrush. These monsters were up to three hundred years old. Their wood was creamy white, close-grained, and strong. In water, the wood floated like cork and was often called cork pine. The pines dominated the forests of Central Michigan, although there also were trees of oak, walnut, chestnut, maple, beech, cherry, cedar, balsam, and hemlock. Through this forest the Chippewa Indians had roamed and hunted and fished and fought long before the white man pushed in to claim the wilderness for his own.

The earliest surveyors had written off Michigan Territory as unfit for human habitation because they saw only its dark swamps and marshes that seemed to breed fevers and illness. Edward Tiffin, the Surveyor General of the Northwest, sent deputies into Michigan to map the area soon after the War of 1812. The surveyors were searching for homestead sites for war veterans. They started north from Detroit between the River Raisin and the Maumee. Soon they were mired in marshlands. The Indians were hostile. The wet, gloomy forests and miasmic swamps seemed a dreary place. Where the land was not marshy, it appeared to them to be barren and sandy, supporting little except stunted oaks. The surveyors turned back, before reaching the pine forests, to make their reports to Tiffin. He in turn asked Congress' permission to halt the survey because "the land is not worth the price of surveying it." Apparently Congress was impressed by Tiffin's report because veterans of the War of 1812 got their bonus of 160 acres in Florida instead of Michigan.

The fur traders and frontiersmen paid little heed to Tiffin's bleak report on Michigan except to jeer at it. They moved deeper into the forests and swamps to trade with the Indians, to hunt the plentiful game, to fish the beautiful lakes and streams, and to hack out home sites. One of the white settlements that grew in the wilderness was located at the junction of the Tittabawassee and Chippewa rivers and later was given the name Midland.

Prosperity came to the region with a rush after a shipment of Saginaw Valley white pine reached Albany, New York, in 1847, ten years after Michigan was admitted to the Union as a state. For years, lumber buyers had considered Maine's pine to be unexcelled, particularly for finishing work in homes. Lumber buyers found the Michigan pine at least the equal of Maine's white pine and some thought it superior. The reputation of Michigan pine spread rapidly. Timber cruisers poured in to stake out huge tracts for lumbermen and speculators, paying as little as $1.25 an acre. They received a bonus of one-fourth of the timberland they found. After them came the choppers and then the sawyers, the riverhogs, the sawmill operators, haulers, cooks, shanty boys, teamsters, and chickadees (the chore of the chickadees was to keep the roads and logging trails clear of horse manure).

Logging camps dotted the forests. Towns sprang up near each big lumbering operation. Great rafts of logs floated down the Tittabawassee, the Tobacco, the Sugar, the Chippewa, the Pine, the Bad, the Cass, the Shiawassee, and the Flint into the Saginaw River. At Saginaw and at Bay City the logs were ripped into lumber at the sawmills. Railroads were built deeper into the forests to haul out logs which could not be floated by water.

The get-rich-quick excitement that accompanied the logging boom was called Michigan Fever and from it came a song whose lines were:

> Come all ye Yankee farmers who wish to change your lot, Who've spunk enough to travel beyond your native plot, And leave behind the village where Pa and Ma must stay, Come follow me and settle in Michigania. Yea, yea, yea, Mich-i-gan-ia!

Historians have estimated that from 1850 to 1897 at least 160 billion board feet of white pine were cut in Michigan—enough to build ten million six-room houses or to build fifty one-inch plank roads, fifty feet wide, from New York to San Francisco.

By the time Dow arrived in Midland, the lumbering boom had moved northward and was nearing its end. The region around Midland was a stumpland with its vast wealth in timber gone. Salt-making and the manufacture of bromine were the major surviving industries and even they were failing. Young people were leaving to seek their fortunes elsewhere. Homes and business houses caught fire and burned under mysterious circumstances. Insurance companies threatened to withdraw all protection. A quip went around town: "If you're going to burn out, better do it now." It wasn't much of a joke. In one week, the volunteer firefighters battled twenty fires.

The timber was gone. The area was poverty striken. But beneath the earth was another treasure left there from an age when shallow, salty inland seas washed across parts of the continent. For millions of misty years a sea covered what is now the Middle West, stretching from Michigan deep into Georga and Mississippi. Then slowly the waters receded, leaving some areas covered with salty lakes. Evaporation of the lakes left behind saline deposits.

Then came the Great Ice Age. A mighty glacier inched down from the north. Like a giant bulldozer, it shoved a layer of earth and stone over the brine deposits and for centuries the land that was Michigan lay buried beneath ice hundreds of feet thick. The Michigan brine deposit was trapped in porous rock formations shaped like a nest of dishes. They underlay all of Central Michigan, a tremendous ocean of brine.

This was the stored treasure young Dow was determined to tap when he came to Midland, although he never dreamed it was as extensive as it later proved to be. He arrived on Thursday, August 14, 1890. After a night at the Larkin Hotel, he arranged for room and board ($15 a month) at a boarding house. He deposited his partner's check for $275 in the bank. And before the week ended he had leased an idle brine well and empty barn next to the Evans Flour Mill at the west end of Main Street. He also had placed an order with a printer for letterheads which proclaimed: Midland Chemical Company, J. H. Osborn, President, Herbert H. Dow, General Manager.

Dow hired a thin, lanky jack-of-all-trades, Julius Burow, at $1.50 a day, to help him build the electrolytic cells from cheap wood painted with tar. Julius' brother, Albert, was also frequently on the payroll. They knew nothing of chemistry, but they were expert with hammer, saw, paint brush, engines, wrench, and shovel. The barn became the "factory." Since electricity had not yet come to Midland, Dow bought a second-hand, 15-volt generator and set it up in the barn to make his own electricity. The generator was turned by a homemade rope belt attached to the steam engine at the flour mill. The belt ran from the generator to the engine through a hole knocked in the sides of the barn and flour mill.

It's little wonder that Dow became known in the months ahead as "Crazy Dow." Few people in Midland understood the mysteries of chemistry and reports of what was taking place down by the flour mill tended to support the view that neither Dow nor his business would ever be much of a financial credit to the town. But Dow ignored the gossip. Through the fall months and into the winter, he experimented with his electrolytic process, tinkered with his tar-wood cells, and saw his mustache grow to impressive length.

January 2, 1891, was a red-letter day. Dow turned on the generator, got the fan going for the blowing-out process, and for twenty-four consecutive hours the little plant produced bromine—the first in the world to be produced electrolytically as far as anyone knows. It was a chemical milestone that passed unheralded except for a brief notation in one of Dow's notebooks. Whatever jubilation Dow may have felt was tempered by the gloomy fact that he was almost broke, unpaid bills were accumulating, and the process was not working well enough to offer any hope of a profit in the near future.

Dow struggled through the winter working as much as eighteen hours a day to improve the operation of the rickety plant. He bought secondhand tools, equipment, and materials. He economized in every way he could, to hoard his dollars. But it was no use. He needed more capital if he ever hoped to make a commercial success of his process.

In the early spring of 1891, Dow started on another search for money. He took his problem to his partner in Cleveland, J. H. Osborn, who had backed him with never a reprimand for failures. Osborn agreed they should expand their partnership and he persuaded two Cleveland businessmen, W. L. Hulbert and B. W. Howe, to join their venture. When the partnership papers were signed, Dow returned to Midland with high hopes that now the money would be available to rebuild the plant and put it on a paying basis.

He immediately began overhauling the plant and building larger cells. But the new partners were not as enthusiastic about supplying money as Dow was in spending it for improvements and expansion. By April, Dow was writing to Howe; "The balance in the bank is $7.64. The boiler has not arrived and we haven't enough money to pay the freight on it when it does come." His itemized inventory of the Midland Chemical Company showed its worth at $3,000.

Almost every week Dow wrote to his partners pleading for more money with which to pay bills or to buy a needed piece of equipment. One crisis came with Albert Burow's threat to quit his job because in working with corrosive chemicals he was ruining his overalls. Dow reported to Howe; "Albert was going to leave us but I got him to stay by agreeing to pay for his overalls." Late in August, a note of desperation began to creep into Dow's letters, indicating that while he had not lost faith in the soundness of his process, he was beginning to doubt his own managerial ability.

"... Every chemist of my acquaintance who understands our method thinks the principle is right and the method is the best one for making bromine," he said in one letter. "I think another manager might make a rousing success of it, but I know that I have done the best within my ability." A week later he was writing; "I don't know what to do. My board bill is running up and I get no ideas from you as to what you intend doing." Dow paid his board bill by persuading his creditors to accept stock in the company.

What Howe and Hulbert intended doing was to remove themselves from the partnership. They had invested $2,115. The company had sold a small quantity of bromine. But nothing had happened to encourage them to continue sending money to Dow when his enthusiasm for his process monotonously outstripped production. And so the partnership began to fall apart in the fall of 1891. It was finally dissolved on August 11, 1892.

During that winter of 1891–92, young Dow returned to Cleveland to place still another plan before his friend Osborn. By this time he was convinced that the secret of success lay in using larger brine cells and a heavier current of electricity in freeing the bromine. He convinced Osborn the process would work this time if only enough capital were raised to equip a new plant properly. With Osborn's help, he began to look for financial backing for still another try.

During these months, Dow found time to pay court to a slender, petite school teacher named Grace Ball, whose father was a farmer-businessman. The Balls were a prominent Midland family with roots in New England and the town watched the courtship with interest. It was an open secret that the two were in love. Their go-between was a small boy in one of Grace Ball's classes. He was often observed leaving the school during class hours, getting on his bicycle and racing to the plant where Dow labored, or to his boarding house, to deliver and receive a note.

"If those two don't get married," one citizen observed sagely, "that boy is going to wear himself out riding that bicycle." Many residents were not so much concerned with the health and stamina of the bicycle rider as they were with the wisdom of Grace Ball in becoming seriously interested in a young man who was a chronic failure hardly able to pay his board bill. It caused quite a bit of talk at the bazaars and picnics and church socials as well as at the bars on Saloon Row.

But things were looking up for Dow. He and Osborn persuaded a group of businessmen to back a new corporation that would have 10,000 shares of stock at $10 par value. Theoretically, at least, Dow would have $100,000 this time with which to build a plant and buy equipment. The articles of incorporation were approved on May 24, 1892. The largest stock subscriber was a Cleveland businessman, B. E. Helman. He paid off the claims of Hulbert and Howe and furnished most of the cash. He also had himself elected treasurer by the board of directors. Dow put his patents into the pot and received in return a substantial bloc of stock, the title of general manager, and a salary of $100 a month.

Dow quickly found that he would have considerably less than $100,000 with which to build the plant. Actually, the stockholders paid into the treasury only $10,000. But then a Cleveland bank advanced a credit of $10,000 to place a more solid financial underpinning beneath the new enterprise.

Dow's first move was to shift the location of the plant from the Evans Flour Mill property to a 10-acre plot of land he purchased with company funds at the east end of Main Street on the bank of the Tittabawassee River. Two brine wells were drilled. New buildings, all of cheap pine, were constructed. New and bigger brine cells were hammered together. Some said that Dow even counted the nails that went into each building, figuring out the stresses so that two nails would not be used where one would do the job.

The greatest single expense was the purchase of a new 50-kilowatt generator which could generate the 100 volts Dow estimated he would need for operating the new and larger cells. The trough-like cells, set in series, were partitioned by tarred boards into a series of smaller cells. Carbon electrodes, bought secondhand, were run through the partitioning boards to carry electric current from one brine cell to the next. In the past, Dow had made ferric or iron bromide from the bromine. Now he planned to make potassium bromide, which was in greater demand by industries.

Two months after the Midland Chemical Company's incorporation, Dow turned the current into his brine cells and began the production of potassium bromide. The product contained impurities which would have to be removed. There were more breakdowns, frustrations and disappointments. But the process was working better and Dow was confident he was headed in the right direction. Perhaps the best measure of his confidence in the future was his marriage in November of that year to Grace Ball. They set up housekeeping in a house that rented for $10 a month. Often in the first months of their marriage, the young bride went with her husband to the plant on cold winter nights to stay with him while he fired a boiler or worked on the cells. They often slept on cots in the boiler room. She also spent hours helping him pick black specks and impurities from the first barrels of bromide crystals.

The fly in the ointment of happiness was Helman, who soon made it clear he was determined to run the Midland operation from his Cleveland office. The new corporation was only a few weeks old when Helman began questioning the smallest expenditures by Dow. Why had Dow spent four cents for two stamps on two letters when the two letters could have been placed in one envelope requiring only two cents' postage? Why had he bought a lock in Midland when it could have been ordered from Saginaw cheaper? Why had a pipe wrench been purchased? Why should the company buy chalk for the carpenters when it was customary for carpenters to furnish their own chalk? Why did Dow include in an expense account 20 cents for "sundries" without explanation?

And Dow's answers went like this: "I had already mailed the first letter when your letter arrived, which I thought needed a prompt reply—thus requiring the use of a second stamp"... "Yale locks cost in Saginaw 29 cents more than the price I paid"... "If I had not needed a pipe wrench I would not have got it"... "You say carpenters furnish their own chalk. Our shingling was not done by carpenters"... "The sundries include only 20 cents that was paid a boy in the woods seven miles from here to show me the way to Mr. Towsley's house through a blinding snowstorm."

Dow ended one letter to Helman by saying; "In conclusion I will say that I will be very much pleased to have you call my attention to 'little expenses or waste that we can remedy' but quoting you again, 'Busy men do not like and cannot afford to waste their time.'"

The bickering-by-letter continued and young Dow found himself trapped in a thoroughly disagreeable situation. The company owned his patents. Helman and his friends held the controlling stock in the corporation. Helman had no faith in Dow's managerial ability and did not even bother to use diplomacy in dealing with him. But the greatest blow of all came early in 1893 when Helman—without the formality of a board meeting—hired a general manager to take over Dow's responsibilities. The new manager was H. S. Cooper, a brother of one of the stockholders.

This period was a galling, bitter time for Herbert Dow. Five years of research and sweat and worry appeared to be going down the drain with little of substance to show for it. His pride was wounded. He had no real authority in the plant he had struggled to build. Worst of all, perhaps, he had lost control over his electrolytic process for making bromides.

These were the months when the people of Midland would see Dow driving a horse and buggy over the back roads of the countryside with his young bride by his side. Whenever the black moods were unbearable, they would leave the town behind to talk things out between themselves. Some said it was the stubborn will of this tiny woman that kept Dow from walking away from the humiliations and defeats. Whatever the truth, their troubles drew them more closely together.

Instead of quitting, Dow continued working at the plant to improve the bromine cells. The production improved. The product became better even though progress was slow. And Helman continued to keep a tight personal control over the smallest expenditures.

During one of Cooper's absences from Midland, Dow wrote to Helman: "Now you write me that the $126.19 I received is sufficient for both last and this week's expenses and refuse to send me more. The result is I am compelled to shut down and stop all output.... The secondary result is that I as nominal manager am spending money without getting a return and thus ruining both my own and the company's reputation. In the last 37 weeks there have been only two weeks when I have been paid in full to date.... You say my salary must not touch on the revenue of the works but must come in as we can make it from time to time, and refuse to send me any for either personal or company use although the company owes me to date $271.65...."

Surprisingly, it was when things looked darkest for him that Dow began borrowing money from friends to buy more stock in the Midland Chemical Company. Perhaps he felt that some way, somehow, his luck would change, he would regain a voice in the management of the company, and would win a measure of control over his patents. But such hopes seemed a bleak prospect at the beginning of 1894. On January 8, Helman called a brief meeting of the board of directors in Cleveland and H. S. Cooper was officially named general manager of the plant. Dow was given a crumb. He was named secretary of the company.

During the fight with Helman, Dow had been quietly at work devising a process to extract chlorine from the brine. The brine was richer in chlorine than in bromine, and chlorine products were becoming more and more important on the commercial market. One of the products was bleaching powder (chloride of lime) used in large quantities by textile mills, cotton mills, and pulp paper mills. Chlorine was also a product with vastly greater commercial possibilities than bromine because it could be used not only in making bleach, but in making a large number of other products.

The Midland brine contained .15 percent bromine, 12.5 percent sodium chloride, 10.1 percent calcium chloride, and 3.6 percent magnesium chloride. In extracting only bromine, the Midland Chemical Company was dumping into the sewer as garbage the greatest part of the brine's wealth. Dow was certain a way could be found to make use of it.

Three months after he was officially deposed as general manager, Dow argued the directors into letting him "spend such money as he may require for apparatus to make experimental tests on chlorate manufacture...." The arguments he used were never revealed. But Helman did loosen the purse strings enough for Dow to carry on his experiment in a small shed on the company property.

Perhaps Helman was generous because the company was now making money at the rate of two to three percent a month. The bromine process was working smoothly. Expenses were being held down. If nothing rocked the boat, the company would pay the stockholders handsomely even though the country was feeling the pinch of a business depression.

Things were going so smoothly that Helman persuaded the directors to send an agent to Europe to try to sell or lease the Dow bromine process to the Germans. Fortunately for Dow, the Germans were not interested. They thought their own manufacturing process was better—a decision which they were to regret within a few years.

With virtually no responsibility at the plant, Dow busied himself with work on the chlorine process. He received encouragement from his former schoolmate A. W. Smith, who had become a professor of chemistry at Case School, and with whom he had corresponded regularly. Smith wrote to Dow in October, 1894: "... I see an enormous future for the company if they will go into a few of the many things that may be developed electrolytically. You go ahead alone and get your plant in tip-top shape...."

Dow did just that. And it must have been around the time that he received Smith's letter that he began trying to figure out a way to free himself from any obligation to give the company his future patents.

Indeed there was stirring in his mind the idea of forming a new company in which he would have more freedom to explore all the commercial possibilities of the Midland brine—and not be limited to one or two products. He had his dreams, too, of a company in which he would have a voice with some authority.

At a meeting of the board of directors on January 22, 1895, Dow announced that his experiment with the new chlorine cell had proved it was ready to be tested commercially. He was stretching the truth without pulling it entirely out of shape. A good deal of work still had to be done to make a success of the process but it did look unusually promising. This time Helman went along with Dow. He made a motion that Dow go to Cleveland and make application for a patent on his bleaching powder process and the motion was carried. Then the board approved a most curious motion "that Herbert H. Dow be released from any obligation to surrender to this company any invention, process or patents except such as may relate to products which may profitably be manufactured from the salt water as pumped from their wells."

It has never been explained whether Helman was moving to tie up all of Dow's patents—or Dow was maneuvering to free himself from the maze of frustration he found himself in. At any event, Dow began work immediately to set up the chlorine plant around the cells he had devised and patented. Two months after getting the go-ahead approval of the board, he switched electric current into the cells. The hour was 11 A.M. Everything seemed to be working satisfactorily when Dow and his crew left the building at 12 noon to have lunch. They had walked a few yards distance when the cells exploded with a cannon's roar. The sides of the building blew out and the roof collapsed. Other buildings were damaged. Firefighters rushed to prevent the flames from destroying the entire complex of barn-like wooden buildings housing the bromine operation.

When news of the explosion reached Helman, he called an emergency meeting of the board of directors and they hurried to Midland to assess the damage. Dow could only speculate that hydrogen had been released in the cells and somehow a spark had caused the explosion. Luckily no one had been injured and the loss was not great although it could have been a disaster.

Helman had had enough of Dow's experiments. He hired a chemist, J. C. Grayes to take over the chemistry problems which had been Dow's responsibility. He ordered an immediate halt to any further work on the chlorine project. A majority of the board agreed the Midland

Chemical Company should stick to what it knew best—making bromine. Profits were good. Expansion into other products was too risky. There was no sense in jeopardizing a sure thing on a gamble that could wipe out the company.

Again Dow found himself cornered. He remained an employee of the firm at a small salary. He continued to hold the stock he had received in exchange for his patents and ideas. He had a minority voice in management. His future with the Midland Chemical Company looked less than promising. He was twenty-nine years old and his seven years in the business world had been largely a series of disappointments. Over it all was a cloud of debts and anxiety for his family. A daughter, Helen, was one year old and Mrs. Dow was again pregnant.

In June of that difficult year, the company's board pushed Dow a little deeper into despondency. He was ordered to go to Syracuse to try to sell his chlorine process to the Solvay Process Company, with any money received to go into the company's treasury. But somehow Dow persuaded the group to agree that in event a sale could not be made within one month, then he would have all rights to the process himself—provided he paid to the Midland Chemical Company one-tenth of the gross receipts from the process.

It is hardly likely that Dow tried very hard to sell his process to the Solvay people. And when the thirty days had passed without a sale, he had at least salvaged his chlorine process from the wreckage—even though there was a ten percent mortgage on its future.

It was during this time that Dow patented a liquid to make bicycle tires puncture-proof and organized a company to develop it. But nothing came of this venture. And then in the fall of 1895, Dow dissapeared from Midland with his family. There were reports that they were in Massillon, Ohio, where Mrs. Dow had given birth to a second daughter, Ruth. A Midlander was heard to say; "Come to think of it, I haven't seen Crazy Dow around lately. What's happened to him?"

"He left town in a hurry," another said. "I don't think we'll be seeing much of him anymore."

But Midland was to see Herbert Dow quite often in the years to come. His absence was a mere interlude.

Chapter Three

Herbert Dow's driving energy and unorthodox ideas always held a fascination for J. H. Osborn of Cleveland. He could ill afford to risk his money on a manufacturing process that was commercially sound in theory only, because he was not a wealthy man. And yet each time Dow came to him for financial help, Osborn was like Ado Annie in the modern-day musical comedy, *Oklahoma!*—he couldn't say no.

When Dow arrived at his office in the winter of 1895 and asked for still more help in starting still another chemical company, Osborn was caught up once more in the whirlwind of Dow's enthusiasm. This time it was Dow's enthusiasm over his electrolytic chlorine process and its money-making potential. But this time Dow did have a solid base from which to make his appeal: the Midland Chemical Company was making money from his bromine process and paying Osborn and the other stockholders two percent a month on their modest investment despite the national depression. Furthermore, he insisted, the chlorine process held a far greater potential than the bromine process.

Once again Osborn pitched in to help Dow finance his new adventure. They did not turn to Cleveland businessmen in search of backers, however. They went to the academic community—more particularly to Case School and men who understood the underlying theory of Dow's process. They talked to Dr. Cady Staley, president of Case, and Professor A. W. Smith, Dow's long-time friend. Dow brought into the discussions James T. Pardee, one of his former classmates at Case who was then a civil engineer working for the City of Cleveland.

These men understood what Dow was trying to do and how he intended to go about it. They knew his theory was sound even if they might have had reservations about Dow's claims that it would take only a short time to get a plant in operation which would produce bleaching powder on a commercial scale. They agreed to dig into their modest savings to back him in setting up the plant. They signed a partnership agreement which said:

1. Herbert H. Dow, James T. Pardee, Albert W. Smith, J. H. Osborn and Cady Staley hereby agree to associate themselves as partners under the firm name of Dow Process Company, for manufacture of and dealing in bleach and caustic under the process discovered and invented by Herbert H. Dow.

2. Herbert H. Dow agrees to furnish $2,000; James T. Pardee, $5,333.33; Albert W. Smith, $3,333.33; J. H. Osborn, $4,000; and Cady Staley, $2,000; all in money to the capital of the partnership.

3. And Herbert H. Dow agrees to transfer and assign to the partnership his entire invention and discovery and process for the manufacture of bleach and caustic, together with any and all improvements he may make in said process . . .

With the money in the bank, Dow did not head for Midland. He set out for Navarre, Ohio, a small town some 300 miles south of Midland. Why he decided to go to Navarre rather than return to Midland no one knows. Perhaps he wanted a place where he could work on his process in secrecy. Almost everyone in the infant chemical industry in those days was highly secretive about laboratory experiments and manufacturing techniques even after his brain-child had been patented. And Dow was no exception.

He put up an eight-foot-high board fence around a plot of land 300 feet long and 300 feet wide on the outskirts of Navarre. Six wooden buildings were constructed, a generator installed and tar-wood cells built. No one was permitted inside the fence without Dow's permission. All deliveries of materials and equipment were unloaded at the plant's gate by wagon drivers to whom chemistry was as dark a secret as a voodoo ritual. When anyone asked Dow what he was manufacturing, he replied: "We're making embalming fluid."

Dow did call one meeting of businessmen in Navarre, suggesting they finance the drilling of salt wells to be leased to the Dow Process Company. A lumberman thought it was a good deal. He offered to put up $1,000 if his neighbor, a German chemist, would put up a like amount. But the German wanted no part of the deal. He was suspicious of Dow and his embalming-fluid story. He arose at the meeting and told his fellow townsmen: "I will gladly give Mr. Dow $1,000 to move his plant out of the community. I don't want a whistle waking me up every morning when I want to sleep." Besides, he argued, what Dow was doing behind the fence was very likely a dangerous operation.

About all the meeting did was to divide the town into rival camps which were pro-Dow and anti-Dow. There was a grain of truth in what the German had said about the danger, because Dow did have several small explosions as he worked to get the bugs out of his process. The explosions in the cells, or "traps" as they were sometimes called, were to plague him for months until their cause was discovered and a remedy found.

Dow's partners in Cleveland soon became upset by the reports from Navarre. Dow had appeared confident of quick success at their Cleveland meetings, but he seemed to be making little progress as the weeks passed. Pardee was especially uneasy because he had most of his savings invested. At one point he wrote to Dow: "I have refrained from writing you for some time in hope of receiving some encouraging news regarding the progress you were making in the work. I have felt so discouraged over the way things turned out, that I haven't felt like thinking about it long enough to write. I thought from what you said that we would be able to start up right away and make some bleach, but it seems from what you have written Dr. Smith that you are not able even to get chlorine part of the time...."

Actually, Dow was making more progress than the partners realized. Part of it was the seemingly negative progress of learning what wouldn't work. The thing he needed most, he felt, was time in which to perfect a continuous bleach process.

Only six months after setting up the Navarre plant, Dow startled and dismayed his partners with the news that Navarre wasn't the best place after all for the plant and that he was moving it to Midland. He reported he had leased a plot of land adjoining Midland Chemical and had worked out a deal with Helman to use their waste brine for a small fee. The bromine would be taken from the brine by Midland Chemical before it reached Dow's plant—but that was immaterial because Dow was now only interested in the chlorine it contained.

The real reason behind the move back to Midland may have been that Dow wanted to keep an eye on Helman's operations. He had learned through H. S. Cooper, his successor at Midland Chemical, that Helman was working on a scheme to gather the major bromine producers of the country into a combine dominated by the Midland company. In a confidential letter to Dow, Cooper said Helman's action seemed "to breathe the rule or ruin spirit" and "it may be best not to get too much under the control of it." He said he had advised Helman he wanted no part in the maneuvering.

Dow learned, also, that Helman had changed his views about producing only bromine. Now he wanted to expand the company's operations into other products. Belatedly, he had recognized the fact that the company was throwing away a potential fortune in the waste brine. In one letter, Helman had written Cooper: "We have thousands of dollars, good dollars, running into the river every year. Probably, too, we may develop Graves into a discoverer by leading him into this, another having suggested the way. Dow is a genius, quick to see and certainly brilliant in his way. We must not stop with bromine. We must get through Graves or Dow or both all there is in that brine that we can turn into money."

Helman was now suggesting the precise course which Dow had tried to get the company to take earlier. Even though Dow held a substantial bloc of Midland Chemical Stock, was the company's secretary, and wanted the company to prosper, he nevertheless had no intention of again playing on the same team with Helman as captain.

It was in early 1896 that Dow returned with his family to Midland. He quickly set up a small plant and went to work on the chlorine process. Gradually he made improvements in the traps and stopped some of the leakage of chlorine which was a nagging problem. He also made some bleach. But more important than anything else was his conclusion that if the manufacture of bleach was to be a success, the process would have to be geared to volume production. Instead of thinking and planning in terms of pounds, the company would have to think and plan in terms of tons. Dow had in mind a plant and equipment that would turn out no less than nine tons of bleach a day, 365 days a year. At the time, bleach was selling for $3.10 a hundredweight with the market price controlled by the British bleach combine, United Alkali. The British were sending bleaching powder into the United States at the rate of more than 100,000,000 pounds a year, paying shipping and handling charges, and still making a profit. The invention of the rotary press and the growth of the penny press had boomed the demand for bleach in the paper industry. Dow knew if he could crack this market the future of the company would be a rosy one. But to compete with the British would take money—far more money than he had been able to raise before.

As the New Year, 1897, arrived, however, there was too much excitement in the Dow household to permit much thought of business. The family doctor came oftener to the Dow home. And on January 4, Mrs. Dow gave birth to a son who was named Willard Henry Dow. The proud father quickly spread the news among his friends.

J. H. Osborn wrote to congratulate the parents, saying: "I am rather sorry that you did not see fit to carry out your idea of bestowing the name of Osborn on the young man. I feel sure that 'Osborn Dow' would have done him credit. . . . I never heard of but one man by the name of Osborn being hung." (The Dows later named a son Osborn, but he died as a small boy.)

When all the excitement had subsided, Dow laid his plan for a larger plant before his partners. He convinced them the time had come to build on a large scale and to move boldly into the bleach market. Dow was certain they could undersell the British and find customers to take all they could produce. The partners were inclined to agree. But Pardee didn't want to rush into any hasty decisions such as the building of the plant at Navarre which Dow had abandoned after only a few months. He suggested that perhaps Dow should get his process in perfect working order—and then an agreement could be worked out to merge the Dow Process Company and the Midland Chemical Company.

It was agreed that J. H. Osborn should sound out Helman on the merger idea. By this time, Dow and Osborn together held almost 50 percent of the Midland Chemical Company's stock, but Helman still swung the controlling interest and a merger on favorable terms hinged on his approval.

With hindsight, it seems naive that the partners of a nonproductive company based on a flawed process could believe that Helman would agree to a merger on equal terms. Nevertheless, Osborn sought a meeting with Helman.

Meantime, the partners outlined their plans for a larger company to Charles Post, the secretary and treasurer of the East End Savings Bank of Cleveland and one of the city's most influential businessmen. By the time Dow had finished talking, Post also was infected with the fever of his enthusiasm. He promised to call together some of his friends who might be interested in backing the venture.

Post cautioned, "Just now is not a very good time to get capital to invest. I think the climate will be better in the spring." Post agreed with Pardee that Dow's process should be put in good working order before any serious move was made toward a merger with Midland Chemical.

But Osborn thought it best to talk to Helman and the two men met in late January. As might have been foreseen, Helman rejected the idea of a merger on equal terms. "In the first place," he told Osborn, "Midland is not the best place for the location of a bleach plant. And no one with capital will go into a deal with the Dow Process Company on an equal footing with the Midland Chemical Company. Such a merger is not even practical."

Osborn reported the conversation to his partners. "It looks to me," he said, "we will have to go on and do the best we can alone and possibly amalgamation may be brought about later."

In a separate letter to Dow, Osborn said of Helman: "Money men always want to have the big end of the hog and if not they won't have anything to do with it. They cannot bear to see some other fellow who is not a capitalist nor has any business standing own a larger share than themselves." Then for the first time in their years of association, Osborn began to waver in his support of Dow. He pointed out that the Midland Chemical Company was an established fact while the Dow Process Company was an experiment—and perhaps the wise course would be for the Midland Chemical Company to take over Dow Process Company.

But even as Osborn was writing this letter, Charles Post was taking charge of the plans to organize a company to take over Dow Process Company. Dow was so certain of success that in March he began to borrow money on his Midland Chemical stock to put into the new company. He wrote a glowing letter to his uncle, Frank A. Curtiss, in New Haven, Connecticut: "If you want to invest I think our new company will offer the best inducements of anything I know of. . . . We have already got some unusually good men who we think are not of the tricky sort. . . ."

Then he added a note: "To change the subject, Grace and all the babies are getting along nicely. Helen is as prim and polite as anyone you ever saw and very neat at the table, but Ruth makes so much noise you can hear her a block away and never forgets to divide what she eats between her mouth and the rest of her face and hair. . . . Willard Henry would fling his whole weight onto his feet before he was two months old. We expect him to be the champion strong man."

These were happy and exciting days for Dow. When not at work on his bleach process, he had been campaigning for election as alderman from Midland's Third Ward. A good bit of his electioneering was carried on in Frank Teal's Main Street barber shop where he stopped each morning for a 10-cent shave and an argument with anyone willing to argue with him. Teal usually was willing. And the campaign was a success.

On April 30, Charles Post mailed letters to several prominent Cleveland businessmen, saying: "Dear Sir: You are cordially invited to meet a number of other representative businessmen at this office on Tuesday, May 4, 1897. at 7:30 P.M. Standard Time. Professor A. W. Smith of Case School and Mr. H. H. Dow, secretary of the Midland Chemical Company, will be present to explain a new process of electrochemical manufacture. Yours very truly, Charles H. Post."

A large group gathered at Post's office to hear Smith and Dow explain the manufacturing process and their hopes for the future. Each was handed a statement which said in part:

"About $2,000,000 worth of Chloride of Lime or Bleaching Powder is consumed each year in the U. S., but none is now made here on a Commercial Scale. We propose to manufacture it by a new electrical process, in some respects similar to our Bromine process that has proved a phenomenal success. We are the first persons, so far as any records show, to make use of electricity in any chemical manufacture, on a Commercial Scale, aside from electroplating of metals. This is quite a different operation and has been in use for many years.... Our method of making Chlorine is extremely simple and does not require expensive apparatus and has been developed to such an extent that we advocate no change whatever in size in the proposed plant...."

There was a touch of pre-Madison Avenue salesmanship in calling Dow's process "extremely simple." In theory the process was relatively simple. But in putting theory into commercial practice, the process was proving stubbornly difficult and would continue to be for months to come. Nevertheless, Dow transmitted his own enthusiasm to the crowd. When he had finished his talk, more than fifty of the businessmen lined up to put their names on the list of stock subscribers.

Nine days after the meeting in Post's office, the subscribers met and voted to form a corporation to take over the operation of the Dow Process Company. The new company was to be called The Dow Chemical Company. It was agreed to capitalize the company at $200,000 divided into 20,000 shares of stock having a par value of $10 a share. At some unspecified time in the future, the company was to pay the Dow Process Company $250,000 in stock for its assets, which were little more than the patents Dow had obtained on his chlorine process.

Dow agreed in a memorandum to devote "my entire time, skill, energy and attention to your company, giving to you the entire product of every kind resulting therefrom...." He was to be paid a salary of $500 a month with the stipulation that only two-thirds of it would be paid until the company was paying dividends.

The Dow Chemical Company was born on May 18, 1897, when the articles of incorporation were filed in Michigan. The board of directors included Dow, Osborn, Staley, Pardee, Smith, and two Midland businessmen. But most of the directors were Cleveland businessmen. They gave the post of president to A. E. Convers, a Cleveland tack manufacturer. Post was named secretary-treasurer and Dow general manager.

If Dow had been a drinking man, the time would have called for a celebration with champagne flowing. In a brief period of months, his fortunes had swung violently from the depths of near-defeat to a pinnacle from which the future had a rosy glow. On paper, he was now moderately well-to-do. If all went well, his days of scrimping and scraping to keep one jump ahead of disaster were over. He was thirty-one years old and he now could afford to hire more than the six men his uncle had once said were needed to keep up with all his ideas.

The company allotted Dow $83,333.33 with which to build the new plant, more money than he had ever had to work with before. And Midland was startled in that summer of 1897 by the fevered burst of construction activity at the east end of Main Street.

Many people in town didn't know what to make of it all. Only a few years before Dow had been having trouble paying his board bill. Now he was spending money in bundles. Not only was he buying large quantities of materials, but he was paying off his workers in cash every week instead of giving due bills as was the local custom. A good many businessmen around town didn't like to see the workers paid in cash. They had been making a tidy profit by buying due bills at a discount. Furthermore, not all the women were enthused by the Dows' new affluence. Word quickly spread that the Dows were paying their maid $3.00 a week while the going rate was $1.50. The Dows were ruining the local labor market.

Some looked at Dow with new respect. To others he still was unpredictable Crazy Dow, upsetting local customs and going his own way. Saloon Row didn't trust him because he was always arguing that those fourteen saloons on Main Street were a disgrace and something should be done about the rowdies who lounged outside their doors. But nobody ignored him as he pedaled his bicycle to and from work with coat tails flying.

Dow plunged into the construction of his new plant. He had cash to spend, but the money had to be spread to cover the cost of land, building materials, expensive new equipment, and labor. Dow designed the first of nine buildings himself, each 40 feet wide and 90 feet long with 16-foot cedar pole supports. His materials were cheap lumber and tar and he still counted the nails. Each building cost him $500, giving him 3,600 square feet of floor space at a cost of 14 cents a square foot.

He persuaded his brother-in-law, young Tom Griswold, Jr., who had married his sister, Helen Dow, to give up his job in Cleveland and come to Midland for $17.23 a week to help design the plant. The tall, lanky Griswold, also a graduate of Case School, was the first of the remarkable group of talented men whom Dow would attract to Midland through the years. Dow also brought his father from Cleveland to help supervise the construction.

He continued to make his chlorine cells of tarred wood and used carbons because of their cheapness. His buildings were designed for utility only. The grinding experience of trying to make do on little money had left its mark. Dow was tightfisted in buying. His father and Griswold argued with him for two weeks before he would invest $125 in a drill press. But in buying a 400-kilowatt generator, condensers, pumps, and air compressors Dow looked for the best. The generator was considered a giant piece of electrical machinery and one of the most advanced of its time.

Through the summer and fall the building went on. The company's power plant was started up on Thanksgiving Day, November 25, 1897, and The Dow Chemical Company produced its first bleach.

Everything went well for a time. But then things began to go wrong. Explosion after explosion jarred the plant as cells blew up. Yellow chlorine poured out onto the floors. Chlorine gas filled the buildings but workers found they could counteract the effects of the gas by inhaling the fumes of grain alcohol. Tom Griswold and chemist Jim Graves, who had left Midland Chemical to join Dow, began a search for the cause of the explosions.

The company sold its first bleach in January, 1898, for $37.48. Sales climbed to around $700 a month and leveled off. At this rate the company was headed for disaster and the Cleveland directors became alarmed. Dow began receiving letters demanding he do something to increase production and sales. The investors were shaken, too, by news that the British bleach combine had slashed the price of bleach in half on the American market. The move was clearly an effort to drive the growing number of American bleach producers out of business. Two members of Dow Chemical's board of directors resigned and put their stock up for sale. Dow borrowed money to buy a large part of it.

The company's first birthday was not a happy one. The plant was running at only half its capacity. Breakdowns often halted work. Even when the plant did work, Dow's process was far from efficient. Bugs developed in the larger operation that had not been foreseen in the smaller plant operations. The gap between theory and practice remained wide. And yet Dow was cheerfully optimistic in his letters to President Convers. To the annoyance of his colleagues, he seemed to regard the gathering thunderheads as nothing more than passing clouds in a blue sky.

During this time a stockholder returned to Cleveland from a trip to Midland and Convers asked; "What's Dow doing up there?"

"He's busy over at the new house he's building."

"He is building what?" Convers demanded.

"He is supervising the construction of a new home. I heard around town that he's building a mansion."

It was true that Dow was building a home. It was far from a mansion, but he had planned a large and comfortable house. He was dividing his time between the plant and the house, changing the architect's drawings and even keeping a critical eye on the installation of the plumbing. No one knew where the money was coming from to pay for the house, but then Midlanders had long before given up trying to account for Dow's activities. The Cleveland stockholders were beginning to believe they had backed the wrong horse.

At odd times Dow also had been working with a few friends to get control of the Midland Chemical Company from B. E. Helman, whose schemes for dominating the American bromine market had collapsed. When the Midland Chemical's board of directors met in June, Dow and his friends held the controlling interest and Dow was elected president. Soon afterward they opened negotiations with Helman to buy his interest in the company.

Early in November, Dow wrote to Convers; "I am not going to let worldly matters bother me today. I'm moving into my new home." The following month Helman sold out his interest in Midland Chemical for $40,000, bringing to an end his long feud with Dow. After three years, Dow once more had a strong position in the company he had helped organize, and he had his family installed in the big, new house on the west end of Main Street—not far from the spot where he had started his first plant near the Evans Flour Mill eight years earlier.

The New Year, 1899, however, brought with it no magical solutions to Dow's problems with the bleach operation. By June, the company had $117,000 invested and sales had not reached a break-even point. The explosions in the chlorine cells continued and the patience of the Cleveland backers was growing more strained. They were looking with misgivings at the contract which called for the payment of $250,000 in stock to the partners in the old Dow Process Company.

Five stockholders, including President Convers and Secretary-Treasurer Post, signed a letter to Dow which said in part: "...developments have shown that the Dow process is not successful and was not a perfect process, as we had been led to believe, and we are of the opinion that it is still in an experimental state.... Our cash reserves are exhausted... and it would be utterly unreasonable to solicit further investment of capital." They put their proposition rather bluntly: cancel the Dow Process claim to $250,000 in stock and accept instead stock to cover only the actual money invested in Dow Process.

Dow simply ignored the letter. He waited for Convers and Post to make the first move. They made it by calling a meeting in Cleveland of Dow Chemical's executive committee late in June. And then Dow argued his case. He told them their fears were groundless, and that he and his men were on the edge of a breakthrough. All he needed to perfect the process was more time. "I am not worried at all now," he said. "I was a year ago. Then we were in trouble. Now we are not." He stalled off any official move to reduce the stock obligation to Dow Process. He played for time because he knew that he, Griswold, and Graves were getting close to a solution of the cell explosions and a serious leakage of electric current.

Graves and Griswold worked in shifts around the clock through August, September, and October. Dow became haggard with weariness and strain. The explosions and leaks had to be stopped or everything would be lost. The plant losses had been cut to $163 a day but the drain could not go on indefinitely. Graves worked from noon until midnight. Then he would stop by Griswold's house near the plant and explain what had happened in the preceding twelve hours. After Mrs. Griswold had given her husband something to eat, Griswold would light his lantern and head for the plant to begin his midnight to noon shift.

It was Griswold who isolated the cause of the explosions. He suspected that the carbon electrodes after long soaking in brine and chlorine became porous, permitting hydrogen gas to seep through to the chlorine gas and form an explosive mixture. He bought some wax at the drug store, melted it on the kitchen stove at his home, and placed the carbons in the hot wax. Then he let the wax cool. When the wax-soaked carbons were installed in several cells, the explosions in those cells stopped.

Graves and Griswold found also that many of the boards holding the carbons had become spongy, which permitted electric current to pass through them without making chlorine. They devised a simple method to test the efficiency of each cell and to check on any loss of electric current. As soon as the efficiency of a cell began to drop, new boards and carbons were installed. The cell efficiency immediately improved.

This was the turning point for The Dow Chemical Company. Production climbed to the nine tons a day that Dow had planned. The quality and strength of the bleach improved. Almost overnight the plant that had been losing $163 a day began to make money. In the new spirit of jubilation that followed, Dow was praised by his Cleveland backers as a man of genius. The harsh words and the fears voiced a few months earlier were things to be forgotten. Dow amiably conceded that perhaps $250,000 was too steep a price to pay for the assets of Dow Process. He suggested that $204,000 would be acceptable to him and his partners and his offer was accepted.

Music sounded through the new Dow home that Christmas. It poured from a Regina Sublima, a polished mahogany music box which Dow had bought as a present for the family. The manufacturers billed their machine as "the only Music Box made which is provided with a mechanism that automatically changes its Tune Sheets.... Without being touched, after once started, it plays successively, by a continuous automatic motion, all the tunes of the repertoire, consisting of a number of disks, which are contained in the lower part of the case.... The Sublima has two large steel combs with 130 tongues tuned in the chromatic scale (and) a long-running Clock Movement which is interchangeable in all parts, and cannot get out of order...."

The disks played such numbers as Wagner's "Grand March," the "Wedding March" from Lohengrin, the "William Tell Overture," "My Old Kentucky Home," Sousa's "The Washington Post March," "Glory Hallelujah Song," and something called "I've Waited, Honey, Waited Long for You."

The end of the century was a large milestone for Herbert Dow. The clawing and scratching for sheer survival in the business world was not over, but the first battles had been won. The ten years of struggle had proved that his bromine and chlorine processes were sound, chemically and commercially. He did not control the companies he had helped start, but at least he now had a strong voice in their management. More important than all else, he had helped pioneer in the first stirrings of an American chemical industry that one day would be free of European domination.

Chapter Four

Across the land, bells tolled, whistles blew, firecrackers exploded, and people gathered to shout and sing—and to pray—as the old century died and the new century was born. There were no major wars being fought around the world. The United States had bounced back from the economic depression of 1893 and times were relatively good.

Wages were low but, then, the purchasing power of the dollar was high. Potatoes were selling for 35 to 45 cents a bushel. Butter was 24 to 35 cents a pound. Wheat was 70 cents a bushel, corn 33 cents, and Texas steers $4.25 a hundred pounds. Ladies' muslin nightgowns could be had for 19 cents, women's shoes for $1.97 (on sale), and "a good, well-made corset in long or short size" could be had for 50 cents. Room and board costs varied according to the locality, but in Midland the rates held steady at $15 to $20 a month.

President William McKinley occupied the White House and it was generally agreed he would be the Republican candidate for a second term. He stood on a platform of protective tariffs, a gold money standard, and conservative policies, which he said were essential to continued prosperity.

Labor was flexing its muscles and demanding recognition, with disputes often ending in bloody riots. Demands were growing for Congress to "do something" about the monopoly practices of the "Trusts." On the Far Left, anarchists were preaching the overthrow of all governments and emphasizing their point occasionally with a tossed bomb.

It was a time of political, social, and industrial ferment—and excitement. There were some 14,000 automobiles chugging along streets and roads, frightening people and horses. But almost everyone agreed with the Literary Digest when it observed: "The ordinary 'horseless carriage' is at present a luxury for the wealthy; and although its price will probably fall in the future, it will never, of course, come into as common use as the bicycle." Nevertheless, there were those who were convinced a cheap car could be built which the average working man could afford.

Europeans had developed the first automobiles. They were low-slung, handmade cars designed for driving conditions in Europe. The Americans were building their cars with an eye to covering long distances and the cars had to have enough clearance to travel rutted roads.

William Morrison of Des Moines, Iowa, was credited with being the first to make an electric automobile. When it made an appearance in Chicago in 1892, crowds clogged the streets to get a close look at the marvelous machine. One account said: "Ever since it arrived, the sight of a well-loaded carriage moving along the streets at a spanking pace with no horses in front and apparently with nothing on board to give it motion, was a sight that has been too much, even for the wide-awake Chicagoan. It is most amusing to see the crowds gather whenever the vehicle appears. So great has been the curiosity that the owner when passing through the business section has had to appeal to the police to aid him in clearing the way." The automobile age was nearer than anyone but a few dreamers imagined. Dow Chemical would be drawn into its mainstream in a manner no one could foresee. Its plants would one day furnish the bromine required for anti-knock gasoline, and other products important to the automobile industry.

In the wider world, Britannia still ruled the waves. But on the first day of the new century a voice was raised in belligerent tones that seemed to issue a challenge to British naval supremacy. Germany's Kaiser Wilhelm II chose New Year's Day to proclaim to the Reichstag in Berlin: "The first day of the new century sees our army—in other words, our people—in arms, gathered around their standards, kneeling before the Lord of Hosts. Even as my grandfather labored for his army, so will I, in like manner, unerringly carry on and carry through the work of reorganizing my navy, in order that it may be justified in standing by the side of my land forces and that by it the German Empire may also be in a position to win the place which it has not yet attained. With the two united, I hope to be enabled, with a firm trust in the guidance of God, to prove the truth of the saying of Friedrich Wilhelm I: 'When one in this world wants to decide something with a pen he does not do it unless supported by the strength of the sword.' "

In that age of America's international innocence, the Kaiser's words were scarcely noted by the man on the street. Europe was too far away and its problems too remote. In all the Midlands of the United States there were other things more important than the posturings and ambitions of an emperor. But then no one, not even in the chancellories of Europe, could foresee that the words spoken in Berlin were one drumbeat in the march toward a great war.

The future looked sunny in Midland, Michigan, as it did in New York and Chicago and San Francisco. The Dow Chemical Company had brought a new prosperity to the town. Main Street was as dusty and rutted as ever and Saloon Row added nothing to the cultural tone of the community. Cows and chickens wandered in the streets. There were no sidewalks except the scarred board walks on Main Street. Not many houses could boast of a bath tub. And yet the gray hopelessness of a decade earlier was gone. The "bleach works" was hiring more men, and money jingled in the workers' pockets on Saturday.

The future looked so promising to the directors of Dow Chemical that they voted an 8 percent stock dividend that was followed by a hefty 20 percent stock dividend. They agreed to Herbert Dow's proposal for further plant expansion. They also agreed the time had come to open discussions looking to a merger of the Midland Chemical Company into Dow Chemical. Dow told his colleagues the union was desirable because it would strengthen his patents and make the company less vulnerable to attack by larger companies; it would secure permanently the source of raw material; the combined fuel costs would be cheaper; operating costs would be lower; and the company would not be so dependent on one product in a market growing more and more competitive. By May an agreement had been reached for Dow Chemical to pay $300,000 in stock for the assets of Midland Chemical. And in August the merger was completed.

The merger was a triumph for Dow. At age thirty-four he owned a one-fourth interest in the chemical company he had created through ten years of hard work. It was true the company was in debt because of the expansions in plant capacity, but it was making money even though the British combine, United Alkali Company, had cut the price of bleach from $3.10 a hundred to $1.65 in the first of a series of moves to freeze out competition.

The year 1900 was also a landmark year because it brought to Dow Chemical two men who were to play a major part in the growth of the company for the next half-century. The first to arrive was Earl Willard Bennett, a small, aggressive young man of twenty, his dark hair parted in the middle and plastered down on his head. Dow hired him as a bookkeeper at a wage of $25 a month, with extracurricular duties of sweeping out the office and running for the daily mail when the train arrived. But one day he would become the company's treasurer and then chairman of its board of directors.

Earl Bennett recalled, "I came to Midland in the early winter of 1900 to visit my grandmother. That was when I decided to apply for a job with The Dow Chemical Company. Before that, when I was 16, I had been a cook in a lumber camp at Hub, North Carolina, which is in the eastern part of the state. I had been going to high school in Grand Rapids where my father was superintendent of supplies for a lumber company. They sent him to North Carolina to supervise a job and he couldn't afford to keep me in school in Grand Rapids. So I went with him.

"Most of the lumbermen working the Hub job were northern loggers. They were a rough lot and when we arrived they were raising Old Ned about the Southern food they had to eat. They weren't accustomed to it. They had been eating greens and biscuits and salt pork until they couldn't bear the sight of it. That was about all the the camp cook knew how to prepare. He dished up greens, salt pork and biscuits one day, and salt pork, greens and biscuits the next day.

"Well, the camp cook died soon after we got there. The men claimed, rather ungenerously I thought, that he had choked to death on his own cooking. At any rate, I went to my father and asked him if I couldn't do the cooking. The job paid $50 a month and I wanted the money so that I could go to business school. I had decided that instead of finishing high school I would take a business course.

"Since there wasn't anybody else in camp who knew how to cook, I got the job. I was about 5-feet tall and in the language of the lumbermen, 'a little short at the top.' We had about one hundred men in the camp and one old stove on which to do the cooking.

"The first thing I did was to start making fresh bread, which the men had been accustomed to in the northern lumber camps. I made my own yeast, too. Instead of serving the men evaporated apples, I cooked the apples down to a sauce and used part of the juice to make jelly. Then I made jelly rolls and jelly cakes, the first they had had in months. They loved that. During the next nine months I saved close to $450. I didn't spend much more than a dollar a month.

"Then I left the camp and headed for Chicago. I sewed my savings in my clothes so nobody could steal it. I entered the Bryant Stratton Business School in Chicago determined to finish their three-year course in six months. I didn't make it in six months, but I did finish it in nine months and just managed to scrape by with the money I had saved. Then I went to work for Marshall Fields for $5 a week. I stayed there for three years.

"When I came to Midland to see my grandmother, I learned The Dow Chemical Company was expanding and I decided to ask for a job. I guess Mr. Dow didn't think I was too short at the top because he hired me."

A few months after Bennett was hired, young E. O. "Ed" Barstow arrived. He had been one of Professor Smith's outstanding students at Case School and Smith had steered him to Midland. He was a broad-shouldered, big-fisted youth who quickly developed a reputation for solving knotty production problems.

"When Mr. Dow offered me $65 a month, I grabbed the job," Barstow recalled years later. "I had two rooms that cost me $1.50 a week and my board bill was $3.50. There were no movies and few places to go to spend money. I was rich."

With the arrival of Barstow and Bennett, Dow had the nucleus of a team that would work together for many years. Tom Griswold was his construction engineer. Bennett was his financial aide. Barstow helped manage the plant, conduct laboratory experiments, and move the experiments from the laboratory into actual production.

By this time Dow had developed a full line of bromides used by the pharmaceutical houses and photographic supply firms, his bleach was at least equal in quality to the British bleach, and he had found an outlet for "mining salts" which were being used in the mining of gold. Crushed ore was saturated with a bromine solution which acted with the gold to form bromide of gold. The gold was then extracted from the solution. Shipments of mining salts were sent to Australia, South Africa, Colorado, and other mining regions and for years were an important source of income for the small company.

In the summer of that sunny year, Dow started a profit-sharing plan for the Dow Chemical employees, persuading his directors to set aside 2 percent of the profit to be prorated among the workers. It was not entirely a benevolent move although it was at this time a revolutionary concept in business. Dow reasoned that if the workers received a profit-bonus, they would be able to buy stock in the company and thus provide working capital. Their interest in the company's welfare would be more personal. And, hopefully, they would do better work, all of which would reflect in greater profits for the stockholders.

Dow was so confident of the business' future that early in 1901 he sold his directors on a $225,000 expansion program. There was no difficulty in the financing. The East End Savings Bank of Cleveland readily agreed to lend the company $100,000. Much of it was earmarked for increased power production by gleaming generators located on the outskirts of a town where electricity in a home was still a luxury.

A few months later Dow convinced the directors that the market prospects were so good he needed an additional $300,000 for expansion to meet the expected demand. Bleach was selling well and he had found a profitable market for bromides in Japan and Europe. He got approval for the expansion.

If Dow expected unqualified admiration for his aggressiveness in locating a foreign market for the company's products, he was disappointed. His old friend J. H. Osborn was upset by the news. He warned Dow that the sale of bromides would very likely antagonize the Germans, who considered the bromide market outside the United States their private domain. Osborn thought it very likely the Germans would retaliate and force The Dow Chemical Company into a costly fight. But Dow refused to take the warning seriously. He continued to export his bromides.

When the first blow came it was not delivered by the Germans. It came from the British, who abruptly reduced their bleach price from $1.65 a hundredweight to $1.25. The aggressor was the United Alkali Company, an association of independent producers in England, Scotland, and Wales. They had held a strong position in the bleach market for years in Europe and the United States, and they intended to defend this position.

For a time Dow tried to hold the price line but he was forced to cut his price as the pressure from his customers mounted. Then the British followed with another price cut to $1.04 a hundred.

The price cut was a staggering blow to Dow Chemical. Dow had planned his expansions on the expectation that the price of bleach would fall no lower than $1.65 a hundred. By midsummer of 1903, the company was $225,000 in debt and $92,000 overdrawn at the bank in Cleveland. Bank officials reluctantly agreed to lend the company money to ride out a short-term emergency—but only after each of the directors personally endorsed the notes.

This money problem had hardly been solved when the British announced that their bleach price for the following year would be 88 cents a hundredweight, a price well below their production costs since it included a 25-cent import duty. The blow was aimed directly at Dow Chemical because virtually every other producer of bleach in the United States had closed down months before rather than engage in a price war.

Dow struck back by contracting to sell his entire 1904 output at 86 cents a hundred. And then suddenly the British pressure ended. United Alkali announced that instead of 88 cents, their 1904 price would be $1.25. But the announcement was not made until Dow had made his commitments.

Dow himself was bitterly resentful that his company had been forced by other American bleach makers to carry the burden of the fight. He wrote to a stockholder, "It seems too bad that we have to bear the entire cost of bringing the United Alkali Co. to its knees."

On the broad waters of American commerce, the bleach fight scarcely raised a ripple. It was important only to those engaged in it and it received scant attention in the financial press. But with the perspective of time, it would become clear that the shots fired were important to the survival of an American chemical industry.

Americans had other things of greater interest to them than the tribulations of an obscure Michigan chemical company. One of these was the endless arguments as to whether or not a man would ever be able to fly in a heavier-than-air craft. In October of 1903, Astronomer Simon Newcomb of the United States Naval Observatory at Washington wrote what many considered to be a reasonable statement: "The example of the bird does not prove that man can fly.... There are many problems which have fascinated mankind since civilization began which we have made little or no advance in solving.... Air mechanicians (may be) ultimately forced to admit that aerial flight is one of the great classes of problems with which man can never cope...."

On the other hand, H. G. Wells, the noted British author and historian, conceded that man might learn to fly but "I do not think it at all probable that aeronautics will ever come into play as a serious modification of transport and communication."

In the midst of such solemn predictions that man would likely remain an earthbound creature, Orville Wright climbed into a strange looking contraption at the base of Kill Devil Hill near Kitty Hawk, North Carolina, and flew it 130 feet in 27 seconds. Later in the day, his brother, Wilbur, climbed into the pilot's seat and flew the craft for 852 feet in 59 seconds. Like the bumblebee, their plane was ungainly and poorly constructed for flight, but it flew nevertheless.

It was beginning to look as though Dow would never get his company off the ground. Not long after the bleach fight had ended, a visitor came to Midland and sought an interview with him. The stranger's calling card identified him as Herr Herman Jacobsohn, representative of the Deutsche Bromkonvention, an organization of German bromide makers. Dow received the visitor and after a few polite exchanges, Jacobsohn got down to business. He said he had reliable information that Dow had exported bromides to Europe.

"What of it?" Dow asked.

"Don't you know you can not export bromides?" Jacobsohn said, as though any informed businessman should be aware of this simple rule of commerce.

"I know nothing of the kind," Dow said.

It was then that Jacobsohn patiently explained he had been sent to Midland from New York by his colleagues to make it clear to Dow that such violations of the accepted rules could not be tolerated. While the amount of money involved in Dow's transactions had been trivial, the Bromkonvention in principle could not overlook the invasion of their territory. Furthermore, he said, if Dow continued such exports, the Bromkonvention would be forced to put two pounds of bromides on the United States market for every pound exported by Dow. And with this ultimatum, Jacobsohn excused himself. He left on the next train for New York.

Dow said later to a friend: "I thought he was bluffing and paid no attention to him."

But Jacobsohn wasn't bluffing. Within a few days, without explanation, a New York City bank notified Dow Chemical that several demand notes it held should be paid immediately.

This warning slap was soon forgotten by Dow because he was under more serious pressure from his own board of directors. The falling profits curve of the company had stirred up some old doubts about Dow's managerial ability. There also was talk that Dow had been wasting his time and energies in an appalling number of activities when he should have been looking after the affairs of Dow Chemical.

One point of irritation was Dow's involvement in a scheme to synthesize chloroform from carbon tetrachloride. The chloroform project had started in 1903 when Dow became convinced that Professor A. W. Smith of Case School and a colleague, Professor William O. Quayle, had found a workable process for the inorganic synthesis of chloroform—something that had not been commercially achieved before. The standard method of producing chloroform was to use a combination of bleach and acetone. Inasmuch as acetone came from the destructive distillation of wood, the process was fairly expensive. The Smith-Quayle process offered the possibility that chloroform could be obtained from carbon tetrachloride much more cheaply—and "carbon tet" could be made from chloride in brine.

Dow decided to transfer the laboratory experiments to commercial production. Inasmuch as some of Dow Chemical's directors were grumbling about too much expansion, he was leery of asking the board to finance the venture. Instead, he organized a new Midland Chemical Company and a plant was set up on land leased from Dow Chemical.

Quayle was brought from Case School to get the plant in operation, but as usual Dow involved himself deeply in the project.

The plant had produced little except headaches for months. Also, some Midland residents living on the windward side of the plants were threatening to sue Dow Chemical because of smelly gases escaping from the chloroform plant built on its property. They said the odors were not only unpleasant but that the gases induced vomiting, and caused vegetation to die, kitchen utensils to rust, and implements to corrode.

Dow blamed Quayle's chloroform plant for most of the odors which he conceded were disagreeable. But he hooted down the claims that the gases were causing all the damages that were claimed. He put Barstow to work to find the cause of the complaints. Within a short time, Barstow located the trouble in faulty pipe fittings. When the joints were sealed properly, most of the odor disappeared and the complaints subsided. It was the beginning of a long and costly effort to minimize air pollution.

It often seemed to some directors that Dow was like an overgrown boy turned loose in a warehouse full of playthings, not knowing where to concentrate his time and energy. He was raising prize pullets and selling eggs. He was planting five thousand fruit trees and trying to prove that the sandy soil around Midland could produce apples the equal of any in the country. He was spending valuable time showing workers how to landscape the grounds around his home and supervising the planting of shrubs, trees, and flowers. He was spending more time in the plant than in his office, frequently stopping to show a worker how to handle a broom, a shovel, a paint brush, or a mop with greater efficiency. On one visit to the plant, a director was startled to see Dow suddenly grab a shovel from the hand of a man shoveling coal into a furnace.

"Let me show you how to do it," Dow said. "You're wasting coal." He proceeded to demonstrate how coal should be spread evenly over the furnace fire rather than piled in a heap. Then he patiently explained to the man why the combustion would be more efficient if the coal was spread evenly over the fire.

Jesse B. Fay, the company's patent attorney and a stockholder from Cleveland, was disturbed because he believed Dow was wasting his time supervising details that employees could do as well or better. He wrote a tactful letter to Dow saying in part:

"In my judgment, your strongest faculty is your originating or inventing faculty. In this line you are superior. Hence, this is the line you should devote yourself to. After you have conceived an idea, it is quite likely that someone else might work out the details of this idea and reduce it to practice quite as well as you could yourself.... Such a person might relieve you from superintendence and leave you free to exercise your inventive faculty.... You have not the time it seems to me to work these ideas out yourself, for your ideas come too rapidly for one man to reduce to practice. Frankly, and without meaning any disrespect, I believe that a very ordinary man of good technical knowledge could under your direction reduce your ideas to practical form at a lower cost, and with much better ultimate results than you could yourself...."

And then Fay got down to the core of the problem as he saw it. "So far as I am able to judge," he said, "your mind does not work according to any normal law. Logic seems superseded by inspiration.... Things that to the ordinary mind appear to be fixed facts and axioms, to you appear faulty and capable of being changed for the better in many ways. You start with one idea and before you can put it into words new avenues of thought open up to you that divert you from the original idea.... You should... not use up your energy in doing something that another man could do as well as you."

Dow replied that his ideas for inventions and improvements did not come from sitting in a chair and forcing himself to think of them. He said they came from the fact that he did become involved in the details of the plant operations. "Improvements of the kind you speak of," he added, "are spontaneous evolutions or outgrowths of this knowledge." In a footnote, Dow solemnly said he had relieved himself of some of the detail work due to Fay's suggestions. He had arranged for the bookkeeper, Earl Bennett, to sign checks for lumber that had been purchased.

The unrest over Dow's management reached a crisis stage in the summer of 1904 when the board of directors named an executive committee to explore the advantages of hiring a manager to take over the direct supervision of the Midland plants.

Dow went to the board with a defense of his management. He argued that his construction costs had been 60 percent below the lowest bids offered by contractors; the company produced its own electric power more cheaply than the highly efficient power plants supplying the city of Chicago; no serious legal blunders had been made; labor costs had been closely controlled; because of automatic control and recording devices, "one man sitting in his office is able to accomplish what twenty foremen observing the operations of the men might fail to do"; and both bleach and bromides were being manufactured "cheaper than anyone else anywhere."

"To sum up the whole matter," Dow said, "The Dow Company, as far as we have any means of judging, is better managed than any other manufacturing plant with which comparison can be made.... I trust the executive board will appreciate what ability may exist in Midland and place as much confidence in the work being done there as results will warrant."

Dow succeeded in blocking the appointment of a manager. He had seen the management of the old Midland Chemical Company slip from his hands and he didn't intend for it to happen again without a fight. But the Cleveland directors did not share his optimism that the company was on a solid base nor were coming events to lessen their pessimism.

Early in 1905, Dow decided to make a trip to Louisiana and Texas to talk to prospective customers. Then he planned to swing north to St. Louis to meet Mrs. Dow and the children. From St. Louis, they were going on to California for a visit with Mr. and Mrs. Osborn. Two years earlier, Osborn had retired from the National Carbon Company and moved to Pacific Grove, California.

In early February Dow was in New Orleans when he learned that the Germans had cut the price of potassium bromide on the American market to 15 cents from 30 cents—while in Europe the price was being held at 40 cents. Other bromide prices were cut in half. He carried this distressing news with him to San Antonio. There he received an urgent message to come to St. Louis to meet with a representative of the Deutsche Bromkonvention.

Dow caught the next train out of San Antonio after wiring his plant manager, Jim Graves, and his sales manager, Rupert Paris, to meet him in St. Louis. On his arrival in St. Louis, Dow went with Graves and Paris to the executive offices of the Mallinckrodt Chemical Works where he found the Bromkonvention's representative to be Herr Jacobsohn—the same Jacobsohn who had issued the ultimatum to Dow a year earlier.

Jacobsohn bluntly informed Dow the price cut in bromides had been made to punish Dow Chemical for invading the German market. He proceeded to lecture Dow on the folly of his trying to disrupt the unwritten but historic understanding that the bromide market in Europe and the rest of the world outside the United States was reserved to the Bromkonvention. He demanded once again that Dow stop the shipments of bromides to Europe and Japan. If they were not halted, he said, then the Germans had no alternative but to flood the American market with bromides priced below the cost of production. He pointed out that the German combine could well afford to do this because it had the financial resources of the government behind it. In a long price war, he argued, the Germans would inevitably be the winner.

Dow refused to stop shipments abroad. He was angered by the dictatorial tone of Jacobsohn, and by the threats. Suddenly he stood up to announce there was no need for further discussion. The time was nearing for him to meet Mrs. Dow and his children and board the train for California.

"You can't do this!" Jacobsohn exclaimed. "You don't know what you are doing!"

"Good day, gentlemen," Dow said and he left with Graves and Paris.

Dow was angry but his anger had not dictated his decision. He was sure he could produce bromides cheaper than the Germans and he was fairly certain the Germans were not in as strong a position as Jacobsohn claimed. For one thing, their 15-cent price included a 25 percent tariff, leaving them only about 12 cents to cover all costs. At such a price, every pound of bromides sold on the American market would be a financial drain.

By the time Dow reached Kansas City, he had his strategy worked out. It was not complicated. He would simply withdraw from the American market and invade the German market. He sent his family on to the West Coast and he stopped overnight at the Hotel Baltimore. He sent a message to Graves and Paris in Midland to keep the bromine plant in full production and to start stockpiling bromides. He authorized the sale of 120,000 pounds of bromides at 12 cents a pound to leave the impression that he was going to fight them on the American market.

These were the preliminary moves to the invasion of the German market. Germany had no import duty on bromides and if he could wedge his way into this market, he would be able to put pressure on the Bromkonvention not only in the United States, but on their own home grounds.

He penned a long letter to President Convers in Cleveland telling him of the meeting with Jacobsohn. "The bromide situation is now getting strenuous," he said. ". . . The whole situation is very spectacular and intended to frighten us. . . . Jacobsohn stated that the European market was theirs and that they would make us trouble until we withdrew from there and left the market free to them. We would not consider his terms. . . . Mr. Paris left. . . for the East where he will arrange to sell 100,000 pounds of bromides in Europe, mainly in Germany. . . ."

With his counterattack organized, Dow went on to California to join his family. One day he spent with the famed horticulturist, Luther Burbank, discussing fruit trees. Dow promised Burbank he would send him some chemicals which he thought were worth testing as sprays and soil nutrients. On his return to Midland, he sent the chemicals and received a note of thanks from Burbank: "The Chemicals which you sent were received all right and I thank you. They are very highly appreciated, and I will give them a careful test as soon as I can find time. I enjoyed your visit with me more than I can possibly tell you...."

Three months after his confrontation with Jacobsohn, Dow wrote to President Convers to report: "We are increasing our crystallizing capacity quite rapidly, and will soon be able to invade Europe with quite a quantity of crystals." By this time he had built up a stockpile of more than 300,000 pounds to throw into the fight. A short time later he was writing to Osborn in California: "There is undoubtedly a long fight ahead but we are absolutely confident of the results."

Dow may have been confident but some of the Dow Chemical directors were frightened and angered by Dow's move into the price war without even consulting them. The company was heavily in debt. There was no market for the stock. And it was obvious that a long war with the Germans would eliminate any chance of dividends.

But in this critical time, Dow found a defender in President Convers. In one hawk-like note, Convers said: "My idea is that we ought to ship bromide to Germany in such quantities as to completely upset the market there. The only way we could bring Jacobsohn to terms... will be to demoralize his market if possible at the point where he is getting his profit."

This was precisely what Dow intended doing. Soon there were tons of bromide crystals moving into German ports. Dow had secretly engaged a German firm and a British firm to sell his bromides. The chemicals were offered to the German trade at prices below those fixed in Europe by the Bromkonvention. The shipments sold quickly. The scheme worked so well that Dow began buying German-made bromides on the New York market for 15 cents a pound. He repackaged them and secretly shipped them back to Germany where they sold for 27 cents a pound. In effect, he had the Germans working against themselves without being aware of it.

Whatever pleasure Dow may have enjoyed from outwitting the Germans, the fact remained that the fight placed a heavy strain on Dow Chemical. Again the banks called their loans and the directors were forced to raise money by signing personal notes. The banking community was not as optimistic as Dow that the Germans could be beaten in a long fight.

Dow tried to convince his colleagues that the situation wasn't as gloomy as some of them thought. In one letter he said: "We are the absolute dictators of the situation." In another he said: "One result of this fight has been to give us a standing all over the world. . . . We are. . . in a much stronger position than we ever were, although the profits are not so great. . . . Practically all the plants on the Ohio River have closed down except one at Allegheny. We therefore know that we have no competitor who can make bromide at as low a figure as we can."

To some who received these persistently cheerful messages, it sounded too much like a man whistling through a graveyard.

Chapter Five

They called it the "Millionaires' Panic," the now-famous money crisis that jarred the nation in 1907. It began with the collapse of an effort by Wall Street interests to put together a huge business combine involving banks, the copper industry, and other enterprises.

The shock from this failure ran through the New York financial community like a convulsive shudder through a fever-stricken man. Then a rumor spread that the Knickerbocker Trust Company was in deep financial trouble. Before dawn on the morning of October 21, frightened depositors began to gather at the marble entrance to the bank. They came by foot, in horse-drawn carriages, by streetcar and some by automobile. The crowd grew from a few score to a milling, scrambling, shoving mob of thousands. Police squads rushed to the scene to restore order. They forced the crowd into long queues which stretched for blocks.

When the bank's doors opened at 9 A.M., the first in line rushed for the tellers' windows to demand their money. Among them was a burly bank messenger. He carried a satchel containing thousands of checks which had been presented during the night to the Night and Day Bank by canny Knickerbocker depositors who remembered the bank stayed open for twenty-four hours a day. Their foresight was paying off.

For six hours the Knickerbocker's tellers counted out sheaves of cash. When the bank closed its doors as usual at 3 P.M., the lines of people outside were as long as they had been at dawn. They were still there the next morning. The bank continued to pay the depositors on demand. But then at noon the tellers slammed shut their cages. The money had run out. The bank's doors were closed against the milling, shouting crowd. Some were screaming in anger. Some were weeping in desperation.

There was no central banking system to support the besieged Knickerbocker. The Federal Reserve System, providing a reservoir of funds for such a crisis, would not be authorized by law for six more years. Each bank more or less stood on its own resources. And these resources were not enough to save many banks from the panic that spread from New York to other parts of the country. Assets could not be converted to cash quickly enough to hold back the tide of fear. The panic spread to the stock market. Prices tumbled.

Onto this scene of disarray in the money market strode J. Pierpont Morgan, the titan of American banking. He called the country's top financiers to an emergency meeting in his office to find a means of restoring public confidence in the banks. These men pledged their resources to support banks and corporations caught short by the panic. They arranged to have $100,000,000 in gold shipped from Europe. John D. Rockefeller, Sr., tossed $10,000,000 in government bonds into the pot of reserves. Secretary of the Treasury George B. Cortelyou announced in Washington that the United States Government would deposit $150,000,000 in federal banks, and more if needed.

The news that the nation's banks had new and powerful support swept the country. Perhaps the most important of all was the news that the mighty House of Morgan was willing to stake its future on the solvency of American business. People reasoned that if J. P. Morgan had such faith, then they had no real cause to be fearful of their savings. The panic subsided. The runs on banks stopped. Depositors began returning their cash to the banks. The hurricane was over in a matter of a few weeks.

Soon people were quoting a statement made by J. P. Morgan at a meeting of businessmen in Chicago. Morgan said his father had once told him; "Remember, my son, that any man who is a bear on the future of this country will go broke. There may be times when things may be dark and cloudy in America, when uncertainty will cause some to distrust, and others to think there is too much production, too much building of railroads, and too much other enterprise. In such time, and at all times, remember that the growth of this vast country will take care of itself."

But while the money crisis had passed like a tropical storm moving out to sea, the business depression that followed was a cycle that had to run its slow course. It reached into every city and town in the country as the wheels of industry slowed. Small businesses were in deep trouble as banks tightened credit and sales fell. The Dow Chemical Company in Midland was no exception. Once again it was struggling to stay alive.

One who never forgot those lean times was Earl Bennett, whose title as assistant treasurer of Dow Chemical in 1907 was far more impressive than his salary of $1,800 a year. He would recall later: "One winter day after the panic, my wife called me at the office and asked me to bring home a loaf of bread for supper. At quitting time, I put on my overcoat and started for the grocery store. I was walking up Main Street when I suddenly realized I didn't have even a nickel in my pockets and it was two more days until payday.

"I could have asked the grocer to give me a loaf of bread on credit. But then I thought: 'If I ask for credit, the word will get around town that The Dow Chemical Company is in such bad shape Bennett can't even afford to pay cash for a loaf of bread.' I suppose it was foolish of me not to ask for credit. But I had borrowed $8,000 at the bank to buy a thousand shares of Dow Chemical stock and I was having a hard time meeting the interest payments. My thought was that if the bank heard I was so broke, they might call the loan and I would lose the stock I had put up as collateral.

"I walked past the door of the grocery store and on up the street, wondering what to do. I couldn't bring myself to stop an acquaintance and ask for a nickel. I said: 'Lord, I'm in trouble and I need help.'

"I crossed the street and walked back down Main Street. The wind was blowing leaves along the walk and then I saw a small ball of green paper roll by. I thought it was the wrapper from a package of tobacco. But I stopped and picked it up. I unfolded it and saw I was holding a two-dollar bill. I said: 'Thank you, Lord, for answering that prayer.'"

Bennett paused to chuckle. "Times were never as bad after that—and I never did think a two-dollar bill was unlucky."

Herbert Dow was feeling the pinch of hard times, too. In the months that followed the panic, the Iroquois Cement Company in which he had an interest failed. He lost the money he had invested in the Ontario Nickel Company of Canada—a venture by which Dow and several colleagues hoped to use a bromine solution in extracting nickel from ore. And once again the directors and stockholders of Dow Chemical were grumbling over the company's poor showing. The $10 par value stock was being offered by some hard-pressed holders at $5.50 a share. The directors did approve a token dividend of one percent for 1907, but only to impress creditors with a show of solvency.

A frightened woman stockholder wrote to Dow during these difficult times: "I am writing to you to see if I can get some information in regards to the Chemical Co. You know it has been some time since I have received any interest. Do you think the small share holders will be frozen out? The amount I have in the Co. would not make them rich, but it would be a big loss to me. Will you please answer this and tell me just how the things are. I have heard a good many things lately but I know what you would say would be so."

Dow assured her "there is no such thing as freezing out small stockholders" and that when conditions returned to normal he hoped the company would be able to pay at least 6 percent. He added: "We think the time will come when we will pay more than this amount."

Perhaps the effects of the depression would not have been so severe had not the Germans continued their pressure on Dow Chemical to force it out of the European market. The price of bromides in the United States was cut from 15 cents a pound to 12 cents and then to 10½ cents. Even though Dow was shipping bromides to Germany and other European countries, profit margins were thin or nonexistent.

And yet Herbert Dow remained optimistic. He felt he was in a stronger position than the Germans in the bromide fight. The reason for this confidence stemmed from observations he had made in Germany and in England during a trip abroad early in 1907.

The year 1907 had begun with a favorable outlook. Business had been good with no indication that a money panic and depression would knock all calculations awry. Dow decided the time had come in the fight with the Deutsche Bromkonvention to go to Germany and see for himself what the situation was.

Dow told friends he was going to Europe for a holiday with Mrs. Dow and their children, who now numbered five. They were Helen, 12, Ruth, 11, Willard, 10, Alden, 2 and Margaret, 1. They sailed for England in January and settled into a rented house near London for one month before moving to an apartment near Buckingham Palace.

While Mrs. Dow and the children remained in London, Dow went to Berlin and New Stassfurt to visit chemical plants. His German hosts proudly showed him the manufacturing plants which they believed to be the most efficient in the world.

The more Dow saw the more he became convinced that in all important respects The Dow Chemical Company had a more efficient plant than the German bromine makers. He also discovered the world demand for bromides was even greater than he had suspected, and that the overseas market offered tremendous possibilities for his own company. In a note to his directors he said: "The fact that this amount is more than twice as great as we had formerly supposed may have some bearing on our future development."

It was while he was in New Stassfurt that members of the bromine syndicate approached him for a settlement of the price war. They offered to withdraw from the United States market if Dow would pull out of the European market.

But by this time Dow could see he was firmly entrenched in Europe. He had representatives in England and Germany to handle his shipments and sales. The buyers were pleased with his products and his prices. Dow later explained to a friend: "The German offer, when you analyzed it, was a one-sided affair. They were willing to withdraw from the American market where we could beat them in a competitive fight on a long-range basis regardless of price. In return, they wanted us to give up a market where we could compete with them at least on even terms. The advantage was all on their side."

It was no sale. Dow refused to end the fight on those terms. He returned to England. A visit to the United Alkali Company's bleach plant at Plymouth convinced him he was making bleach more efficiently than the British.

In a memorandum to the Cleveland office, Dow reported the primary benefit from his trip: "We know the people to whom we are selling goods. We also know our competitors and have in general a clearer knowledge of the whole situation than we had before, thus enabling us to act more intelligently in the future."

A good many things came into focus for Herbert Dow during his trip to Europe. The most important by far was the realization that The Dow Chemical Company was leaning too heavily for survival on bromides and bleach. The company had other profitable lines. The mining salts sold well. There was a market for chemical fertilizers and food preservatives. The demand was good for sulfur chloride, benzyl chloride and benzoic acid. The Midland Chemical Company's carbon tetrachloride was selling fairly well and the company had no trouble in selling its small output of chloroform.

But Dow knew he was taking from the brine only a small portion of its chemical wealth. The greater part of it was still being flushed down the sewer in waste sludge. He felt this waste had to be turned into useful products and the time had come for a bold step in this direction.

When faced with knotty problems, Dow frequently left the plant and went to his apple orchard to shovel soil around the base of the trees. He had a theory that piling the sandy soil around the tree trunks helped their growth and also he seemed to think better while engaged in physical exercise. Often when absorbed in a problem he would grab a shovel and start working without shedding his hat or coat.

Perhaps it was in the apple orchard that Dow came to the conclusion that the old chlorine cells which had been the workhorse mechanism of the company for so many years had to be replaced with a new type of cell capable of extracting more chemicals from the brine.

He sensed the day was coming when the company would have to increase and diversify its chemical mix if it was going to survive in the competitive race. He had to face the fact that the old chlorine cells were not as versatile as the cells that were being used by some of his competitors. While his cells produced only chlorine, the newer cells were producing both chlorine and caustic soda.

He was bothered, too, by Dow Chemical's dependence on the Germans for an important raw material. To make potassium bromide, he had to purchase potash from Germany. Almost all the world's supply of potash came from the great Strassfurt deposits. Some way had to be found to avoid this dependence on a raw material controlled by a foreign syndicate. Some way had to be found to use the sodium, calcium, and magnesium in the Michigan brine which were going to waste.

Dow upset his already disgruntled board of directors by asking them for money to finance the development of a new cell. They grumbled but they gave him the money.

There were some bright spots in that dismal depression year of 1908. Early in January Dow closed a contract with the Eastman Kodak Company to supply 100,000 pounds of bromides a year for five years, the beginning of a long and close business association.

He was more than pleased with the promising work of a young chemist named Charles Strosacker, another graduate of Case School. Strosacker had come to Midland after the collapse of the Ontario Nickel Company venture. He had worked on the nickel extraction process and his quick mind had impressed Dow. Dow had predicted a bright future for Strosacker. He had written his friend, Professor Smith: "The one good thing that came out of the Ontario venture was Charles Strosacker. He is going to be a great asset to the company."

Dow's faith was justified. Strosacker and the equally brilliant Ed Barstow gave Dow a strong research and development team. They not only were able in the laboratory, but they could translate laboratory results into commercial production. Combining their talents with the engineering skill of Tom Griswold, they had steadily raised the efficiency of The Dow Chemical Company plant—one of the keys to the company's survival in the depression.

Another bright spot for Dow was a report that the Germans were weakening in their offensive to force Dow to an agreement in the bromides war. Rumor had it that the German bromine producers were squabbling among themselves and the syndicate was becoming unglued.

The rumor had some substance. During the late summer the

Germans put out peace feelers through their New York representatives. They wished to talk to Dow again and explore the possibility of a compromise.

Dow met a German delegation in St. Louis in May. But the "peace feelers" proved to be another ultimatum. The Germans demanded that Dow limit his sales to the United States and leave the rest of the world market to them. In addition, Dow would have to permit them to sell a token 15,000 pounds of bromides on the American market.

Dow made a counter proposal. "My proposition is this," he said. "Germany for the Germans. The United States for American manufacturers and the rest of the world on an equal footing."

The Germans appeared to be aghast at such a proposition. They made the old argument that no manufacturer could match their production costs and it would be suicidal for Dow not to accept their proposition.

Dow refused. He wrote to President Convers: "The Germans could not realize that it was possible for anyone else to make bromides as cheaply as they could."

It soon became apparent the St. Louis conference had been merely an opening gambit by the Germans to see if Dow was weakening after two years of price slashing. A few weeks later, they asked for another meeting. This time, Dow left the preliminary discussions in the hands of The Dow Chemical Company's Cleveland secretary, H. E. Hackenberg. Early in November, Hackenberg advised Dow that he had agreed to a meeting with the Germans at the Savoy Hotel in London on November 24.

The conference was agreeable to Dow. He had nothing to lose. If a reasonable settlement could be reached, a great deal of pressure would be lifted from him and his company during one of the worst depressions the country had ever known.

Hackenberg advised Dow to keep the trip secret. The conference might amount to nothing, and nothing could be gained from publicity. He advised Dow to travel to Europe under the name "Herbert Henry." If he traveled under his own name, it might cause a flurry of comment in the chemical trade press.

One reason Hackenberg wanted no publicity was this: if the news spread through the Ohio Valley that a settlement of the bromide war was imminent, bromide makers who had closed their plants rather than fight the Germans would prepare to start up production again. It was just as well to let sleeping dogs lie.

Dow wrote Hackenberg: "In accordance with your request, I will sail as Herbert Henry. If I should happen to make a mistake in signing my name, and should start to write 'D' I will put another D at the end of it." It is not known whether Dow ever made the slip and was mistaken for a doctor of divinity.

Dow also had a bit of advice for Hackenberg. "When I was in London," he said, "I had a continuous cold until I bought an English pair of shoes. As you would probably not like these shoes, I would suggest that you get the heaviest pair of shoes you can buy before you leave here. The roads and sidewalks there are always damp in the winter, and rubbers are considered effeminate and are not worn at all by men."

Dow spread the word in Midland that he was leaving town "looking for trade in the East" and it was so noted in the Midland newspaper when he left. He and Hackenberg sailed from New York at 10 A.M. on November 14 aboard the White Star line's *Arabic*, a 15,801-ton ship carrying 400 passengers. On the passenger list Dow was "Herbert Henry, Cleveland, Ohio." His cabin on the promenade deck cost him $90.

There was a touch of theater in the cloak-and-dagger charade: the bearded, forty-two-year-old chemist-manufacturer from the little Michigan town of Midland enroute to great London Town on a secret mission, using an assumed name, to settle an international dispute with barons of world commerce. Broadway had seen plays with a thinner plot.

There was also an element of drama. Twenty years had passed since Dow had left Case School. Those years had been a struggle that often bordered on the desperate to build a business based on the idea of chemical discovery. There hadn't been much time for play. He had taken the idea of freeing bromine and chlorine from brine by electrolysis and made it work through ingenuity and dogged persistence. He managed and owned a large share of a chemical plant housed in some one hundred wooden buildings, with assets estimated at $2,000,000.

On the surface of things, Dow had achieved security and a strong position in the United States' developing chemical industry. But the truth was that his guaranteed salary was only $3,000 a year—plus a percentage of profits that didn't exist at the moment—and there was no market for the company's stock.

(Years later a colleague would say: "We were bankrupt, but thank God nobody knew it.")

Certainly the Germans were not fully aware of the precarious financial condition of The Dow Chemical Company on the eve of the London conference and Dow had no intention of showing any weakness.

The *Arabic* docked at Liverpool on November 23. Dow and Hackenberg went on to London where they registered at the Savoy Hotel. The next morning at ten o'clock they met with four German representatives of the Bromkonvention. One of them was the same Herr Herman Jacobsohn who twice had issued ultimatums to Dow which he had ignored. They gathered in a room with a name on the door that must have brought a smile to Dow's lips. It was the "Patience" room.

For three days the group discussed formulas for ending the price war, with no firm commitments made. From London, Dow and Hackenberg traveled to New Stassfurt and Berlin, where further talks were held. But the talks settled nothing. The members of the Bromkonvention insisted that in all "neutral territory"—the countries outside Europe and North America—the Germans should control two-thirds of the markets.

Dow and Hackenberg returned home in early December after a rough Atlantic crossing. On the face of things, the conferences had not brought the war to a formal ending. But they did bring about a stalemate and they did result in an odd sort of undeclared armistice as the months passed. The Germans finally withdrew from the American market and Dow gradually halted his shipments of bromides to Germany. The rest of the world market became free competitive territory and remained that way. Prices began to rise in late 1909 to their prewar levels.

It was a costly victory for Dow but it had its rewards. The reputation of the small Michigan chemical company was enhanced. The trips to Europe had satisfied Dow that his manufacturing processes were sound by any comparison. And he had learned that the market for chemicals which he could produce was a far greater market than he had ever imagined.

All this knowledge was not very helpful as the economic depression continued on into 1909. Nor did it cheer Dow's directors that he was spending money on the development of new chlorine cells and encouraging Barstow, Strosacker, and their laboratory aides to search for new products which had little if any immediate commercial value. They thought this research was a diversion of money and energies from the primary function of the company to make bromides and bleach.

Dow had other ideas. He saw brine as a potential source of a great many products. Depression or no depression, he was determined to push research into creative chemistry. Among other things he encouraged his chemists to try to find a synthetic rubber even though their first efforts produced a substance that was either too hard, too soft, or too gummy for any practical commercial use. There were many failures. But in the failing Dow and his men accumulated a storehouse of knowledge that would serve them well in future years.

Dow's research projects were not limited to the laboratories directed by Barstow and Strosacker. Many of his ideas were passed on to Case School of Applied Science to be tested by students in the school's laboratories. This working arrangement through the years had made Case School virtually an extension of The Dow Chemical Company. It was one of the most remarkable industrial-academic relationships in the country.

Dow was a Case graduate. All of his first team with the exception of Bennett had come from Case. He recruited promising young talent from Case. And he often turned to Professors Smith and Morley of Case for help when he encountered a particularly knotty problem of chemistry or production.

American industry one day would form close alliances with colleges and universities to tap their resources of brainpower. But Dow did it from the time he entered business, totally unaware that what he was doing was one of the secrets of German successes in industrial research. As time passed, he would turn to the University of Michigan for many of his recruits. But during these early years his ties were entirely with Case.

Professor Smith had an intimate knowledge of Dow Chemical's operations and he generally supported Dow's ideas on research and expansion. But even Smith became alarmed in 1909 as he watched Dow stubbornly continue to fight with the Germans and in the depth of the depression push harder and harder into research, spending money that otherwise might have been available for dividends.

Smith became so agitated that he wrote Dow: "I am extremely anxious for all of us who have our whole means in the Dow stock, that the company should make a fair return during the next five or ten years, rather than begin ten or twenty years hence. Whether we beat the world or not is a secondary matter. It seems to me that you have, like our mayor of Cleveland, fought so long, that you are obliged to continue when there is no real need, solely from habit."

Others, too, were upset by Dow's continual search for new products and new methods of production. One stockholder wrote to President Convers, who passed the letter on to Dow: "When I learn of Mr. Dow's buying apparatus costing thousands of dollars just to try once and throw aside, I wonder where his conscience is. Allowing a margin for exaggeration I have reason to think Mr. Dow is better fitted for a laboratory than as Superintendent. Had he some rich patron of science who had plenty of money to expend in investigation 'twould be a worthy use to put it to. Mr. Dow no doubt has a gift of discovery. He is an enthusiast along that line, but not a safe man to expend the money of poor widows and orphans."

Part of Dow's troubles came from stockholder unhappiness over the operations of the Midland Chemical Company on Dow Chemical property. The company had not turned out to be the profit maker that Dow had predicted. Its problems with chloroform and carbon tetrachloride had cost a good deal of time and money. Dow Chemical stockholders and directors who had no direct stake in the plant saw its operations as a drain on their own company.

It was true that Dow, Barstow, and Strosacker frequently were involved in Midland Chemical's problems. Dow himself was not without blame for some of the confusion in the company's management. For one thing, he had developed a dislike for the plant's manager, W. O. Quayle, who had been Professor Smith's associate at Case in developing the chloroform process.

It annoyed Dow that Quayle came to work each day wearing a neatly pressed pinstripe suit, white shirt with stiff collar, a tie, and bowler hat. He managed the plant mostly from his office while Dow thought he should be getting his hands dirty in the plant, finding out for himself why production was lagging. He wanted Quayle to conform to his own ideas of how a plant should be managed. He and Barstow rarely entered their offices. Strosacker carried his office around with him in his hat. And Dow thought that was the way it should be done.

Quayle must have had a streak of stubbornness in his makeup because he refused to change his habits. The relationship went from bad to worse.

The coolness between Dow and Quayle dated from the time Quayle came to Midland from Case to set up the plant in 1904. After the plant had been in operation for two years and still was not turning a profit, the personality clash deepened. Dow was inclined to blame Midland Chemical for troubles which may well have been the responsibility of Dow Chemical.

Professor Smith often chided Dow for "being too hard" on Quayle and he sought to ease the friction. But the relationship continued to deteriorate. Very likely there would have been a showdown at the end of two years except for Smith's interventions. The blowup came in 1908 when Dow insisted that Dow Chemical take a lease on the Midland Chemical Company. Within a matter of months after the lease was signed, Quayle was released. He went on to a distinguished career in the chemical industry and later enjoyed a friendly relationship with Dow. But the friendship came later.

The row over the Midland Chemical Company brought new criticisms of Dow's management. For a time he ignored them. Then he wrote to James Pardee in Cleveland: "From a number of remarks I infer that reports have been made that I have some other business besides The Dow Chemical Company that takes part of my energies and time.... The stockholders of The Dow Chemical Co. in this town who are now receiving dividends have many other criticisms as to how I should run the plant.... It seems to me that an investigation is in order and that the person who is bearing the tales should be stopped if an investigation proves his statements to be untrue. We make bromides better and cheaper than anyone else. We make bleach better and probably as cheap as any American maker.... We have fallen down on our ability to sell enough of any of the above to keep running full and therein lies our great weakness. Costs and quality are proof of how well a manufacturing plant is run. Dividends depend on many things besides the operation of the plant."

There was reason for the stockholders' uneasiness. In fiscal 1909 the company's net income totaled only a little more than $50,000. The darkest cloud hanging over the stockholders was a $300,000 bonded indebtedness which would come due in three more years. Unless earnings improved, this debt could not possibly be met.

And then, slowly at first but with gathering speed, the nation began to shake off the economic depression. The ponderous, jovial presence of William Howard Taft in the White House may have been a reassuring factor. The business community liked Taft. On the other hand, recovery may have been nothing more than a downward business trend running its course. Whatever the reasons, The Dow Chemical Company's recovery kept pace with the upswing across the country. In one year net income doubled. Hope for renewed dividends sprouted among the stockholders like spring blossoms on an apple tree. The criticisms of Dow's management were stilled. It's always hard to knock success.

The months of research were paying off, too. The company began the production of lime sulfur and lead arsenate sprays, iron chloride for engraving and rotogravure work, and zinc chloride for use as a soldering flux. Bleach and bromine were selling well. The sales of carbon tetrachloride climbed with its acceptance as a household cleaning agent and fire extinguisher. The latter sales were so good and offered such promise that Dow asked and received authority from directors to double the capacity of the carbon tetrachloride plant to 150,000 pounds a month. It was the first time in many months that he had dared suggest any spending for expansion.

By late November of 1910, Dow was looking for reliable foremen to handle the increased work force. He wrote to Professor Smith: "If you can get a good football captain sometime who is looking for a job, I think we can use him here. I believe we are more in need of foremen who can handle other men than we are of professional men without this ability."

With the pickup in business, Dow Chemical had no trouble refinancing the $300,000 bond issue which had seemed such a terrifying burden a few months earlier.

The boom swung through 1911 and into 1912 with increasingly good sales. Herbert Dow celebrated in 1912 by buying a Ford touring car and learning how to drive. He paid $590 for the machine. But he never seemed as comfortable behind the steering wheel as he had been in a buggy behind his horse. Pedestrians took to cover when they saw him coming down Main Street. Too often they had seen him rear back in the seat, pull on the wheel, and yell "Whoa!"--rather than step on the brake pedal.

The economic upswing continued into 1913. And then it was that Dow dropped a bombshell early in the year. He called Barstow, Strosacker, Griswold, and Bennett into his office.

"We're going out of the bleach business," he said.

Barstow never forgot the impact of the announcement. "We thought he was mad," he later said. "Bleach was one of our big money-makers and had been for years. We had three plants making bleach. At first I couldn't understand the decision."

Dow explained the reasons for the move. He told his aides the real future of the company lay in the use of its chlorine for products other than bleach. As a raw material, it was too valuable to sell in the form of bleach.

There was another explanation. After five years of research that included untold failures, Barstow and a young electrochemist named Louis E. Ward had come up with a cell far more sophisticated and efficient than the old wooden chlorine cell which had served Dow so well for so long.

In the old plant a current of electricity—together with the

blowing-out process—had been used to liberate bromine from the brine. Then the bromine-free liquor was passed into the chlorine cells where an electric current freed much of the chlorine. In both of these steps, Dow had deliberately avoided evaporation.

In the new plant, evaporation was the key function. After the bromine had been removed, the brine flowed into a vacuum evaporator or sealed vat. Boiling forced the sodium chloride or common salt to sink to the bottom of the evaporator where it could be removed. The liquid passed into the next evaporator which forced out magnesium chloride. The last evaporator freed calcium chloride. Where once only two chemicals had been obtained from the brine, there would now be five chemicals.

But the chain did not end there. The salt was dissolved in water, fed back into the new cells and charged with an electric current. The products that came from this process were caustic soda and chlorine. Hydrogen also resulted, but for a good many years the hydrogen was allowed to escape into the air. After 1928 the hydrogen would be combined with nitrogen taken from the air to manufacture ammonia.

The magnesium chloride opened new vistas. It could be treated with lime to produce magnesium hydroxide which, reacted with sulfuric acid, made Epsom salts. It could be converted to magnesium oxychloride for use as a flooring or as a hardener for stucco. It could be fed into cells to become metallic magnesium.

The calcium chloride was a versatile chemical that in a short time was being sold by the trainload. It became widely used to control dust on unpaved roads, to settle coal dust in mines and coal yards, as a refrigerant, and as an agent to melt ice and snow on streets.

With the new plant, the possible combinations of chemicals were multiplied many times. Through the year 1913 there was a burst of construction at The Dow Chemical Company as the plant was overhauled and new cells installed. One by one new products came into production. Dow was driving hard not only to catch up with his competitors but to shape the plant to a new concept of manufacturing.

No one realized it at the time, but Herbert Dow had won the race of his life.

PART TWO *1914-1930*

Chapter Six

The man who captured the imagination of America in the first days of the violent year 1914 was neither President, King, Czar, Emperor, nor Potentate. He was a slender, little-known Detroit automobile maker named Henry Ford whose classically simple, four-cylinder Model T was rattling over streets and rutted roads in fast-growing numbers.

The Model T was sturdy. It was cheap. It could be repaired easily. And its high road clearance gave it a practical advantage on the dirt roads which rains often turned into muddy lanes stretching across rural America.

Model T's were selling as fast as they could be rolled off the assembly line. In 1913 Ford's profits had reached a spectacular $20,000,000 and the best years were ahead. He had won the race to produce a popular, mass-produced, low-price car. But little was known about Henry Ford himself until the red-letter day of January 5, 1914. That was the day Ford announced he was going to raise the basic wage of his workers from $2.40 for a nine-hour day to $5.00 for eight hours of work. He explained the pay rise was a means of sharing profits with his thirteen thousand employees. He also had a theory that if workers were paid better, they would be able to buy more Fords.

Five dollars was a fantastically high wage for eight hours of work in 1914. Ford's action sent shockwaves of surprise, wonder, and consternation through the country. The New York *Herald* called it "an epic in the world's industrial history." The New York *Sun* exclaimed: "It was a bolt out of the blue sky, flashing its way across the continent and far beyond, something unheard of in the history of business." *The New York Times* said in almost disbelieving tones: "The lowest-paid employees, the sweepers, who in New York City may claim from $1.00 to $1.50 a day, are now to receive $5.00 in Ford's plant."

Reporters rushed to Detroit to interview the man of the hour and explain his philosophy to the public. One of the many reactions to Ford's announcement was a suspicion that he harbored some dark, unspoken motive. He was roundly accused of being a Socialist bent on destroying the capitalist system. Then a mass meeting of several hundred Socialists denounced Ford in a unanimous resolution which said, "Ford has purchased the brains, life and soul of his men by a raise in pay for a few dollars a week."

To the man in the street, Henry Ford became a hero.

As the swarm of Model T's grew, so did the jokes about the little car. There was the garbage collector saying: "The life of a garbage man is gettin' harder every year; dead cats is bad enough and broken bottles is hell, but the worst on the temper and the fingers is sortin' out them damned little Fords."

The vaudeville comedian said: "Ford is going to paint his cars yellow so that the dealers can hang them in bunches and retail them like bananas."

A straight man would ask: "Why do you want to be buried with your Ford?" And Mr. Bones would reply: "Because I never been in no hole yet that my Ford didn't get me out of." The stories multiplied as the number of Fords increased.

North of Detroit in the little town of Midland, less spectacular but revolutionary advances were being made in chemistry in the laboratories and plants of The Dow Chemical Company. At the time, the manufacture of automobiles and the making of chemicals from brine had no conceivable connection. And yet the day was coming when Dow chemists and engineers would have to go to the sea to get the vast quantities of a chemical required for the fueling of high-compression automobile engines. What Henry Ford was doing and what Herbert Dow was doing—not so many miles apart—were not unrelated. The chemical industry as well as the automobile industry was on the move toward changing the old patterns of living.

What was happening at Dow Chemical reflected the forward leaps being made in the world of science toward an understanding of the arrangement of atoms in simple molecules, the basic unit of chemical compounds. More and more was being learned of how to take molecules apart, how to put them together again under controlled conditions, and how to rearrange molecules to produce new products. They were learning, as science writer Lawrence P. Lessing would note, that "molecules could be built up, linked, cross-linked, and rearranged in an endless series of chemical changes, adding or substituting such other elements in the molecules as oxygen, nitrogen, sulfur and chlorine, to form a vast variety of different compounds."

Of the more than ninety elements found in the structures of the physical world and chemistry, the dominant ones were (and still are) carbon (from coal and petroleum), hydrogen (from petroleum and water), sodium and chlorine (from salt), and oxygen and nitrogen (from air). Together with calcium (from limestone), sulfur, and phosphorus, scientists had the building-block elements for putting together countless products and compounds useful to man. Of the four great basic raw materials—air, water, salt, and hydrocarbons—Dow Chemical had three of them (air, water, and salt) in almost inexhaustible abundance. Herbert Dow had been fully aware of this when he turned from the manufacture of bleach in order to use the chlorine from salt as a starting material for an infinitely greater variety of products.

When the century turned into its fourteenth year, it could be said that the American chemical industry was stepping from knee breeches into long pants. The transformation from boy to man was speeded by the war in Europe which started on August 1, 1914. With the Continent aflame, small chemical businesses literally were forced into an unprecedented expansion and development. It was the beginning of their independence from the German chemical giant which had long dominated the world markets and had been the leader in the application of science to industrial production.

The act of violence that sent millions of men marching to war and spurred the chemical industry's development occurred in an obsure place. Germany's Prince Otto von Bismarck had gloomily predicted after the Franco-Prussian War that the next great conflict in Europe would be touched off by "some damned foolish thing in the Balkans." And the damned foolish thing happened on June 28, 1914, in the little Bosnian town of Sarajevo.

Archduke Francis Ferdinand, fifty-one-year-old heir apparent to the throne of the Austro-Hungarian Empire, and his wife, Sophie, had come to Sarajevo to join in the Serbs' celebration of the Feast of Saint Vitus and to observe their fourteenth wedding anniversary. To mingle with the Serbs on this day was good public relations in an empire with discontented minorities.

The visit of Ferdinand and his wife was well publicized in advance. Crowds cheered them as their small motorcade passed through the streets enroute to a ceremony at the City Hall. But along the route were seven young assassins pledged to kill Francis Ferdinand in the cause of Serbian nationalism. They did not hate the archduke. They hated the empire he represented, an empire which dominated Serbia's economy and refused the Serbs an outlet to the sea.

As the car bearing Francis Ferdinand and Sophie reached the

Cumuria Bridge, one of the conspirators tossed a bomb at the archduke's green-feathered helmet. The bomb was deflected and exploded in the street behind the car, wounding several onlookers. The motorcade sped on toward the City Hall.

Francis Ferdinand was shaken and angered by the attempt on his life but he continued with the ceremony at City Hall. After the speeches were over, he insisted he must go to the hospital to visit those who had been wounded by the bomb. He urged Sophie to stay behind but she refused to leave his side.

Their motorcade headed for the hospital. The driver of the archduke's car made a wrong turn at an intersection into Francis Joseph Street. He quickly braked the car to make a turn-around. The maneuver placed the automobile within a few feet of Gavrillo Prinzip, one of the assassins.

Prinzip drew a pistol and fired twice. One bullet struck Sophie and the other struck Francis Ferdinand. For a few seconds, the two sat upright in the car as though nothing had happened. Then blood spurted from the archduke's mouth and Sophie crumpled in the car's seat. Within a few minutes they were dead and Bismarck's prediction was taking form.

Austria's anger over the assassination, fanned by political opportunists, turned against Serbia where outspoken enemies of Austria were encouraged by Russia. With a nod of consent from Germany's Kaiser Ferderick Wilhelm II, the Austrians declared war on Serbia.

The flames spread like fire in a dry forest. Troops flocked to battle stations. Old jealousies, fears, unfulfilled ambitions, and treaties created the opposing alliances. Ultimatums were issued and rejected. On August 1, the German army marched into neutral Belgium and World War I had started on its bloody course.

Britain's fleet steamed into action to choke off Germany's trade by sea. Germany sent her submarines out in packs to hunt down enemy warships and freighters. The war had been underway only a few weeks when industry in the United States began to feel the pinch of shortages in chemicals. The demand on the small American chemical industry for more production steadily increased. Buyers bid against each other to shoot prices up in the open market. As an example, phenol or carbolic acid quickly climbed from 55 cents a pound to $1.70 a pound, before production by American chemical companies could bring down the price.

Three months before the war began, a small block of Dow Chemical stock sold for $5.25 a share. One year later it was $140 bid with few shares offered. One reason was that Dow Chemical had the largest stockpiles of bromides in the United States and the plant was expanding to produce other war-short chemicals. Dow Chemical also had absorbed the Midland Chemical Company and its relatively large chloroform-carbon tetrachloride production.

Some thought the Germans would conquer France and Russia in a matter of a few months. Herbert Dow was convinced it would be a long war and his company had better be prepared for it. The fighting had been underway scarcely a month when Dow wrote to President Convers: "Ideas as to the duration of the war are not very much better than pure guesswork.... It is my personal opinion that the war will last more than a year and that the present plan of campaign consists in letting the Germans get near Paris or possibly surround Paris to compel them to have a long line of communications, whereby they will be easily vulnerable to the almost unlimited reserves of Great Britain and that ultimately the Germans will have to retire within their own boundaries and will then be so strong that it may be years before peace will be established."

Dow's analysis of Allied strategy may have been faulty but he was correct in judging the duration of the war. He pressed for expansion, over the objection of some of his directors, to produce a wider range of products.

The stockpiles of German-made chemicals in the United States dwindled rapidly as the war ground on. Potash, dyes, and pharmaceuticals quickly disappeared from the open market. The demand for more chemicals was not easily met. The American industry was largely made up of small plants scattered around the country. They had depended for years on Germany to supply them with most of their intermediate chemicals. Now the supply line was being choked off by the British naval blockade and the industry was being forced to rely on its own research and manufacturing resources.

Dow's expansion program forced him to look around for another qualified chemist-manager to share the work load with Barstow and Strosacker. He found his man at Case School. He was Mark E. Putnam, a professor of chemistry, whose contributions soon were to equal those of Barstow and Strosacker.

Early in 1915, Dow saw there would soon be a serious world shortage of dyes used by the textile makers. The Germans had been supplying at least 80 percent of the dyes sold on the world market and now this source could not be depended on. Dow had the chemical building blocks for making a synthetic indigo—the most widely used of dyes—if a manufacturing process could be worked out. He brought Dr. Lee H. Cone of the University of Michigan, an organic chemist, to work on the development.

Dow didn't ask his directors for permission to develop the synthetic dye process. This time he bulled ahead on his own, taking no chances of being refused the authority. In the summer of 1915 he wrote to Professor Smith at Case: "The best new thing in sight is indigo. Every step has been worked out and they are turning out a few ounces regularly every day, and there is nothing in the whole proposition from beginning to end that is going to call for any great amount of money or that appears to be problematical."

Dow was reverting to his old habit of putting a high gloss of optimism on any new adventure that excited him. The process was neither fully developed nor was it going to be inexpensive. The fact that the process worked in the laboratory was no guarantee it would work profitably on a large-scale commercial basis.

Smith knew the indigo plant would be no small investment. He wrote to Dow: "It seems to me that... so large an investment in the indigo plant is not warranted by the present experimental development.... I think a mistake was made in going so fast."

But Dow already was moving from laboratory experiment to commercial production without the intermediate testing of the process in a pilot plant. He realized the urgency of the need for a new source of dyes and that the first to reach this market would be handsomely rewarded. He was willing to gamble his process would work.

Dow was not aware that the Germans at this time viewed their dye monopoly as an economic weapon that could be used against the United States. In March, 1915, before the British blockade had sealed off all German exports, Count Johann-Heinrich von Bernstorff, German ambassador to the United States, had cabled Berlin: "Serial No. 432 of March 13, 1915. It is reported to me by Hossenfelder, telegram No. 4, that the stock of dyes in this country is so small that by a German embargo about 4,000,000 American workmen might be thrown out of employment. (signed) Bernstorff."

Whatever the real value of this weapon, Dow helped take it from the hands of the Germans. Eighteen months after the laboratory experiments had begun, the first synthetic indigo ever made in the United States left Midland on its way to the Proximity Manufacturing Company at Greensboro, North Carolina. Du Pont and National Aniline soon followed with their own shipments of American-made dyes—and the crisis had passed. The German monopoly was smashed.

Dow did not hesitate to spend large sums on equipment, new processes, and expansion when plunging into a new venture. His spending often frightened some of his directors. But a curious streak of frugality cropped out when he had to spend money on what he considered to be a nonessential. This penny-pinching habit—a holdover from the hard years in the past—showed itself when he reluctantly asked his board to give him $15,000 for a new office building. To him, the office was the least important part of his plant.

He wrote to President Convers: "I have not been especially enthusiastic about a new office at any time, but am beginning to think that it is going to become an absolute necessity. The room adjoining mine is a passage way between other parts of the office and outdoors, as well as to my room. It is 13x18 ft., and contains the Superintendent's desk, Assistant Superintendent's table, my stenographer's desk, and the Purchasing Department, which includes Mr. LeFevre's desk and table, and a number of racks for catalogs, a Dictagraph, and Mr. Beckert's receiver and typewriter desk. Under these circumstances, it was decided some time ago that this room was less crowded than other parts of the office, and the cabinet for stationery was therefore put in there.... Mr. Van Winckel's room (sales) contains three people, each with a desk, and is 12x13 feet. It was impossible to find a place for another table in Mr. Griswold's room some time ago, even though we tried very strenuously to see if another table could be put in...." Apparently Dow saw nothing amusing in his picture of a corporate mad house.

Dow was deep in the supervision of the plant expansion in early December, 1915, when he received a sudden shock. He was called to Cleveland and informed that a majority of the board of directors was in favor of selling The Dow Chemical Company to an Eastern syndicate. The syndicate had offered $500 a share for stock that only nineteen months before had sold for $5.25. The sale hinged on Dow and his team of managers remaining with the company.

Dow returned to Midland to think over this offer. On paper he was a moderately wealthy man. The sale of the stock at $500 a share would make him more than a millionaire at age forty-nine. Taxes would take only a small share of the profits. He could live the rest of his life in comfort and provide generously for his family. The long struggle would be over.

H. E. Hackenberg, the company's secretary, was one of those who favored the sale along with President Convers and others. Hackenberg wrote to Dow:

"We feel that it is tempting fate to not try to get together on a basis that will permit us to take at least a part of our money out of the business. We are all of us past middle life when health is more precarious and we are less able to stand the strain of the hard work of creating and if it should turn out that the war were suddenly terminated, it is very likely that the readjustment in competition plans abroad might make the business just an ordinary manufacturing proposition.

"The difference between the price... proposed to us and what our stock would be worth during several years of depression would make such a difference in our individual fortunes that it is a serious thing to contemplate and as the matter stands at present we are in the position of refusing to take the certainty which offers today, for the speculator's dream of getting out at the top. We fear we may all have cause to regret it. . . . We trust that you can come to see this as we see it. . . ."

No one knows the thoughts with which Dow struggled in the days that followed. But shortly before Christmas, he called together the men who had worked with him so long to build the company, each of whom had his savings invested in Dow Chemical stock. There was Griswold who had been his chief engineer since the first days of the company's development; Bennett, the shrewd money-man who had started out as a bookkeeper and part-time office boy; Barstow, the genius at making things work when others couldn't; and Strosacker, the scholarly bachelor with one of the best minds in the industry.

"I want you to go with me to a meeting in Cleveland," Dow told them. He did not disclose to them that the board of directors had called a meeting for a decision on the sale of the company.

The five men traveled to Cleveland by train. When Dow entered the board meeting, he asked his Midland companions to wait in an adjoining office. They still didn't know what the mysterious meeting was all about. Minutes passed and only the sound of loud voices came through the heavy door. Then Dow stepped from the meeting and closed the door behind him.

He said: "I can tell you now that a majority of the board wishes to sell The Dow Chemical Company to an Eastern syndicate. They will pay $500 a share for our stock—and they want us to remain with the company and direct its management and operations. I am not going to oppose the sale. If this is what the directors want, I will not fight it.

"You have several choices. You can continue in your jobs. You can resign. Or you can come with me. I am not for sale. If the company is sold, I'll start another chemical company. Do you wish to stay with the company or come with me?"

For a time there was a startled silence. Then Bennett said: "I'm staying with you. "Strosacker, Griswold, and Barstow echoed Bennett's decision. If they went, they would go as a team.

Dow returned to the board meeting and announced the decision. It was the blow that ended the matter. The syndicate was not interested in The Dow Chemical Company without its management brains.

As the war in Europe moved toward its second anniversary, the Dow Chemical plants were working at capacity. Employment had jumped in one year from four hundred workers to twelve hundred, including a team of one hundred chemists. The town of Midland simply could not house that many men and their families comfortably. Under this pressure, Dow got approval from his board to spend $100,000 in building houses for married employees. The company's Stag Hotel in Midland was expanded with beds and meals for three hundred men—and even then men slept in the beds in shifts.

Saloon Row had disappeared, wiped out in 1908 when the town had voted for prohibition by a majority of 127 votes. No little anti-saloon sentiment had been generated when Barstow walked past a saloon with a young lady one evening only to have a ruffian make a slurring remark. Barstow left his companion in a store with friends, returned to the saloon, and thrashed the lout.

With the passing of the saloons, there were few places the workers could gather during their off hours for amusement. Barstow sponsored a Midland Community Center and Dow helped the town obtain a Carnegie Foundation grant to start a library. A company training school was opened to teach new skills to workers who flocked from the farms of central Michigan to the better-paid jobs in Midland. It was one of the first schools of its kind in the industry.

Watching the development of the war in Europe, Dow noted the increasing use of airplanes for observation and combat. He became convinced that magnesium metal, alloyed with aluminum, was certain to be the primary material in airplane construction. Years before, he had put Barstow to work to develop a process to make metal from the magnesium chloride found in the Michigan brine. The project had been dropped largely because there was no market for the light, bright metal even though it was one-third lighter than aluminum. It had remained an oddity in the family of metals.

Once again Dow put Barstow in charge of devising a process to manufacture magnesium. This time he gave him a team of able young helpers who later were to make their own mark in the chemical industry—W. R. Collings, E. C. Burdick, and W. R. Veazey, a chemist on loan part-time from Case School.

They quickly devised a crude electrolytic cell. Their first laboratory effort, in the basement of a building known as the Old Mill, produced small particles of magnesium which they showed to Herbert Dow. "I want to see one pound of magnesium in one piece," Dow said, and walked away. The problem was to get the magnesium particles to unite into a solid piece.

On a blazing June day, six weeks after they had begun their work, the electric current was sent through a molten salt bath. Small globules of magnesium began to float to the top. This time they knew how to bring the globules together.

Veazey recalled later: "We had been working at such a determined pace on the problem of getting the small pieces of magnesium to coalesce that when we finally succeeded in getting one whole piece, we suddenly realized nobody had thought about how to cast it or get it out of the cell. Somebody grabbed the first thing he could find, which was a piece of sheet iron. It was heated and bent into the shape of a crude ladle. A piece of pipe was attached for a handle and the piece of magnesium metal was scooped out of the magnesium bath. There was no mold, so we set the ladle on the floor to get the magnesium cool. And that's how we got the first ingot of magnesium."

This was the beginning of one of the most remarkable episodes in American industrial history. For years Dow Chemical produced magnesium metal at a loss while trying to interest industry and the United States government in its use. Only through the stubborn persistence of Herbert Dow and his son, Willard, would the United States be ready in 1942 to meet the fantastically large demand for magnesium in World War II. But that is a later story.

The ability of Dow's chemists and engineers—isolated from the centers of commerce and learning—to keep pace and often a step ahead in the early-day competitive chemical race was once explained by Tom Griswold when he was in a mood to reminisce. "When I came to Midland," Griswold said, "I felt painfully lonesome for lack of communion with other engineers, and because of separation from engineering libraries and other engineering undertakings. I figured I would be hopelessly behind the times in five years. So I took steps to prevent such a dire event.

"Out of my salary of one thousand dollars a year I set aside one hundred dollars which I used to buy technical books and magazines in three languages. Mr. Dow gave me a set of Roscoe and Schorlemmer and I acquired a copy of Watt's *Chemical Dictionary*. I read them from cover to cover. I distributed my books and magazines at all points in the house where I might have a few moments for reading. Newspapers, fiction, and current literature were put aside. I devoured the British abstracts in the *Journal of the Society of Chemical Industry,* the German *Zeitschrift fur Elektochemie,* French books on alkali, *Engineering Magazine, Engineering News-Record, Iron Age, American Machinist, Municipal Engineering, Electrical World, Scientific American* and Supplement, Patent Office *Gazette,* and other publications.

"After about eighteen months of this I was in the office of a noted engineer in Cleveland. This man was explaining a design for a coal-handling plant he was working on. I asked if he had seen one being built at Duluth. He was surprised and said he had not known of it. I asked if he knew of a like project at Fairport Harbor. He did not. I began to sit up and take notice. I seemed to know things in his line he might logically be expected to be familiar with. He took me into a friend's office to show me a hoist hook being designed to weigh the load lifted. I asked his friend, an engineer, if he was familiar with one developed by the Brown Hoist years before. He was not. I asked him if he had seen one published in a recent Patent Office *Gazette.* He had not.

"I asked a lot of questions and found that these men spent over two hours a day on street cars reading newspapers and in the evenings relaxed in activities planned by their wives. I contrasted their two-hour ride with my three-minute walk to the office, with my reading of technology, and felt fairly safe against becoming very stale as to what was doing in my line."

Dow Chemical's surge of growth in 1916 was not entirely the result of the war. It was largely based on the months and years of research that preceded World War I, and on the explosive growth of scientific knowledge. These resulted in new products broadening the base of the company which once had depended for survival solely on bromides and bleach. The new products included anilin oil (for dyes), monochlorbenzene (for high explosives), salicylic acid (for aspirin), oil of wintergreen (for flavoring), and calcium chloride (for laying dust on roads). Most of Dow's sales were chemicals sold in bulk to the chemical industry. He was content to leave the fabrication and sale of finished products to others.

In Europe, the new year 1917 arrived with the big guns thundering death and destruction. The armies on the Western Front were bogged down in the winter mud with troops living like moles in trenches and dugouts.

On the Eastern Front the Russian armies were collapsing. Troops were throwing down their rifles and deserting. Revolution was spreading under the whiplash of the Marxists. Russia was dissolving as an effective fighting force against Germany.

In Washington, President Woodrow Wilson continued to preach peace and neutrality. Without doubt he voiced the hopes of the majority of Americans. The Germans were encouraged to believe that the United States would not enter the war under any circumstances and, with the collapse of Russia, they could turn the full force of their might against France and Britain.

With the tide of war seemingly turning in its favor, the Imperial Government made its fatal mistakes. On January 9, the Kaiser sent a secret message to his navy: "I order that unrestricted submarine warfare be launched with the greatest vigor on February 1. You will immediately take necessary steps."

The United States State Department was formally advised of this action on January 31, too late for a protest to have any effect. The United States government was further advised, "All sea traffic will be stopped with every available weapon and without further notice." The only exception was that the United States would be permitted to send one passenger vessel to England each week.

The German leaders were confident their arrogant action would not bring the United States into the war on the side of Britain and France. Arthur Zimmerman, the German Foreign Secretary, said to United States Ambassador James W. Gerard in Berlin: "America will do nothing because Wilson is for peace and nothing else." On that same day, Wilson announced he was breaking off diplomatic relations with Germany.

American public opinion began to turn against Germany. But perhaps the policy of unrestricted warfare at sea would not have led the United States into the conflict had the Germans not made a second blunder.

On January 17, British Naval Intelligence intercepted a wireless message signed by Foreign Secretary Zimmerman. It was addressed, by way of Ambassador von Bernstorff in Washington, to the German ambassador in Mexico City. Cryptologists toiled over the message until they broke the code. Its important passage said:

> WE INTEND TO BEGIN UNRESTRICTED SUBMARINE WARFARE. WE SHALL ENDEAVOR TO KEEP THE UNITED STATES NEUTRAL. IN THE EVENT OF THIS NOT SUCCEEDING, WE MAKE MEXICO A PROPOSAL OF ALLIANCE ON THE FOLLOWING

BASIS: MAKE WAR TOGETHER, MAKE PEACE TOGETHER, GENEROUS FINANCIAL SUPPORT, AND AN UNDERSTANDING ON OUR PART THAT MEXICO IS TO RECONQUER THE LOST TERRITORY IN TEXAS, NEW MEXICO, AND ARIZONA.

For days the British kept the message secret as they checked its authenticity. Then at the moment when they believed it would have its greatest impact on neutral America, they passed the message on to President Wilson. He had the original ciphers checked against those transmitted by Bernstorff to Mexico City. The ciphers matched exactly. There could be no doubt of it—the message was not a fraud, and the Germans so admitted later.

Wilson made the Zimmerman note public and the storm of anger that followed overwhelmed the small minority in Congress who had been filibustering for neutrality.

On April 5, 1919, Congress approved a joint resolution which said "the President is hereby authorized and directed... to carry on war against the Imperial German Government and to bring the conflict to a successful termination." The day following, President Wilson issued a formal declaration of war.

Although the war had been underway in Europe for more than two years, the United States entered the conflict with shortages in almost everything from artillery shells to clothing for the armies. The demand for chemicals became desperately urgent. Dow stepped up the production of indigo to 2,000 pounds a day and planned larger production. A phenol plant was built and expanded to produce fifteen tons a day and then thirty tons as munitions plants called for more and more phenol for the manufacture of picric acid, used in explosives.

It was during this time that Herbert Dow startled his employees and the townspeople of Midland by coming to work one day clean shaven. The beard was gone. Even his close friends didn't recognize him at first.

"It looked too Prussian," Dow explained.

In pictures and cartoons, the "Prussian look" was being identified with arrogance and Herbert Dow wanted no such personal image. His sympathies were with England in her struggle on the Continent, and he wanted this made clear.

The war brought the first real stirrings of a magnesium industry. Dow's experiments with magnesium metal—after a good many false starts and failures—were beginning to show promise. A year after the first ingot was produced in 1916, Dow reported to his directors, "We will soon be making metallic magnesium which will probably find a great market in airplane production as an alloy with aluminum." At that time, magnesium was used primarily in flares to illuminate battle areas.

Dow was convinced the airplane would become an instrument of war that would do away with heavy battle cruisers and change naval strategy. He wrote Michigan's Representative G. A. Currie soon after the United States entered the war, urging him to support appropriations for fleets of airplanes.

He said: "I have a great deal of confidence in the ability of Americans to accomplish wonders with aeroplanes, and I think that aeroplanes are going to do away with the enormously expensive battle cruisers with a 35-mile-an-hour speed, as the hydroplane would prove a better eye for a fleet than a 35-knot cruiser. I think the whole idea of naval strategy that calls for these cruisers is knocked out if an ordinary super-dreadnaught and a hydroplane will take their place. . . .

"I think there is every reason in the world why very large amounts should be spent on air fleets in preference to other lines of expenditures."

Dow was too conservative in his estimates of air power. He could not foresee that one day the plane would not only shatter the old concepts of naval strategy but it would make the "super-dreadnaught" obsolete. Unfortunately, it would take another war to convince Washington that "very large amounts should be spent on air fleets."

By 1918 Dow Chemical had become a virtual arsenal with almost all of its chemicals going to the government. Its phenol production was the largest of any manufacturer in the nation. More than 3,000 workers labored in the Midland plants.

When President Wilson named industrialist Bernard Baruch to head the War Industries Board and bring some order out of the chaos of production and priorities, Dow was named a member of the board's chemical section. He became a regular commuter between Midland and Washington.

Dow lobbied hard for tariffs on chemicals that would protect the young American industry from German competition after the war. He predicted that when the fighting ended, the Germans would be certain to try to regain the monopoly positions they had held before the war and, without protection, many of the small American chemical companies would not survive. He recalled that without the tariff on imports of bromides and bleach, he would never have been able to compete with the British and Germans in the bleach and bromine wars.

In June, 1918, the Dow Chemical board of directors elevated Dow to the presidency of the company and he retained the title of general manager. Convers was moved up to become chairman of the board. It had taken twenty-one years, but Dow was finally sitting securely in the management saddle.

By this time it had become increasingly clear that Dow's decision in 1913 to shift production heavily to chlorine products had been one of the most important of his career. The war years had set off a chain reaction in the production of chemicals by American manufacturers. The production of one resulted in by-product chemicals which could be linked with others for even more products. Chlorine was one of the most versatile of them all.

But there was a block to unlimited expansion into new chemical products. The needs of the United States government restricted Dow Chemical largely to manufacturing the products it could supply in large quantities to war plants. The war effort came first.

When Germany used mustard gas on the Western Front in a move of desperation to shatter the Allied defenses, the United States government called on Dow Chemical to manufacture the gas. Professor Smith at Case School worked out a process to make the gas from ethylene, sulfur, and chlorine. At war's end it was being produced at the rate of ten thousand pounds a day, but little of it ever reached Europe and the stockpile left after the war was buried at sea. More important than anything else was the knowledge gained by Dow's researchers in the production of ethylene—a product that would become tremendously important in peacetime research.

Dow's plants poured into the war effort 30 million pounds of caustic soda; 2 million pounds of monochlorbenzol for use in explosives; 1 million pounds of acetic anhydride used in making the varnish which coated the fabric wings of airplanes, stiffening them and making them water and fire resistant; 23,500,000 pounds of phenol used in the manufacture of picric acid, also required in explosives; 1,000,000 pounds of chloroform; 22,900,000 pounds of carbon tetrachloride used as a solvent and for the manufacture of other war materials; and bromine and bromides by the millions of pounds.

Other important products were Epsom salts, used as a medicine and in the tanning of leather; aspirin; insecticides for crop protection; and magnesium for battle-front flares.

Dow knew the feverish pace of expansion and production would not continue indefinitely. One day the war would end, the abnormal demand for chemicals would drop, and his company would be left with many of its plants standing idle. He warned his directors in the summer of 1918 that difficult times were ahead.

For almost four years, selling had been no problem. Buyers had clamored for products and asked for more. Sales had been automatic. As a hedge against a post-war slump, Dow started expanding the sales organization which for years had been centered in Midland. He opened a New York office and adopted a trademark—the name DOW enclosed in a four-pointed diamond.

When September rolled around, he wrote his old friend, J. H. Osborn, in California, "I suppose it is hard for you to realize that I am now 52 years old and beyond the draft age. Willard was 21 last January and came in the Spring registration and enlisted in the Engineering Reserves. He is a senior at Ann Arbor, taking the Chemical Engineering Course, and they returned him to college to finish his course before going into service. I think he is anxious to get into service, and I am more than pleased that his mother has raised no objections, but we all sincerely hope that the war will be over before long and I think as soon as American machinery gets in full swing, that the end will be near."

The end was nearer than Herbert Dow imagined. The armistice was signed on November 11 and the guns were stilled.

Chapter Seven

The end of World War I brought peace to the United States, but it was peace flawed by an economic depression and social and political unrest.

The abnormally high demands for goods and labor had ended abruptly with the signing of the Armistice. Many factories which had sprung up to supply materials for war closed their gates. In others, the machines idled at a slow pace. Millions of workers found themselves out of jobs. The federal government was not prepared, by law or precedent, to ease the impact of the sudden work stoppages on American industries or the workers.

As the Depression settled over the nation, anarchists preached violent overthrow of government. The Communist Party of the United States emerged after failing in a fight to capture control of the Socialist Party. The left-wing Industrial Workers of the World (IWW) was involved in head-thumping strikes and civil disorders.

Assassins planted a bomb at the doorstep of United States Attorney General A. Mitchell Palmer which wrecked the front of his home on Washington's fashionable R Street, N. W. Palmer and his wife were not injured but the assassins were killed in the explosion. Bombs were sent through the mails in packages to John D. Rockefeller, Sr., J. P. Morgan, three cabinet members, four United States senators, two congressmen, a federal judge, and two governors. Fortunately, the bombs were intercepted or failed to reach their intended victims.

In 1920, Prohibition went into effect across the nation and spawned a lawless era of rum-running, speakeasies, and underworld empires of hoodlums. Big, bluff, amoral Warren G. Harding was swept into the Presidency on an ungrammatical slogan, "Back to Normalcy."

Midland was outside the main currents of the social and political tempest. But the town was hard hit by the postwar business depression. When the government cancelled its contracts at war's end, Herbert Dow was forced to cut back his operations. While three thousand men had worked overtime to keep the plants running during the emergency, only four hundred were needed to manufacture the chemicals that could be marketed in 1919.

One of Dow's first moves was to junk plants built solely for war production and to scrap obsolete equipment. At Earl Bennett's urging, Dow quickly settled claims against the government in order to get on with his peacetime plans.

"A lot of companies haggled with the government for years after the war over the contracts," Bennett recalled. "We settled as fast as we could at whatever price we were offered. We cleared the decks in a hurry and it was one of the best moves we ever made."

Dow did not cut back on research even in the worst of the Depression. He told his board of directors six months after the war ended: "We have as many research men at work now as we had at any time during the war. In years gone by our research has been the basis of practically all our profits. That is to say we have not made money by picking up old processes from our competitors and others. Our processes have been originated and developed by our own chemists and engineers..."

He badgered his board into giving him $300,000 to expand bromine production even though there was no immediate demand for increased capacity. This was the pattern that had proved successful in the past: build in bad times for the good times ahead. It was a reflection of the elder J. P. Morgan's philosophy: "Any man who is a bear on the future of this country will go broke."

While many companies were pulling in sail to weather the economic storm, Dow expanded and overhauled his war-worn plant. With his curious talent for reaching into the manpower pool and pulling out the right man, he picked young, tough A. P. "Dutch" Beutel for the job of modernizing and mapping the network of pipes through which the chemicals flowed. The miles of pipelines had been installed through the years in crisscross confusion.

Beutel was a chunky, square-jawed graduate of Case School who had worked briefly as a coal mining engineer before joining Dow in 1916. He had had experience with pipes and pumps in the mines. He might have stayed with coal mining except that he fell in love with a girl who refused to marry him unless he quit mining.

"I had been in a couple of smash-ups in the hole that left me with a limp," Beutel would explain, "and my future wife, Belle Armstrong, wanted me to get out of it. She said, 'If you don't get out of the coal mines I'm not going to marry you. I don't want to be a widow.' So I promised her I'd get another job. The day before our wedding, Tom

Griswold called me at St. Charles, Michigan. He said, 'Get over here. I want to talk to you about working in Midland.' I said, 'I'm going on my honeymoon.' He said, 'Oh, to hell with the honeymoon.' And I said, 'Not me.'

"I came with Dow after the honeymoom.... One day in 1920 I was called in to talk to Herbert Dow and Fred Lowry, his general plant superintendent. Dow said to me, 'I want someone to go into the plant and put our pipelines and equipment in some kind of shape. They're in a mess. We've never had any engineering in our piping system. I'll give you a crew to help.' I said, 'I've never run a crew.' He said, 'You've got to learn sometime.' "

Dow also enlarged his research staff. He was determined to move more boldly into the field of organic chemistry which the Germans had exploited so skillfully before and during the war. He gave the job of organizing an organic research laboratory to his argumentative, apple-cheeked son-in-law, William J. Hale. Hale had married Dow's eldest daughter, Helen, in a wartime wedding.

The first move Hale made was to put together a company chemical library. He had studied chemistry in Germany prior to the war and he knew the value of a library well-stocked with technical books, papers, and reference material. Dow's chemists and engineers had their own personal libraries but there was no central source of research material in Midland from which all the researchers and engineers could draw. The library he started eventually grew into one of the largest chemical libraries in the United States.

After a time Hale persuaded Edgar C. Britton to leave his teaching job in the University of Michigan chemistry department and join him at Dow Chemical. But before coming to Midland, Britton wrote to ask about living conditions and how much vacation time he would be allowed.

Hale replied: "For heating a cook stove, we use kerosene and it seems to be the only practical thing. Electrical rates are very high and all you will use in that line will be a hot plate and toaster. There are many here who use a common coal stove, but no enterprising person would think of such a thing. [We use] the best kerosene range made, namely the Puritan, put out by the same concern in Cleveland that puts out the Perfection....

"As for your vacation, each chemist is allowed about two weeks a year with, of course, holidays extra. You should choose your two weeks though at a time when your work is not too pressing. The real chemists soon get over that obsolete three months' summer vacation idea. That scheme works all right possibly for those who are unaccustomed to real work, but I can't imagine a real live grown-up man desiring seriously to follow the custom. It really is detrimental to your development as a chemist, let alone the harmful effect it has upon your associates among the living."

Britton soon found himself swept into the competitive research and development race that had become a way of life for Dow's chemists and engineers. New products, new machinery, new processes and expanding knowledge of the atom were opening wider fields to explore. Herbert Dow prowled the plants and laboratories, suggesting experiments or ways to improve old processes. He encouraged the competition.

Veazey would recall: "He encouraged everybody to find out things in their own way. It was not uncommon for him to put several people or a group of people to work on the same problem at the same time, and run the whole show like a horse race to see which one would come up first with the answer."

The research was not as helter-skelter as it might seem. Ed Barstow was the man to whom Dow turned in a time of crisis to get a new product on the market ahead of a competitor, to build a new plant in a hurry, or to find a way of doing things when others said it couldn't be done. Cost was not as important to Barstow as quick results.

Charlie Strosacker was the penny pincher. He would come along behind Barstow, pick up the pieces of a plant torn down by Barstow, and end up making a different product that could be sold at low cost.

Putnam became the perfectionist, turning out products such as aspirin, that required refinement to their greatest possible purity. It was Putnam to whom Dow turned in 1918 to give his son Willard his first shake-down training in managing a chemical plant after his graduation from the University of Michigan.

An oldtimer commented, "I think Herbert Dow had a more subtle sense of humor than any of us imagined at the time. He started Willard out in the aspirin plant—learning how to cure headaches."

The rough, tough in-plant competition among these strong-minded men developed a high degree of pride and enthusiasm among the employees. They identified themselves as a "Barstow man," a "Strosacker man," or a "Putnam man" and fought for priorities in research projects and materials. The stabilizer who kept the research from flying off in all directions was Dow. He spent as much time with his research teams as he did in his office looking after the management.

Dow's main interests in the months following the war centered on phenol and magnesium metal, two products which were to play an important part in the company's climb to a position of leadership in the chemical world. No one knows why Dow became so deeply interested in phenol at a time when there was comparatively little demand for it. In the years before World War I, only about 1,000,000 pounds of phenol were sold in the United States. Most of it went into carbolic acid, to be used as a general antiseptic or into Bakelite, one of the pioneer plastics. Almost all of this phenol was imported from England, where it was manufactured as a by-product of coke.

When war came, synthetic phenol plants sprang up across the country to supply the munitions makers. Production rose to 320,000 pounds a day. Then suddenly the war was over and demand for phenol dropped back to its prewar level—a demand hardly great enough to stir excitement over potential profits.

Dow could not possibly have foreseen that within a few years phenol would be required in tremendous quantities for the manufacture of a wide range of plastics far more versatile than the hard, brittle Bakelite. And yet he set Hale and Britton to work in 1919 to devise a new phenol process at a time when its future looked anything but promising.

Dow had been dissatisfied with his old phenol process even though it had met the demands of the time. For one thing the process required huge amounts of sulfuric acid which Dow did not produce himself. The acid had to be bought from others and this didn't fit into Dow's ideas of efficient manufacturing.

Dow turned the problem of finding a better phenol process over to Hale and Britton. The objective was a process that would bypass the use of sulfur and depend on chemicals found in Dow's plants. As a starter, they had the notes made by Strosacker and chemist Robert Dreisbach during some preliminary research work in 1915 on a phenol process involving the use of chlorbenzol, caustic soda, and hydrochloric acid. The idea was not new. Chemists in England and Germany had made small amounts of phenol in their laboratories from these three starting agents. But no one had found a way to convert the laboratory experiments into a commercial process.

The Hale-Britton research team set out with Dow's blessing to prove a workable process could be found. They labored for months with failure after failure. But in 1922 they came up with a process that looked promising on paper. It called for an apparatus that could withstand internal pressures of 5,000 to 6,000 pounds per square inch when the chlorbenzol reacted with caustic soda. No chemical manufacturer—and indeed no manufacturers of any product—had worked successfully with such tremendous pressures. Many experts said it couldn't be done and wrote papers to prove it. Usually, chemical production was carried out at normal atmospheric pressures or, at the most, pressures of a few hundred pounds.

Dow sent to Chicago for special reactor coils designed to withstand the high pressures but, when put to the test, the coils burst. The research team reached the conclusion that if they were ever going to get a reactor, Dow Chemical's own people would have to design and build it.

With Mark Putnam and Dutch Beutel giving big assists, they solved the pressure problem by having the chemical reaction take place in a thick iron pipe with a small bore. The small-bore pipe was coiled in a larger tube through which the starting materials were fed. A small amount of heat helped keep the reaction going. Once the reaction started in the small pipes, the self-generated heat raised the temperature of the starting materials to the level necessary for efficient and economical production of phenol.

Beutel remembers: "We put the heating and reactor coils in a big tank so if they blew up we wouldn't kill anybody—6,000 pounds of pressure was a hell of a lot of pressure at that time. They started making these coils in Chicago and shipping them out to us. They blew up as fast as we put them in. I looked into the problem and found that the welds were poorly made. I said, 'Let me try making some.' So I made some coils with ordinary acetylene welding and then got the group to buy a flash welder. I set it up in the shop and started making pipe coils. Then Paul Cottringer and I got together and we decided the coil design was all wrong and we had to start over. We finally figured out how to make the coils—and we put a little better than a mile of pipe in the heating coils and reactor coils. Once we figured out the mechanical details, the thing worked beautifully."

The breakthrough in the Hale-Britton process was a sensational advance for Dow Chemical. It bypassed the need to buy sulfur in large quantities, used chemicals readily available to Dow, and gave him a lead in the manufacture of phenol that the company would never relinquish through the years.

But the success of the process was not wholly in the production of phenol as an end product. The process also produced four useful by-product chemicals that helped reduce the cost of the phenol.

One of these was salt, which was fed back through the chlorine-caustic cells to make caustic soda, hydrogen, and chlorine. Two others were never-before-seen chemicals called orthophenylphenol and paraphenylphenol. They became the base of a line of germicides, fungicides and insecticides marketed under the trade name Dowicides. They were effective against pests ranging from termites to fungus growths plaguing the paper, leather, and glue industries. Paraphenylphenol also became the base for a new lacquerlike varnish used on the hulls of vessels to help them slip through water with a minimum of friction.

The fourth by-product from the line was diphenyloxide. At first it was regarded merely as a troublesome waste matter. Then the discovery was made that diphenyloxide could be converted into a material useful in manufacturing processes requiring an agent that could hold high temperatures at low pressures with great stability. This product became known as Dowtherm.

The geranium-smelling diphenyloxide was sold in huge quantities to the makers of soaps and perfumed toilet goods. But perhaps the most remarkable quality of this chemical oddity was its ability to do a disappearing act. Researchers found that when diphenyloxide piled up in unmanageable quantities during the phenol-making operation, it could be fed back into the phenol process to help make more phenol. Thus the production of diphenyloxide could be turned on and off at will, without disturbing the production of phenol or the other by-products.

At the same time the phenol process was being worked out, a team of Dow researchers under Barstow's general direction labored to improve the process for making magnesium even though there was little demand for the metal in the United States. Industry generally knew nothing of the properties of magnesium or how to work with it, although the Aluminum Company of America (Alcoa) was experimenting with magnesium as an alloy with aluminum. Alcoa obtained its magnesium from its subsidiary, the American Magnesium Corporation (AMC) at Niagara Falls. In 1919, Dow Chemical and AMC were the only two producers of magnesium in the country, other producers having dropped out of the business when the war ended. Dow Chemical sold its magnesium under the trade name, Dowmetal.

In that first postwar year, Barstow's men devised a process that produced 50 to 60 pounds of high-quality magnesium a day. The process was relatively crude but it worked for weeks without a breakdown. Dow was so pleased with the results he had sixteen vat units installed. By this time he had some $225,000 of the company's money invested in magnesium and the returns had been small.

The new units worked smoothly for six weeks. Then on February 1, 1920, one of the big metal vats in the production line cracked. More than 300 pounds of molten salt gushed out. It poured across the wooden platform on which the vats stood and reached the wooden supports of the building. Within minutes the plant was an inferno. Fire fighters managed to keep the fire from spreading to other buildings.

When the flames subsided, Herbert Dow surveyed the charred wreckage and said to Barstow, "I guess these things have to happen. Go ahead and rebuild it."

There was heavy pressure from Cleveland to halt the magnesium experiments. The product had been a drain on the company's treasury except for one year of the war when 3,852 pounds had been sold to the government. Sales in 1919 had dropped to 859 pounds.

Dow overrode the opposition. He had gone too far to back out now, or so he argued. He insisted that a use for magnesium would develop in the United States as it had developed in Germany and Dow Chemical had to be ready to meet this demand. Already Germany had begun to experiment with magnesium in airplanes.

The Germans had a twenty-four-year lead over Americans in accumulating knowledge of how to produce and work with magnesium. They had built the world's first electrolytic magnesium plant in 1886 at Hemelingen near Bremen, using carnallite—a double salt of magnesium chloride and potassium chloride—as a raw material. Later a large plant began operations at Bitterfeld. The Germans called the new metal Elektron.

They learned how to use magnesium as an alloy with aluminum, zinc, and other metals. Because of their limited supply of bauxite—the ore from which aluminum is made—the German chemists began to alloy aluminum with magnesium rather than to alloy magnesium with aluminum.

The most important German advances had not been made in the production of magnesium, but in its fabrication. They knew how to melt and cast the alloys with a minimum of waste. The cheapness of the finished product depended largely on the cost of fabricating. The Germans protected their processes by having them patented around the world.

When Dow persisted in exploring magnesium, he was pushing into uncharted territory as far as his chemists and engineers were concerned. This was metallurgy, and they had had little experience in it. The field was alien to them. But Dow had no choice except to move in this direction if magnesium was to be developed as a structural material. Someone had to learn how to fabricate and alloy magnesium and then teach others in industry how to do it.

A few of Dow's people had gained a measure of expertise in alloying the metal in 1918 when they built a small foundry and experimented with alloying magnesium with manganese. Methods of casting had to be found that would not infringe on German patents or the patents held by the American Magnesium Corporation. The most important German patent—the one that gave them an advantage—involved the use of sulfur. Sulfur formed a protective shield around the metal while it was being melted and cast. This process was simpler than Dow's and as a consequence gave the Germans an edge.

The German advantage may well have driven Dow from the field had not Congress passed the Fordney-McCumber Tariff Act in 1922 which gave the young chemical industry in the United States a measure of protection from German imports. Magnesium was included in the tariff list.

Dow tried to interest the automobile industry in magnesium pistons. But engineers were afraid the pistons would burst into flame at high temperatures. They had heard of magnesium powder and magnesium shavings burning. They thought solid magnesium would do the same and no amount of argument by Dow would impress them—even after he put an ingot of magnesium into a gasoline fire to prove it would not burn.

To dramatize the safety and durability of his pistons, Dow arranged in 1921 to have them placed in the engines of three of the cars entered in the 500-mile Memorial Day Race in Indianapolis. Tommy Milton drove his Frontenac to victory in a near-record 89.62 miles per hour to win with Dow's pistons. The other cars finished third and fifth.

The flurry of publicity from the achievement at Indianapolis helped sales for a time. Garages and service stations bought Dow pistons as replacements in rebuilding worn-out engines. This business reached a peak of $100,000 a year. But the pistons never won over the automobile makers and the costs of research, fabricating, sales, and promotion outstripped the returns.

Magnesium was used in small quantities in automobile horns, portable tools, wheelbarrows, and specialty items in the early 1920's. A Dow employee even fashioned a violin from magnesium but its tone hardly had the quality of a Stradivarius. The greatest demand for magnesium was as an alloy in aluminum, and this field was dominated by the American Magnesium Corporation.

Barstow would recall: "If we had spent as much time, effort and money on developing some other product as we spent on magnesium, the company would have been better off financially in the long run.

Few people can imagine how stubborn Herbert Dow was about developing magnesium. It was an obsession with him—and it was lucky for the country that he didn't drop it."

An upswing in business in 1922 eased some of the pressure on Dow and he was able to spend more time with his family, his apple orchard, and the gardens which were becoming a Michigan showplace. He rarely went to church although he was a member of the Presbyterian church. Some wags said he stopped going to church with his wife because he couldn't get up during a sermon and argue with the preacher.

Dow loved to argue—politics, business, literature, religion, education, or apple growing. The subject didn't matter as long as someone had a viewpoint and defended it. Once when he came home downcast, Mrs. Dow said, "My, you're grumpy. What's the matter? Did you lose an argument at Frank Teal's barber shop?"

Frank Teal's place had been one of Midland's forums for arguments for many years and when Dow couldn't find a good argument at the plant he knew he could find one at Teal's. The friendship with the barber had lasted for more than twenty years although there had been a period when Dow refused to set foot inside the door.

The rift came one day when Dow entered the barber shop and found Teal busy cutting the hair of a customer. Dow sat down to wait his turn. He settled himself comfortably and put his feet in another chair.

"Dow!" Teal barked. "Were you raised in a stable? Get your feet off that chair!"

Dow stalked out and for weeks gave his business to another barber. But things weren't the same. This fellow wouldn't argue with him like Teal, who stood in no awe of the town's leading industrialist. Teal remembered Dow from the days when he could barely scrape up enough money for food and rent, and people were calling him "Crazy Dow."

Finally Dow capitulated. He returned to the barber shop and found Teal alone. He sat in the chair and Teal began trimming his hair as though nothing had happened between them. They talked of this and that and then Dow said, "Teal, how would you like to go to work for me?"

Teal stopped his snipping and said, "Dow, I wouldn't work for you if you were the last man on earth."

Dow grinned. He said, "I was only wondering."

Chapter Eight

January 25, 1924, was a cold, raw, gray day in Midland. Low-flying clouds scudded across the sky, driven by a stiff wind out of the northwest. Snow piled in drifts along fence rows. Only a few people ventured onto the streets. It was much like a thousand other wintry days in that part of the country.

And yet this day was different because it brought to Midland two men who would open the way for The Dow Chemical Company to link its fortunes—at least in part—to the booming young automobile industry. Herbert Dow had failed to interest automobile makers in his magnesium pistons. But now another door was swinging open.

The visitors were Charles F. Kettering, director of the General Motors Research Laboratories, and his associate, Thomas Midgley, Jr. Both were pioneers in the development of the automobile.

In 1912, Kettering had invented the electric self-starter. This gadget was most particularly a boon to women drivers because it eliminated the necessity of hand-cranking an engine to get it running. The starter was first adopted by Cadillac. Then one by one other manufacturers made it standard equipment. Henry Ford was a long-time holdout but he, too, eventually came around to the self-starter.

Midgley had found in the laboratory the secret to anti-knock gasoline.

Kettering and Midgley arrived in Midland at a crucial time in the history of the automobile's development. The industry was in the midst of its first great boom. Better automobiles and better roads were helping shove sales upward. Detroit's prosperity had given the entire country an economic shot in the arm.

Henry Ford had led the way in converting the automobile from a rich man's plaything into a necessity. His Model T dominated the market as the country headed into the Roaring Twenties. But General Motors was climbing fast and others were fighting for a share of the market. Filling stations were sprouting at crossroads. Dealers were opening showrooms and stocking automobile parts. Manufacturing and selling automobiles had become the biggest industrial operation in the United States. Before the decade would end, the industry would be taking 20 percent of the nation's steel output, 80 percent of the rubber imports, and 75 percent of the plate glass. The petroleum industry was being shaped to supply the needs of the automobile.

This happy scene was not without its flaw—a serious one that worried the car makers and brought a torrent of complaints from automobile buyers. The flaw was in the gasoline that went into the tanks of cars and trucks. The low-octane, poorly refined fuel of the day caused engines to knock. The gasoline, instead of exploding in the cylinders with a rhythmic surge of energy, exploded in too-fast, uneven bursts that turned the crankshaft with jerky movements and produced a knocking sound. The knock was annoying to the driver, hard on engines, and wasteful of gasoline.

Kettering and Midgley started a search in 1916 for an inexpensive chemical that could be added to the gasoline to slow down the combustion and eliminate the knock. They tried hundreds of different combinations. They found that iodine would do the job but iodine was impractical. It cost $4.50 a pound and the world market was dominated by Chilean producers who could manipulate the price practically at will. Aniline proved to be another additive that worked, although not well enough.

Then Midgley, in 1920, discovered that a knocking engine could be soothed to a purr by adding tetraethyl lead to the gasoline. Road trials confirmed the laboratory tests. It appeared for a time the problem of the knock had been solved.

However, the solution to the knock created still another serious problem: the leaded gasoline left behind a metallic deposit that fouled cylinders, valves and spark plugs. The clogging action of the lead was worse than the knock it had eliminated.

Another search was begun, this time to find a chemical that would prevent the lead from fouling the engines. Herbert Dow heard of the search in 1923 and sent Charles Strosacker to the General Motors Research Laboratories at Dayton, Ohio, with several samples of chlorinated compounds. "Tell Midgley to be sure to try bromine," Dow said.

Midgley already had tried ethylene dibromide, a derivative of bromine, and it had worked. When two parts of ethylene dibromide were mixed with three parts of tetraethyl lead, the knock disappeared and no lead deposit was left behind in the engines. This combination looked like a winner.

Ethylene dibromide could be bought for about one-seventh the cost of iodine. Yet Midgley had reservations about using the chemical. He told Strosacker he was afraid there wasn't enough bromine in the country to meet the demand that was certain to develop for an efficient, knockless gasoline.

Strosacker insisted Dow Chemical could supply the need. "We can dig more wells," he said.

Before committing themselves, Kettering and Midgley began a search for a source of bromine on which they could depend in the years ahead. They sent scouts across the United States and to Mexico, Germany, North Africa, and the Middle East. When all the reports were in, Midgley was satisfied the Michigan brine deposits were the most favorably located and The Dow Chemical Company would be the most dependable supplier. Dow Chemical had been producing ethylene dibromide for some time without finding a market for the product.

It was the decision to turn to Dow Chemical for ethylene dibromide that brought Midgley and Kettering to Midland that cold January day. Herbert Dow was away at the time so they discussed their problem with Willard Dow and Lee Doan. Later, Herbert Dow assured them he could meet their immediate needs. But he conceded that if a tremendous demand developed for knockless gasoline, the production of bromine would pose a serious problem: to pump vast quantities of brine merely to remove the bromine would throw Dow Chemical's production out of balance and it would be almost impossible to dispose of the waste brine.

"When that time comes," Dow said, "we'll have to mine it out of the ocean."

Dow suggested it might prove feasible to pump water from the Pacific Ocean into a desert basin, let the sun's rays evaporate it, and then obtain the bromine from the concentrated brine.

At first Midgley was amused by the thought of going to the sea for bromine. But Dow was serious. Later Midgley came to the conclusion that perhaps the sea was a logical source after all for the chemical needed in anti-knock gasoline—if a way could be found to take the bromine from the water cheaply.

In later years, Midgley would recall in a letter to Willard Dow: ". . . It was fully recognized that bromine would some day become the limiting factor in the use of tetraethyl lead. Your Father was consulted and kept fully informed of the factors which surrounded the problem. In the beginning we secured all our bromine from The Dow Company, and as you know, this soon developed into the requirement for more wells. During this time we had a chemist by the name of Fisher from Standard of New Jersey go to the Dead Sea and survey the possibility of securing bromine from that source, and at about the same time Mr. Kettering visited the Sebkas of Northern Africa and inspected what the French had done during World War I to get bromine from this area. We also asked our various oil company customers to send us samples of brine from their drilling operations and we analyzed this for bromine content. There was a large percentage of bromine in the brines from the Tampico region in Mexico, and as you know, some of the brines from Ohio were rich in bromine. However, the Ohio situation did not look promising and aside from this no other area within the United States, excepting the territory operated by The Dow Chemical Company, showed anything worth while. Throughout the time of this survey, I kept insisting that our bromine must come from within the United States. I could not see any sense in getting our internal combustion engines developed to operate on a product which could be cut off by war. At the termination of these surveys, we had a conference with your Father in Midland... Your Father stated that the only solution to the problem of securing adequate quantitites of bromine from the United States for further expansion would require sea water as the raw material, and since the concentration in the sea water was so low, it would be necessary to concentrate the sea water by evaporation. He proposed a method of pumping Pacific Ocean water over the Rocky Mountains, forming an inland salt lake in some of the arid desert land and letting this water concentrate by solar evaporation. Rather jokingly, I suggested that we might consider this problem to be merely the pumping of the Pacific Ocean over the Rocky Mountains and letting it dry out, to which he replied that was just about what it amounted to...."

The conferences with Kettering and Midgley led to Dow agreeing to furnish them with 100,000 pounds of ethylene dibromide a month at a cost of 58 cents a pound. Dow immediately stepped up the pumping of brine to meet the contract requirements, even though he suspected it was a stopgap measure.

The idea of getting bromine from the sea intrigued him. The bromine was in the sea in almost limitless quantities, with each million parts of sea water being 67 parts bromine. The problem was how to pump 1,000,000 pounds of sea water to obtain most of its 67 pounds of bromine—and do it cheaply. The separation couldn't be done with electricity or heat because the cost would be prohibitive.

Soon after Kettering and Midgley left Midland, Dow started the first of more than two hundred experiments looking to the extraction of bromine from sea water. During 1924, he had samples of brine brought from the Atlantic, the Pacific, and the Dead Sea. Chemists began working on the problem of removing the bromine without the use of electricity or heat. When Dow saw an analysis of these brines, he noticed that the concentration of bromine was about the same as it was in the waste brine at his bromine plant.

In July, Dow wrote J. S. Crider, a director of The Dow Chemical Company: "...The 'sewer' brine from the bromine plant normally contains about the same amount of bromine as the oceans. We have just made some tests to see how good an extraction we can get under extreme conditions and have been able to reduce the bromine down to a point where it is running 40 per cent of the amount in the oceans. This would seem to indicate that we could extract bromine from the oceans and recover 60 per cent of the bromine in ocean water. However, bromine made in this way would not be cheap."

Dow was encouraged in the experiments by word from Midgley that ethylene dibromide continued to look better than any other chemical as an additive to control the lead problem. And then Midgley and Kettering returned to Midland in early August to tell Dow all doubts had been resolved in favor of the bromine product. They wanted Dow to start a crash program to supply the Ethyl Gasoline Company with 600,000 pounds of ethylene dibromide each month—an increase of 500,000 pounds over the shipments Dow had been making. On the face of it, the proposition offered a big breakthrough for Dow Chemical into the automobile market that had been closed to them for years except for minor sales of magnesium.

Dow moved cautiously, however. To supply that volume of a single chemical would require new wells and construction of a new plant. Even after these costs, there was always the possibility some other chemical would be found more efficient than tetraethyl lead. Such a discovery might eliminate the need for bromine.

Dow agreed to the expansion provided he received enough for his ethylene dibromide to cover the cost of the emergency construction program. With this formula as a bargaining base, a quick agreement was made.

But getting anti-knock gasoline to the market place became a nightmare. Two months after Dow reached his agreement with Midgley and Kettering, scare headlines sprouted on the front pages of newspapers across the nation: "Mystery Gas Crazes 12 in Laboratory"—"Poisonous Gas Drives 5 Men Mad, Two Die"—"Looney Gas

May Menace Motorists"–"New York Prohibits Sale of Looney Gas."

The victims in this tragedy were workers in a Standard Oil Company laboratory near Elizabeth, New Jersey, where experiments were being carried on with tetraethyl lead in the search for the best combination of anti-knock compounds. The men had been poisoned breathing gas fumes.

The immediate reaction was fear that the entire population of cities would be menaced by deadly fumes if automobiles were permitted to burn anti-knock gasoline. New York City banned the sale of leaded gasoline. The Board of Health made it a misdemeanor for anyone to use the new gasoline within the city. Other cities followed New York's lead. State and federal agencies began investigations into the causes of the workers' deaths and illnesses.

For more than a year production of anti-knock gasoline was halted while the United States Surgeon General sifted fact from rumor. Out of this investigation came the quieting report that the leaded gasoline itself was harmless. The tragedy had resulted from a breakdown in laboratory safety precautions.

The bans on anti-knock gasoline were lifted. Gasoline stations once again filled their tanks with the high-potency fuel and sales boomed. During this time, du Pont fitted out a ship as a floating chemical plant and sent it into the Atlantic Ocean in an effort to extract bromine from the sea water. The ship made only one voyage and nothing more came of the experiment.

With the cloud removed from anti-knock gasoline, Dow moved rapidly to increase production of ethylene dibromide. He put his son, Willard, in charge of the expansion. Wells had to be drilled miles from the production plant and pipelines laid to gather the brine. Power lines had to be strung and powerhouses built to supply the energy for the pumps.

When the job began to lag behind schedule, Willard came to Dutch Beutel and asked him to take charge of the pipeline job. "Dutch," he said, "you take on the job of being a pusher for me. Get these fellows in line so they will get the job done in a hurry. The way we're going, we'll never get it finished."

Dutch Beutel would later recall: "So I took on the job of being the expediter. We pushed out twenty to thirty miles from the plant with our wells and pipes. We got up to two miles a day in laying pipes—using hand labor to dig the ditches. But this was too slow. I went to Willard and said, 'Let me buy a ditching machine. They can just spin this dirt out of the ground and we can do this job a lot quicker.' And that's what we did."

Meantime, Herbert Dow had a team working on a scheme to extract bromine from sea water by acidifying the brine and passing it through a blowing-out tower. This process, in the laboratory stage, was beginning to look hopeful as 1926 came to a close.

— — —

In those first years of the tempestuous Twenties, Dow once again found himself at odds with his board of directors. A majority wanted him to slow down his research and ease up on the building of new plants to produce chemicals for which there was no immediate demand. Dow insisted the company must push forward with its research and new products or else it would limp along in the shadow of aggressive competitors.

Stripped to its bare bones, the issue between them was whether the board sitting in Cleveland was going to run The Dow Chemical Company through control of the purse strings—or whether Dow was going to be the boss in research and production.

This tug-of-war had started at a meeting of the board in 1922. The board had startled Dow by voting to limit his spending authority in construction to $2,500—except in cases where he had specific approval of the board to exceed that amount.

Dow protested the limitation was a deliberate effort to slow up the company's operations. He argued it was impractical to be running to Cleveland for board approval to spend comparatively small amounts of money when on-the-spot action could mean the difference between a profit and a loss. He asked the board to rescind the action, but the vote stood.

Except for the strained relations between Dow and his board, things were going so smoothly in the winter of 1922—23 that Dow decided to take Mrs. Dow on a cruise to Japan by way of Hawaii. They sailed to Hawaii where Dow spent most of his time relaxing in the warm sun. He wrote to Professor Smith at Case that he had surprised himself by going to church with Mrs. Dow three Sundays in a row.

Smith replied: "... Strange you spoke of going to church for three Sundays and the letter arrived a few days after Molly and I had gone to church for the first time in about a year. It makes me think of the little ditty: 'Old Solomon and David led merry, merry lives; they had many, many lady friends and many, many wives; but when they grew older, they had many, many qualms; so Solomon wrote the Proverbs and David wrote the Psalms.'

"Have you and I and the gray-haired men of Honolulu reached the period of 'many, many qualms' and will this phenomenon recruit men for church services in the future?"

Dow's reply to this query has been lost for the record.

From Hawaii, the Dows sailed to Japan where Dow visited a few Japanese chemical plants. But the making of chemicals did not interest him as much as the Japanese gardens, the beauty of which he could never forget and which he would duplicate in his own garden in Midland.

Dow celebrated his fifty-seventh birthday in Japan and then returned to Midland to find that new production and sales records were being set. He wrote to his friend, James Pardee, in Cleveland: "Of course, prices are so much lower than they were during the war that the dollars do not mount up as fast, but these figures (a 50 percent increase in tonnage shipped) are an indication of the large amount of development and the construction work that has been completed since the war, and it is this work that is now earning a good share of our dividends."

During the trip to Japan, Dow came to a decision on his dispute with the board. He concluded that he would continue to be hamstrung in his management of the company unless control of the board was shifted from Cleveland to Midland; the best thing to do was to see that directors were elected who shared his views on research and expansion.

In lining up support, Dow wrote to Professor Smith: ". . . It has not been my intention at any time to do important construction work without the authorization of the board of directors. . . . But if the Board wants to exercise its undoubted right in matters of this kind, it is going to seriously injure The Dow Chemical Company, and I do not think either you or I should stand for that. It can be easily prevented by electing several members on the board from Midland, who could be easily got together on short notice. I have been figuring over the holdings of stock, and find that the Dow family without including their friends, owns a little over one-third of the entire stock, and about 58% of the entire stock is held or controlled from Midland without including Mr. Pardee's stock which is about 9%. . . . Dow stock would be worth almost nothing now if this policy had been carried out during the last four years; and there is less reason why retrenchment should take place from now on than there has been in the past."

Dow knew he could depend on Smith, Pardee, and Chairman of the Board Convers to vote their stock with him in electing new board members Smith assured him of his support, writing, "I fully agree with you that the Midland operators should have entire control of the details of the plant and it is the Board's business to consider broad questions only."

This was the beginning of the end of the Cleveland influence in The Dow Chemical Company. Gradually Dow shaped the membership of the board to give it a strong Midland representation.

What offended Dow most in the Cleveland-Midland relationship, perhaps, was having men miles removed from the actual operation make decisions on how the company should be run. He believed the best manager of a machine or a company was the man close to his job, whether he was a director, a manager, or an engineer. Dow despised "remote control" even in running a machine.

He enlarged on this subject in a letter to Professor Veazey, saying:

"I am no believer in an engineer having an oiler. He no sooner gets this oiler than he sits down and the oiler becomes the man who is in intimate contact with his job and therefore knows his engine and the engineer proceeds to be the equivalent of a man sitting in the office.

"When they put the addition on the power house, they had a room with all the control instruments in it; all the records appeared there and they proceeded to operate the power house from this little office, called the control room. I objected to it because the men would control the machines that they were not in intimate contact with, which constitutes another phase of the tendency everywhere of fellows to migrate to an office with a desk and easy chair, but I was not sure of my position to arbitrarily head it off. It has been on my mind ever since and I cannot help thinking it is a bad idea for the engineers to have an office and desk from which they can control their equipment and issue orders without themselves being in as intimate contact with the subjects as it is possible for them to be.

". . . I would bank my whole reputation as a plant manufacturer on the fundamental basic idea that wherever possible keep a man in as close contact with his job as possible."

Dow's ideas on how to get the best work out of men and machines often confused even his employees. Such was the case once when a mechanic failed to oil his machine on schedule. The bearings burned out and the production of an entire plant came to a halt for hours before the damage could be repaired. Ed Barstow gave a full report of the shut-down to Dow.

"Where is the operator now?" Dow asked.

"Home packing, I guess," Barstow said. "I fired him."

Dow said, "Barstow, you'd better hurry out and hire him back because we've just invested several thousand dollars in his training."

Subscribing to Abraham Lincoln's theory that "the man who hoes the corn should eat the corn," Dow encouraged his employees to invest their savings in Dow Chemical stock. He would interrupt a man at his work to ask, "How many shares of Dow stock do you own?" If the man owned no shares or fewer than Dow thought he should own, he would say, "You don't have much faith in the company, do you?" It was a technique that goaded many men into becoming financially independent despite themselves.

As Dow's hair became streaked with gray, he became "The Old Man" to his employees when he was out of hearing. They never knew what he would say or do in any given situation, but whatever he said or did usually turned out to be the unexpected.

Once Dow stopped by a cutting machine and asked the operator, "Why don't you sweep these steel shavings off the floor?"

"I'm busy," the operator said, not even looking up from his work. "Why don't you sweep them up yourself?"

Dow got a broom, swept up the shavings, and left.

An observer said, "Why didn't you fire that man?"

Dow said, "He was too busy."

Another time in the late evening, Dow walked into a shop where several chemists had been working late on a difficult problem. All of them jumped to their feet when Dow entered the room, except one. He was lying on a bench and he didn't shift from his comfortable position.

Dow checked over the operation and then turned to the man lying on the bench. "Why didn't you get up like the others?" he asked.

The chemist said, "Because I'm very tired and I know everything is going all right."

Dow thought it over a moment. "I guess that is as good an answer as any," he said. And he walked out.

To Dow, an idea was not something to deal with as an abstraction. It was a call to action. When he heard of a drought in the Los Angeles area, he wrote to an acquaintance, H. L. Payne: "I have been hearing numerous stories about the shortage of water in Los Angeles and have a wild dream that possibly water could be distilled from the ocean in multiple effect evaporators at a price that might make it attractive. I think we have the largest evaporating pans in existence. One pan will evaporate and condense about 100,000 pounds of water per hour with a very low heat head. Please wire me collect, upon receipt of this letter, what the wholesale price of water is per thousand gallons... and the price per ton of fuel oil and I will do some more figuring. This is more interesting to me than crossword puzzles."

Payne wired back: "Forget that dream and stick to the crossword puzzle. There is a shortage of rain but no shortage of water."

Dow replied: "Columbus didn't have all the dreams. There are other cities beside Los Angeles. Is water worth more or less than sixty cents per thousand gallons?"

In a following letter he added: "I might add further that distilled water for irrigating purposes is not half as foolish as supporting a heavy vehicle on a bubble of air inclosed in rubber, and at the same time putting the rubber next to the road where it will get all the grief that the road can impose. A cost of 50 cents per thousand gallons of water is not an impossibility—this price including overhead but not taxes, and enough return on the investment to more than pay for any bonds that a municipality might issue."

Dow never got around to working on a scheme to evaporate sea water for irrigating arid areas but the idea was not as fantastic as Payne thought.

One of Dow's dreams at this time in the mid-Twenties was to make Midland a more attractive place in which to live. During his trip to Japan in the winter of 1922–23, one of his fellow ship-passengers was Paul Tonow, a landscape artist renowned for the work he had done on Tokyo's parks. Dow asked him to come to Midland, at Dow's expense, and re-create some of the gardens which Dow had admired so much in Japan.

Tonow came to Midland in 1925. He helped Dow reshape his acres of lawns and pools and shrubs. Then Dow announced that Tonow's services would be available free of charge to any Midland resident who wished to have a landscaping plan drawn for his residence.

Dozens took advantage of the offer and soon Midlanders were in a lively contest to see which could have the most beautiful grounds. Sunken gardens appeared where none had been before. Tiny waterfalls splashed into sheltered pools. Miniature bridges were built over small steams and a touch of Japan was found in many a backyard retreat.

"My idea of a beautiful garden," Dow said in a bulletin, "is one in which there is a small pool, some stones on one edge, a fine mist from an invisible source dropping on the stones and dripping off into the water, and all of it surrounded by shrubbery or plants, the background being high enough so that the eye could not see the ugliness that might be beyond..."

When Midland County officials decided the rickety, 1856-vintage courthouse had outlived its usefulness, Dow persuaded them to let him bring Architect Bloodgood Tuttle of Cleveland to Midland, at Dow's expense, to design a distinctive building. Tuttle produced a Tudor-style building of stone and stucco which resembled a country manor rather than a public building. It remained through the years one of the most unusual public buildings in the United States.

Artists from New York and Detroit were commissioned by Dow to paint murals inside the courthouse. Detroit artist Paul Honore was brought in to do exterior murals depicting the pioneer days of Indians, lumbermen, trappers, and traders. The panels were done with magnesite stucco colored with pigment and mixed with ground glass.

By 1926, Midland had a population of eighty-five hundred. Paved streets had replaced the old cedar paving blocks, the sawdust, and the sand. Most of the residents were comparative newcomers—chemists, engineers, technicians, and white-collar workers. They had no memory of the town when it sat in the stump-covered ugliness of a ravaged countryside and when men were glad to get a job that would pay them $1.25 for eight hours of work.

In a little more than a third of a century, "Crazy Dow" had become known as "Doctor Dow"—an honorary title having been conferred on him by his alma mater, Case School. The ramshackle plant he had started in a rented shed had grown into a substantial business with sales of $8,461,000, giving employment to sixteen hundred people.

Merchant Ewart L. Gardiner summed up the changes pretty well in a homespun article written for a special edition of *The Midland Sun* in 1926: "These newcomers ... have built this newer and better Midland.... From sand and sawdust roads to asphalt pavements, from cow paths and plank contraptions to cement sidewalks, from the pleasant smell of freshly cut pine to the odor of innumerable chemicals, from kerosene lamps to electric lights, from the church concert to the movies, and from red flannel underwear to B.V.D.'s, a number of us old timers have lived through the several stages of Midland's ups and downs and are quite content to accept our share of applause for a job well done. We may have been a trifle stingy in the personal effort expended, but we will show no timidity in accepting any extra credit that is lying around loose.

"Midland has arrived. It has arrived while some of us were asleep. Newspapers and magazines print articles about us and strangers drive up to our doors and take us for an inspection tour of our own city—the city that our fathers hewed out of the wilderness. We look at it and expand. We smile and say: 'Oh yes, we've a fine town here,' and then we hurry home and ask the wife if she has ever seen Ed Teal's evergreens, Bert Carter's back yard, or Earl Stein's sunken garden...."

Midland was changing rapidly and perhaps it was in anticipation of changes ahead in The Dow Chemical Company that Herbert Dow named his son, Willard, to the post of assistant general manager in 1926. Dow was sixty years old. Gradually he began to shift some of the responsibilities of management to Willard.

For a time it appeared that both Willard and his younger brother, Alden, would follow in their father's footsteps. Alden had gone to the University of Michigan in 1922 to begin the study of chemical engineering. But his heart wasn't in his studies; he wanted to be an architect. After three years he dropped out of the university to work for a year in the chemical plant. Then he entered Columbia University's School of Architecture.

Alden Dow would one day recall: "Even as a boy I wanted to be an architect. I remember once I was swinging on the gate at home and the girl who lived nearby said, 'What do you want to do when you grow up?' I told her I wanted to be an architect. She said, 'Nobody can make any money being an architect.'

"When I was at the University of Michigan, I didn't know much about what was going on in chemical engineering—but I knew everything that was happening in the architectural classes. Father agreed the best thing to do was to work for a time in the plant. One morning I came downstairs determined to tell Father that I was going to be an architect. He was to leave that day on a business trip to New York. I said, 'Father, I'm going with you to New York. I want to enter Columbia University's School of Architecture.' If he was disappointed, he didn't show it. He said, 'All right, get your things packed.' That's how I broke the news to him that I wasn't going into the business of making chemicals. I wanted to do something creative on my own."

Unfortunately, Herbert Dow did not live long enough to see his younger son win international recognition as a student of the famous Frank Lloyd Wright.

Chapter Nine

In nominating a Vice-Presidential candidate in 1920, the Republican National Convention chose Calvin Coolidge as running mate for Warren G. Harding in his campaign aimed at bringing the country "back to normalcy."

One of the observers at the convention hall was the caustic Baltimore critic H. L. Mencken, who later reported:

"I left the press-stand and went to the crypt below to hunt a drink. There I found a group of colleagues listening to a Boston brother who knew Coolidge well, and had followed him from the start of his career.

"To my astonishment I found that this gentleman was offering to lay a bet that Harding, if elected, would be assassinated before he had served half his term. There were murmurs, and someone protested uneasily that such talk was injudicious. . . . But the speaker stuck to his wager.

" 'I am simply telling you,' he roared, 'what I KNOW. I know Cal Coolidge inside out. He is the luckiest goddam * * * in the whole world.'

"It seemed plausible then and it is certain now. No other President ever slipped into the White House so easily, and none other ever had a softer time of it while there."

Mencken was right. From the time of Harding's death on August 2, 1923, until Herbert Hoover moved into the White House in March, 1929, Coolidge had to deal with remarkably few crises. Millions of citizens gaily ignored the national Prohibition laws. The underworld prospered. Young people whooped it up in the Jazz Age of hip flasks, rolled stockings, bell-bottom trousers, and the Charleston. There was a revolution in morals and manners. But these goings-on were never laid at Coolidge's doorstep.

There was a paradox in business. The farmer found "normalcy" to be a prolonged period of depressed prices for farm products; but, in general, industry prospered. Small investors plunged into the stock market and the prices of stocks climbed steadily. The economic future had a rosy glow and most economists saw no reason for alarm.

Industry's appetite for chemicals appeared to be insatiable. The demand rose steadily and the American chemical industry entered a spectacular period of growth. Research and engineering technology combined to pour new products onto the market.

The Dow Chemical Company was well prepared to ride with the tide. Herbert Dow had laid a solid base in research and plant expansion during and after World War I. His old policy of using bad times to prepare for good times ahead was paying off.

Automation was one of the keys to Dow's success. Most of his chemicals were being produced, in part or entirely, by continuous processes roughly comparable to the automobile industry's assembly lines. Large tonnages of such chemicals as Epsom salts, aspirin, and calcium chloride came from production lines which were automatically controlled from start to finish.

From 1920 to 1930, Dow Chemical's sales multiplied almost four times from $4,000,000 to $15,000,000. The stock was split 4-for-1 in 1923 and by 1929 had climbed to a peak of $500 a share. The backbone of the business was the sale of bulk chemicals to the makers of rubber, leather, drugs, paints, varnishes, textiles, and anti-knock gasoline. Also, the company had established itself in direct-to-consumer sales of agricultural chemicals and calcium chloride for laying dust on roads and curing concrete.

The growth of Dow Chemical in this period did not go unnoticed in the East. In 1927, E. I. du Pont de Nemours and Company made a move to buy a controlling interest in the company and add the Midland plant to its growing chain of chemical subsidiaries. The Du Ponts had begun their expansion into chemicals prior to World War I by buying several small companies. The purchases had continued after the war.

While taking a winter vacation in Florida, Dow received a letter from Secretary James T. Pardee in Cleveland disclosing that "some strong financial interests" were interested in buying Dow Chemical stock.

"Last week Monday," Pardee wrote, "Mr. Convers, Mr. A. R. Harr, Mr. Crider and I had lunch at the Union Club. Mr. Harr wanted an opportunity to 'sound out' what kind of a reception a proposition from some strong financial interests to buy into the Dow Chemical Co. would receive from some of the Dow Company officials. No names were mentioned, but Mr. Harr stated that the suggestion came from one of the strongest financial groups in the country; men whom he thought we would be glad and willing to have associated with us. He stated that it was not a stock-jobbing proposition, and that a permanent interest was desired...."

After Dow returned from Florida, a representative from Du Pont came to Midland to discuss the matter with Dow.

One of Dow's associates would one day recall: "Dow really didn't want to discuss the matter with the Du Pont representative. He took him on a tour of the plant and led him from place to place—the last thing this fellow wanted to do. He wasn't interested in plant tours. But neither was Herbert Dow interested in talking about selling—and this was his way of avoiding the subject."

Dow did go to New York for a conference with Du Pont representatives. On his return to Midland he wrote Du Pont's Vice President R. R. M. Carpenter: "With reference to the subject matter of our conference at the Vanderbilt Hotel, we are now able to state that the principal stockholders of the Dow Company do not desire to sell an important part of their common stock...." And that ended that matter.

This time there was no division among the board members as there had been in 1915 when Dow refused to sell, threatening to walk out and take his team of aides with him. The future looked too promising.

Two years after this incident, Ed Barstow reported to Dow that he was convinced his team of scientists and engineers had unlocked the secret of taking bromine from the sea cheaply even though it meant handling 1,000,000 pounds of water to get some 55 pounds of bromine.

Six years of research had gone into this project with three chemists—Ivan Harlow, Ray Boundy, and John J. Grebe—giving the final push that achieved the breakthrough. The key was in the discovery that a precise addition of a small amount of hydrochloric acid and chlorine to the seawater liberated the bromine. The hydrochloric acid first neutralized the alkaline salts of the seawater and for a time no bromine was liberated; but the continued action of the acid freed 70 to 80 percent of the bromine. It could then be recovered by putting the seawater through a blowing-out process.

In his physics laboratory, Grebe also had found a way to measure the alkalinity of the seawater automatically and to adjust the acid feed accordingly. The same equipment measured the amount of bromine that was freed in the seawater.

These developments came just as the demand for anti-knock gasoline increased across the country by leaps and bounds, a demand which called for more and more of Dow's ethylene dibromide.

Once Dow saw that the bromine process could be made automatic, he was confident he could use the sea as a source of raw material. He had no doubts about the laboratory process working in a full-scale commercial plant. Harlow had figured the cost of taking bromine from the sea would run about two cents a pound more than bromine taken from Michigan brine; and volume production possibly would reduce this figure.

"We can go to the sea at any time for bromine," Dow advised Thomas Midgley.

But Midgley was skeptical. He brought a team of his own scientists to Midland to check on Dow's claim. A demonstration of the laboratory process failed to convince them that Dow had solved the problem. Their conclusion was that Dow was in no position to supply all of the ethylene dibromide the market would require.

Midgley began working with the Texas Company to develop a process for taking bromine from the waste brine pumped from Texas oil wells. For a time it appeared the Ethyl Corporation was determined to make its own ethylene dibromide and Dow would lose all or part of this market.

Dow was reasonably certain Midgley would not find a reliable source of bromine in Texas. In June, 1930, he sent one of his men on a scouting trip to the East Coast to locate the most favorable site for a plant to take bromine from seawater.

The scout, Roy Osmun, took hundreds of samples of water from the ocean along the eastern seaboard. The highest concentration of bromine was found in the waters off North Carolina's Kure Beach on the Cape Fear Peninsula. At this point, the Gulf current swept close to the shore, undiluted by fresh river water. Seawater could be pumped from the ocean on the eastern side of the peninsula and after the bromine had been freed, the waste water could then be dumped into the Cape Fear River on the western side.

Dow reported to his stockholders: "The big expansion in the use of Ethyl gas has caused an increased demand for bromine that is largely supplied by your company. Should this demand continue to expand, it is quite likely that the added amount of bromine would be secured from sea water. Your company has therefore done considerable work on this subject and has a small plant operating on a synthetic sea water with very satisfactory results.... We have received considerable quantities of sea water for test purposes and have found that we can get the same extraction from the actual ocean water that we produce from the sea water that is made artificially...."

The thought of going to the sea for magnesium as well as bromine had not yet occurred to Dow, probably because there had been no pressure for greater magnesium production. Magnesium had not lived up to Dow's bright hopes that it would become competitive with aluminum despite his efforts to persuade industry to use more of it.

Nine years after World War I, Dow Chemical and the American Magnesium Corporation (AMC) remained the only producers and fabricators of the metal in the United States while France and Germany were the only producers of the metal outside the United States.

The American magnesium market was a small one but the German chemical combine, I. G. Farbenindustrie, was then exploring the possibility of moving into the field to compete with the American producers.

Directors of I. G. approached Dow in 1926 with several propositions. The first called for Dow Chemical to sell its entire magnesium output to I. G. exclusively at a favorable price, plus $900,000 for Dow's patents and goodwill. Another was that I. G. and Dow pool resources and know-how in a jointly owned plant to be built at Midland. Still another was that Dow join them in forming a worldwide chemical combine, merging his interests with those of the combine.

There was a threatening undertone in these proposals. The Germans implied that Dow was not only infringing on their patents in the production of magnesium—but that his patents were invalid.

Dow refused to join in a combination and he rejected the notion that his patents were invalid. He reported his conversations with the Germans to Professor Smith at Case School who replied, "They are certainly wise bluffers with an infinity of nerve.... We have so often been deceived by German spies that I do not think we can be too careful about them."

Dow was doing some bluffing, too. He was concerned over the possibility of the powerful I. G. Farbenindustrie entering the American market at a time when magnesium was not even paying its way with only two producers. But whatever the magnitude of the threat, it was shoved into the background when Dow Chemical collided with AMC over patent rights in the heat-treating of magnesium alloys.

A legal battle threatened until the companies agreed in 1927 to a cross-licensing arrangement. Dow granted AMC rights for a heat-treating and forging patent. In return, AMC granted to Dow the rights to one extruding patent and two heat-treating patents. Each could sublicense the patents but only to customers who purchased magnesium from Dow Chemical or AMC. In effect, the buyers of imported magnesium could not use the Dow-AMC patents.

After this agreement, AMC began buying its magnesium from Dow

Chemical, which was producing the purer product. AMC received a discount of 10 cents a pound below the general market price for quantity buying. The arrangement was pleasing to Herbert Dow because his sales and service costs had been running slightly more than 10 cents a pound.

Dow immediately ordered a $175,000 expansion of the magnesium plant and made plans for another $250,000 expansion the following year. At this point, AMC decided to drop the manufacture of magnesium altogether and concentrate on the alloying and fabrication of the metal.

Almost overnight, Dow Chemical found itself the sole producer of magnesium in the United States, a monopoly position that in time would be damned by one voice of the federal government while the company received grateful praise from another government voice for persisting in the development of a magnesium industry.

Willard Dow would later say: "[When] AMC chose to stop producing magnesium... Dow was left as the country's sole producer. This was either a privilege or a burden. Up to that time, neither Dow nor anyone else had succeeded in making any money out of the production of magnesium. Dow, in effect, was presented with a monopoly by default. Dow had the same kind of monopoly in producing magnesium as Henry Ford had during the early days of producing the Model T—the monopoly which comes as a matter of course when anyone makes a thing better and cheaper than anyone else."

Having a monopoly in magnesium production was one thing. Making money on magnesium was another. For ten years aluminum production per pound in the United States had outpaced magnesium 1,200-to-1. And yet Dow clung to a bullheaded faith that his gamble on magnesium would be justified eventually.

In the 1928 annual meeting of stockholders, he said: "Metallic magnesium is now being taken up by aviation engineers the world over and promises to be one of the most important lines Dow has ever developed. That research work had cost more than any other research work ever undertaken."

The picture Dow painted was tinted with the brighter shades of his own optimism. Actually, while magnesium was being used by engineers in Europe to lighten the weight of airplanes, very little of it was being used in American-made planes. A few civilian planes in the United States were equipped with magnesium propellers and magnesium crankcases but neither industry, nor the Army Air Corps, the Navy, nor the public was showing any great interest in the lighter-than-aluminum metal.

By 1930, Dow was producing slightly more than 1,000,000 pounds of magnesium a year. The price had dropped from $5 a pound in 1917 to 48 cents a pound. The hitch was that Dow Chemical could sell only about three-fourths of its production and the ingots were piling up in warehouses. But it was cheaper to keep running the plant than to shut it down.

During this period of the struggle with magnesium, Herbert Dow decided to challenge the Chilean monopoly in the production of iodine. Most of the world's iodine was being made as a by-product of Chile's nitrate industry and a British-Chilean syndicate controlled the price which fluctuated slightly below $5 a pound.

This decision came when one of Dow's chemists, C. W. Jones, developed a process that held the promise of taking iodine from oil-field brine. It involved the use of the blowing-out process which Dow had used so successfuly with bromine.

Dow turned this project over to his son, Willard, to manage. The Jones Chemical Company was formed and, backed by Dow Chemical money, the tall, angular Jones set out for Louisiana in 1929 to find a site for the operation. He located his plant at McDade, Louisiana, near Shreveport, in a crude shed built of rough planks. The process worked and within a few months Jones sent his first shipment of iodine to Midland, a small amount worth $19.45.

The achievement in Louisiana went unnoticed for months in the chemical world, possibly because Jones was having trouble with his plant and he could not get a satisfactory volume. But this was Dow's first move outside Midland—and in the years ahead the repercussions from this venture would shatter the Chilean iodine monopoly and bring the price of iodine down from more than $4.50 a pound to 81 cents a pound.

As the 1920's came to a close, organic chemistry in the United States was developing rapidly. Herbert Dow told the stockholders in June, 1929: "Probably nothing but the long continued war, followed by a protective tariff, would ever have established organic chemistry in the United States in competition with the German industry where every by-product was the raw material for another by-product, and the by-products of the new reactions were again raw materials for still other products. But today the interlocking of by-products is as marked in your company's plant as it is in any foreign plant and the mechanical equipment is undoubtedly better...."

Business boomed in that strange summer of 1929. And yet the depression on the farms was unbroken after eight years, jobs were scarce in the textile towns of New England, and there were pockets of unemployment in many sections of the nation.

The stock market ignored the shadows. Small investors rushed into the market to get their share of the bonanza. The bull market was a money tree in full flower.

The voices of caution were drowned out in the full-throated roar of the bulls. Economist Roger Babson among others warned that the frenzied speculation was building a paper house that could not stand. But few listened. The paper profits climbed and the majority of prophets saw no reason why the wave of prosperity should not roll on unbroken into the 1930's.

One who did sense danger in the climbing market was Dow Chemical's Earl W. Bennett, who had risen from his $5.93-a-week job as clerk to assistant treasurer. For several years Bennett had carried the responsibilities of treasurer without the title, which remained an honor reserved for a Cleveland stockholder, J. C. Crider. Bennett began to put the company's financial house in order—just in case.

The bull market reached its peak in early September. On September 3, United States Steel nudged above 261. Radio Corporation of America, which had split 5-for-1, was quoted at its new price of 99. American Telephone and Telegraph stood at 302, General Electric at 395, and Anaconda Copper at 130 7/8. Dow Chemical stock sold over the counter for $500.

The market wavered and then began to sag. Prices rose, dipped, rose and then dropped lower as the days passed. A wave of selling hit the market during a short session on Saturday, October 19. Another hit on Monday and another on Wednesday. Selling orders poured in by the thousands on Thursday and panic was growing.

In this crisis, the leaders of five great financial institutions in New York City met at the House of Morgan to pool their resources in support of the market and to shore up public confidence. They were from J. P. Morgan and Company, National City Bank, Guarantee Trust, Chase National, and Bankers' Trust. No doubt they recalled the panic of 1907 when J. P. Morgan, Sr., had formed a multi-million-dollar combine which halted bank runs and quieted the fears of depositors.

For a few hours it seemed the prestige and power of these financiers might turn the tide. Prices steadied and even rallied feebly. But then the dam burst and nothing could hold it. On Tuesday, October 29, a blizzard of selling orders hit the offices of stock brokers. Officially,

16,410,030 shares were sold that day but no one probably knew the true total in all the confusion. Through September and October, more than $30,000,000,000 in stock values vanished. Dow Chemical stock, priced at $100 after the 5-for-1 split, quickly slid to $35.

The panic spread to Europe and the Great Depression was on.

The first shock waves of the Depression passed over Midland. Eight months after the market collapse, Dow reported to the stockholding: "During the past year your company has not experienced the hard times that many industries have had. Up to Nov. 1, the company did in round numbers, 21 per cent more business, measured in dollars, than it did during the corresponding period of the previous year. Since November, the increase has been less, but it is still 16 per cent ahead of the average of the corresponding months a year earlier. . . ."

At this time, Herbert Dow was making plans to shift control of the board. These plans called for Charles Strosacker and Ed Barstow to be elected to the board to join Earl Bennett, who had become a director four years earlier. Bennett later was to be named treasurer. Strosacker and Barstow were elected to the board in June, 1931, and Bennett became treasurer in 1934.

In 1929, Dow had placed his sales department under the control of Leland I. Doan, a tall, gregarious young man who had married Dow's daughter, Ruth, in 1917. Doan had been graduated from the University of Michigan in 1916 and after a year with the Michigan Bell Telephone Company he had served an apprenticeship in the plant before moving into sales.

After thirty-three years, The Dow Chemical Company was at last firmly under control of Herbert Dow and the men who had helped him build the company from a venture on the edge of bankruptcy into a multi-million-dollar business.

It was in that first year of the Depression that the American Section of the Society of Chemical Industry paid Herbert Dow an extraordinary tribute by choosing him as "the American chemist who had most distinguished himself by his service to Applied Chemistry."

Dow was the choice of a committee of scientists representing the American Section of the Society of Chemical Industry, the American Chemical Society, the American Electrochemical Society, the American Institute of Chemical Engineers, and the Societe de Chimie Industrielle. He was presented with the coveted Perkin Medal Award "in recognition of his achievements in the fields of bromine, alkalies, magnesium and its salts, phenols, and other developments of his organization." The first Perkin medal had been struck in 1906 in honor of Sir William H. Perkin for his discovery of the first aniline dye, mauve—and Dow was the twenty-fourth recipient of the award.

The award came none too soon. In September of 1930, Dow fell ill. He entered the Mayo Brothers Clinic at Rochester, Minnesota, where it was found he was suffering from cirrhosis of the liver. His condition rapidly became worse. He seemed to rally after an operation but then he sank into a coma and died at 5 P.M., October 15.

A special railway coach carried Dow's body back to Midland. A crowd of at least a thousand townspeople huddled in a cold rain on the station platform to pay a silent tribute. One of those waiting in the rain was Elzie Cote, who had worked for Dow from the time he had started his chemical plant in an old barn.

Cote talked to a reporter about those early years: "When Mr. Dow came here as a young man, I well remember when he stayed with the late Sherman Olmsted. He didn't have very much of this world's goods, and Olmsted, I think, used to help him along.

"Midland people who knew Mr. Dow regarded him as a curiosity when he came here. I remember when he used to be experimenting in the old barn right over there, where the water tank is now. Some of the people used to think that he was a little off, but that supposition was mighty wrong.

"He was always quiet and very unassuming. He was never what you would call a man about town. He was either at the plant or home. Those were his two interests—at least the two I could see best."

Dow was buried in the Midland Cemetery, not far from the site of the old barn where he had struggled with his dream forty years earlier. For Midland and The Dow Chemical Company, it was the end of a remarkable era of discovery.

PART THREE *1931-1949*

Chapter Ten

As the country sank deeper and deeper into the Depression in 1930, it was becoming more and more apparent to economists that this was no ordinary recession from which business would rebound after a slight breathing spell. The bread lines in the cities lengthened. More businesses failed. More banks closed. More factory owners slowed their production, laying off workers and cutting the wages of those who remained.

On the farms, the situation simply moved from bad to worse. Farmers had never recovered from the 1920–21 depression when wheat fell from $3.50 a bushel to $1.00, corn from $2.00 to 42 cents a bushel, and cotton from 42 cents to 11 cents a pound. The farmers' problem was complicated by the increasing migration of young people to the cities. A song writer had sensed the trend from farm to city as early as World War I when he wrote the words, "How you gonna keep 'em down on the farm, after they've seen Paree." The young were lured not only by the bright lights but by the jobs which offered them higher wages than they could earn by dawn-to-dusk labor in the barns and fields.

These were difficult times even for a company with the most seasoned and mature management—and now The Dow Chemical Company was without the leadership of the man who had guided its every move for more than a third of a century.

For five days after Herbert Dow's death, Midland waited and watched to see who would move into the presidency of the company whose assets had grown to $30,000,000. Some thought the directors would choose Ed Barstow, the solid production man. Others believed the post might go to Charles Strosacker, who inspired such great loyalties. Still others nominated the canny Earl Bennett or James Pardee, the company's secretary and Herbert Dow's long-time backer and friend. But when the directors emerged from their meeting on October 20, 1930—five days after Dow's death—they announced their choice was thirty-three-year-old Willard Dow, the handsome and extraordinarily able elder son of the company's founder, whose wit and humor had made him a popular figure in the plants and in the community.

Others may have wondered if Willard Dow had the maturity and the diplomatic finesse to lead men who had watched him grow from a shy boy to manhood. But Willard himself had never doubted that he would succeed his father and while working in the plant he had formed his own ideas on how the company should be run.

There was no battle over the presidency as might have been expected among strong men accustomed to speaking their minds. The veterans closed ranks behind young Dow. And he quickly made it clear that he intended to be the boss, taking over the titles of both president and general manager.

In all the time he headed Dow Chemical, Herbert Dow never had an organization chart. The lines of authority were loose and overlapping. But in general, Barstow, Strosacker, and Putnam were the production men, Bennett handled finances, and Dow directed research with overall control of production. There was no fixed budget for research. The money went to the ideas that appeared most promising.

Willard Dow did not disturb the rough working arrangement which had proved so successful in the past. But gradually he placed more emphasis on research than on either production or sales. He made it clear that he considered research the key to the company's progress—and that nothing must interfere with research. He did not have his father's inventive genius, but he shared his faith in research.

At his first annual meeting with the stockholders after his election, Dow reported: "While on the subject of development, it might be well to comment that we maintain a large and expensive research organization, which is constantly developing improvements on our present processes as well as new products and processes to come. The successful developments over the past years are results of this policy of extensive research and it is not the intention of the management to curtail in any way the development program."

While many others in industry were cutting back on research to wait out the business retreat, Dow pushed ahead. He encouraged more research into petrochemicals and plastics. And as this research continued, Dow put surplus dollars to work modernizing the plant, improving product quality, and testing new processes.

One of his first moves after his father's death was to make certain that Dow Chemical held onto its position as the chief supplier of ethylene dibromide for anti-knock gasoline. Early in 1931 he persuaded the Ethyl Gasoline Corporation to enter into an agreement to form a jointly owned company "for the purpose of manufacturing bromine from sea water."

It was a canny move. Both Ethyl and Dow Chemical had everything to gain and nothing to lose from such an agreement. If the process for taking bromine from the sea proved successful, then both would profit from the venture. If it didn't work, Dow Chemical still had the Michigan brine to fall back on and Ethyl was free to shop for bromine whereever it wished.

Dow sent Barstow and Ivan Harlow to North Carolina to check on the report by Roy Osmun that Kure Beach on Cape Fear was the best place to locate a bromine plant. They confirmed Osmun's judgment and a strip of land was purchased, three-fifths of a mile wide and extending from the Atlantic to the Cape Fear River.

The announcement of this purchase—and the intention of tapping the sea's resources—caught the imagination of newspapers and trade magazines. The *American Business World* was starry-eyed in its reaction: "American industry will congratulate the enterprising spirit of the Dow Company. It is engaged in a romantic role, but it will successfully prosecute this assignment in a practical, scientific manner. We commend such praiseworthy and vigorous action as indicative of the leadership which has been attained by the Dow Company in the American chemical manufacturing industry."

There were some at the time who thought perhaps the flowery commendation was premature. The bromine process still had to be proved in large-scale operation. It was a risk being taken at a time when prudent men were avoiding risk. Some of Dow Chemical's stockholders saw no cause for tossing bouquets. They wrote to Dow that they were alarmed by the announcement. They argued the company was in no position financially to undertake a project that would require at least a $500,000 investment—and perhaps more—with no guarantee of success.

Willard Dow replied: "Our stockholders should realize that The Dow Chemical Company is not operated on the basis of a banker's opinion about a chemical process. On the contrary, our activity is controlled by the results we can show in the laboratory as well as in the financial earnings of our processes. The details of organization are not entirely matters that should properly concern our stockholders as long as satisfactory results are obtained and provided they know that the results are obtained by fair and satisfactory means. . . ."

Despite his public show of confidence in the seawater process, Dow wasn't willing to take the gamble of jumping from the laboratory into a full-scale effort in North Carolina. He favored investing $100,000 in a pilot plant at Kure Beach which, if it worked satisfactorily, could be replaced by a full-size plant.

Barstow and Harlow argued for going directly into commercial production. "Let's go the whole plant or none," Barstow said.

But Willard overrode them. He ordered the pilot plant built to give the process a thorough test.

His caution perhaps was the result of the continued slide in business during 1931. By early June Dow Chemical's sales were off 15.5 percent from the previous year, earnings were down to $3.44 a share from $4.08 and the stock was selling at 35.

No doubt this caution was wise because the Depression grew worse in 1932. More than thirteen million men were idle across the United States. Fear of violence and revolution spread. Capitalism was under heavy attack for failing to provide the people with jobs and security.

Big Business became the villain in this drama of conflict. Politicians looking for a whipping boy to blame for the collapse of the economy turned to Wall Street and the big names of finance. The investigations came one after another and those who were questioned at one hearing included the Du Ponts, J. P. Morgan, and General Electric Chairman Owen Young. Historian Adolf A. Berle would recall: "They sat around the room, stunned at the havoc, many with tears in their eyes as they saw the nation's banking power irrevocably pass from Wall Street to the Capitol."

And there was the famous "Bonus March" on Washington in 1932 by thousands of World War I veterans. They demanded that the money due them in 1945—the $1,600 cash value of matured insurance policies—be paid immediately. The so-called march began in May when unemployed veterans in Portland, Oregon, decided to take their case directly to the Congress. They rode the rods eastward and by the time they reached Washington they had been joined by thousands of others. They swarmed on the Capitol, determined but disciplined.

They bivouacked, twenty thousand strong, in the marshy Anacostia River flats, their presence a silent threat as Congress considered a bill to pay the bonus they demanded. The Senate killed the bill and hundreds of the veterans went home. But some fifteen thousand remained on the flats. They lived in tents, shacks of tar paper and tin, and whatever else they could find for shelter. "Stay until 1945" became the watchword.

For weeks there was little trouble. Then a Communist-led group seized an opportunity to start a brief riot in which two men were killed and two wounded by pistol fire. From the White House came orders for federal troops to move the veterans out of the Anacostia flats. General Douglas MacArthur led troops in the march to force the veterans from their camp. The shacks and tents were burned to the ground and the Bonus Army dispersed—an action praised by some and bitterly condemned by others.

The situation highlighted the desperation of the times and the unrest which marked those last months of the Administration of President Herbert Hoover, who tried but could not stem the economy's toboggan slide.

This was, by any indicator, a poor time to start a new business enterprise. And yet Willard Dow decided early in 1932 to launch Dow Chemical into the business of helping oil companies increase productivity by treating oil wells with acid.

The idea of treating wells with acid to stimulate oil flow was not new. In 1895, Herman Frasch at Standard Oil's Solar refinery in Lima, Ohio, had theorized that muriatic or sulfuric acid forced into a well would dissolve obstructions in limestone strata and increase oil flow. Several wells were treated without much success and the idea was laid aside. Others tried it in the late 1920's. But one of the major difficulties was that the acid destroyed the well pipes.

About this time, Dow Chemical's John Grebe began experimenting with an arsenic compound as an inhibitor that perhaps would prevent the acid from destroying well pipes. The inhibitor worked. Then with Ross Sanford and an aide, Noland Poffenberger, Grebe tried the inhibited acid on one of Dow Chemical's old brine wells—and the flow of brine increased 30 percent.

Willard Dow reached an agreement with Pure Oil Company to treat some of their Michigan oil wells. The first one selected was an old well near Chippewa Township which Pure Oil was preparing to abandon because of its falling production.

On a cold February morning, Dow Chemical's Robert Quinlan hauled a wooden tank filled with 500 gallons of inhibited acid to the well site where two Pure Oil men waited. They used a rubber hose as a siphon to pour 250 gallons of the acid into the well casing, then flushed it down with 6 barrels of oil. The next day the well was cleaned out and the acidizing process repeated.

The treated well began pumping 16 barrels of oil a day, nothing spectacular but enough to encourage both Dow Chemical and Pure Oil to try again. The second well they treated was in better condition than the first. The well's production jumped from 30 barrels of oil a day to 125 barrels. The production at a third well was increased from 90 barrels to more than 800 barrels.

News of these successes swept through the oil industry. Inquiries poured into Dow Chemical headquarters from all parts of the United States and Canada. Crews were organized and sent into the field with tanks of acid and pumps mounted on flat-bed trucks or on trailers. At first the crews operated only in the Michigan oil fields.

One day Willard Dow dropped by the office of Dutch Beutel, who had been promoted to the post of assistant general manager. He dumped an armload of letters onto Beutel's desk. "Dutch," he said, "You are now president of the Dow Well Service."

The demand for the service became so strong during that summer of 1932 that Dow decided to organize a subsidiary which could operate legally in all the states. The name Dow Well Service was shortened to Dowell Incorporated, and a new business was born.

From this crude beginning grew a business that in later years would gross more than $75,000,000 a year. From acidizing oil wells, the service expanded into the acidizing of gas wells and the acid-cleansing of industrial boilers and pipes. The brilliant Grebe's laboratory found a whole new family of inhibiting agents and chemicals to help drillers obtain a greater yield from their gas and oil fields.

Through the years Dow's researchers developed an admiration for Grebe that amounted almost to awe. The man was a fountain of ideas and bubbling enthusiasms.

An oldtimer in Dow Chemical recalled: "The trick was to sort through Grebe's ideas and choose the ones that held the greatest promise. It wasn't possible to explore all of them. Ray Boundy had become Willard's right-hand man in research and he was a wizard at checking Grebe's ideas and putting the best of them into production."

Also in that dark year of 1932 Willard Dow decided to invest more money and effort in the development of the iodine process which had proved workable in Louisiana—but which had lost money from the time C. W. Jones had started the small Louisiana plant. Mechanical failures, corroded pipes plugging brine wells, and faulty construction had plagued the efforts of the Jones Chemical Company. Dow took Beutel off the Dowell operation temporarily and sent him to Louisiana to see if he could whip the production problems.

Beutel would one day recall: "The plant was just a bunch of junk. I was amazed at what I found. I said to myself, 'Oh, God, how can you make anything in a place like this?' The blowing-out tower was leaning and it was supposed to be level so that the brine would trickle down uniformly over the lath-filling in the tower. The brine was being blown out with gas, like an air jet, but the pipes would corrode, break off and drop into the well. It would take a week to fish the pipe out and put a new pipe down—and meantime the plant would be shut down."

There wasn't much that could be done with the plant as it was built. Beutel brought Ivan Harlow from Midland to check on the operation, and after figuring costs, Harlow said, "Dutch, it's costing us more to pump these wells for the brine than we're getting for the iodine."

The Louisiana operation looked hopeless. But Willard Dow refused to give up. Then Jones suggested perhaps it would be best to move the plant to Long Beach, California, where he had found that the oil-field brines were much richer in iodine than the brines of Louisiana. Surveys in California confirmed Jones's findings.

The move to Long Beach was made and for a time the Jones Chemical Company shifted to a silver process for making iodine. Beutel directed the construction of the first plant in record-breaking time and within six weeks the plant was in production and making iodine well. But it was having trouble making potassium iodine as a second product until a fellow named Fred Lusk wandered into Long Beach from Louisiana without a job.

The silver iodide process made iodine, part of which was converted to potassium iodide in batch lots. The difficulty was that nobody knew how to control the color of the iodide crystals. The batches came out all colors of the rainbow when they should have been a pure white.

Beutel recalls: "We had a nice white tiled room with Monel metal trays so there wouldn't be any rust. It was built like a beautiful hospital room and we were turning out junk. This process was more of an art than it was chemistry—and that's about the size of it.

"I was sitting in my office one day wondering what to do next. Lee Doan was calling about sales. Willard was calling and raising hell because we didn't get out shipments.

"In the middle of all this, my secretary walked in and said there was a man from Louisiana, Fred Lusk, who wanted to see me. When he walked in I said, 'Fred, what in hell are you doing here?' He said, 'I was working as an oil pumper in East Texas but I got tired of it. I'm taking a little vacation.'

"I said, 'You made potassium iodide back there in McDade, didn't you?' He said he had, so I told him to report to me the next morning. He said, 'But I'm on vacation.' I said, 'Nuts to the vacation. You be here in the morning.'

"Next morning, Fred walked through the plant and said, 'You're doing it all wrong.' In about two days he had the thing running and he was turning out beautiful stuff. He knew how to treat the brine so he could knock down all the impurities that produced the color. So we made Fred the head operator. This was one of those things that happen once in a lifetime. I got more credit for getting the iodine plant into quick production than I deserved."

Even though Fred Lusk got the bugs out of the silver iodide process, it proved to be only a stopgap operation. In Midland, Grebe, Ted Heath, M. F. Ohman, and others had succeeded in developing a blowing-out process, superior to the old Jones method—and the new process required no silver.

The new process had barely been perfected in Midland in 1933 when an earthquake rocked Long Beach and left part of the iodine plant in ruins. The rolling of the earth ripped houses apart, buckled roads, and flattened the huge brine tanks at the Jones Chemical Company.

Beutel rushed from Midland to Long Beach to survey the damage. He reported that except for the tanks, the damage could be repaired within a short time. "Well," said Willard Dow, "fix it up and get it going again."

But at this point Dow decided to rebuild with a new Grebe-Heath process and to take the plant directly under Dow Chemical control. He negotiated with C. W. Jones to buy his interest in the Long Beach operation. A deal was made and the Jones Chemical Company became the Io-Dow Chemical Company, a wholly owned subsidiary of The Dow Chemical Company.

Within a few weeks the new plant was in operation with a spurt in iodine production that eventually would shatter the Chilean monopoly and give Dow Chemical 90 percent of the iodine sales in the United States. But Dow Chemical would not reach this position without a fight in which the price of iodine would be battered down from $4.50 a pound to 81 cents. In addition to laying the ground work to capture a share of the United States iodine market, Dow Chemical now had a toe in the door of the West Coast's growing chemical industry.

The economic storm of 1932 forced Willard Dow to trim the company's sails a bit—but not much. Early in the year he cut 250 men from the company's payroll of 2,025 workers and reduced salaries across the board by 10 percent. Four six-hour shifts were ordered to spread the employment as much as possible.

"We could do with even fewer workers," Willard Dow told his board, "but we must balance the needs of The Dow Chemical Company against the needs of the community. It is a responsibility we can not ignore."

Quietly he passed the word to Midland banks that the resources of Dow Chemical were available to help any employee in a financial squeeze. No mortgages were to be foreclosed or Dow Chemical stock held as collateral sold through undue pressure. Many employees wondered, without knowing and not daring to ask, why banks renewed notes on request with no questions asked.

And then in September of 1932 a strange thing happened. While every indicator pointed to lower chemical sales and a further slowing of production, Dow Chemical's sales began to increase steadily. Workers were called back to their jobs. Plants began to approach capacity production. For Midland, the hard times were over less than a year after they had begun and it would be called "the town that never knew the Depression."

But Midland's relative prosperity was the exception. Angry waves of unrest swept Herbert Hoover out of the White House and brought election victory to Franklin D. Roosevelt. In the early months of 1933, the number of jobless climbed to more than fifteen million. Banks continued to close their doors and industries were mired deeper in trouble. One quarter of the entire state of Mississippi had been lost in foreclosures of mortgages. One out of every two railroads was in bankruptcy. Earlier, Calvin Coolidge was moved to make the despairing remark, "I see nothing to give ground for hope."

The day of Roosevelt's inauguration dawned cold and bleak. *The New York Times* reported, "A sense of depression had settled over the capital so that it could be felt." But thousands gathered on the wind-chilled Capitol plaza to witness the ceremony.

"This is a day of national consecration," Roosevelt began. And then he went on with the lines which would be quoted for years: "Let me assert my firm belief that the only thing we have to fear is fear itself—nameless, unreasoning, unjustified terror which paralyzes needed efforts to convert retreat into advance. . . ."

Among those who listened by radio to the address as they sat in the Cosmos Club in Washington was Willard Dow. After the inauguration he sat in the stands opposite the White House and watched the inaugural parade.

Dow later wrote to his mother and sister Dorothy in Midland: ". . . . I will say this about it all; that I came back being much more enthusiastic about our new President than I was when I went. . . . I have a great deal of confidence in the way the new Administration is going after everything and the apparent regulations that are being made seem to be very constructive and very proper. There is nothing radical at all in the actions and I don't think any of us has any reason to be the least bit concerned about the various conditions that confront us. . . . The redeeming feature about it all is that we undoubtedly have a better and stronger Federal Government than we had during Hoover's administration."

Roosevelt did start his Administration advocating a conservative course of action to stem the tide of the Depression. But as the New Deal developed, Willard Dow's enthusiasm waned. He began to feel—as did many conservatives—that too much power was being concentrated in Washington.

However, young Dow was not a political animal and there was too much to be done to waste time brooding over politics. He and Bennett had managed the company's finances so well during the first three years of the Depression that he was able to report to the stockholders in June that the company had no bank debts and cash reserves totaled more than $500,000. Most of the men who had been laid off the year before were back at work and wage cuts had largely been restored.

"During this past year," he said, "your company has maintained its policy with regard to research. It has not curtailed its research investment and although many processes have been developed in the laboratory and put on the shelf, we have not felt it wise to follow the principle of so many of our competitors, who have entirely eliminated research. We have, on the other hand, developed some important processes which in the days to come we believe will continue to keep your company in the lead as one of the most modern chemical companies in the country."

By this time, Dow's emphasis on research was beginning to produce some spectacular results. New compounds, liquids and solids, were being developed faster than Lee Doan's sales department could find a market for them. There was no known use for some of the products. Later they would find their way into the stream of commerce—but until then they were "put on the shelf."

Dow hired consultants from colleges and universities to find practical applications for the products. A special products catalogue was printed and sent to manufacturers to see what they could use. Research men were called from Dow Chemical laboratories and drafted into the sales force to help find markets.

One of these draftees was William Allen, who had come to Dow Chemical as a chemist in organic research. "One day," Allen recalled, "Willard Dow called me into his office and explained there was so much research developing and so many new products that the company had to find an outlet for them. He asked me if I wouldn't transfer into sales where technical knowledge was needed. I said, 'I've never sold anything in my life but *The Saturday Evening Post* when I was a boy.' But he persuaded me to take the job."

The progress of Dow Chemical in the early 1930's was not without its disappointments. The product which caused the greatest concern was magnesium. The reason was that after almost twenty years of trying, Dow Chemical had failed to interest either the government or industry to any great extent in the possibilities of the metal even though it had become increasingly important in the European airplane industry.

In Germany and Italy, planes were being built with magnesium landing wheels, shock absorbers, landing gears, motor cowlings, gasoline and oil tanks. One English firm listed 102 aircraft parts made of magnesium alloys. In the United States, the Navy and Army Air Corps left magnesium research to industry and showed only casual interest.

Part of magnesium's difficulty was the cost of fabrication. Dow Chemical had brought the price of the metal down from $5.00 a pound in 1917 to an average of 26.3 cents a pound in 1934. But the sand castings of alloys cost 94.8 cents a pound and die castings cost 53.8 cents a pound. The only way fabrication costs could be reduced was to create a volume market.

The largest buyer of magnesium in the United States was the American Magnesium Corporation, the Alcoa subsidiary, which signed a five-year contract in 1933 to buy not less than 1,500,000 pounds of magnesium from Dow Chemical. In that year Dow Chemical for the first time sold more magnesium than it produced, dipping into the stockpile to fill orders. The business came close to showing a profit.

But trouble was brewing for Dow Chemical in the magnesium market. In 1932 the AMC had reached an agreement with the I. G. Farbenindustrie to use German fabrication patents, and the two companies formed the Magnesium Development Corporation (MDC). They then tried to induce Willard Dow to use the German sulfur patents on a royalty basis in fabricating metal.

When Dow refused, the MDC filed suit claiming Dow Chemical's fabrication processes infringed on the German patents. Before the suit reached trial, attorneys for MDC suggested a compromise.

Dow wrote to MDC outlining his company's position:

"We believe that our success in the magnesium industry is not dependent on patents now controlled by the Magnesium Development Corporation.

"We believe that magnesium will be made by The Dow Chemical Company just as cheaply in this country as by any competitor.

"The idea which was expressed that The Dow Chemical Company has no patents which are of interest to the Magnesium Development Corporation seems ridiculous to us. We have thirty - seven issue patents and thirty - one applications relating to fabrication methods and alloy composition and we regard them as of more value than the patents controlled by the Magnesium Development Corporation. Any proposal which does not take proper cognizance of the value of these Dow Chemical Company patents will not be of interest to us.

"We believe that by cross-licensing of the Dow Chemical Company and Magnesium Development Corporation patents, more profits can be made by each party and that greater progress is possible than otherwise."

With further dickering, the suit was settled out of court on January 1, 1934. Dow agreed to pay a royalty of 1 cent per pound on its domestic sales, with minor exceptions, for the right to use the I. G. fabricating patents owned by the Magnesium Development Corporation.

While this dispute was going on, Dow decided the time had come to push ahead with construction of the plant to take bromine from seawater. The pilot plant had proved successful and Dow called on Dutch Beutel to oversee the construction of the finished plant.

Beutel would recall: "I hadn't had a vacation in a long time so I planned to take my wife to California, where I would finish up the job on the iodine plant. Then we would return to Midland by way of Banff and Lake Louise. We talked to Lee and Ruth Doan about it and Ruth said; 'Dutch, you've got that trip twisted around. If you go to Long Beach first, you'll never get to Banff and Lake Louise.'

"We decided to follow her advice. We turned the trip around and went to Canada first. We finally landed in Long Beach and went to the Blackstone Hotel where we got an apartment with a kitchenette. Belle went out and bought some nice California fruit and groceries.

"We had just finished dinner when the telepone rang. It was Willard Dow. He said, 'Get on the train in the morning and come on home right away.' I said, 'What's going on?' He said, 'I'll tell you when you get here. Let someone else handle the iodine job.'

"So we left Long Beach the next day and started for Midland—leaving all those groceries in the hotel."

In late July (1933), Willard Dow and Beutel left Midland by train for Wilmington, North Carolina. Crews were already at work with bulldozers, mule teams, and scrapers, clearing the land, when the two arrived at Kure Beach. In the thickets were crumbling trenches which had been dug by Confederate troops during the Civil War. Rusted gun barrels, minnie balls, and bits of metal were strewn over the ground where one of the last battles of the war had been fought.

Willard Dow said, "Dutch, we've got to get this plant built by the first of the year. The Ethyl people are pushing us hard."

"Who can I have from Midland?" Beutel asked.

"You can have anybody you want," Dow said.

The Cape Fear plant was given top priority in manpower and materials. Within days, construction engineers from Midland and their crews were swarming over the Cape. Hotels in Wilmington and at Cape Fear were jammed to overflowing. Beutel leased an old fifty-two-room hotel near Kure Beach to house some of the men.

The first time Beutel walked into the hotel with the owner to look it over, scantily clad women scattered to their rooms. "We broke up a flourishing business there," Beutel would recall with a chuckle. "But we had to have a place for our people. When we got the women out, we cleaned up the place, had it painted and put in some heat. Norris Coalwell was my assistant. Carl Branson was head of the construction gang. Charlie Short was in charge of building the ethylene plant. Harland Sherbrook had the blowing-out tower. Herman Smith and Leo Glesner handled the sewer and pipe work. Brick Dressel, who was to take charge of the operation when the plant was finished, looked after the finishing end of the ethylene plant."

The crash program continued through the fall and into the winter. Two huge piers were built out into the ocean and a channel was dug some 200 feet inshore. At this point the sea water was pumped—30,000 gallons a minute—over a dam into a mile-long canal and storage pond. The bromine plant was located in two 5-story-high brick buildings, each 200 feet long by 85 feet wide. The water was pumped from the canal to the tops of the blowing-out towers at the rate of 26,000 gallons a minute.

The plant was operating in January and some called it "the miracle at Kure Beach." This conquest of the sea was a bench mark in the development of the American chemical industry. Never before had man taken from the sea such a treasure. With minor adjustments, the process worked as efficiently as Barstow and Harlow and Grebe had predicted it would.

The plant was formally turned over to the Ethyl-Dow Chemical Company on January 19, 1934, and Herbert Dow's dream of "going to the sea" was a reality.

A visiting scientist looked over the operation of the plant and shook his head in disbelief. "This is disgustingly simple," he said. "It doesn't do justice to research."

The "simplicity" of the operation was the result of thirty-five years of research in Midland and the know-how gained in untold hours of perfecting the process. News of the spectacular achievement shot the price of Dow Chemical stock to a new Depression high of 95. This price was almost back to the level the stock had reached before the market crash in 1929.

Earl Bennett would recall: "When I was in England some time after the bromine plant went into operation, an English chemist said: 'My friends and I have a question to ask of you if you do not think it impertinent. We want to know frankly if taking bromine from sea water is profitable or if it is something in the way of an advertising or publicity stunt which gets bromine—but at a tremendous cost.' I told him it was profitable."

For a time, there was a flurry of excitement over the possibility that Dow Chemical might be planning secretly to take gold from sea water. If bromine could be recovered, the reasoning went, then why not gold? The metal was in the sea in minute amount.

Ethyl Corporation's Art Mittnacht—who had consulted with Beutel in the plant construction—jokingly heckled Brick Dressel to recover both gold and bromine from the waters of the Atlantic. News of this heckling filtered back to Midland where Don Gibb, then operating the company's magnesium alloy foundry, decided to come to the aid of his friend Dressel.

Gibb obtained a small lump of magnesium and put it through a treatment which gave it the color of gold. He sent it to Dressel and the next time Dressel was in New York he stopped by Mittnacht's office.

"Art," he said, "you've always said we should get something other than bromine out of all that sea water. We've done it—and I want you to be the first to know." He tossed the golden nugget onto the desk. "What do you think of that?"

Mittnacht seized Dressel's hand. "Congratulations!" he exclaimed. But then he felt the lightness of the nugget, and laughed.

In June of 1934, Willard Dow reported to the stockholders that, despite the Depression, earnings per share had climbed from $2.95 in 1932 to $5.39. Cash on hand had tripled to almost $1,500,000. The company was three years ahead of schedule in retiring its obligations. The plants were running almost at capacity with employment up from 2,012 workers to a record 3,019. The directors voted not only to continue the regular $2.00 dividend, but to give stockholders a 50 percent stock dividend.

Referring to the bromine plant at Kure Beach, Dow said: "The construction of this plant was accomplished entirely by our own engineers and may properly be classed as one of the many unique things your company has accomplished in its history. This accomplishment is without doubt one of the most novel developments in chemical engineering in the world. . . ."

Dow knocked down stories that the Ethyl-Dow Chemical Company might try to extract gold from sea water. "When the details of this project were first made public," Dow said, "newspaper writers stressed the idea of the possible extraction of gold from sea water... rather than the more important and pertinent fact of the actual, successful commercial extraction of the more profitable bromine and this naturally gave some an erroneous idea of the operation. For this reason, it should be stated that we are not extracting gold... nor do we anticipate we will extract it."

The simple arithmetic of the situation was that for every $300.00 worth of gold in the sea water there was $6,000 worth of bromine.

By the end of 1934, the country was edging its way upward from the depths of the Depression which had touched Midland so lightly. Dow's aggressive research and plant expansion had placed the company in a more solid position than anyone—even Dow himself—could possibly realize. The impetus which these programs gave the company was to be felt for another twenty years.

Much of the progress was due to the explosive developments in organic chemistry. Discoveries of new products and processes were multiplying at a breathtaking rate, particularly in the field of plastics.

Dow underlined his enthusiasm for organic chemistry research in a talk before a group of Midland scientists. He said: "It is impossible to intimate the number of possibilities there are in the organic chemical field. One of the famous German chemists illustrates organic chemistry by saying—'Go out on a starry night and you realize how infinite is the number of stars that are visible. Suppose each star is an organic compound. Then suppose you were to go to any one of those stars and imagine the infinite number of new stars that would then become visible.'

"This in a way illustrates our conception of the possibilities of the multiplication of organic compounds. Each compound itself suggests others and each one of these suggests still more. Then in the second or third generation from the original it is possible to intermarry compounds and get entirely new series that are again infinite in number. Just for a guess let us say that the possibilities run into the billions. I believe there is hardly a chemist in the world who does not feel that the big future of the chemical industry is tied up with organic chemistry...."

Chapter Eleven

The death of an eccentric, sixty-seven-year-old multi-millionaire at Lake Placid, New York, on June 8, 1936, provided a startling footnote to the record of The Dow Chemical Company's thirty-nine years of growth. He was Colonel E. H. R. "Ned" Green, son of old Hetty Green who bore the title of "richest woman in the world" at her death in 1915.

News of the Colonel's passing and the fortune he left to be fought over by heirs and tax collectors stirred the memories of some of Midland's oldtimers. They recalled his mother's brief visit to the town shortly before the turn of the century when bearded young Herbert Dow was struggling to get the company started. They remembered the stories of Hetty sitting on the barrel at the general store on Main Street, eating cheese and soda crackers, asking questions about "Crazy Dow" as he drove by in his buggy, and listening to the talk of his efforts to make bleaching powder by a process which passed a current of electricity through brine.

Hetty had bought 100 shares of the company's stock for about $10 a share after she left Midland and she had tucked it away. After her death, half of her fortune of more than $100,000,000 had gone to her only son, Ned. When Ned Green died, Dow Chemical stock certificates were among the securities left in the estate. The 100 shares had multiplied through stock splits, purchase of subscription rights and stock dividends to 6,143 shares worth $766,339.25 at the quoted price of $124.75.

One Midlander remarked, "No one ever came to Midland who stayed a shorter time, asked more questions, spent less, and made more money than Hetty Green."

At the time of Colonel Green's death, Dow Chemical was growing at a faster rate than any other major chemical company in the United States. It was one of the paradoxes of the Depression, churning ahead with research, expansion and production of new products while many American businesses were fighting for survival. By 1939 Dow Chemical was the fifth largest chemical company in the country behind Du Pont, Allied Chemical, Union Carbide, and American Cyanamid.

Much of the growth stemmed from Willard Dow's realization that the company's potential was far broader than his father had imagined. With the spread of Dowell's oil field service, the success of Io-Dow's California plant, and the achievement of taking bromine from the sea, Dow was quite certain that opportunities for growth were not limited to Midland and Michigan's brine.

Dow told the stockholders at their 1935 meeting: "Your company has grown so rapidly in the past decade that most of us intimately associated with its operations are not apt to see the importance of its size. The depression brought home to us that our sphere of operation is not limited alone to Midland . . . . The depression taught us that it is wiser to spread our prosperity to a larger area and thereby benefit more people. The depression taught us that our company was one of the outstanding if not the most prosperous company in the State of Michigan throughout the depression period and having developed such a reputation, our responsibility is necessarily much greater than formerly . . . . The facts of the case are that we are now engaged in one of the most ambitious programs we have yet undertaken. . ."

This ambitious program was one of more expansion, based on the discoveries made in the laboratories which now included a Metallurgical Laboratory, an Organic Laboratory, a Physics Laboratory, an X-ray and Spectroscopy Laboratory, a Lubrication Laboratory and a Biochemical Laboratory. The strong research teams of chemists, physicists, metallurgists, and chemical engineers were headed by Ed Barstow, Charles Strosacker, Mark Putnam, Ray Boundy, E. C. Britton, John Grebe, William Collings, W. R. Veazey, and Ted Heath.

In the 1930's, one of the most exciting developments in Dow Chemical—and throughout the chemical industry—was the research into plastics, the hooking together or polymerization of "giant molecules" to imitate simple natural products such as rubber, cellulose, and plant and animal fibers. This research got underway on a large scale in the 1920's and rapidly gained momentum.

The complex chemistry involved in making plastics was closely linked with heat and pressure as means of controlling the actions of atoms and molecules. Sir William Bragg in his *Concerning the Nature of Things* described the critical nature of chemical reactions in this way:

"We have seen how it can happen that when two atoms approach each other at great speeds they go through one another, while at moderate speeds they bound off each other like two billiard balls. We have to go a step further, and see how, at very low speeds of approach, they may actually stick together. We have all seen those swinging gates which, when their swing is considerable, go to and fro without locking. When the swing has declined, however, the latch suddenly drops into place, the gate is held and after a short rattle the motion is over. We have to explain an effect something like that. When the two atoms meet, the repulsions of their electron shells usually cause them to recoil; but if the motion is small, and the atoms spend a longer time in each other's neighborhood, there is time for something to happen in the internal arrangements of both atoms, like the drop of the latch-gate in its socket, and the atoms are held."

In their latching and cross-latching of atoms and molecules, Dow Chemical scientists looked for plastics which could be made largely from raw materials available in the plant and which would be different from those made by any other company. They first concentrated on two plastics. One combined wood cellulose with ethyl chloride, a petroleum product which Dow Chemical had learned to manufacture cheaply and in large quantities. The other was styrene, a material derived from benzene and ethylene.

The chemical world had known of styrene for almost a century before Dow Chemical's scientists began investigating it. In the late 1920's the Germans were shipping some monomeric (liquid) styrene into this country but the quantity was small and the product impure. The objection to styrene was that when converted into polystyrene (a solid), it became cloudy. This flaw made it unsuitable for most kinds of manufacture. No one had found a way to produce high-purity styrene on a commercial basis. This is what Dow Chemical's scientists set out to do.

The ethyl-cellulose plastic found a ready market. It was exceptionally tough, transparent, shock-resistant, and water-resistant. Its first uses were in transparent foil and in lacquers which had to be tough and pliable. It sold under the trade name Ethocel.

Ethocel looked so promising by 1934 that Willard Dow decided the time had come to stake out a future source of cellulose. He opened negotiations to form a joint company with the Cleveland Cliffs Iron Company at Marquette, Michigan. Cleveland Cliffs, which had large timber reserves near Marquette, had started in business in the 1850's making hardwood charcoal and using the charcoal to convert Michigan iron ore into pig iron. Later the smoke from the charcoal kilns was trapped and converted into methanol and acetic acid. By the late 1920's, the chemical by-products had become more valuable than pig iron.

Main Street in Midland, Mich., as it appeared about 1898, the year after Herbert Dow established the new Dow Chemical Company here. At the other end of Main Street (below) was the Midland Chemical Company Bromide Plant, Dow's first plant, which he was shortly to acquire for his new company. No. 1 brine well is at right.

In 1897, at age 30, when he founded the Dow Company, Herbert Dow wore a handlebar mustache because he felt it made him look older. Below is an early photo of the house he built for his young family a few years later. It is notable for its lack of shrubbery; Dow used the grounds for experiments in landscaping. House still stands in Midland's Dow Gardens.

Herbert Dow's earliest work in Midland was done in the Evans Flour Mill, which stood at the west end of Midland's Main Street. The tower housed a brine well. Here he proved his bromine process would work.

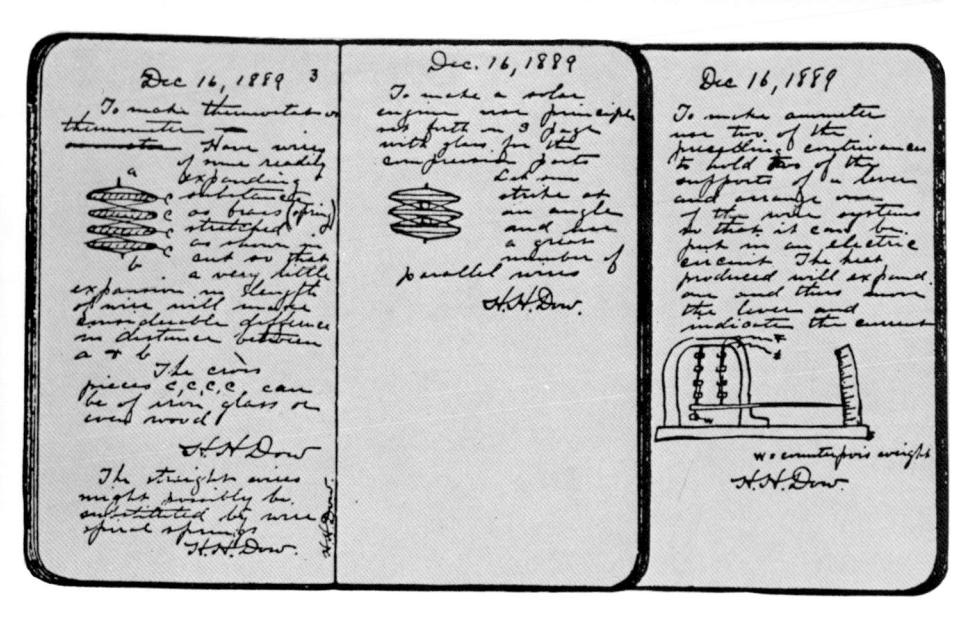

Herbert Dow's early notebooks are crammed with ideas for devices and inventions. The pages above are notes for a thermostat, a solar engine, and an ammeter. At right is promotional material for one of his ventures, a compound poured into bicycle tires to seal punctures from the inside. The company that marketed it collapsed when tiremakers removed their guarantee from any tire filled with the compound. The cyclist is believed to be Dow.

Panoramic photo of Dow plant was made in two segments on June 5, 1902, from roof of Bromide Plant, by Tom Griswold, Jr. Numbers indicate: 1. Carbon house; 2. Bleach warehouse; 3. Wood shop; 4. Brick warehouse, bleach plant, tin shop; 5. Limehouse; 6. Experimental gas producer; 7. Storeroom; 8. Blacksmith shop.

Most of the office force, about 1904. L. to r., F. N. Lowry, James Smith, E. W. Bennett, E. O. Barstow, E. O. Cross, J. E. LeFevre, Fred Vance. J. C. Graves (rear), G. Lee Camp. Lowry was early plant manager; Bennett became board chairman; Barstow was "the father of magnesium"; LeFevre was first purchasing manager; and Camp was later sales manager.

Julius Burrow (holding the bicycle) worked with Dow from the latter's earliest days in Midland. Probably most of the work force of the Midland Chemical Company in 1894 were: (L. to r.) Julius Stark, Burrow, Roscoe Dunham and Alfred Burrow (Julius' brother). The bearded man on the steps was Henry S. Cooper, a former Midland mayor.

In about 1913, Herbert H. Dow posed with sons Willard, then 16, and Alden, 9.

Willard Dow looks on as first magnesium is poured at wartime plant built at Marysville, Mich., in 1943.

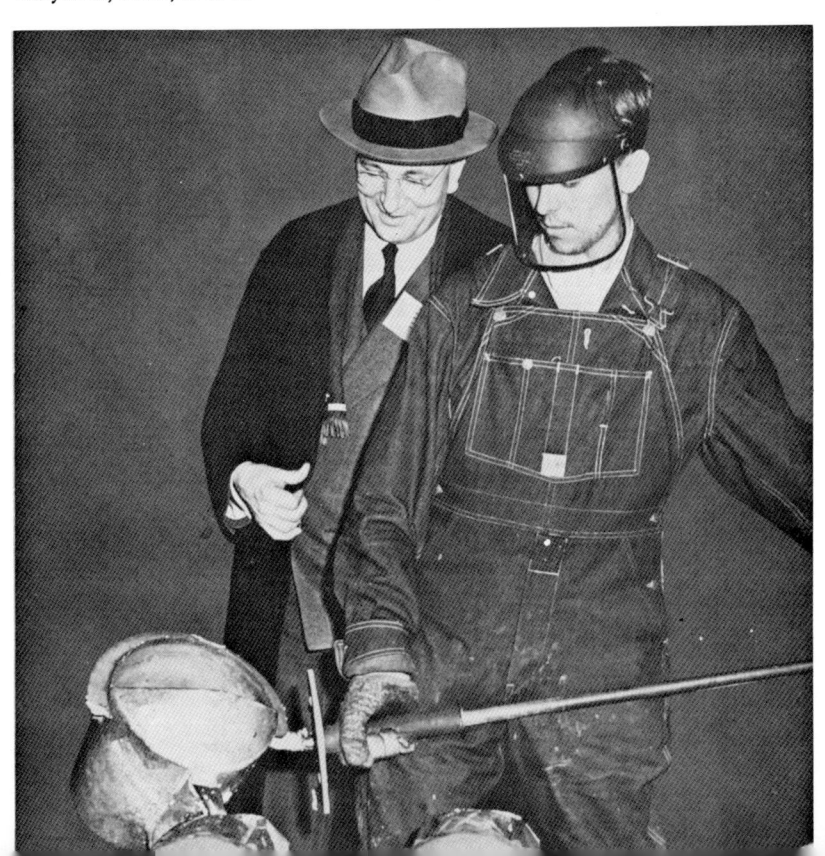

At Lake Jackson, Texas, Dow workers in 1944 were housed in duplexes like these along Grapevine Turn.

At 50th anniversary dinner in 1947, G. F. Kettering ("Boss Ket") of General Motors paid tribute to Dow accomplishments. Willard Dow brought his mother, Mrs. H. H. Dow, into limelight.

In 1945, a Russian colonel and his aide, and Dow's Ray H. Boundy (right) and his American interpreter posed before a meeting with the Quartermaster Corps Plastics Team to discuss arrangements in the Russian Zone of Germany. Boundy was responsible for building of polystyrene plastic plants for Dow during war.

Early artist's rendition of Midland shows town as it was in 1884, five years before Herbert Dow first saw it. ✓ indicates where he established first plant in 1890, ✠ where he moved it later, and where its world headquarters remain.

In 1917 this photo of the first shipment of indigo to leave the Dow plant in Midland was recorded. World War I had cut off United States supply, which until then came from Germany. Company's first locomotive is shown (below) in 1905 delivering coal to Dow's "E" Power House.

Treatment of waste by Dow began in 1935. It emerged as a really large-scale operation in 1946 when this general Waste Disposal Plant was put into operation at Midland.

Some of the Dow pioneers;

Dr. E. O. Barstow

Dr. E. W. Bennett

Dr. A. P. Beutel

Dr. R. H. Boundy

Dr. E. C. Britton

Dr. Wm. R. Collings

Dr. John J. Grebe

Dr. Mark E. Putnam

Dr. C. J. Strosacker

On June 21, 1961, Pres. John F. Kennedy pushed a White House button activating the nation's first plant for converting salt-water into fresh, located at Freeport, Tex., site of Dow's Texas Division. He was flanked by Dr. Leland I. Doan, Dow president, and Dr. A. P. Beutel, Dow Gulf Coast vice president. At Freeport (below) Dow extracts bromine and magnesium from sea water.

In the post-World War II years Dow Chemical launched one of the greatest expansion drives of its history, building plant after plant. In 1952 Dr. W. R. Veazey broke ground for the company's new Texas research complex, now called the Veazey Research Center. Veazey was one of the company's research leaders.

On his first anniversary as Dow president, in 1950, Leland I. Doan was presented a letter signed by more than 5,000 Midland and Bay City employees congratulating him on "a job well done." L. to R.: C. C. Payne, Dr. Doan, Patricia Yack, Frank Jacobs, and Ross Gordon.

Recent years have carried Dow to far places. Above, Dow Aerospace Services team helped with firing of Saturn booster rocket at Cape Kennedy. Below, New Zealand's largest producer of agricultural and veterinary products is Ivon Watkins-Dow, located at New Plymouth, N.Z., jointly owned by Dow Chemical.

Present leadership of Dow Chemical took reins in 1962. Left to right are C. B. Branch, executive vice president; H. D. Doan, president; and Carl A. Gerstacker, board chairman.

At Terneuzen, The Netherlands, is Dow's main producing plant for the Common Market. Present in 1964 when street leading to plant was named for H. H. Dow were (l. to r.) Macauley Whiting, president of Dow International; Alden B. Dow; H. D. Doan; Zoltan Merszei, president of Dow Europe; Terneuzen Burgomaster H. Rypstra; Herbert H. Dow II; and A. F. C. de Casembroot, Queen's Commissioner for Zeeland.

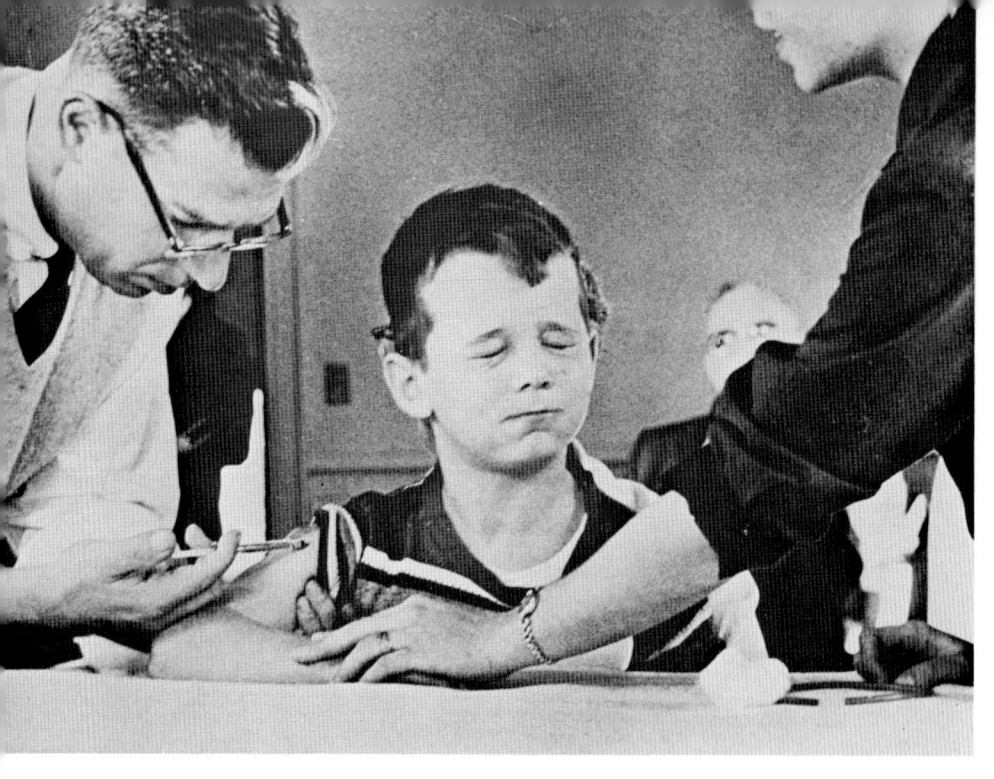

In 1967 the U.S. Public Health Service launched a campaign to eradicate measles in the United States, and the scene above was repeated millions of times. Most of the vaccine used was the new one-shot Schwarz strain developed by Dow Chemical. During the same year Dow was the object of dozens of campus demonstrations (below, at University of Wisconsin) as students protested its manufacture of napalm for the war in Vietnam.

A deal was made in May, 1935, and the Cliffs Dow Chemical Company began as a subsidiary of Dow Chemical and Cleveland Cliffs Iron Company. Willard Dow sent managers and technicians to Marquette to modernize the plant and improve the yield of chemicals through new wood distillation processes.

One of those he sent to Marquette was Nelson Griswold, the son of Herbert Dow's first engineer, Tom Griswold. Nelson Griswold would recall: "They were losing from $10,000 to $20,000 a month up there before depreciation when we took over the plant. We got it turned around and earning a profit in eighteen months.

"It took me six months to get the Cliffs people to say what they thought about anything. I wasn't accustomed to this sort of relationship. All of us at Dow Chemical were used to open discussions where you said what you thought. That was one of the key elements in the company's success. Gradually the Cliffs people learned they could speak without fear of reprisal and without having to be a yes-man. Then they opened up.

"There are hazards in such frankness as we have at Dow Chemical. In a small town people are inclined to speak freely. In such open talk there is always the hazard of giving away information to outsiders. But this hazard is not as great as not discussing problems."

Dow Chemical chemists and engineers had no great difficulty finding a commercial process for the production of Ethocel. But they searched for months to find a way to make high-purity styrene on a commercial scale.

At one point, Willard Dow was ready to shove the styrene research aside and concentrate on the cellulose plastics. He called in Strosacker, who headed the styrene research with Britton, and told him to stop work on styrene. The money was going on cellulose.

And then followed a strange episode in the history of The Dow Chemical Company. The research on styrene continued behind Willard's back, due in part to the behind-the-scenes maneuvering of Treasurer Earl Bennett. And the result led Dow Chemical to become the major producer of one of the most vital ingredients in the synthetic rubber produced for World War II.

Earl Bennett remembered: "Willard's decision to drop styrene hit Strosacker, John Grebe, Ray Boundy, and Bobby Dreisbach a hard blow. They had been working hard on this project and they were convinced they were close to a solution.

"Bobby Dreisbach didn't have much finesse. He was hot-tempered and sometimes he even got into fist fights in the laboratory. One day he came to me in a rage. He said, 'Mr. Bennett, we're not going to stop work on styrene. I know Strosacker has his orders, but we just can't stop because we know we're right. Can't you do something to help us?'

"I said, 'Bobby, I've got my orders, too. I've got orders to close the account number. But I'll tell you what you can do. You can go back and think up a name other than styrene. Continue working on styrene—but under another name. I'll issue you a new account number.'"

Bennett chuckled. "I did it, too, because I thought they were both good processes."

Such shenanigans would have been impossible under Herbert Dow. Hardly a day passed that he wasn't in the laboratories and plants checking on what the men were doing and following in detail the progress on every process. But Willard controlled research through conferences with his top research people. The company had grown too large in size for one man to check on what was taking place in each building of the sprawling plant.

The subterfuge engineered by Bennett paid off. Mrs. Sylvia Stoesser and Jim Pierce, together with Grebe, developed an inhibitor that was the key to a commercial process for producing styrene of great purity and low cost. It could be polymerized to what became the most important plastic in the Dow Chemical stable. The polystyrene was given the name Styron. It was a plastic so clear that it resembled crystal. It was adaptable to many uses, clear or colored. Through another chemical combination, styrene became Styraloy, a useful plastic with slightly different qualities than Styron.

In his mistaken judgment on styrene, Willard Dow could very well have excused himself on the grounds that he had the same right to be wrong that was granted to others in Dow Chemical. And this right had been granted to an astonishing degree from the earliest days of Herbert Dow.

Willard Dow conceded that mistakes and failures often were necessary. He put it in this way to a class of young recruits:

"A large percentage of failures on a problem is necessary for its solution. We have a right to be wrong. Many an industry has come into existence through results gleaned from failures; indeed it may be said that negative results often determine the correct procedure. . . ."

Willard Dow was a typical conservative Midwestern businessman in many of his attitudes. But in research he was a radical. He encouraged his researchers to attack the impossible, to question the old ways of doing things, to challenge textbook theory, and to look for the unorthodox approach in solving a problem. There were times, he once said wryly, when management had to adopt the method "of carrying on research by supplying chemists with plenty of so-called patient money while maintaining a prayerful attitude."

The primary problem, as he saw it, was to achieve a balance between radical research and conservative production practices. On this point he said: "Our research organization must be a group of extremists. They must imagine developments in the so-called 'impossible range.' In contrast, the production men must be conservative because they must maintain their production and quality of goods to satisfy their customers. The chemical industry is a changing business. A product selling in tons today may a year or two hence be a dying industry. It is our requirement that we must maintain big research staffs; we must... be willing to discard the old process and be equally willing to take up the new."

The American chemical industry was not only changing in the late 1930's, but it was also the fastest growing industry in the country. As business conditions improved, the pressure for growth and expansion to meet consumer demand increased steadily.

Dow Chemical and Ethyl Gasoline Company had built the Kure Beach bromine plant in 1933 with expectations that its yearly production of 6,000,000 pounds of ethylene dibromide would meet the market requirements for several years to come. But two years later the plant capacity had to be almost doubled to 10,000,000 pounds. It was doubled again in 1937 to 20,000,000 pounds. Twelve months later the increasing sales of anti-knock gasoline forced Dow Chemical's engineers to add another 10,000,000-pound unit—bringing total capacity to 30,000,000 pounds.

In this period, too, Europe began its grim preparations for war. Orders for magnesium poured in from England, France, Germany, Poland, Holland, Mexico, and Japan. Germany halted its purchases in 1936 to conserve its foreign exchange but other nations continued buying. On the domestic front, the American Magnesium Corporation took almost one-third of Dow Chemical's magnesium production. Sales of magnesium jumped from some 2,000,000 pounds in 1934 to 6,500,000 pounds in 1938.

Most of the magnesium going abroad was to be used in planes and the foreign buyers of American-made planes were specifying that many parts had to be made of magnesium or magnesium alloys. Yet the United States military establishment showed little interest in magnesium.

Despite the slowness of American manufacturers to accept magnesium, Willard Dow sensed that the demand for the metal was not a temporary war-scare phenomenon, but the beginning of an era that would see magnesium accepted as a basic structural material. His father had gambled that magnesium would become an important metal, and Willard Dow was no less sure of it.

As the threats of war grew more ominous in the late 1930's, Willard Dow persuaded his directors to set aside $300,000 for more intensive research into magnesium production and fabrication. He got them to vote another $650,000 for expansion of the magnesium plant.

Then Dow stepped up his efforts to get the Navy and the Bureau of Aeronautics to follow the lead of European manufacturers and to incorporate more magnesium parts in United States military aircraft. But he got little encouragement. The Bureau of Aeronautics advised Dow Chemical's engineer, stationed in Washington, that it had reached the point in its tests where it was ready to turn down all use of magnesium alloys in naval construction.

For months an argument-by-letter went on between Washington and Midland. The Navy contended there was an "inherent lack of resistance to corrosion" in magnesium parts. Dow Chemical's tests showed that these parts had resisted corrosion up to eighteen months—and Dow argued the corrosion problem could be licked entirely if the Navy would only work with Dow Chemical on a program of developing protective coatings to meet Navy specifications.

In April, 1939, a ranking officer in the Bureau of Aeronautics wrote Willard Dow, saying in part: "Your company may or may not be engaged in research of a fundamental character leading to the development of data of direct interest to the Bureau of Aeronautics. However, if you are engaged in such research, information on the status of certain magnesium developments hereinafter listed would be helpful. If no developments of scientific significance are being made, this Bureau may find it necessary to decelerate the introduction of magnesium into naval aircraft applications until such time as substantial engineering information is available."

When Willard Dow read the questions listed by the bureau's spokesman, he commented: "Practically all of that information, and indeed all important information, has long been available—but not availed of." As for "research of a fundamental character," the bureau should have known by this time that Dow Chemical was the only company in the country that had been researching magnesium continuously for more than twenty years.

Dow's representative in Washington reviewed the efforts of Dow

Chemical to get the government interested in the use of magnesium and summed up the situation in this way:

". . . The Dow Chemical Company has supplied thousands of samples for cooperative tests free of charge. It has sent its own engineers and laboratory men to the government laboratories and testing stations wherever desired, as well as on regular trips. It has sent these same engineers and research men as well as officers of the company to confer many times with Navy personnel in Washington, offered the facilities of the Dow laboratories to the Navy, arranged with the Bakelite Corporation to supply free of charge large quantities of coating materials for the protective coatings under study. The company has conducted continuous tests and studies in its own laboratories to develop protective coatings as well as purer magnesium."

The prewar effort to get the government interested in magnesium made little progress. But when war came, the magnesium requirements for American planes for one year alone soared to more than 140,000,000 pounds—more than twenty times Dow Chemical's 1939 production.

Willard Dow had seen the possibility of magnesium consumption in the United States increasing to as much as 12,000,000 pounds a year, which was about the limit that could reasonably be produced at Midland. Anything beyond 12,000,000 pounds would call for the pumping of so much brine that the company's balanced production of other chemicals would have been thrown out of kilter. But as a precaution, he put Barstow and other magnesium experts to work to perfect a process that would take magnesium metal from seawater. He reasoned that if bromine could be taken from the sea, then the sea also would yield up its magnesium with the proper coaxing. There was one pound of bromine in every 1,700 gallons of seawater but, theoretically at least, there was one pound of magnesium in only 90 gallons of seawater. If a new magnesium process could be developed and if the demand for magnesium continued to grow, then Dow Chemical would be ready to supply the need.

An amusing contrast to the government's reluctance to encourage magnesium in plane construction was the eagerness with which scientists embraced the idea of using equipment made of magnesium on an expedition to Russia in 1936 to photograph an eclipse of the sun.

The idea originated with Dr. Donald H. Menzel, professor of astrophysics at Harvard University, when he came to Midland in 1934 to lecture on cosmic chemistry. He had never seen magnesium in metallic form until that visit.

"I remember calling for a lantern-slide pointer," Menzel later wrote, "and was both surprised and dismayed when they produced what appeared to be a glorified furnace poker, about six feet long. I groaned at the thought of lifting it and let it lie at my feet until I was well into the lecture. There came a time, however, when I could not proceed with the lecture without the aid of a pointer and I stopped to pick it up. The force I exerted would have been enough to raise a crowbar. The pointer flew ceilingward and I had difficulty holding it back. Such was my introduction to Dowmetal and its most obvious property: lightness.

"That moment provided the inspiration for a new idea: Why not use Dowmetal for eclipse equipment and for other scientific purposes where lightness is an asset? This idea bore fruit a few months later."

Menzel had been chosen as a member of a scientific team from Harvard and Massachusetts Institute of Technology who were going to the remote Russian town of Ak-Bulak, east of Moscow, to observe a total solar eclipse. He discussed with Willard Dow the possibility of Dow Chemical making a box-like container for spectroscopes, tripods, supports, and other equipment of magnesium to reduce the expedition's weight problem.

Dow was enthusiastic. He offered to fabricate the equipment in the company's shop without charge as his contribution to the scientific expedition. Menzel built models of the various instruments from wood and cardboard and sent them to Midland where they were duplicated in magnesium. The magnesium equipment was shipped to Ak-Bulak by ship, train, truck, ox cart, and camel cart early in the spring of 1936. In appreciation of Willard Dow's help, they called their camp "Camp Dow."

Menzel wrote of the camp: "Dowmetal itself came in for a large share of the interest. The Russians must have thought us the original 'Supermen,' when they saw us toss from one end of the tent to the other a large Dowmetal casting. They laughed heartily when we let them in on the secret and allowed them to lift the eighteen-foot I-beam that was used in one of the instruments. I frequently saw boys, raising the massive appearing Dowmetal equipment, showing off before their girl friends or posing for pictures.

"Another property of Dowmetal that made it extremely useful for field work was the ease of machining. From the various blocks and sheets of the material we readily formed, even with the limited shop facilities that we had carried with us, numerous auxiliary apparatus that we had not had time to construct before our departure. It was surprising what one could accomplish with a drill, a file and a hacksaw."

The bulkiest piece of equipment was a large rectangular box of magnesium which housed four spectrographs. Thousands of Russians gathered around Camp Dow on July 19 to watch the Americans and to see the eclipse.

Menzel recalled: "The Soviet has popularized science to an extent that only we who have actual contact with the Russians can appreciate. They used the eclipse as a means of scientific education. Thousands of lectures were given in all parts of the country and in many tongues and dialects. The government distributed pamphlets printed in thirty or more of the major native languages that the Soviet is trying hard to preserve. These leaflets told the story of the eclipse, what to expect, and how to observe it. They gave wide distribution to an inexpensive pin-hole camera, to which was attached films, developers, hypo, and full directions for taking eclipse pictures. In consequence, eclipse day found the people prepared to understand and enjoy the great spectacle. There was no repetition of the incident of the 1914 eclipse when the unprepared Russians thought that the world was about to end and fell praying on their knees in the fields."

"Camp Dow" was soon dismantled but magnesium had played its part well in lessening the burden of the scientists.

Willard Dow's aggressive policy of pushing out in new directions placed heavy pressure on the company to finance the expansion program. The company's cash needs for more than thirty years had been handled through Cleveland banks. Soon after he became treasurer, Earl Bennett had realized the time was coming when the company would have to turn to a larger money market. He began visiting New York banking houses to make himself and the company known.

Bennett would recall: "I went to New York cold, without any introductions, and I started making the rounds of the banking institutions. I introduced myself and explained that I represented The Dow Chemical Company. Remember, I was only 5-feet-6 and weighed no more than 110 pounds. A good many of those people found it amusing that so small a man should be walking around such a big city talking about future credit for a company few of them knew anything about. Our stock for years wasn't listed in the New York papers. It was quoted on the Cleveland market.

"I wasn't able to get through the layers of secretaries and vice presidents in many houses to reach the top men. But I did get a very warm reception and a hearing from Smith, Barney & Company, and from Lehman Brothers. As a result of this trip, we developed a very close relationship with Smith, Barney that lasted through the years."

To improve the company's financial position, the directors decided early in 1937 to list Dow Chemical stock with the New York Stock Exchange. The number of shares was increased from 945,000 to 2,000,000 and on June 30 the stock appeared for the first time on the Big Board, closing that day at $135.

Dow Chemical's listing with the New York Exchange came in the forty-first year of its operation and was a belated birthday present for Willard Dow, who had celebrated his fortieth birthday a few months earlier. Dow was a nervous bundle of energy, driving himself harder than he did the men who worked under him.

Willard Dow once tried to explain to a friend why it was he that pushed himself so hard and why he felt the expansion of the company was necessary.

"It's difficult to make people understand," he said, "that money is not the motive. A company must make money to exist. But the company that exists only to make dollars can not live very long. If you produce something that is useful—and do it better than anyone else—then the dollars will take care of themselves. There is a responsibility involved in management that has nothing to do with money, although I don't expect many people to believe that."

Competitiveness, pride, the desire to create, or the pleasure of the so-called race—whatever the compelling reason, Dow had brought the Dow Chemical Company in 1938 to a point where it had to expand outside Midland or else turn over growing markets to competitors.

Dow saw this clearly and his decision was to expand—as fast and as far as it was necessary and safe. He saw that the movement of the population was westward and he discussed with his business intimates whether the company should locate a chemical plant in Denver, Colorado, or in California.

An opportunity to expand into California developed unexpectedly. During a trip to the West Coast, Dow learned that the majority stockholders of the Great Western Electrochemical Company were interested in selling the property. The plant was located at Pittsburg, California, at the junction of the Sacramento and San Joaquin rivers, near San Francisco.

Great Western was a subsidiary of the Great Western Power Company and was a pioneer manufacturer of electrolytic caustic soda and chlorine west of Detroit, having started operations in 1916. The chlorine had been used in the manufacture of bleaching powder.

Strangely enough, the first cells used by Great Western to make bleach had been built from drawings bought from Herbert Dow. They were the same cells Dow had used so successfully in Midland. But the cells which operated efficiently in Midland's cool climate were not suited for the long, hot summers of California.

Not long after this purchase, Great Western's chief chemist, Wilhelm Hirschkind, visited Midland to study the Dow Chemical operation. He mentioned to Herbert Dow that the cells installed by Great Western made excellent bleach during the cool winter months, but they had proved to be unsatisfactory during the long, hot summers.

Herbert Dow said, "I sold the cells to Great Western at their request. I didn't guarantee their operation in that climate."

With the installation of refrigerated chambers, the cells worked as well as they did in Midland. But Great Western eventually dropped the bleaching powder business and used the chlorine to produce a wide number of products. Hirschkind directed production into the field of xanthates, chemical compounds used by the western mining industry to separate minerals from sludge. Chemicals were developed for the western newsprint industry, and processes found for a wide range of chlorinated products.

Willard Dow was interested not only in the Great Western properties but in Hirschkind as a scientist. He was a brilliant, peppery little man who had once worked in Germany with the legendary Fritz Haber, discoverer of the process for extracting nitrogen from the air. Hirschkind had left Germany in 1912 and had come to the United States to become an instructor in chemistry at the University of Illinois.

Hirschkind would recall: "When I came to the United States, the scientist looked down on the inventor and the inventor was in turn contemptuous of the scientist. So were some of the men of business who backed the inventors in successful enterprises.... [This] story illustrates the popular attitude toward scientists. At the time of the United States' entry into World War I, representatives of the American Chemical Society called on President Wilson's Secretary of War, Newton Baker, offering the services of the chemical profession in the conflict. The Secretary thanked the committee for the offer and promised to investigate the matter, asking them to return the following day. On doing so, Mr. Baker informed them that he had looked into the situation and while he appreciated the offer, he found it was quite unnecessary because the War Department already had a chemist."

Willard Dow had a chemist, too, but he wanted more. In December, 1938, an arrangement was worked out for The Dow Chemical Company to take over the Great Western Electrochemical Company. In this move, Dow Chemical not only obtained the services of an outstanding scientist, but it got an outlet for its products on the West Coast and an aggressive research center that had developed several important processes.

While negotiations were underway with Great Western, Willard Dow came to the conclusion that the time had come to go to the sea not only for more bromine but also for magnesium. The growing demand for magnesium was piling up trouble for the Midland operation. The primary trouble was in disposing of the waste brine which could not be cycled through other chemical processes. Part of the waste was pumped back into the ground, a trick of "vertical storage" that had been pioneered by Dutch Beutel.

As Beutel recalled: "I set up a rig in Midland to pump the waste brine down vertically in what they call the Parma sand formation, which is one level higher than the Marshall formation. The Parma sand was in the range of about 900 feet deep. I got some tanks from salvage and some big high-pressure pumps that went up to about 600 pounds of pressure. I hooked the pumps up to brine-filled tanks and began pumping the brine into a well. After a time, the pressure was building up but nothing was happening—the brine wasn't moving out of the tanks. Then suddenly everything let go. The pump started to pump like hell and you could see the brine level going down. I couldn't get enough brine into the tanks. I had to shut off the pumps, and refill the tanks. We left the valve open and the brine poured down the well. My first thought was that we might be pushing brine through the sand all the way to the outcroppings at Saginaw Bay.

"But what I had done with that pressure was to lift the earth and fracture the zone. The brine wasn't being forced into the sand—it was pouring into this fracture. If we had known enough at the time, we could have gotten a patent on this process. Actually, this fracturing of the earth became the basis of Dowell's oil field operations with pressures running up to 10,000 pounds."

But underground storage of brine supplemented by surface settling tanks was not the complete answer to the waste brine problem. There was growing danger that pollution control would get out of hand and create serious problems on the Tittabawassee River.

In addition to the waste brine problem, the production costs at the Kure Beach plant were causing growing concern. Electric power at Kure Beach was costly and the cost of getting large quantities of soda ash and sulfuric acid to the plant site by ship and lighter was becoming prohibitive.

Late in 1938, Dow and Beutel set out on a scouting trip to Texas to look for possible sites for a Gulf Coast plant that would produce both bromine and magnesium from sea water. The lure of cheap fuel from the natural gas fields drew them to Texas. Both Dow and Beutel had driven through the state several times checking on operations of Dowell crews who were acidizing oil wells. They had been fascinated and appalled by the sight of mile after mile of towering, gas-fed flames lighting the skies at night as the gas was "flared" after separation from the oil. It made them groan to see all this potential energy going to waste.

Beutel recalled: "At one place in Texas, we saw the gas roaring up out of 6-inch and 8-inch pipes into the air. They produced the oil out of the wells with the gas, put it through a series of separating tanks, and the gas was flared into the atmosphere. The gas came out of those gas separator vents with such force you couldn't hear yourself talk. It was all going to waste, and the same thing was happening all through the oil fields at that time. You could actually drive from Houston to Freeport at night and read a newspaper by the light from the flared gas."

Dow and Beutel drove from New Orleans across Texas to Brownsville checking on possible plant sites. On their return to Midland, a team of chemists and engineers set out for Texas to test the bromine and magnesium content of Gulf water.

And so it was that Willard Dow prepared to make the biggest gamble of his life—the creation of a giant chemical complex many miles removed from the birthplace of the company. The secret for taking bromine from the sea already had been solved; whether the sea would give up its magnesium and other chemicals without staggering losses was the unknown factor. Laboratory experiments and cost analyses said yes. But the paper analyses could not possibly anticipate all the difficulties that would have to be overcome.

Dow's confidence that his researchers, engineers, and production men could create a new manufacturing center from the ground up was bolstered by the record which the company had made during the eight years of his management:

...Sales had increased from $16,033,000 in 1930 to $24,871,000 in 1938 while assets had grown from $22,474,000 to $38,484,000 over the same period.

...The key to taking bromine from the sea had been found.

...Dowell Incorporated had increased oil production across the nation with its acidizing process, adding untold millions of dollars to the value of oil fields which were nearing depletion.

...Research had turned up useful plastics made from combinations of wood, brine, and oil.

...The joint venture with the Cleveland Cliffs Iron Company had given Dow Chemical an important new source of raw materials.

...The subsidiary Io-Dow Chemical Company had broken the Chilean iodine monopoly and the price of iodine had been driven down from $4.50 a pound to 81 cents.

...The Midland plants during the Depression had been overhauled, production expanded, and debts paid from earnings generated during the nation's worst economic recession.

...The financial position of the company and its prestige had been strengthened by the listing of the stock on the New York Stock Exchange.

...Demand for magnesium was growing for the first time in twenty years and appeared to be nearing a point that would justify the heavy investments in research and in plants.

...Key employees had stuck by the company loyally through the hard times and they formed a tough, experienced, able management corps around which to build.

...Training programs had discovered unsuspected talent in the ranks of Dow Chemical employees and strengthened the reserves on which management could draw to fill key posts from within.

...The number of employees had increased from eighteen hundred in 1930 to more than four thousand and the community of Midland had felt few of the shocks from the Depression which had paralyzed so many towns and cities across the country.

The record was reassuring, but neither Willard Dow nor anyone else could foresee that the decisions to expand production in 1938 would prove vital to the success of the Allies in the war that was to come.

Chapter Twelve

In 1938, the statesmen of Britain and France tried to buy peace in Europe with appeasement. They paid the price Adolf Hitler demanded—freedom to seize Czechoslovakia. But appeasement only whetted Hitler's appetite for conquest and made him contemptuous of the leaders of Britain and France.

And so it was that Europe rushed toward war. The first shock of 1939 was not a warlike move, however, but a political maneuver. On August 24 Fascist Germany and Communist Russia signed a ten-year military and political nonaggression pact. The net effect of the agreement, as far as Hitler was concerned, was that it gave him the guarantee of protection from attack by the Soviets, freeing divisions for offensive operations.

Seven days after the pact was signed, German armor, infantry, and aircraft lashed out at Poland and World War II was underway. The attack began about 5 A.M. on September 1 when dive bombers began blasting targets across Poland. An hour later, the infantry and tanks poured over the border.

Britain and France declared war on Germany on September 3, but they could not save Poland. On September 17, the Russians invaded Poland from the east and the Polish army was caught in a vise. Warsaw took a fearful pounding and fell to the Germans on September 28. Shattered Poland was divided between the partners to the nonaggression pact.

The marching of the armies in Europe and the preparations for war had their reverberations around the world in capitals and in villages. Some had foreseen the conflict. Others had not. In Midland, Willard Dow and his managers had sensed that war was coming long before the Germans crashed into Poland. Their decision was to speed up expansion with priority given to building a chemical complex in Texas that would ease pressures on the Midland plant and help meet the demand for basic chemicals which they saw developing.

The expansion program was the most ambitious that Dow Chemical had ever undertaken. More than $7,000,000 was to be poured into new plants and processes. Plans for the Texas plant called for an integrated production line that would take from seawater and petroleum 12,000,000 pounds of magnesium a year, 330,000 pounds of chlorine a day, and (yearly) 68,000 tons of caustic, 25,000,000 pounds of ethylene, 15,000,000 pounds of ethylene dichloride, 15,000,000 pounds of ethylene glycol, 15,000,000 pounds of vinylidene chloride, and 28,500,000 pounds of ethylene dibromide for anti-knock gasoline.

During the summer and fall of 1939, Dow sent chemists and engineers to make further tests along the Gulf Coast at the sites recommended by the team which had made the exploratory study some months earlier. They were instructed to look for a site that offered: seawater not too much diluted with fresh water; large deposits of seashells from which to make lime; a good freshwater supply; availability of electric power, gas, and oil; land at a reasonable price with room for expansion; good transportation; and a means of disposing of the waste brine.

The early reports favored two places, Corpus Christi and Freeport, the latter a small fishing village sixty miles south of Houston.

Beutel would recall: "In the summer of 1939, Willard decided he wanted to take another look at Freeport and he asked me to go with him. We were careful not to overdress because we didn't want anyone to know why we were there. We stopped in the Brockenbrough Drug Store to get a Coke. Old Man Brockenbrough was behind the counter. He gave us our Cokes and said, 'Where are you folks from?' We gave him a vague answer. We talked for a while and he said, 'This looks like a dying town. The Freeport Sulphur Company is going to move out. They've mined out the sulphur dome here and the one up the way will be worked out soon.'

"We found out what we wanted to know by talking to Texans and studying the reports of our own people. We found there was land to be had at a reasonable price. We could get gas, oil, and electricity. There were salt domes in the area. There was an unlimited supply of oyster shells in Galveston Bay. The Brazos River and Oyster Creek flowed by the town. There was a good supply of underground water and a good deep river channel into the Gulf, with a jetty already built. There was sulfur nearby. As far as I was concerned, this was it."

A split developed among board members over the choice of a site. Dow and Beutel leaned toward Freeport while others were insistent that Corpus Christi was the better place to build. Corpus Christi did have many advantages over Freeport. It offered schools, hospitals, housing for employees, and good shopping facilities. Freeport was a mere village surrounded by a sea of salt grass, herds of roaming goats, and marshland. Yet Freeport's location on a peninsula, having sources of raw materials nearby and easy disposal of waste brine, was an attraction.

As it turned out, a cold wave that moved deep into Texas to freeze the Corpus Christi area played a part in the final decision. In January, 1940, Dow called for the board of directors to meet at the Driskill Hotel in Corpus Christi to decide on the plant location. Prior to the meeting, he and Beutel took their wives on a Mexican holiday. Then after a few days in Mexico City, they headed for Corpus Christi to meet the board members. They arrived just as a "norther" hit south Texas.

Beutel remembered: "Lordy, but it was cold when we got there. There wasn't much heat in the hotel. When we went down to breakfast, we found the others shivering in the dining room. They had gone out the day before to explore the country. They'd been stuck on icy roads with no heaters in the cars. The windshields would ice over, and every few minutes they had had to stop and scrape ice off the glass. Nobody was dressed for such weather."

The meeting in Corpus Christi was brief. Someone said: "Let's get out of here and go over to Freeport." It could hardly be said that the sudden turn in weather was the decisive factor in Corpus Christi losing out to Freeport as the site for the new plant. But it helped. The board members went by train to Houston and drove to Freeport under warmer skies to look over the lay of the land. When they returned to Houston to make their decision, the vote went to Freeport.

In the next few weeks, Dow Chemical bought about a thousand acres of land along the Gulf and the Brazos River before a speculative boom could develop to skyrocket prices.

A Texan involved in the land purchase would recall: "There was one large beach section that had been divided years before into 5-acre plots and 25-foot-wide lots by a land company. Those plots were strung all over hell's half acre. The promoters advertised these as city lots, but they were nothing but salt grass from the beach on back. The come-on was that you'd build a home on your plot and have orange groves and fruit trees right on the Gulf. You can't raise oranges or anything else on that land except salt grass and goats. It was the damndest land promotion you ever saw. It took a bit of doing to run down all the owners of those little plots—but the agents managed it."

While the land purchases were being made, Dow sent a team of engineers and technical people to work with Austin Company engineers in getting the plant on the drawing board. The construction at Midland and the planning for the Texas complex were more than Dow Chemical's own engineering department could handle alone.

The use of outside engineers on a Dow Chemical construction job was one of Willard Dow's breaks with tradition. From the time Herbert Dow had hired Tom Griswold as his engineer in 1897 until his death in 1930 he had insisted on his own engineers designing plants, processes, and equipment. But with the fast growth of the company during the Depression, Willard Dow often turned to the Austin Company for help.

Later the engineering staff moved from Cleveland to Houston as work crews broke ground for the first major chemical plant to be built on the Texas Gulf Coast. This was the beginning of the great Texas petrochemical complex. Years later it would stretch from Louisiana to Brownsville as other companies followed in the wake of Dow Chemical.

Dow knew the hurry-up program in Texas had come none too soon when Hitler sent his armies into action on the Western Front after a winter of inaction that had become known as "the phony war." In April, 1940, Hitler seized Denmark and Norway, blocking any chance of a British invasion on his flank. And then on May 10 the Germans struck into Holland, Belgium, and Luxembourg. They smashed on into France with blitzkrieg tactics that demoralized the Allied defenders, and threw the battle front into confusion. Panzer divisions broke through at Sedan, swung toward the Channel, and trapped nine divisions of the British Expeditionary Force and ten divisions of the French First Army in the area of Dunkirk. These forces seemed doomed. But in an almost unbelievable saga of the sea, thousands of small craft swarmed across the Channel and evacuated 338,226 British and French soldiers from the beaches, saving them to fight another day.

In six weeks it was over. France capitulated on June 25 and Hitler stood astride most of Europe. Soon the Battle of Britain would begin, the savage air war in which Hitler would seek to blast Britain's defenses with explosives and fire bombs and open the way for invasion.

President Roosevelt, in early January, had called for a preparedness program to cost just under $2,000,000,000. But with France under attack and reeling, the President asked Congress to almost double the preparedness spending. Airplane production was to be increased from 5,000 to 50,000 planes a year.

The President's request for 50,000 planes came as a shock, largely because it underscored in a tangible way the tremendous production task ahead for American industry which still had not fully recovered from the Depression of the 1930's. The program would place a heavy burden on The Dow Chemical Company in supplying magnesium.

Chapter Twelve

The President's Secretary of State, Cordell Hull, described in his memoirs how the decision was reached to fix airplane production at 50,000 planes:

"Of one point the President and I had not the slightest doubt; namely, that an Allied victory was essential to the security of the United States. . . .

It was also evident to the President and me that the enormous superiority of the German Army revealed by the lightning occupation of Holland and the break-through at Sedan required the revising of all of our estimates for the rearming of the United States. The President discussed with me the project of a special message to Congress requesting a virtual doubling of the military appropriations for the year, in which I fully concurred. [Ambassador William] Bullitt had sent me a cable for the President on May 13 stressing the importance of increasing our production of planes, because of the vital part planes were playing in the German advance. I thereupon suggested to the President that he tell Congress that the United States should aim for a production of 50,000 planes a year. I had already mentioned this figure to my associates. The reaction of Mr. Roosevelt was the same as that of my associates—he was literally speechless, for 50,000 planes was ten times our current annual production.

I argued, however, that it was best to aim at a high figure and take the long view. Such a production did not seem so impossible to me as it seemed to others. I felt that the mere mention of the figure, with our tremendous productive capacities known to the world, would have a good effect on stimulating our own people, in comforting the Allies, and in giving cause for worry to the Axis.

The President forthwith agreed. In his message to Congress on May 16 he said he would like to see the nation geared to a production of 50,000 planes a year. He asked for additional appropriations for all branches of the armed forces totaling $1,182,000,000. But, significantly, he asked Congress not to hamper or delay the delivery of American-made planes to foreign nations that had ordered them or might seek to purchase more planes. In other words, our own rearmament must not be at the expense of the democracies we were seeking to aid. . . ."

This was the atmosphere of urgency in which Willard Dow moved as he pushed for fast construction of the Texas plant. Chemicals would be needed in huge volumes to meet the demands in the expansion of the armed forces.

Dow turned to Dutch Beutel to ramrod the Texas construction. He gave him some of his ablest engineers and production men to speed the building—among them George McGranahan, Harland Sherbrook, Nelson

Griswold, C. M. Shigley, J. R. Stein, Leo Glesner, C. A. Branson, Russ Crawford, and Roy Smithers.

Priority was given the magnesium plant. Once it was in operation the chlorine, bromine and other units would fall into place.

Fortunately, the summer and early fall of 1940 were dry in Texas and the work moved rapidly. But in October the rains came, heavy rains turning roads into quagmires and making lakes of building sites. The oyster-shell topping on roads sank from view. Trucks mired in the greasy mud. Huge tanks tipped over in the soft earth. A flood on the Brazos River slowed the digging of a drainage canal.

But somehow the dog-tired crews and their bosses got their jobs done. Gas lines were laid. Power lines were strung. An intake pipe was extended into the Gulf with the opening 30 feet below the surface—and giant pumps installed to draw 300,000,000 gallons of water a day into the plant.

In the midst of this building drive, representatives of the British Government came to Midland with an urgent plea for Dow Chemical to supply Britain with the magnesium desperately needed for her airplane construction. Britain's magnesium plant could not possibly supply all the metal required.

Dow agreed to produce 8,400,000 pounds of magnesium a year for the British. He ordered an addition to the Midland plant to produce 2,400,000 pounds. The remaining 6,000,000 pounds were to come from an addition to the Freeport plant.

Britain's air fleet had suffered heavily in the weeks of aerial combat with German bombers and fighter planes—the air war which had become known as the Battle of Britain. The battle had begun in July, one month after the fall of France. Hitler's Air Marshal Herman Goering had a fleet of 1,314 bombers, including 316 dive bombers, and 963 fighter planes to send into the battle. The British had between 700 and 800 fighter planes to defend the island.

The German bombers thundered across the channel in waves with swarms of fighters to protect them. During the first weeks they came in daylight, hitting mostly airfields and military targets. Between August 24 and September 6, an average of 1,000 planes a day were over England bombing and strafing. The Royal Air Force lost more than half of its fighters, destroyed or damaged beyond usefulness. But the German losses were so heavy that Hitler was forced to drop his invasion plans, known as Operation Sea Lion.

On September 7, the Germans switched to night raids, concentrating mostly on London. Tens of thousands of men, women, and children were driven to air raid shelters by wailing sirens and the pounding of anti-aircraft guns. The skies were lit with the fires set by bombs and incendiaries. London was mauled. Coventry was destroyed and Plymouth left in ruins. But the men of the RAF won the Battle of Britain in the gallant stand which moved Winston Churchill to say, "Never in the field of human conflict was so much owed by so many to so few."

For a time during this air war, British air experts were puzzled by the large number of bombs which the German planes were able to carry. But then they found the answer in the wreckage of bombers shot down on English soil. The German planes had been built with magnesium alloys as a major structural material and not as a minor material. The weight displaced by the light magnesium alloys gave the planes their greater-than-expected ability to carry large bomb loads.

About the same time that the British were making this discovery, the Assistant Chief of the Army Air Corps in Washington was reporting that magnesium was merely an incidental requirement in American-made planes. He wrote in the August issue of *Aviation Magazine:* "Magnesium—Less than 1.2 per cent of the composite total raw materials constitute the average engine requirements and less than 1 per cent of the airframe and propeller requirements are magnesium."

On this basis, American-built planes would require only 80.4 pounds of magnesium per planes—and the 50,000 planes which President Roosevelt had called for in May would require only about 4,020,000 pounds of magnesium. (As it later developed, the government needed not merely 80.4 pounds per plane, but as much as 2,000 pounds per plane, and the aircraft program leaped from 50,000 planes to 125,000 planes a year.)

Building the added capacity into the Freeport magnesium plant for Britain caused no appreciable delay in the Texas construction and in early January the giant plant was nearing completion.

In later years, Willard Dow would say of the Texas venture: "Dow Chemical seemingly was venturing into the great unknown. It was not for Dow really an adventure into the unknown, for much had been learned at Wilmington. But it was a venture of high daring, for nature has a way of her own and will not always conform exactly to the plans laid for her. That is why research has to be supplemented by experience. That is why also the story of the building of Freeport is not told by a mere recital. There is an epic quality involved in the peopling of a flat, narrow tongue of waste land with strange shapes of structures and having them combine to take a ladle of gleaming metal out of a curling, white-capped ocean wave. Not even the old alchemists, in their wildest fancies, ever got that far.

"Freeport grew prosaically out of concrete and steel, and it had to be described in such terms, but, when all the contrivances have been exactly described and fitted into their places as mere chemical facilities, there still remains a touch of the fairy wand."

By mid-January, 1941—less than a year after ground was broken— the plant was ready for testing. The cell feed was brought from the Midland plant in cake form to be melted in the new cells, because the start-up procedure was a critical operation which determined the proper functioning of the cells.

The process for converting seawater into metal was a complicated series of steps that has been described as "about ten times as formidable as that at Midland." The seawater was pumped into huge settling tanks to be mixed with a milk of lime. The lime came from shells dredged from Galveston Bay, washed, put through a lime kiln, and slaked. The magnesium chloride and magnesium sulphate in the seawater reacted with the lime and formed magnesium hydrate, or milk of magnesia. The heavy milk of magnesia was drawn off into a filtering tank, passed into other cleansing tanks and treated with hydrochloric acid to form magnesium chloride—the same raw material obtained from the Michigan brine through a simpler process. Then the raw material was treated and dried to become cell feed for the electrolytic cells which extracted the pure magnesium. And through this process a barrel of seawater became a third of a pound of magnesium.

On January 21 at 1:45 P.M., big, barrel-chested Clarence Hock—a Midland-trained magnesium operator—dipped a ladle into a vat of molten magnesium and poured the first ingot of magnesium metal to be taken from the sea.

Hock turned to Willard Dow and grinned. He said, "Well, Willard, we've done it!"

But only the small group of Dow Chemical technicians, operators, and officials clustered around Clarence Hock knew of the achievement. No one had thought to notify the newspapers or the wire services in order to publicize the history-making event. The first public notice that magnesium had been taken from seawater was a brief statement by Willard Dow given to "*The Freeport Facts*—Brazoria County's Most Complete Newspaper." The statement appeared in print two days after the ingot was poured.

It was not until three days after the event that the news reached Midland. A telegram was sent from Freeport to the editor of the *Dow Diamond,* the company's family magazine, which said:

Chapter Twelve

```
                    WESTERN UNION
                        TELEGRAM
                     W. P. MARSHALL, PRESIDENT
```

        FIRST MAGNESIUM METAL FROM SEA-WATER WAS POURED JANUARY 21, 1941,
    AT 1:45 P.M. AT FREEPORT, TEXAS. CLARENCE HOOK, MIDLAND OPERATOR,
    POURED THE FIRST BILLET.

        THOSE PRESENT INCLUDED W.H. DOW, G.M. MCGRANAHAN, E.O. BARSTOW,
    HARLAND SHERBROOK, RALPH SCHNEIDER, S.B. HEATH, WILLIAM SCHAMBRA,
    LEWIS WARD, JACK STEIN, R.M. HUNTER, DAVE LANDSBOROUGH, JOE GLESNER AND
    JOE O'CONNOR.

        MIDLAND OPERATORS WERE JAKE SCHWEIGERT, CLARENCE HOOK, ANTON SUNDEOJ,
    PAUL HOLZINGER AND BILL RAVE.

        FREEPORT OPERATORS WERE JORDAN L. MARIAN, DON C. LINSAY,
    GRADY LAWSON, BRANTLEY WALER, JAMES BRYAN, EWING F. EDWARDS.
    EARL SHENK, CLARENCE W. PATTERSON, MARCUS KRUEGER, PHILIP KENDRICKS,
    FLOYD HONEYCUT, LEO HELLMAN, LUTHER WALDEN, LEE HELLUMS, CHARLES
    MEYER, CLYDE PATTERSON AND W.W. CECIL.

The announcement and folksy listing of all those present was hardly an example of high-pressure public relations and communication. The editor of the *Dow Diamond* was flabbergasted and chagrined. No one had told him the historic event was to take place. And he was not prepared to handle the flood of inquiries that poured in from newspapers, magazines, columnists, and science writers asking for details of the startling accomplishment.

This was a time for elation. But the elation was short-lived. A few days after the first ingot was poured, the magnesium cells began to boil over. An unfamiliar sludge began to form in the cells, as much as a ton a day. Cells designed to produce 1,000 pounds of magnesium a day were producing 100 pounds. And the old saying that "Maggie is a temperamental bitch" was holding true.

Nothing like this had been experienced by Dow Chemical in its twenty-five years of making magnesium metal. Shock waves ran through the company. Just as pressures were building for more deliveries of magnesium, the Texas giant appeared to have failed.

Beutel would recall: "Willard would call and ask about our production and I'd tell him. He would say, 'What's the matter with you people down there?' I explained there was something mysterious in the brine that wasn't making anything but sludge. He said, 'There is nothing mysterious about chemistry. All you have to do is find out what it is.' I was losing my temper, too. I yelled back, 'What do you think we're doing? We're trying to find out what it is.'"

Not only were the cells giving trouble, but the shelf dryer was not functioning properly. Beutel called Barstow in Midland. "Ed," he said, "come down and help me out. I'm in misery."

Barstow hurried to Freeport to lend a hand. Samples of the Gulf water were sent to all Dow Chemical laboratories and to several private laboratories to see if they could isolate a chemical substance, not found in Michigan brine, which could be causing the cell difficulty.

Someone suggested the plant be shut down, the cells cleaned out, and the operation started over again.

"Listen," said Beutel, "I'll shoot the first man that pulls a switch on a mag cell. At least we're getting a hundred pounds of mag—and a hundred pounds is better than nothing. If we don't keep running we'll never find out what went wrong." Barstow agreed with Beutel: Keep the plant running.

Early in March, Chemist Leo Greene in Freeport called Dow Chemical's magnesium cell expert, Ralph Hunter, and reported, "I don't know whether this is significant or not, but I've noticed the percentage of boron in Texas cell feed is going up." Boron had been found in the Gulf water in the ratio of 150 parts per million.

Hunter bought, at a grocery store in Midland, a box of borax—a household product that contains boron. A small amount was added to the feed in one of the Midland magnesium cells. And boron was found to be the culprit.

Robert Blue, one of those involved in the search for the trouble, would recall: "The cell test started about four o'clock in the afternoon of March 7. Charlie Wiles came in late that evening and asked the men in the cell house how the cell was doing. They said it was doing terribly and Charlie said, 'That's wonderful!' The operators couldn't see anything wonderful about it. They had a very horrible mess on their hands. But it was on that evening that we established conclusively for the first time what impurity was causing the trouble in Texas. It was boron."

The next step was to find a way to eliminate the boron. Soon the chemists in Ted Heath's Chemical Engineering Laboratory found that boron could be knocked out of the cell feed by adding lime during the hydrating process. The over-liming kept the boron in solution and it flowed off in the waste water. The remedy was simple and inexpensive. And with the boron and shelf-dryer problems solved, the production of magnesium jumped to the planned level.

There was trouble piled on trouble for Willard Dow in those first hectic days of 1941. Even as the boron problem was developing in Texas, The Dow Chemical Company's monopoly position in the production of magnesium was under attack from the Department of Justice.

On January 30, nine days after the first magnesium was poured at Freeport, a federal grand jury in New York, acting at the request of Assistant United States Attorney General Thurman Arnold, returned an indictment charging the company had achieved its dominant position in magnesium illegally. More specifically, the indictment charged that Willard Dow and Treasurer Earl Bennett, the American Magnesium Corporation, and the Magnesium Development Corporation (with certain of their officers) had entered into a conspiracy as far back as 1927:

(a) To prevent any person other than Dow Chemical from producing magnesium.
(b) To limit the production and sale of magnesium products to the defendants and the defendants' sublicensees, and to eliminate competition among fabricators in the solicitation, obtaining a retention of customers.
(c) To control the price of magnesium and magnesium products and to prevent price competition.
(d) To pool patents relating to the production of magnesium and fabrication of magnesium products in order to prevent competition and control prices.

The Department of Justice issued a press release which, in summary, gave these five reasons for the action:

1. The existence of inadequate facilities for producing magnesium.
2. That an alleged conspiracy between the American companies and the German firm had "restricted, restrained and discouraged" development and use of magnesium in airplane manufacture.
3. A serious shortage of foundry facilities for fabricating magnesium products that has "seriously impeded and delayed" aircraft production.
4. The price of magnesium in the United States has been maintained at an artificially, unreasonably high level in contrast to prices abroad.
5. The alleged conspiracy had resulted in maintaining a single producer in the United States.

Willard Dow did not dispute the monopoly charge for, indeed, The Dow Chemical Company did have a monopoly position. But he denied the conspiracy charge and the other allegations. His position was that the monopoly had developed from the fact that after World War I all the magnesium producers dropped out of the field simply because they saw no profit in making the metal; Herbert Dow had refused to drop out because he was convinced that magnesium would one day take its place as an important metal alongside aluminum and steel. He insisted the cross-licensing agreements neither had limited production nor blocked others from entering the field. To the charge of inadequate facilities, he maintained the plant capacity existed to produce even more magnesium than the government's own agencies estimated would be needed. Furthermore, he pointed out that the company had lost money on magnesium for more than fifteen years before turning a profit.

Perhaps to nail down his point about the adequacy of production, Dow called Washington a few days after the indictment was returned. He offered to step up magnesium production by another 100,000,000 pounds a year, with Dow Chemical financing the expansion, if the government would agree to buy the metal. The offer was not accepted.

There was never a trial to settle the conspiracy issue in court.

Late in 1941, Dow called Thurman Arnold in Washington and sought to have the case adjourned until the war emergency was over. The substance of the conversation as taken down at the time was this:

"Dr. Dow stated that he was disturbed over the fact that on next Tuesday, October 21, the Department was going to set the case down for trial next April unless all parties indicate their willingness to enter into a plea of nolo contendere assuming that a satisfactory decree and fines could be worked out. Dow said that it was impossible for the Dow Company to make magnesium and at the same time defend an anti-trust suit. Arnold said it is necessary to do both and that the Department could not nolle pros our case on the above grounds. Dow asked for an adjournment of our case until after the emergency. Arnold said that this could not be done. He said that if they did it for the Dow case, he would have to postpone all of the cases until after the emergency. Dow said why shouldn't they do this. Arnold suggested that his advice was for one individual to plead and no doubt satisfactory fines could be worked out at a later date."

Dow and the other defendants chose not to contest the government's charges. They entered a plea of nolo contendere after criminal charges had been dropped by the government and an equity suit substituted.

In the case of Tucker v. United States, 1912, 196 Fed. 260, there is this definition of nolo contendere: "The plea is in the nature of a compromise between the state and the defendant—a matter not of right but of favor. Various reasons may exist why a defendant conscious of innocence may be willing to forego his right to make defense if he can be premitted to do so without acknowledging his guilt. Whether in a particular case he should be permitted to do so is for the court."

The defendants paid fines totaling $140,000 and for the time being that was where the matter rested.

Government and military men first began to realize the importance of magnesium for plane-building as information from the Battle of Britain gave a clearer picture of how the Germans were building their planes. In March, 1941, the government's Defense Plant Corporation—a subsidiary of the Reconstruction Finance Corporation—asked Dow Chemical to add an 18,000,000—pound addition to its magnesium plant in Texas. The addition was in production within eight months at a cost to the government of about five cents a pound in terms of annual capacity.

Then it seemed that Washington suddenly was seized by a magnesium panic. The British were asking for more magnesium, not only for planes but for incendiary bombs with which to strike at Germany's war plant. The Office of Price Administration (OPM) earmarked 400,000 pounds of the 18,000,000 pounds from Texas for the British.

The OPM in June went all out to increase production of magnesium to 400,000,000 pounds—a figure later expanded to 600,000,000 pounds. Cost was no object. Production was all-important. Special incentives in financing and priorities were offered to companies which would turn to magnesium production for the government's account. The Army Air Corps's estimate of 40.8 pounds per plane in August, 1940, had leaped to more than 1,000 pounds per plane in June, 1941.

By this time, America's plane production was beginning to climb. Bombers built for the British were being flown into Canadian airfields and then ferried to England. The American air fleet was taking on muscle, too, and the country that could use only 480,000 pounds of magnesium in 1938 now wanted more than 500,000,000 pounds of the metal produced on quick order.

The government asked Dow Chemical to make its know-how in magnesium production and fabrication available to other companies on request. Willard Dow agreed. Within a short time ten companies had contracted with the DPC to build and operate magnesium plants for the government. Two companies chose to use the Dow process. They were the Diamond Magnesium Company of Painesville, Ohio, and the International Minerals and Chemical Corporation of Austin, Texas.

They planned to get their raw material from crushed dolomite ore rather than brine.

The government began to pour some $515,000,000 into an expansion of the magnesium industry in an unprecedented crash program. Fortune magazine would say of this drive:

The technology of magnesium production suddenly proliferated in all directions. There was no longer time for hunting the most efficient process. The single, governing factor was production—fast, expense no object. From 1940 through 1942, OPM and WPB (War Production Board) authorized construction of fourteen new magnesium plants.... Perhaps no other program in the entire war effort has provoked more scientific criticism, political investigation, and plain back-fence gossip....

Among those who entered the field were Mathieson Alkali Works, Lake Charles, Louisiana; Basic Magnesium, Incorporated, near Las Vegas; Permanente Metals Corporation, Permanente, California, a subsidiary of Henry J. Kaiser; and Ford Motor Company.

Meantime, Willard Dow pushed the expansion of other Dow Chemical manufacturing units, rushing to completion the third styrene plant to be built in two years. He gambled that styrene was going to be a basic product in huge demand, and Dow Chemical was the sole producer in the country.

Early in 1941, Dow had tried without luck to interest the government in a synthetic rubber program. Dow Chemical and the Goodyear Tire and Rubber Company in 1940 had formed the Goodyear Dow Corporation to produce synthetic rubber from styrene and butadiene—the same primary ingredients used by the Germans to free Germany from dependence on the raw rubber of the Far East. Dow proposed to the Reconstruction Finance Corporation that the Goodyear Dow Corporation produce annually 10,000 long tons of synthetic rubber for the government, either of the Buna-N or Buna-S type.

The offer was premature. Washington had not yet become alarmed over the possibility of a rubber shortage although President Roosevelt was watching, with growing concern, Japan's conquests in the Far East. The rubber scare would not explode for another year.

At the annual meeting of the Dow Chemical stockholders on August 21, 1941, Willard Dow could not resist making an I-told-you-so comment on the sudden importance of magnesium.

"It was twenty-seven years ago," he said, "that Herbert Dow said, 'There must and will be a major use for a metal as light as magnesium.'

As you have seen, magnesium in the past three years has risen from a relatively obscure material to one of the most strategic and talked of metals in the world."

The military men who had virtually ignored magnesium three years earlier were now calling for more and more of the metal for planes and incendiaries and flares. And in November the Defense Plant Corporation contracted with Dow Chemical to build a 72,000,000-pound plant for the government at Velasco, Texas, only a short distance from Freeport. This was in addition to the 18,000,000-pound plant which was starting production for the DPC.

In a small way, Willard Dow received some balm for the bruises in 1941 when in early December *Chemical and Metallurgical Engineering* magazine presented its Chemical Engineering Award to The Dow Chemical Company for the achievement of taking magnesium from the sea.

In accepting the award for the company, Dow said: "There is not a single engineer in the world who alone could have handled this complicated job. It was only through group cooperation, with every engineer contributing his own individual talent, that results were made possible in so short a time."

(Note: At this time, Dow singled out sixteen of his men for special recognition in the development of the Texas plant. They were: E. O. Barstow, W. R. Veazey, A. P. Beutel, S. B. Heath, F. R. Minger, L. E. Ward, R. M. Hunter, I. F. Harlow, E. R. Stein, L. J. Richards, E. R. MacLaughlin, G. M. McGranahan, C. M. Shigley, George W. Greene, N. D. Griswold, and G. F. Dressel.)

The strains and stresses of that last year of peace for the United States were only the signals of greater pressures to follow. For on December 6, 1941, a task force of the Japanese fleet steamed secretly into the unguarded waters northwest of Hawaii. At dawn the next day, war planes swept from the decks of aircraft carriers, sped low over the water to the Island of Oahu, and caught the ships of the United States' Pacific Fleet unguarded at Pearl Harbor.

For 110 terrible minutes the Japanese pounded warships, airfields, and oil storage tanks. When they left, the fleet was shattered and the United States was at war.

Chapter Thirteen

In the first weeks after Pearl Harbor, there were fears the Japanese were preparing for an invasion of the West Coast. Coastal cities were blacked out at night. Civil defense teams took their stations to be ready to protect homes, businesses and industries from fire bombs. With the Pacific fleet a battered wreck, the oceans no longer offered security from attack. Or so it seemed.

Japan's armies seized Indo-China, Malaya, Sumatra, Java, and Bali—giving the invaders control of 90 percent of the world's production of crude rubber. And then, five months after Pearl Harbor, the Japanese forced the surrender of the American defenders of Bataan. Japan, for the time being, was the master of the Pacific.

On the other side of the world, Hitler dominated most of Europe while his partner, Mussolini, carved out an empire in Africa and claimed the Mediterranean as his own lake.

As Americans answered the call to arms, the government sent an urgent plea to The Dow Chemical Company to rush construction of the 72,000,000-pound magnesium plant which Willard Dow had agreed to build for the government. It was decided the plant would be located at Velasco, Texas. Drawings of the new plant, virtually a duplicate of the Freeport operation, were completed in December.

Once again the job of pushing the construction fell to the hard-driving Dutch Beutel. Fortunately, he had around him the same experienced men who had helped build the Freeport plant—McGranahan, Shigley, Griswold, and others.

The government recruited men in Texas and even in distant states to work on the Velasco plant. They began to arrive in January by train, truck, bus, and wheezing secondhand automobiles. Some brought their own trailers and staked out home sites beside the road. They came by the thousands to dig ditches, hammer nails, lay pipes, string electric lines, pour concrete, drive trucks, and do the jobs that had to be done. Freeport and Velasco could not possibly house the small army. The first arrivals lived in shacks, tents, automobiles, and houses as far away as Houston. Rents charged for shacks, garages, and rooms skyrocketed.

The Dow Chemical Company and Defense Plant Corporation moved swiftly to get the workers into houses and to provide reasonable comforts. This job fell to Alden Dow, the younger brother of Willard who had chosen to follow a career in architecture rather than go into the chemical business.

Alden Dow had been graduated in 1931 from Columbia University's School of Architecture. For five months in 1933 he had studied under the famed Frank Lloyd Wright. Then he had opened an office in his home in Midland from which he could look across the garden vistas landscaped by his father. He had won international recognition in 1937 when awarded the Diplome de Grand Prix for residential architecture in the United States. The competition was sponsored by the Paris International Exposition.

Within a matter of weeks, Alden Dow had plans drawn for a workers' community dubbed Camp Chemical. The design called for twenty-one-hundred fabricated one-room cottages for the married workers and forty-six barracks for the single men; a central cafeteria to seat one thousand; a community entertainment hall; a library; a large community store the size of a modern supermarket; barber shop, beauty parlor, firehouse, and police station; and laundries and bath houses. The whole was tied together with shell-topped roads and walkways, gas mains, electricity, running water, and sewer lines.

Carpenters—two thousand of them—hammered together sections of walls, roofs and flooring and fitted one section to another. The speed with which Camp Chemical rose on the flat, sandy acres was a triumph of planning. Construction began on February 20, 1942, and thirty-one days later Camp Chemical was officially opened.

The same urgency spurred the construction of the magnesium plant. With the experience of the Freeport building behind them, Beutel and his men were able to pare weeks from the time that the work normally would have taken. This time, shortcuts were taken. Gas and water pipes were laid on top of the ground. Roadways were built on fills above ground level and topped with concrete, eliminating the old problem of trucks and equipment bogging down in mud during the winter rains.

Beutel had promised the plant would be in operation by July 1. But when June came, some of his engineers said it would be impossible to meet the deadline.

"We'll meet the deadline," Beutel said. "I've already invited people from Washington and Midland to be here June 26 to see the first magnesium poured."

The first ingot of magnesium was poured at the Velasco plant, as Beutel promised, on June 26. This time not even a belated public announcement was made that the plant had gone into operation to take magnesium from the sea. Secrecy cloaked much of the wartime effort across the nation.

Beutel would recall: "When we started the Velasco job, I said to myself, 'I've got to be an athlete to live through this.' I quit smoking and I didn't have a highball all through that six months. Willard came down for the ceremonies when the plant started production and when he and the Washington brass left late that afternoon, I found myself all alone. I was bushed from the excitement of the day and the long strain of the job. I said to myself, 'Hell, I haven't had a cigaret or a drink for months and that's bad.' So I went out to the kitchen, got a bottle of Scotch, sat down at the table, and opened the Scotch and a package of Camels. I think I smoked the whole package of cigarets and had about three big drinks before I went to bed. I slept like a log."

The most urgent need for Camp Chemical passed with the completion of the Velasco plant and the release of many of the workers. But Alden Dow still had a job ahead of him the likes of which come to few architects: the planning and designing of a permanent town from the ground up.

This was to be no Camp Chemical, hastily put together as a temporary solution to a transient labor problem. This was to be a small city with shopping center, stores, services, utilities, and homes primarily for the men and women who worked for The Dow Chemical Company and would make the town their home.

The site that intrigued Dow was an area of more than 5,000 acres inland from Velasco near Lake Jackson. This freshwater lake stood on what once had been a large plantation. Across the land meandered Oyster Creek, a clean, clear stream where lunker bass lay under lily pads and wild ducks settled for the winter.

In Civil War days, the acreage had belonged to Major Abner Jackson. It was part of an estate of three plantations sprawling over 70,000 acres in South Texas. A brick mansion sat among moss-draped pin oaks with slave quarters nearby. Fat cattle and a herd of one hundred and fifty horses and mules grazed in pastures fenced off from the cotton fields and orchards. In the woodlands roamed deer, wild turkeys, opossums, coons, and an occasional bear.

Legend has it that after the Major's death, his two sons quarreled over the division of the estate. One shot the other fatally and then died himself two weeks later from wounds and exposures suffered during the

Civil War. No one ever knew the whole story of the family tragedy. But the old mansion crumbled away. A jungle grew up about Lake Jackson and Oyster Creek. The Jackson estate passed from the family into the hands of strangers, was divided and redivided.

The area was a jungle when Alden Dow first saw it. But in the thickets of brush and dewberry, blackberry, ivy, and grape vines stood towering, gnarled old trees of oak, cypress, and elm which in his mind's eye he could see casting shade over winding streets and homes. The land stood well above flood levels, offering protection from high water as well as the Texas sun and the winds from the Gulf.

The first bulldozers, and mule teams pulling scoop shovels, began ripping into the jungle early in 1942. Before the summer ended there were paved streets winding among the trees—streets called Winding Way, Azalia, Yaupon, Bluebonnet, Lantana, and Lupine. And, with a pixie sense of humor, Dow named on street Thisway and another Thatway. All the streets curled and circled in a pattern that left no angles.

The houses that soon began to border the streets of Lake Jackson had the distinctive, modern appearance of all Dow-designed homes. Private builders moved in, too, to help the development. Federal Housing Authority loans helped buyers finance home purchases. And within less than two years Lake Jackson was a thriving town of 2,800 population, generating its own growth and government so rapidly that Dow Chemical could withdraw to the sidelines.

The fast growth of the chemical plants at Freeport and Velasco, and the creation of a modern town in a jungle, were hardly noticed by the rest of the country in the hurly-burly of those first months of war. Too much was happening too fast at too many places.

Fear of Japanese raids on coastal regions by carrier-borne bombers lingered for months after Pearl Harbor. The psychological impact of the attack was such that the military for some time had little faith in its ability to defend the continental United States from another hit-and-run raid. As a result, the War Department circled on its maps the areas considered "safe" for new or expanded war plants and the areas considered "unsafe." No plant was considered in a safe area if it stood within two hundred miles of the border.

The net effect of these early and exaggerated fears was to drive new war plants inland, separating them from natural sources of raw materials and hiking the cost of war production.

Willard Dow would recall: "After the war started it was a great handicap to us in going to Washington to develop priorities for materials, to find in every office a War Department map with zones marked favorable for further development and expansion and other zones marked unfavorable or where no expansion should be made. In the early maps it is interesting to know that Detroit was marked as a zone for no new developments. . . . The Army program started out with two strikes against it on all its stipulations, with their saying no new developments should be made within 200 or 300 miles of our borders. However, from the standpoint of actual production and economic factors involved, this stipulation threw so many stumbling blocks in the way, it tended to slow things up, as red tape necessarily does. . . ."

These restrictions came into play in March, 1942, when the government asked Dow Chemical to add still another 72,000,000 pounds of production to its magnesium plants. Willard Dow suggested that the Velasco plant, already being built, be expanded to take the magnesium from seawater. But government authorities insisted it could not be built near the coast.

The upshot was that Dow Chemical was authorized to build the plant at Ludington, Michigan, northwest of Midland, where brine could be pumped from the underground reservoir. The project was plagued with war-related difficulties from the start. Shortages of materials developed and the Defense Plant Corporation could not find the electric generating equipment needed for a plant of that size.

The problems were solved by building the first-stage plant at Ludington and the final-stage plant across the state at Marysville, where power was available from Detroit. The cell feed was made at Ludington, shipped across the state, and then fed into the cells at Marysville to produce the finished magnesium metal. By June, 1943, these plants were in operation, raising the nation's total magnesium-making capacity to 576,000,000 pounds a year. Of this total, Dow Chemical and the plants using the Dow process were responsible for 258,000,000 pounds.

At Bay City, Michigan, the company's magnesium foundry and fabricating division was a hive of activity. It had started in 1934 as a small plant building Dowmetal trailers for hauling new cars from automobile factories to dealers. It had developed into the nation's largest center of research into the engineering, design, and use of magnesium.

One of the more important developments during the war emergency came when the Bay City center proved to the Army and Navy that airplane structures could be made safely of magnesium. They designed and built wings for a trainer plane used by both services. The wings passed all government tests with a 17 percent saving in weight.

The magnesium plane wings were possible because the Dow Chemical researchers had discovered ways to form magnesium into sheets, to bend the sheets with heat to desired forms, to weld them and to rivet them.

Dow Chemical turned over to other companies its accumulated knowledge in magnesium fabrication. The techniques of sand and mold casting were given to 192 companies which had contracts to make plane parts. Sixty-eight other companies were taught the tricks of incendiary bomb casting, rolling mill operations, forging practices, and die casting.

The forced growth of the magnesium industry in the United States after Pearl Harbor was a mixture of remarkable achievement and costly failure. The sorriest record was in the story of Basic Magnesium organized by Basic Refractories of Cleveland, Ohio, to take part in the drive for magnesium. The company started with a $24,000 investment in magnesium-bearing ore lands, obtained a $70,000,000 contract from the Defense Plant Corporation to build a plant near Las Vegas, Nevada, and failed dismally in the production of the metal. The eventual cost to the government was later estimated at $133,000,000.

The management of Basic Magnesium had no experience in magnesium production and attempted to use a copy of a British plant which had been licensed under German patents. The plant site itself—halfway between Las Vegas and Boulder—was 950 miles from the company's ore deposits. It cost $6 to ship one ton of ore from the mill to the plant.

A government investigation forced a transfer of the management from Basic Magnesium to the Anaconda Copper Company in October, 1942, and Anaconda soon had the plant in production. But Basic's performance was by all odds the worst blot on the magnesium record during the war.

A Senate investigating committee would say of the Basic operation: "In the opinion of the committee this was one of the most unjustified contracts which was proposed in connection with the war program and represented a wholly unwarranted advance of Government funds to a newly organized corporation which had no financial resources and only the most meager experience and talent."

This report came from a special Senate committee appointed to keep watch over the huge wartime spending programs. The committee was headed by the then Senator from Missouri, Harry S. Truman, and it became known as the Truman Watchdog Committee.

During the Truman committee's inquiry into magnesium production, Willard Dow saw an opportunity to defend himself and The

Dow Chemical Company from the conspiracy charges which had been made by the Department of Justice in 1941. The accusation that rankled most was that he had entered into a conspiracy which had the effect of giving Germany indirect control over Dow Chemical's prewar magnesium production and prevented others from entering the field.

On March 6, 1944, Dow went before the committee to testify. He had spent weeks organizing his testimony and when he sat in the witness chair he launched a fighting defense of Dow Chemical's record, with no apologies.

"In the twenty-two years from 1918 to 1939," he said, "Dow made and sold magnesium at a loss in all except four years. In 1939 Dow was the only surviving American producer and had been for more than ten years. No one else cared to take the punishment. It had steadily expanded production to reduce costs and had brought the price down from $5 a pound in 1915 to 21 cents in 1939, in the hope of increasing consumption. But still it could not in most years dispose of its production.

"No one in authority in 1940 recognized magnesium as a vital war material or that Dow had created a national asset. Although Washington refused to recognize that magnesium could be a vital element in the national defense, Dow knew that inevitably it must be and in full faith and courage doubled the production capacity at Midland and greatly expanded research to cover the needs of national defense.

"Dow boldly conceived a project to recover magnesium from the waters of the sea and in March, 1940, began the erecting of a plant on the Gulf, at Freeport, Texas, to do what man had never done before, and at the same time it began further additions to facilities in Michigan. By the end of the year, Dow had under way facilities for the production of thirty-six million pounds of magnesium a year and had spent around twenty-five million dollars of money raised by selling stock and by borrowing. . . .

"The war side of Washington went all out for magnesium with a $400,000,000 program designed to produce from six hundred to seven hundred million pounds of magnesium a year. These were the same war authorities who had been content with six million pounds only two years before and fourteen million pounds only a few months before.

"The war side of the Government turned to Dow, asking the help of its technicians to teach others how to make magnesium and at the same time asked Dow to erect and operate for the account of the Government a seventy-two million pound plant using sea water at Velasco, Texas. This Dow agreed to do.

"Dow in 1942 also agreed to build and operate for the Government a seventy-two million pound plant at Ludington-Marysville, Michigan, using brine as at Midland.

"With the Dow skill available and with Government money also for the asking, only two concerns chose the Dow services.

"Eight other concerns going into magnesium with Government money followed processes other than Dow's. . . .

"There is another side. While the Government's right hand was pressing Dow for more production and more plants, its left hand was stretching out as a barrier. Through the second half of 1940, as Dow was building plants, an Assistant Attorney General was presenting evidence to a Federal Grand Jury. In January, 1941, while Dow was getting the great Freeport plant into producing from sea water, this Grand Jury brought in an indictment charging Dow with monopoly.

"The Dow Company and its chief officers were forced by the Government—its right hand unmindful of its left—to choose between defending themselves and putting their skill in the service of the nation. They could not at the same time be in a court defending their honor and be in a factory defending their country. They had no choice, in April, 1942, but to placate by pleading nolo contendere and agreeing to a consent decree. They had to submit to indignity in order to get on with the business of the war. . . ."

Dow outlined the history of magnesium production in the United States from its earliest days, and then he concluded:

"The magnesium program of the Government, and consequently the source of supply to the Allies, was made possible by the foresight of The Dow Chemical Company in having ready the facilities for production when and as the materials were needed.

"In 1942, the critical year in magnesium production, Dow produced 84.2 per cent of all the magnesium output in the country, and the Dow Group as a whole produced 91.2 per cent. . .

"Here are the facts for the year 1943:

". . . The rated annual capacity of all magnesium metal plants in the country was 580,000,000 pounds.

"The Dow group had 44 per cent of this rated capacity, and yet during 1943 they produced 60 per cent of all magnesium made.

"The Dow group produced 87 per cent of its rated capacity [others 46 per cent]. . . .

"On the assumption that the Government had spent $400,000,000 on its magnesium program and that the Dow group had $150,000,000 of the total, the Dow group had 38 per cent of the money spent. On this basis:

"The Government has an investment of $.80 for every pound of magnesium produced in 1943 by the Dow group.

"The Government has an investment of $1.67 for every pound of magnesium produced in 1943 by the others.

"The Government received 1.2 pounds of magnesium in 1943 for every dollar invested with the Dow group.

"The Government received only half as much [.6 pounds] in 1943 for every dollar invested with the others."

When the Truman Committee made its official report one week later, it conceded that the cross-licensing agreement which Dow Chemical had made with the Magnesium Development Corporation had not limited production.

One paragraph said in part: "Dow Chemical never has been a licensee of Magnesium Development Corporation production patents but only of fabrication patents, under a cross-licensing agreement. Therefore, Dow Chemical was never limited in the volume of its production. . . ."

The Committee added: "The committee is interested in this past history, not for the purpose of assessing blame for any possible violation of the antitrust statutes, but for the purpose of understanding the background of the magnesium industry. Both Dow Chemical and Alcoa were active in that industry. Dow Chemical incurred original losses in order to produce magnesium and to improve the production techniques. Both Dow Chemical and Alcoa incurred initial losses in order to find and develop the use of new techniques of fabricating magnesium. Without their efforts, we might not have had any magnesium industry, or again the absence of any price differentials or cross-licensing agreements might have induced others to enter the field and to make greater contributions than either Dow Chemical or Alcoa. . . "

The committee then praised Dow Chemical for its wartime record, saying: "The magnesium plants owned or operated by The Dow Chemical Co. and the magnesium plants for which The Dow Chemical Co. acted as consultant and adviser reached 100 per cent production within 5 to 7 months from the start of operations. Other companies, new to the magnesium field, with processes heretofore not utilized in this country, took a longer period to reach capacity operation, and even at the present time there are a few of the projects which are still experiencing production difficulties and have not reached capacity operation. The extent to which magnesium requirements were met is due in no small part to the established production of The Dow

Chemical Co. and the speed with which additional projects using the Dow process were brought into production."

On the Sunday following the committee's report, the New York *Herald Tribune* had an editorial comment to make:

In its report on war-time magnesium production, just made public, the Truman committee has high praise for the Dow Chemical Company, to which it gives the major share of the credit for the nation's success in meeting its requirements. However, some of the edge is taken off this citation by what the committee has to say about the company's prewar record. Noting that Germany's production in 1933 was 33 million pounds, against only 7 million pounds for Dow Chemical, the sole American producer, the committee issues a dictum to the effect that it is "incumbent" on any firm holding a monopoly on any type of production to make certain that the United States at least equals other countries in output of that material.

Commenting on this latter suggestion, Dr. Willard H. Dow, president of the chemical company, notes pointedly that "Germany and the countries preparing for war, as opposed to the United States, operating entirely for peace, represent two entirely different modes of living, two entirely different approaches to the development of markets, and in no sense is there any comparison between the two."

In the rather ungracious observation of the Truman committee two criticisms seem to be implicit: first, that Dow Chemical enjoyed a monopoly in the field of magnesium production which enabled it to determine the amount produced in the prewar years; second, that it was lacking in foresight with respect to war-time needs. It is true that in the middle of the war effort the Justice Department brought monopoly charges against the company, but Dr. Dow has denied these emphatically, and certainly the record, on its face, seems to sustain him. It shows, for example, that in the twenty-two years, from 1918 to 1939, despite the fact that the company was reducing prices from $5 a pound to 21 cents a pound, it lost money on its magnesium activities in all but four years and could not dispose of its production. Dr. Dow's statement that his firm enjoyed no basic patents which would give it a monopoly seems to be borne out by the events of the war.

In 1940, according to the unrefuted testimony of Dr. Dow, this company alone foresaw the importance of magnesium in the war effort and proceeded on its own convictions and with its own resources to construct additional facilities with a productive capacity of 36 million pounds of the metal. In December of that year the advisory commission of the Council on National Defense, on the advice of the Army-Navy Munitions Board, was reporting to the President that 1941 requirements would be only 14 million pounds, those of 1942, 22 million. It was not until the early months of 1941 that the Office of Production Management awakened in a panic to the realization that earlier estimates should have been at least ten times higher than they were. The Dow company was called in to help get a $400 million program under way, and in 1942—the critical production year—the group of plants which it organized produced more than 91 per cent of the nation's metallic magnesium. And it produced it twice as economically as competitors following other processes.

In the light of this record it can hardly be said that the head of Dow Chemical is overstating the case when he declares that his company has "served the country in spite of, and not because of, the government."

In that same week, *Time* magazine played the committee report prominently in its Business & Finance section under the heading "Dow Up, Jones Down." The article said in part:

When World War II caught the U. S. desperately short of magnesium, a No. 1 component of incendiaries and planes, the Federal Government spilled out $515,000,000 to expand the infant industry. Last week, the Senate's wallet-watching Truman Committee ended a two-year probe of: 1) whether the U. S. got its money's worth; 2) what will happen to the new industry at war's end. Its report:

Praised Michigan's Dow Chemical Co. which, with its licensees, turned out 61% of all U. S. magnesium last year.

Roundly condemned the contract made by Jesse Jones's Defense Plant Corp. with Basic Magnesium, Inc., to build the country's biggest magnesium plant at Las Vegas, Nev.

Gave Henry Kaiser a pat on the back for his Permanente project which, despite WPB pessimism, has produced 19,000,000 lb. and has 'future possibilities.'

To Dow Chemical (only prewar U. S. magnesium manufacturer) the mild praise was sweet. But even sweeter to the company's white-haired president, Dr. Willard H. Dow, was the deathblow the Committee gave to the popular belief that the U. S. magnesium shortage was due to an agreement between Dow, Alcoa and Germany's I. G. Farben. Under that deal—so the libelous rumor ran—Dow magnesium manufacture was limited while German production was kited. Other agreements brought antitrust indictments down on the heads of Dow and Alcoa in 1941, forced them to pay $140,000 in fines after pleading nolo contendere ("We couldn't spend months in court and still have time to expand production").

The Committee had now found that the agreement "probably assisted in fabricating magnesium and increasing its commercial use in the U. S. though price differentials may have kept newcomers out of the field." "Dow Chemical was never limited in its production."

Rather, it "incurred original losses in order to produce magnesium Without (Dow's) interest the production of magnesium in the U. S. might not have been so great". . . .

The generally favorable stories in the press were, indeed, sweet to Willard Dow. But he was not yet willing to let the matter rest. He felt that the committee report, and some newspaper stories based on the report, left the impression that Dow Chemical had done something illegal or unpatriotic in selling 1,525,027 pounds of magnesium to Japan in 1938.

Dow wrote to Secretary of State Cordell Hull, saying:

"During 1938, The Dow Chemical Company accepted in the ordinary course of business orders from Mitsui & Company, Ltd., 350 Fifth Avenue, New York City, totaling 1,525,027 pounds of pure, ingot magnesium and in accordance with instructions, duly shipped the orders to them f.a.s. New York. We did not inquire whether or not the magnesium was for the account of the Japanese Government or the use to which it was to be put, since we were not asked for technological service.

"On Monday, March 6, 1944, while testifying before the Senate Committee investigating the National Defense Program, I was asked by counsel for the Committee if we had obtained clearance for the shipment from the Department of State and also why we had not investigated the use to which the magnesium was to be put. The inference or innuendo was that we had in some fashion neglected our duty as citizens.

"I am writing to discover if you will be good enough to inform me whether or not this Company failed to perform any duty in the premises which it should properly have performed. . . ."

Secretary Hull replied: ". . . The President's Proclamation of May 1, 1937. . . proclaimed a list of articles to be considered arms, ammunition and implements of war. Magnesium is not included in this list which was in effect throughout 1938. There was no other law administered by the Secretary of State requiring such a license at that time."

With Secretary Hull's permission, Willard Dow sent copies of the correspondence to editors throughout the country. And so the bitter magnesium dispute was laid to rest.

But the magnesium production drive was only one of the emergencies into which Dow Chemical was swept in those years of crisis. The war caught the nation with an alarming shortage of crude rubber reserves. And suddenly there was a frantic scramble to find a synthetic rubber that would meet not only the expanding needs of the military, but the requirements of a people who now traveled on rubber-tired wheels.

The government finally decided to concentrate on producing a synthetic rubber known as Buna-S which also became known as GRS (Government Rubber, Styrene). This plastic material could be made from butadiene and styrene, both relatively inexpensive materials.

Once again—as in the magnesium crisis—Dow Chemical held the key to immediate large-scale production of a critical war material. It was the only company in the United States producing styrene on a commercial basis.

President Roosevelt became concerned over the nation's natural rubber stockpiles after the outbreak of war in Europe. When Germany invaded Poland in September, 1939, the United States had a reserve of only 125,000 long tons of crude rubber—and there was no synthetic rubber industry.

By 1940, the only producer of synthetic rubber in any quantity was Du Pont, which manufactured 2,468 long tons of a synthetic called neoprene. Du Pont had begun a serious search for a synthetic rubber in the mid-twenties. By chance the company heard of research by the Reverend Julius A. Nieuwland of the University of Notre Dame which suggested a new approach to the problem. And by 1931 Du Pont was producing neoprene in commercial quantities.

But while the United States in 1940 was using 2,560 long tons of synthetic rubber, it was consuming 648,500 long tons of natural rubber. In contrast, Germany was using more synthetic rubber than natural rubber and was producing fifteen times more synthetic rubber than the United States.

Alarm over the rubber situation began to grow as Hitler's divisions slammed into France and the Japanese advanced in the Far East. In June, 1940, President Roosevelt created the Rubber Reserve Company under the Reconstruction Finance Corporation. Its job was to build up the nation's stocks of crude rubber.

Leaders of the rubber industry met in Washington in August with the National Defense Advisory Council to discuss the rubber situation. The result was a suggested program to increase synthetic rubber production to 100,000 long tons per year. But the government was not willing to plunge into any such spending and after months of discussion, the program was scaled down to 40,000 long tons per year. Plans were advanced to build four plants, each to have a 10,000-ton capacity.

It was during this period that Dow Chemical and the Goodyear Rubber Company offered to build a 100,000-ton plant for the government to manufacture the butadiene-styrene type synthetic from which tires would be manufactured. But the offer was rejected.

During 1939–41 Washington talked endlessly of a rubber crisis but did little about it. The harsh realization that the war effort was in peril from a rubber shortage came when the Japanese attacked Pearl Harbor and seized the Far East's rubber plantations. Fear of a shortage spread through the country. People began buying and hoarding tires for automobiles and trucks. Tire stocks soon disappeared from dealers' shelves. The government searched in neutral countries for crude rubber, buying whatever they could find at premium prices.

The government's plans for the production of 40,000 tons of synthetic rubber were doubled to 80,000 tons and then to 160,000 tons in early 1942. Rubber and chemical companies were asked to pool their patents, processes, and know-how for the common cause.

In August, 1942, President Roosevelt named industrialist Bernard Baruch to head the Rubber Survey Committee to study the rubber situation and to make recommendations. Baruch underlined the gravity of the situation by reporting: "Of all the strategic materials, rubber is the one which presents the greatest threat... to the success of the Allied cause." His committee recommended, among other things, the rationing of fuel and tires.

President Roosevelt created the Office of Rubber Director under the War Production Board to supervise a synthetic rubber program. Plans were made that would pour more than $700,000,000 into creating a synthetic rubber industry. Forty-nine rubber, chemical, and industrial companies were called on to build and operate fifty-one plants for the government's Rubber Reserve Company. The nation that had produced only a little more than 8,000 tons of synthetic rubber in 1941 was now rushing desperately to build an industry that would be producing more than 800,000 tons three years later.

In the magnesium program, Dow Chemical shared its know-how in production and fabrication with others who possibly would be competitors after the war. And it did the same in the synthetic rubber program. The company shared with others its hard-won secrets of manufacturing styrene, one of the most versatile materials in the chemical world. Dow Chemical engineers and scientists helped competitors install the necessary equipment and taught them all they had learned in years of research about styrene production.

The company received a small royalty of .125 cent per pound on the styrene produced by others using the Dow process—but the sum was little more than a token payment compared to the value of the process had it remained Dow Chemical's exclusive property.

With Ray Boundy directing the program, Dow Chemical built and operated styrene plants for the United States government at Velasco, Texas, and Los Angeles, and for the Canadian government at Sarnia, Ontario. More than half of the styrene manufactured in World War II came from these plants and from Dow Chemical's own plants at Freeport and Midland. Dow-built plants also supplied large quantities of the butadiene needed in the synthetic rubber program.

For a time in the early war years, it appeared that Dow Chemical would not only produce styrene and butadiene for GRS rubber, but also a synthetic rubber with the trade name Thiokol.

Willard Dow had become interested in Thiokol in the early 1930's when the Thiokol Corporation of Trenton, New Jersey, arranged for Dow Chemical to manufacture the latex required in the synthetic process. Within a few years Thiokol was being widely used as a substitute for rubber in hosing for tank trucks, typewriter rolls, valve seat discs, washers, and a large number of other products which originally had been made from rubber.

Thiokol had been discovered in the Twenties by Dr. J. C. Patrick, a chemist-physician in Kansas City, Missouri, while he was experimenting with an antifreeze solution. Patrick had mixed ethylene dichloride and sodium polysulfide in one experiment, and the reaction had brought forth a gummy substance with some of the qualities of rubber. The synthetic looked so promising that a processing plant was built in Trenton. Then in 1938 Dow Chemical obtained a license from the Thiokol Corporation to produce the synthetic.

After Pearl Harbor, Dow Chemical's chemists experimented with Thiokol as a substitute for rubber in whole tires and retreads. They found a chemical combination they called Thiokol-N which stood up well under tests. Whole tires fabricated from Thiokol were found to have a useful life of 10,000 miles while retreads lasted for 5,000 miles. The most objectionable feature of Thiokol was its slightly skunkish odor.

The road tests impressed the Rubber Reserve Company which gave Willard Dow the go-ahead in May, 1942, to build a pilot plant in which to perfect a process for large-scale production of Thiokol. While the construction was underway, War Production Board Chief Donald Nelson told the Truman Committee: "Thiokol will fill an important gap between the exhaustion of the natural crude rubber supply and volume production of synthetic rubber. But its use will be limited to retreading tires on vehicles whose operation is deemed absolutely necessary...."

A committee of the Rubber Manufacturers Association endorsed Thiokol as a rubber substitute and so did many of the industry's technical men. The result was that in October (1942) the Rubber Reserve Company gave Willard Dow the go-ahead signal to build a Thiokol plant for the government at Velasco. It was to have a capacity of 33,000 long tons—enough to retread 10,000,000 tires a year.

Through the winter of 1942–43 workers rushed construction of the plant at Velasco. But when it was 85 percent completed, the government ordered a slowdown and then abandoned the project entirely as the rubber shortage eased with the production of Buna-S rubber.

As the United States began its third winter at war, The Dow Chemical Company was geared almost entirely to the needs of the government. Research was directed to finding ways for chemicals to aid in the war effort—and there was little time for looking ahead to the shape of the world at war's end.

Chapter Fourteen

The Dow Chemical Company's first move into international operations came in 1942 when the Canadian government asked Willard Dow to help with the production of synthetic rubber.

The government at Ottawa was shocked—just as Washington—by the attack on Pearl Harbor and Japan's swift conquest of the rubber plantations of the Far East. As far as rubber was concerned, Canada was in the same leaky boat with the United States. It had little crude rubber in stock and no synthetic rubber industry.

Shortly after Pearl Harbor, the Canadians set up a Rubber Substitute Advisory Committee whose members included the presidents of Canada's major rubber companies—Dominion Rubber, Firestone, Goodrich, and Goodyear. The committee was headed by Canada's Deputy Comptroller of Supplies, John R. Nicholson.

This group met in Washington in late December with leaders of President Roosevelt's emergency rubber program. It was agreed the Canadian effort to produce synthetic rubber would be linked with the United States' program. The Canadians would build a $50,000,000 plant at Sarnia, located on the St. Clair River at the southern tip of Lake Huron, and use the butadiene-styrene process.

The Canadians moved swiftly after the Washington meeting. Minister of Munitions and Supply C. D. Howe authorized the organization of the Polymer Corporation Limited as the agency to administer the program under the direction of Nicholson. Nicholson had no precedents to guide him. He swept aside red tape with Howe's backing and organized Polymer into four divisions, one to produce styrene, one to produce butadiene and ethylene, one to manufacture the materials into synthetic rubber, and one to coordinate and supervise the operation.

The St. Clair Processing Corporation, a subsidiary of Imperial Oil, was chosen to produce the butadiene and ethylene. Canadian Synthetic Rubber, jointly owned by the Goodyear, Firestone, Dominion, and Goodrich rubber companies, was organized to manufacture the finished products. Polymer itself was the coordinating and supervising unit.

Nicholson came to Midland in February, 1942, to discuss with Willard Dow the possibility of Dow Chemical taking over the design, construction, and operation of the styrene unit. The two men quickly came to an agreement. And out of their conversations came the organization of Dow Chemical of Canada, Limited.

The operating agreement between Dow Chemical of Canada and the Canadian government was dated May 1, 1942. The "party of the first part" was described in the contract as "His Majesty the King in Right of Canada (hereinafter called 'His Majesty') herein represented by the Honourable the Minister of Munitions and Supply (hereinafter called 'the Minister') acting through Polymer Corporation Limited. . . ." The party of the second part was merely termed "Dow Chemical of Canada, Limited (hereinafter called 'Operator')." A charter of incorporation was issued by the Secretary of State of Canada on June 5. The new company's five directors were Willard Dow, Earl Bennett, Leland I. Doan, Charles Strosacker and Mark Putnam—with Dow holding the office of president.

The choice of Sarnia as a site for the synthetic rubber plant was a fortunate one. The town, with a population of some 20,000, had good rail and water transportation facilities. Brine deposits underlay the area. The primary industry was a large oil refinery owned and operated by Imperial Oil. And the St. Clair River provided an inexhaustible supply of fresh water out of Lake Huron.

The region had a colorful history. Not far from Sarnia a man named Charles Tripp had struck oil in 1854 or 1855 while digging a well with a shovel, trying to find water. There was no railroad or road through the wild country over which to transport the oil to market and the news of the oil strike created little excitement. However, Canadians boast that this was the first oil well on the North American continent.

Tripp sold his holdings to an enterprising neighbor, James Miller Williams, and Williams dug more wells. He managed to get some 350,000 gallons of oil through the swamps to shipping points, hauling the oil out two barrels at a time.

The Sarnia *Observer* of 1858 observed: "The ingredient [i.e., mineral oil] seems to abound over a considerable tract of land where it was discovered, and in fact that earth is so saturated by it, so that a hole dug 8 or 10 feet in width and the same depth, will collect from 200 to 250 gallons a day, the supply seemingly inexhaustible." The supply, of course, was exhaustible and the field gradually lost its importance.

It was from Sarnia that the news spread in later years of giant albino turtles being found in nearby Talfourd Creek, arousing the interest of local inhabitants and naturalists.

R. M. McPherson and R. W. Ford, two historians of Lambton County, recalled the excitement aroused by this discovery. They recorded in a booklet:

"Ed and Fred Davis, who ran the ferry between Corunna and Stag Island, would organize launch trips to see the famous turtles when business was slack. But they had to warn people to be careful.

" 'My God,' Fred would say. 'Don't you know a white turtle's bite is worse than a rattler's? Why an Indian from Walpole Island caught one, and the next day he was gone.' Still, if people looked carefully, they could see them swimming about in the creek.

"But one day a brave young wag caught one despite the warnings, and the jig was up—Ed had attempted to stimulate business by collecting hundreds of mud turtles and painting them with white enamel. As for the Indian who had been bitten, he was gone, true enough—gone back to Walpole Island. But perhaps the ghosts of albino turtles still roam the refinery property."

The Canadian government brought more than five thousand French Canadians into Sarnia to build the synthetic rubber plant. Almost overnight the town was changed from a relatively quiet shipping center into a seething center of building activity. The plant site outside town was a section of 130 acres taken over from the Chippewa Indian Reserve. Tree-bark tepees were relocated and in their place sprang up a work camp much like those of the earlier lumberjack days. The camp at night was a brawling, poker-playing, crap-shooting, whiskey-drinking shack town.

Ground was broken in August but then the winter rains turned the area into a sea of mud, mud so deep that it pulled off the workers' boots as they waded through it and it mired bulldozers. Some swore that they saw bulldozers bog down in mud holes and then slowly sink from sight.

When it was obvious the main steam plant would not be ready on schedule, engineers improvised a steam plant. They searched the United States and located several old locomotive boilers in Texas. They converted them to oil burners, set them up in series on heavy timbers, and fashioned a make-do steam plant that bridged the gap.

Dow Chemical's project manager, Charles Sanford, had his styrene unit in operation by late June, 1943, one month ahead of schedule. He turned it over to John Hacking, a Canadian engineer who had been trained in Midland. And on September 29, 1943, the Sarnia plant began the manufacture of synthetic rubber. It had been designed to produce only 10,000 short tons of GRS rubber a year, but within a few months production had been expanded to 35,000 long tons.

This chain of events established Dow Chemical of Canada as one of the pioneers among the companies which built the Sarnia area into what would become known as "Chemical Valley"—the greatest petrochemical complex in Canada.

That action-packed year of 1942 which brought the creation of Dow Chemical of Canada also brought into being a partnership which was the beginning of the American silicone industry—an industry producing fluids, resins, and rubbers unlike any ever seen before. The partnership was between the Corning Glass Works of Corning, New York, and The Dow Chemical Company.

This relationship could trace its origin to the early 1930's when Corning researchers began investigating silicones for possible use in glass manufacture. Silicone was a name coined by chemist F. S. Kipping of Nottingham University, England, in his nineteenth century experiments with compounds made from silicon.

There was no lack of raw material for this research because silicon is found in silica, a main ingredient of quartz or common sand. It is one of the most abundant elements found in the earth's crust. But learning to tear the atoms of silicon apart and to put them together again in combination with carbon atoms to form a useful product was quite another matter.

Some of the keys to manipulating the silicon and carbon atoms were found in years of research by J. Franklin Hyde at Corning Glass and Rob Roy McGregor and Earl L. Warrick, the latter two working on a Corning Fellowship at the Mellon Institute in Pittsburgh. They produced laboratory resins, fluids, and rubbers which had no counterpart in nature—materials with the ability to resist extremes of cold and heat and which were impervious to moisture.

Corning's Eugene C. Sullivan brought the results of these experiments to Midland in 1940 and discussed with Dow Chemical's E. C. Britton the possibility of manufacturing the products. Further experiments directed by Dow Chemical's Shailer Bass in the Midland organic laboratory convinced Britton and Willard Dow that the products were far more than mere laboratory curiosities, and that they should be produced commercially.

At this point the project was placed under the direction of Dow Chemical's William R. Collings who guided the development of the commercial processes. By late 1942 a Midland plant was producing several silicone products and one of them was to solve a critical problem for the Army and Navy air corps. This problem was the tendency of airplane engines to fail while flying in the cold, thin atmospheres above 20,000 feet. Also, ignition systems sometimes shorted out in low-level flights over water.

The frequent power failures in the planes at high altitudes were traced to a corona or often-luminous discharge of electricity in conductors, caused by reduced air pressure. The low-level failures were resulting from moisture shorting the electric circuits.

The Germans had a sealant to prevent such failures in their planes and for a time this gave the Luftwaffe an advantage over United States combat aircraft which had a flight ceiling imposed on them by the corona fault in the ignition systems.

Then it was found that a silicone product which Midland researchers had named DC4 (Dow Corning 4) prevented these power failures. Fortunately the discovery came as the Army Air Corps prepared to send flights of Thunderbolt fighter planes to North Africa to support the Allied invasion force of General Dwight D. Eisenhower and the desert army of British General Bernard Montgomery.

The silicone-protected ignition systems in the Thunderbolts permitted them to fly the Atlantic by way of South America, cutting weeks from the time that would have been required to ship the planes by surface transport. The ignition systems worked perfectly. And so it was that DC4 came to be used as an ignition sealant in all United States combat planes, including the high-flying B-29s which raided Tokyo as the war drew nearer a close. It also was used to seal disconnect junctions of radio and radar systems.

In addition to DC4, the Midland plant turned out silicone resins and varnishes used to insulate electrical equipment in factories and aboard Navy ships. Test motors were built with silicone insulation and put through "torture tests" at temperatures ranging from 392 degrees Fahrenheit to 590 degrees—temperatures that normally would burn out motors. The ordinary insulation would have quickly deteriorated under such heat but the silicone-insulated motors were still running at the end of two years.

The Corning Glass–Dow Chemical partnership was formally legalized in February, 1943, with the organization of the Dow Corning Corporation. Corning's Eugene C. Sullivan was chosen as the first president. Dow Chemical's William R. Collings was named general manager, and Shailer Bass director of research.

Wartime secrecy imposed from Washington forbade any publication of the discovery and use of DC4. It was months before Midlanders knew that the brightly colored plant on the east side of town was the world's first center for the manufacture of silicones and the birthplace of a new industry.

The coming of war revolutionized the entire plastics industry, forcing chemists and engineers into a race to find substitutes for metal and rubber, and to develop new methods of producing and fabricating plastic products required in the war effort. In many ways, the development of the plastics industry was one of the most significant achievements of the chemical industry during the war.

Dow Chemical had three versatile plastics in its storehouse as a result of the research carried on through the 1930's. The most important was based on the monomeric (liquid) styrene which made possible the nation's swift production of synthetic rubber in huge quantities. But the polymeric (solid) Styron, a child of styrene, was also in such demand for war-related uses that none was available for nonessential civilian uses. Styron was used as an insulation material, molded into battery cases, and fashioned into parts for radio transmitters, receivers, altimeters, direction finders, homing devices, radar, and other military equipment.

The company's easy-to-mold Ethocel became a workhorse among the plastics that went to war. Its toughness, resistance to shock at low temperatures, excellent electrical characteristics, lightness, and other qualities made it adaptable to many military needs. It was formed into control knobs, telephone head sets and mouthpieces, dust goggles, canteens, and airplane parts to name but a few. A liquid Ethocel was used to impregnate soldiers' tents, bags, and clothing to make them water and chemical resistant.

In these days that demanded almost instant solutions to critical needs, Dow Chemical came up with one of the most important packaging techniques of the war. This was the sealing of spare parts for planes, tanks, jeeps, and other equipment in a quick-drying coating of Ethocel. The parts were dipped into a vat of molten Ethocel. The plastic dried in a matter of minutes, forming a tough skin which protected the parts from salt water corrosion, dust, grime, and high humidity. The coating could be slit with a knife and peeled from the part like pulling off a rubber glove. The simple process saved untold man-hours in labor alone.

Dow Chemical's other heavily used plastic was Saran. It could be extruded into pipe and tubing, injected into molded parts, made into sheets of varying thickness, or woven into a fabric. In later years this material would become known to housewives across the country as Saran Wrap.

Researchers stumbled onto Saran in 1933 while working on chlorinated dry cleaning solvents. For a time they believed they had found a new compound. But then it was discovered that the clear liquid which became cloudy when it changed into a solid was the same "monomeric vinylidene chloride" which the French chemist, Regnault, had made in his laboratory a century earlier.

Regnault wrote an article on his find which was preserved in scientific literature available to any researcher. But through the years no one paid much attention to his work. A German chemist, H. Staudinger, investigated the compound in 1929–30 while doing research on synthetic rubber, but he apparently concluded it was not worth much as a commerical product.

Dow Chemical's researchers spent six years investigating the compound. In that time, they found the processes for converting it into a useful synthetic resin which they first called VC Plastic. It was a substance that could be forged, drawn, rolled, blown, stamped, and welded. It could be made into a heavy cable or a strong thread as fine as silk. Slight variations in the molecular structure produced resins with different characteristics, all of them resistant to water, acids, alkalies and other corrosive chemicals.

In 1940, the sales and advertising departments produced a trade name for the new plastic—Saran. Not everyone in the company liked it. Some quipped the name reminded them of "a new breakfast food." But most employees liked the word.

Explaining how the name was chosen, the company's magazine, the *Dow Diamond*, said:

So we tried a new tack, and suddenly out of thin air appeared the gleaming magic word, Saran. What did it mean? Nothing, obviously. And that is the word's greatest virtue. It could have meant almost anything, until it got into the hands of your Patent Department, your Sales and Advertising Departments. By legal document, by word of mouth, by the printed page, they made it mean just one thing, and today that Dow plastic which we have known variously as "Vinylidene Chloride," "Polyvinylidene Chloride," "Plastic VC," etc., for convenience in handling it, has been definitely christened "Saran." From now on, in fact, any one caught referring to Saran by any of its former names will be tried for heresy, and if found guilty will suffer the usual penalty.

Saran products began moving onto the domestic market in the form of men's suspenders and belts, handbags, and heavy-duty seat covers for buses, trains, and subways. Seats in New York City subways were fitted with woven Saran covers. Saran found a growing use where pipes, tubing, and fittings were required to handle corrosive chemicals, oils, and waste matter.

But after Pearl Harbor, almost all the Saran produced by Dow Chemical was siphoned into the war drive. It was woven into insect screening for Army use in the tropics and humid climates where metal screening would have rotted away. It was used to impregnate fabrics and fashioned into scores of parts for airplanes, tanks and military equipment. Sheets of Saran film were used for packaging machine guns, airplane and automotive engines, magnetic instruments, and other equipment requiring protection from the elements while being shipped to the fighting forces. The parts were placed in Saran bags containing a chemical agent to absorb all moisture. The air was drawn from the bags and then they were sealed. Machine guns were sealed into heavy Saran tubes along with a moisture-absorbing agent, guaranteeing the weapons would arrive at their destination ready for use. This latter technique was developed by the Frigidaire Division of General Motors.

One Styron product was molded into the first successful radar housing for submarine-hunting airplanes. And the discovery of Styrofoam—the rigid, lightweight, buoyant, air-filled plastic—made possible lightweight pontoon bridges and virtually nonsinkable life rafts.

Dow Chemical's products went into incendiary bombs, flares, and tracer powder, camouflage paints, germicides, fungicides, and preservatives, gun muzzle covers, water purifiers, greases and oils, dyes, shoe polish, shaving cream, shell casings, map protectors, soaps, explosives, and other products too numerous to list.

By the tens of thousands of tons, chemicals poured from the Dow Chemical plants at Midland, Marquette, Wilmington, Freeport, Velasco, Los Angeles, Pittsburg, and Sarnia. They were in the form of products that perfomed at least one necessary function for almost every industry in the United States.

In these years, the general public had not been awakened to the importance of the chemical industry in the war effort, or the role it would play in the postwar world. Without a well-developed chemical industry the United States could not have competed with the German war machine, backed by a strong chemical industry.

The War Department was well aware that much of Germany's strength lay in her ability to produce chemicals. But in planning bombing raids against this industry, the question arose as to where the most crippling blows could be struck. An advisory committee of chemical and industry leaders was enthusiastic in 1942 over a report which advocated bombing the German ammonia plants. If ammonia plants were wiped out, the report reasoned, Germany could not produce nitrates, and without nitrates the Germans would soon be without explosives.

The committee, meeting in Washington, was sailing to unanimous approval of the report, with compliments to the author, until the report was passed around the table to Willard Dow.

"It's a lousy report," Willard said, startling the assembly with the brusque frankness to which he was accustomed in his Midland surroundings. "Whoever wrote it doesn't know anything about the chemical industry."

For a moment there was a shocked silence. Then a committee member turned to Dow and said, "You don't understand, Mr. Dow. Ammonia makes nitrates and nitrates make explosives."

Dow said, "That's the way it was in the last war, but if we took away all their ammonia plants, Germany could still be as aggressive as ever."

"I'm afraid you don't understand nitrates or explosives."

Dow snapped, "If you don't know what I'm talking about, I don't see why I should explain the chemical industry to you."

Recalling this clash later for the benefit of a friend, Dow wrote:

"I was pretty warm under the collar. Just prior to that meeting we had been talking in Midland about the peroxides and how the explosives of the future would be peroxides, but it was not until sometime after the buzz bomb came out that people finally realized they were using peroxide instead of nitrate explosives. I contended at this time the only way to control the chemical industry in Germany was by the control of the amount of electric power permitted to be generated. It would not matter if they used chlorates, perchlorates or peroxides or whatever, the factor of power would enter into it somewhere and would be a definite controlling point. No chemical plant could be controlled in itself, because the imagination and ability of the chemists would go beyond the control of any specific product."

He added wryly, "Like a darn fool, I didn't realize that report had been written by a friend of mine who wasn't a member of the committee. But then he never could understand what I was talking about."

Dow did not win his argument in the committee meeting. But as the war progressed, it became apparent that the most damaging blows to

German production were the bombings of electric power facilities. Without power, all manufacturing was disrupted.

In the fall of 1944, even the most pessimistic conceded the great war was in its final stages. Allied troops on the Western Front were fighting on German soil with complete mastery of the air. The Russian armies were driving the Germans back on the Eastern Front. In the Pacific, American land, sea, and air forces were closing in on Japan. Already the leaders of government and industry were thinking of the adjustments that would have to be made with the closing of war plants and the dismantling of the war machine which had consumed the people's energies and taxed the nation's purse for more than three years.

There were many industrialists and economists who predicted the country would have to endure a severe economic depression at the war's end. Factories would be closed and men laid off from their jobs. Soldiers, sailors, marines, and airmen would be returning home by the millions—and there would be no jobs for them. The postwar period, they said, would be bleak until the nation could adjust to a changed world.

But Willard Dow saw the future in quite a different light. He was convinced that the war—while it had demanded tremendous increases in production facilities—had been a brake on research, business initiative, and opportunity to develop normal markets. He had fretted under the wartime restrictions and controls and was eager to see them ended. He foresaw only a temporary slump at the end of the war and then a spurt in business that would call for production even greater than the production achieved in the war years.

In December, 1944, he told a gathering of scientists in Midland:

"We already have in mind many new additions to Midland as well as Texas and California. We have much more development work to be accomplished. When that is achieved, new operations and new lines of research will open up.

"Some of us ask why it is that we want to keep on growing. The average fellow will say, 'Because we want to make money,' and although we have to make money in order to continue in business, I do not believe that this is in any respect the controlling factor. Any enterprise which exists purely for profit can never be long enduring, because it lacks the basic spirit and responsibility which is an absolute necessity to all progress. I believe that the average American, if he has any spark in him, is born with a sense of responsibility to his country and to himself, and a consuming desire to make a success of any venture he tackles. . . .

"I think that one could say that in place of the company multiplying ten times in ten years as during the past decade, it would be very surprising if we did not multiply ten times again in the next twenty years. There is every reason to suppose that after the war is over, there will be a decline in business, but with the demand that the market of the United States can offer, there is no reason to believe that within five years after the war we should not be producing at a greater rate on all major items than during the war period. And I think we can back up this statement. An analysis of our normal markets and the increasing interest on the part of the public in new products with all their outstanding advantages, indicates that this is no wild dream."

With the surrender of Germany and Japan in May and August, 1945, Dow Chemical was ready, not for retrenchment, but for expansion.

Through the war years, Dow Chemical regularly received the Army and Navy awards for excellence in production. But there was no commendation that meant as much to Willard Dow as the letter he received from the War Production Board's Rubber Director Bradley Dewey on September 6, 1944. Dewey wrote:

"I know that it is a source of great satisfaction to you that the synthetic rubber problem is now solved and that the contributions of The Dow Chemical Company to the solution of this problem have been of major importance. The production of styrene has been largely based on the experience of your company and I feel that the success of this part of the program is largely the result of this experience.

"The contributions of The Dow Chemical Company to the synthetic rubber program, however, have not been limited to the field of styrene. Your early work in connection with the production and purification of butadiene and in the production of various polymers which are suitable as rubber substitutes has been of major importance.

"I am particularly appreciative of the cooperation which you and your associates have shown by willingly aiding others in the production of both butadiene and styrene. . . .

"Without your contribution the country might well have suffered disaster."

Chapter Fifteen

There was something of the incredible in the fiftieth anniversary of The Dow Chemical Company in 1947—almost too much of the poor-boy-makes-good theme to be wholly believable. And yet that was the story.

For one dealing in fiction, the plot was overdrawn. There was the young man coming from college to start a business in a remote, rundown village in the Michigan backwoods.... The ridicule and suspicion of the townspeople.... The struggle against financial disaster.... The battle for survival against international cartels.... The drawing together of exceptional talent far from the centers of commerce and learning.... The discovery of new processes.... The dream of going to the sea for bromine and magnesium.... The son taking over from the father in the midst of the nation's worst economic crisis.... The discovery of new processes for making products vital to the synthetic rubber program.... And the explosive growth placing the company among the top leaders in the nation's chemical industry.

The contrasts between the founding of the company in 1897 and its position in 1947 were startling.

In 1897, Herbert Dow was constructing his first buildings and chlorine cells from rough, tarred lumber, counting the nails that would go into each. He had to count nails and count pennies to stretch his building budget as far as possible.

In 1947, Willard Dow was spending more than $100,000,000 in a postwar expansion and building program. The company had more than $200,000,000 in assets, sales of more than $130,000,000, and the fastest growth rate of any major chemical company in the United States. The one product produced in 1897—bleaching powder—had become more than 500 products. The tar-wood cells and handmade equipment had been replaced by automated equipment of sophisticated design. The fewer than 30 full-time employees had grown to 12,500 workers. The Midland plant itself employed 7,000 people—more than three times the entire population of the town when the company was founded. The single crude laboratory had become 32 laboratories. The single paid chemist had become 1,500 researchers. The lone engineer had become teams of chemical engineering experts.

The Midland plant in 1947 was housed in 400 buildings spread over 785 acres of a 2,800-acre tract on the bank of the Tittabawassee River. The company owned its own railroad system with 24 miles of track inside the fences. Seven locomotives shunted carloads of coal, supplies, and chemicals within the enclosure. There were 850 tank cars for carrying chemicals to factories across the country. And beyond Midland were the plants at Ludington, Bay City, and Marquette, Michigan; at Sarnia, Canada; at Freeport and Velasco, Texas and at Long Beach and Pittsburg, California. (The Ethyl-Dow Chemical Company plant at Kure Beach, North Carolina, had been closed down and the operation transferred to Texas.)

From 1930 to 1947, Willard Dow had lifted the company's assets from $22,474,000 to more than $213,000,000 through research, the marketing of new products, and expansion of basic chemical production. World War II had given tremendous impetus to plant expansion. But the growth would have come even had there been no war because the United States had moved into an era in which chemicals were to play a more and more important role in industrial production, medicine, farming, and everyday living. It was the beginning of "the chemical age."

The growth of the entire chemical industry had been a runaway development through the 1930's and 1940's. In 1937 the seventeen largest chemical producers in the country had total sales of $931,000,000. By 1944, the peak year of the war boom, sales had climbed to $2,177,900,000, in part reflecting the swift growth of the organic chemical business. The climb continued after the war with only a slight pause in 1946. By the middle of 1947, the demand for basic chemicals had out-distanced the industry's capacity to produce them.

The seven-fold growth of Dow Chemical under Willard Dow's direction had brought the company to a point far beyond the dreams of Herbert Dow and established a production base for an even greater growth to come.

On the basis of this record, it was difficult for anyone to fault the management of Dow Chemical. It seemed the son's batting average was topping that of the father who had explained his success on the basis that "I was right more than 50 percent of the time."

But there was a weakness. Willard Dow was grooming no one to take his place. He held all the reins in his own hands. He retained for himself the titles and powers of general manager, president, and chairman of the board. He was, in fact, director of research, and he handled the company's public relations. It was a crushing load for any man and perhaps that is why between the ages of thirty-three and fifty, Willard Dow's dark hair turned to snowy white.

Willard's strength was in his willingness to push into uncharted areas of research and enlarge the frontiers of the company's activities. He could move with confidence because he had behind him a team of strong men who were one of the most formidable combinations of brains, energy, and experience in the chemical industry. They were the veterans who had gathered around Herbert Dow in the young days of the company and they had rallied around Willard when he moved into the top command after the father's death.

The nine-man board of directors had only two members who were not in key positions in the company's management. They were Willard's brother, Alden Dow, and John S. Crider, one of the early investors in Dow Chemical. The others were Earl Bennett, treasurer; Leland I. Doan, director of sales; Ed Barstow, production; Charles Strosacker, production; Mark Putnam, production; and W. R. Veazey, research.

In the Texas Division, Willard had tough, aggressive Dutch Beutel as general manager, and in the Great Western Division he had able Russell Curtis. Both of these men had grown up with Willard in the company.

This team made Willard's ideas work. They operated within a loose framework of authority with no formal organization chart. Areas of responsibility overlapped. Financial writers who came to Midland to see what made the company tick invariably left town with only a hazy picture of who was responsible for what.

The system worked largely because an informal atmosphere brought management close to research and production and no department was walled off from another. It worked, also, because the managers stayed close to plant problems and the company avoided both absentee ownership and remote-control management.

The company's operations meshed in a team effort. But, curiously, while Willard Dow insisted on teamwork and helped develop it in the company, he was hardly a team player himself. He was the coach, involving himself in innumerable details.

An older colleague of Willard would say of him in this period: "As an individualist, and as a man of great energy and amazing capacity for detail, he found it difficult to delegate authority. I think he never quite escaped the feeling that every detail of operation of the entire company with which he had grown up was his own personal responsibility. His judgment convinced him of the impossibility of the thing, yet instinctively he could not resist keeping his hand in the most unexpected details of operation."

Willard realized during World War II that the company was getting far too big and sophisticated an operation for the one-man control he had exercised for so many years. He began in 1944 to shift some of the management burden to others by naming Mark Putnam as head of a board to coordinate the growing geographical divisions. He moved to coordinate research through a General Research Group composed of the heads of Dow Chemical's laboratories.

In the field of selling, Willard did not build on what his father had started. Herbert Dow had paid his first sales manager a larger salary than he received himself, explaining to Bennett, "If that fellow sells as much as I hope he does, he will make money for all of us." He had gone on to develop direct-to-market sales of magnesium products, agricultural chemicals, and chemicals such as calcium chloride for laying dust on roads.

For several years, Willard was content to let the sales department operate in a narrowly restricted area. The huge sales were in basic chemicals such as phenol and caustic soda which were used by other industries in their manufacturing processes. Their sale required no specialized techniques. And even though Dow Chemical produced a lion's share of the aspirin consumed in the United States, it was sold to others to be packaged under their trade names. Dow Chemical did not have to work hard to find customers for products which were in scarce supply.

Nevertheless, Lee Doan had built through the 1930's an aggressive sales force made up of men with backgrounds in chemistry and chemical engineering. They understood not only the company's operations and its products, but the application of chemicals to the needs of industry. They saw that the broader opportunities were not merely in taking orders for chemicals, but in identifying the problems of industries and then helping to find a chemical solution to these problems.

Donald Ballman, who started his career in Dow Chemical as a chemist and then went into selling, recalled: "Sales opened a good many doors and vistas in research and production. For example, we were selling chemicals to the paint industry. This led to further research that ended with us being in latex, and from latex we got to working with the synthetic rubber, Thiokol."

The coming of World War II forced Dow Chemical into a greater appreciation of the need for more knowledge about the end use of the company's products, particularly in plastics. Industries were looking for substitutes for rubber, metals, cotton, wool, and other materials which had been diverted to the war effort. It was up to the chemical industry to replace the things taken out of the economy.

Quite suddenly, Lee Doan's men were more involved with helping businesses to solve their problems than with selling as such. Circumstances had turned them into a service organization. Salesmen were spending most of their time in industrial plants studying a specific problem and then working with Dow Chemical's researchers and production men to find the solution.

Ballman recalled: "You had to have a certificate of necessity from the government to sell anything in those days. There simply was no creative selling—but there was a hell of a lot of creative non-selling. We gained a tremendous amount of know-how we hadn't had before, working with people to help solve their problems and studying the end products."

Lee Doan explained the sales philosophy in a joint meeting of chemists and engineers in Midland in 1947:

"There are a number of old line chemicals which require little or no 'servicing,' but as we have found new uses for these old materials, and as we have developed new chemical products we have found it necessary to base our selling upon customer service.

"Merely offering our chemicals for sale is not enough. We have found that we can sell best by helping our customer to use our materials to improve his product or process, or to make them more economically. To do this properly we have not been able to rely upon middlemen or distributors. Rather we have had to develop our own groups of sales personnel, trained not only in a knowledge of their own products but in a knowledge of the function of those products in industry and the problems of the industries they serve."

Industrial managers, engineers, and chemists flocked to Midland to seek Dow Chemical's help in the war years. Businessmen were threatened with shutdowns unless they could find a plastic pipe that could replace a metal pipe, a synthetic hose to replace a rubber hose, or other raw materials that would substitute for something that had gone to war.

Such pressure pushed applied research forward, particularly in the field of plastics. The enormous expansion of plastics production and the public's ready acceptance of substitutes—often as good as or better than the original—built a broad base for the growth of this new industry.

Lee Doan made a tentative move in 1942 to set up a Market Research and Technical Service to back up the salesmen in handling agricultural chemicals and new products. But Willard was less than enthusiastic. He was fearful that such moves would tend to place too much emphasis on sales.

Nevertheless, when the war came to a close, the younger men were conscious of the need for moving Dow Chemical closer to the needs of the market. They also wanted a continuing survey of market trends and what Dow Chemical's competitors were doing. The Texas Division's E. B. Barnes, an assistant to Beutel, wrote Willard Dow proposing the appointment of a research subcommittee to keep the researchers informed on what competing chemical companies were doing. Dow reluctantly agreed to give the subcommittee a try even though he did not think much of the idea. He wrote Barnes:

". . . I cannot get very enthusiastic about the idea of putting too much emphasis on what competition does, for the reason that just as soon as we start doing that, it will be bound to reflect on our own original thinking. There has been a great tendency in the past number of years to refer to what the Germans are going, or the Russians or our competition rather than going out and doing the job ourselves. I get very much out of patience with the thought of always having to find out what the literature says before we attempt to carry out a development of our own. I admit it is foolish not to be informed on the literature, but what we want to do all the time is stimulate new, original thought on the part of our research organization. As a secondary consideration we ought to think in terms of what competition is doing, and the third, last and least important consideration would be the market. Somebody will misinterpret this last comment as meaning we might develop a wonderful product, build a plant and then tell the Sales Department it is available for sale. Of course, we would not be as foolish as all that, but I feel there is a very nice balance between original thought, market demand and the research necessary to the work; and it can easily be thrown out of balance by the man who talks the most—the salesman. . . ."

An oldtimer would say: "You got the feeling that Willard looked on sales as a necessary evil and certainly salesmen felt they were third-class people in the organization. But the trend was toward greater recognition of the need for knowledge in the end use of products and competition was growing. The use of new thermoplastic resins got a tremendous boost during the war and opened up a new field of chemistry, based on the needs of the customers and not what Dow

Chemical wanted to sell. These things helped stimulate the growth of our sales department."

In the field of research, Dow Chemical's fiftieth anniversary found the company with fifteen hundred people working in more than thirty laboratories located in Midland, Ann Arbor, and South Haven, Michigan; Freeport, Texas; and Pittsburg and Long Beach, California. Two-thirds of the laboratories were in Midland, with experts in such specialized fields as chemistry, biology, botany, geology, medicine, mathematics, metallurgy, radiology, physics, and nuclear energy.

Willard Dow leaned heavily on Ray Boundy—together with the General Research Group—to direct the flow of research toward specific objectives and to choose the discoveries which would be taken into production.

The moving from discovery to production required a high degree of team work. The necessity for working together and sharing knowledge was drilled into recruits from the first weeks of their employment. The veteran W. R. Veazey had the task of explaining to recruits that their best chance for advancement was in becoming a member of the team.

"Good research," he said, "may be preceded by a lot of imagination, discussion and argument but it always terminates in a lot of plain, tedious, hard work. A good researcher is the fellow who can add reality to the poet's dream. Industrial research requires another factor, for the industrial process is too complex for any one man to comprehend. Industrial research requires the cooperation of many different types of minds and skills. It takes team work of the highest order. Ability to work well with all sorts of other people is more important to industry than any other single ability. It takes a lot of people all pulling together to make a successful Dow Chemical Company."

The Golden Anniversary year was a time for taking stock. In balancing the gains and losses of the war years, it was evident to Willard Dow and his managers that the war had cost Dow Chemical heavily in terms of competitive advantages. The secrets of commercial production of styrene and butadiene—the primary ingredients in the most widely-used synthetic rubber—were no longer the sole property of the company. This knowledge had been shared with others who now had become competitors. Promising research and market development programs had been postponed or abandoned.

Despite all this, Dow Chemical had emerged in a strong position to ride with the rising tide of the postwar demand for chemicals. Among the major products, which accounted for roughly 50 percent of sales, were: ammonia for general industrial uses; aniline, used in the manufacture of dyes, rubber accelerators, and pharmaceuticals; butadiene and styrene, used in the manufacture of synthetic rubber and plastics; bromides and iodides, used for medical and photographic purposes; calcium chloride, used for laying dust on roads, ice control, concrete curing and refrigeration; carbon tetrachloride, used in making dry cleaners and fire extinguishers, and in solvent extraction; caustic soda, used in the manufacture of soap, paper, and petroleum; chlorine, used in the manufacture of organic chemicals and paper, and for water purification; Dowicides, used in the treatment of lumber, fabrics, glue, and paints, and also as germicides; Epsom salts, used for medical purposes and in the manufacture of leather and rayon; ethylene dibromide, used in anti-knock gasoline and in soil and grain fumigants; ethylene and propylene glycols, used in antifreeze, explosives, dyes, plasticizers, and solvents; ethylene oxide and propylene oxide, used in the manufacture of organic chemicals, detergents, plasticizers, and insecticides; ferric chloride, used in photoengraving and sewage and water treatment; hydrochloric acid, used throughout industry; magnesium chloride, used in the manufacture of stucco, cements, and magnesium metal; organic chlorides, industrial solvents used for waxes, tars, greases, and extraction of fats; phenols, used in the manufacture of plastics, resins, and pharmaceuticals, and in oil refining; sodium sulphide, used in the manufacture of rubber, paper, and leather; and vinyl and vinylidene chlorides, used in the manufacture of plastics. And this was only a partial list.

Pharmaceutical chemicals accounted for 10 percent of sales, agricultural chemicals for 10 percent, magnesium and fabricated magnesium alloys for 10 percent, and plastics for 20 percent.

Willard Dow and his managers had read the situation correctly when they predicted there would be no slackening of demand for chemicals with the coming of peace. While war had forced a large expansion in chemical production, the war also had shut off the normal consumption of chemicals for non-war purposes. This market had lain dormant for four years as research and production focused on war needs. And this pent-up consumer demand proved to be even greater than the demand created by war.

It was the end of the war that opened the way for Dow Chemical to start a manufacturing operation in Canada on a permanent basis. At that time the Canadian government had to decide whether to close down its synthetic rubber operation at Sarnia or continue production on a reduced scale until supplies of natural rubber were available. The decision was to continue the operations of the government-owned Polymer Corporation.

This meant that Polymer, while cutting back on synthetic rubber production, would have excess styrene from the plant which Dow Chemical had built and operated for the Canadians. Willard Dow quickly reached agreement with the Canadian government in late 1945 to purchase the excess styrene and convert it into Styron.

Through Dow Chemical of Canada—the war-born corporation formed to help the Canadians with their synthetic rubber program—a tract of 113 acres was purchased near the Polymer plant. Dow reached into California for an executive to take his place as president of the Canadian corporation, a title he had held merely for corporate purposes.

He wrote to N. R. "Russ" Crawford, manager of the Dow-built, government-owned styrene plant at Los Angeles: "This company needs a man who is willing to spend the time and live in Canada and see the operation develop and grow. Would you be interested in taking over the job as President of the company? ... The whole thing is a pioneering project, with everything more or less starting from scratch, but there is a bigger picture involved than appears on the face of it."

Crawford was willing. He came to Sarnia in early January, 1946, and took over the presidency. He brought along LeRoy D. Smithers from the Los Angeles operation to be his general manager. And the two supervised the construction of a $1,000,000 Styron plant which began production in February, 1947.

This plant, as Willard had said to Crawford, was a "pioneering project." By the end of World War II, Dow Chemical's researchers had discovered a way to produce both crystal and colored Styron in a continuous process. The Sarnia plant was the company's first full-scale use of the process. It proved so successful that a similar but larger plant was built two months later in Midland.

With the Styron plant operating smoothly, Willard arranged to buy the excess ethylene produced by Polymer. Crawford began building a second plant to produce 1,500,000 pounds of glycols per month. This plant cost $2,750,000 and went on stream in January, 1948.

The "bigger picture" which Willard Dow had mentioned in his letter to Crawford was a plan to develop Dow Chemical of Canada into a major supplier of basic chemicals for Canadian industry. The Styron and glycol plants were only the beginning. Within ten years the Sarnia operation was not only turning out Styron and glycols but caustic soda, styrene, ethylene, chlorine, hydrochloric acid, and ammonia. The plant site had grown to more than 300 acres along the St. Clair River with another 1,500 acres nearby for future expansion.

The start-up of the Sarnia plants was only a small part of Dow Chemical's big postwar expansion drive. It was a drive which required Treasurer Earl Bennett to raise more cash in a shorter period of time than Dow Chemical had ever attempted before. Bennett proposed to raise $30,000,000 through the sale of public debentures, $40,000,000 through an issue of preferred stock, and $35,000,000 through private financing. These were eyebrow-raising sums to be sought by a man who less than fifteen years before had ventured into New York banking houses as a total stranger representing a little-known company.

Willard wanted the money in hand as quickly as possible. He was dickering with the federal government to buy the huge styrene plant at Velasco, the magnesium plant at Freeport, and the magnesium plant at Ludington. In addition, expansions were planned or underway for Midland, Texas and California.

Bennett had no difficulty arranging for the debenture sales and the private financing. But complications arose with the preferred stock because Dow Chemical was still operating at the end of fifty years under its old small-company Michigan charter. It was not possible to issue securities without a time-consuming process to meet all the legal requirements of the charter.

To sidestep this roadblock, Dow Chemical's board of directors directed General Counsel Calvin "Tink" Campbell to transfer the company's state of incorporation from Michigan to Delaware. The shift was made on July 23, 1947, and the following day the company placed on the market the $40,000,000 issue of preferred stock.

The greater part of the new capital was earmarked for the Texas Division where Dutch Beutel's hard-charging outfit had plans on the drawing board which would make the division's production of big-volume, basic chemicals even larger than that of Midland. This expansion was underway in 1947 when Campbell closed a deal with the government to buy the styrene plant at Velasco for $35,000,000. In that same year the company also bought 265,000 acres of gas and oil leases in Texas and California to be operated by a wholly owned subsidiary, the Brazos Oil and Gas Company. Most of the leases were in Texas.

Soon the mushrooming Texas Division was being called "Beutel's Empire." When Beutel walked out of Willard Dow's office on one of his trips to Midland carrying in his briefcase still another set of plans for a plant, a wag remarked, "Well, there goes Beutel with all of Dow's money wrapped up in that briefcase."

The jibe wasn't far from its mark. And the reason why Texas was getting favored treatment was simple. The Texas Division had unmatched sources of raw materials—sulfur, gas, oil, salt, lime, and seawater.

A colleague of Willard and Beutel would say: "Willard had a lot of admiration for Beutel because he was a take-charge guy. You remember they worked together in the Midland plant when Willard was learning the business. Dutch knew how to talk tough to Willard and get away with it. But he also backed up his arguments with facts and figures and when he asked for a plant he could show where he could produce a product cheaper than anyone else. So Willard let Dutch run his own show pretty much in his own way—although nobody ever doubted who the boss was. It was Willard."

For two years after the end of the war, the one product that troubled Dow Chemical most was magnesium. Optimistic predictions that the metal would be in enormous demand after the war proved wrong. The war-born plants closed. Dow Chemical closed down its magnesium production for several months. The market was overhung by surplus scrap selling for 3 cents a pound.

Nevertheless, Willard Dow began negotiations with the federal government to buy the Freeport magnesium plant which the company had operated alongside its own magnesium plant. But the government's decision was to let Dow Chemical continue operating the plant, for a time, to produce a magnesium stockpile.

Not many of those who rushed to produce magnesium for the government during the war were interested in risking their own capital after the war. By 1947, Dow Chemical once again was the only producer of magnesium ingots in the country.

It was on July 6, 1948 that Dow Chemical's record of almost fifty years of continuous production was broken. On that day, Willard Dow wrote in his diary: "Plant closed by strike. First time in history." He made no other comment.

The Midland plant's hourly workers were members of the United Mine Workers Union, District 50. They had voted in June, 2,809 to 1,702, to strike unless their wage and cost-of-living bonus demands were met. When negotiations broke down over the union request for an 11-cent hourly raise and the company's offer of 7 cents, the workers refused to return to their jobs after the July 4 holiday. Pickets permitted office and maintenance workers through the gates, but the company made no effort to keep production going.

There was no violence. Picketing was peaceful and even good-humored. At the end of four weeks a compromise was reached with both sides giving a bit, and the men returned to work.

A company oldtimer said: "Willard got stubborn in his dealings with the union and they got stubborn with him. I guess it was a good thing the blow-up came when it did. The strike cleared the air of a lot of grievances on both sides with no serious damage done. We became more conscious of the union's gripes and the union began to help us with some of our plant problems. It was the beginning of a realistic relationship that worked with remarkable smoothness after the flare-up."

The strike reflected only one of the changes that were taking place in The Dow Chemical Company in that period. Willard Dow had decided the time had come to shake up his top councils, and make plans for the future. One phase of the company's development had ended and another was beginning.

Dow explained to a friend in 1948: "Following the war there was a big demand on all of us for peacetime requirements, and we feel the war set us back ten years in definite progress. The only way we could put ourselves back into the position we had held was to get right in there and do as intensive a job as possible after the war. It is pretty well accomplished by now, or at least we are beginning to see the end of postwar requirements. From now on, beginning with the fiscal year 1949, the principal investments we make will be along the line of developing new activities and new fields. Up until now we have had to fortify our base position on everything we had produced up until the close of the war."

Dow did not intend to lose the momentum gained in the three years following the war. He explained his position further in this way:

"I don't believe it is possible to take an organization as big as we are and say you are going to stop growing at any given point. I just don't think it is feasible, nor do I believe it is proper. The greatest obligation we have for ourselves as well as for our fellow men is to use what we have and make it multiply and increase, not for the purpose of earning money alone, but because it is our responsibility to use our assets constructively.... In no sense can we take the position that there should be any stagnation so as to create dry rot from within. I cannot believe it is possible to stand still and yet be modern and aggressive...."

In preparing for his next moves, Dow enlarged the nine-man board of directors to fourteen members. He brought in Beutel of the Texas Division; Curtis of the Great Western Division; Calvin Campbell, general counsel; Nelson Griswold, an assistant general manager in the Texas Division and son of the company's first engineer; and, the youngest of them all, thirty-two-year-old Carl Gerstacker, who also was made a member of the finance committee.

Gerstacker was the first of a team of younger men who would rise to the top in Dow Chemical and take the places of the Bennetts, Barstows, and Strosackers. He had come to Dow Chemical in 1938 after his graduation from the University of Michigan with a degree in chemical engineering. His uncle, James Pardee, had been an intimate friend of Herbert Dow and one of his early backers in organizing Dow Chemical. Gerstacker started work with the accounting staff of the Dowell Division but when war came, he entered the army where he rose to the rank of major in the Ordnance Department. After the war, he returned to Dow Chemical as a production engineer and then was placed in the company's purchasing department while being groomed for administrative work.

In starting his reorganization at the top, Willard Dow had no premonition that his own time was running short. He was only fifty-one, in good health, and was planning years ahead. His primary concern was that Dow Chemical remain imaginative and avoid complacence.

"The greatest concern I have," he said, "is that we stay original thinkers—imaginative—with no patience in copying the other fellow or copying competition. There is nothing worse than to become self-satisfied and complacent. Then you start to rot. There is always a better way to do things, and sometimes we have to kick ourselves to realize it."

Dow watched with sympathy the postwar struggles of the Ford Motor Company to overcome its management problems. In analyzing the position of Dow Chemical in relation to the Ford Motor Company, Willard wrote to a friend:

"Our whole foundation is basic and fundamental, and unless we are all a bunch of dumbbells, we cannot help developing as the years go by. Our company is so much bigger than any one individual that it necessarily has to be a combination of brains working together rather than any single dominating figure. Our strength lies in just this feature, because in the event of a catastrophe where half a dozen prominent people in our company were wiped out, the organization could still carry on. As I see it, that is the basic difference between us and the way the Ford Company is operated. Henry Ford, and my father, too, through sheer force of personality started and developed a wonderful thing for succeeding generations. If we are to take advantage of that original development, we have to operate on a different basis than did the founders. The only thing wrong with the Ford Company was that Henry Ford got many personalities around him who were principally interested in bigger, better and more production all the time, instead of considering there might be other factors involved in manufacturing. That idea soon became outmoded, and had Edsel Ford outlived his father, I am sure the organization would have been modernized, because he was a very human individual and I have always considered him a much more capable man than his father. It is too bad the public will never know this, because his death at such an unfortunate time gave the impression he was nothing more than a stuffed shirt. Mrs. Edsel Ford and her son Henry reflect Edsel's more human qualities, and I am only hoping to see the organization eventually shape up to be one of the most respected in the country.... But theirs is a mechanical manufacturing company and nothing like ours. Once again, I believe ours is more basic...."

Perhaps Willard Dow never realized how strongly he did dominate the management of The Dow Chemical Company. Perhaps, given time, he would have shifted to others more and more of the responsibilities he had assumed from the day he took over as president and general manager. But time was not on Willard Dow's side.

In early March, 1949, Dow received an invitation from the Massachusetts Institute of Technology at Cambridge, Massachusetts, inviting him and Mrs. Dow to the school's Mid-Century Convocation. Since Dow was a member of the school's corporate board, he and his wife, Martha, were to be among the honored guests who would hear an address by Sir Winston Churchill, the former British prime minister.

Dow accepted immediately. The trip would give him and his wife not only a chance to meet Churchill, but also an opportunity to visit with their son, Herbert Henry Dow II, who was studying chemical engineering at M.I.T. Dow made arrangements to fly to Cambridge in the company's plane and he invited his general counsel, Calvin Campbell, and his wife, Alta, to join them. The Campbells had planned to go East by train because Mrs. Campbell had never overcome a fear of air travel. But Martha Dow persuaded her to make this one trip by air.

The morning of March 31 was a cold, gray morning. The two couples drove to the Tri-City Airport over roads bordered by trees from which icicles hung. They found the plane waiting for them, the engines warmed up and ready to go. The plane was a twin-engine Beechcraft Executive which could accommodate eight passengers plus Pilot Arthur

J. Bowie and Co-Pilot Frederick C. Clements, both veteran pilots of Midland.

The Dows took seats looking to the rear of the plane and facing the Campbells. They pulled their seat belts tight and the plane took off, boring into the leaden, bumpy clouds. Mrs. Dow soon fell asleep.

About an hour after takeoff, the plane made a turn to the right and began to descend. Campbell could see nothing through the window except the gray of low-hanging clouds. Then Co-Pilot Clements looked back at him and pointed his thumb downward. Apparently they were going in for a landing at the London, Ontario, airport. The plane came out of the overcast at about 800 feet. Rain was falling, cold rain that turned to ice on the wings and controls.

The plane roared low toward the airstrip and then started to climb again. Willard Dow looked at Calvin Campbell with sudden alarm and shook his head. Mrs. Campbell reached out and took her husband by the hand. No one said anything. Then came the jarring, grinding crash.

Campbell would recall: "I remember the quietness and the sound of fire crackling in the front end of the plane. I knew Willard and Martha and Alta were dead. The crash had broken my seat belt. I tried to get my wife loose from her belt... and that's the last I remember until I awoke, lying on the ground beside the plane. It was burning."

Farmer Joseph G. Carpenter and his two sons saw the plane crash into one of their fields about a mile from the London airport. "The plane apparently was coming down for a landing," Carpenter said. "It looked like the landing gear was down. It hit a knoll in the field about fifteen feet high, then went over the top of the knoll and skidded for 250 feet. One engine was driven right back to the rear of the fuselage. Parts were scattered for about 400 feet."

The Carpenters ran to the scene and saw a man staggering away from the blazing plane. The man was Campbell. One arm was burned and a heel was fractured but, miraculously, he had survived.

From a hospital bed in London, Campbell called a friend in Midland to report the crash—the first news of the tragedy to reach the town which less than nineteen years before had mourned the death of Herbert Dow.

Chapter Sixteen

The death of Willard Dow on a rain-sodden field in Canada marked the end of one cycle and the beginning of another in the life of The Dow Chemical Company.

The beginning of the new cycle came when the company's board of directors met in Midland on April 5, 1949, and chose fifty-four-year-old Leland I. "Lee" Doan as president. He was a soft-voiced diplomat-salesman who would lead the company through a growth period that would dwarf all past achievements and catapult Dow Chemical into a global operation.

It was not an easy time for a growing company to change captains, reorganize management, and alter its direction even slightly without losing momentum in the confusion of change. The country had not fully recovered from the war. Europe was struggling to rebuild in the wreckage left by bombs and cannon. And the Cold War between the Communist and non-Communist nations cast its pall of unease and uncertainty over the entire world.

But Doan was not intimidated either by the times or the responsibilities he was assuming. He had literally grown up with the company, starting as a twenty-two-year-old plant helper under the stern eye of Herbert Dow. For twenty years he had been general sales manager and director of sales for Dow Chemical. And then as a member of the board and a vice president, he had shared in the decision-making through Willard's regime. His easy-going ways were in sharp contrast to those of Herbert and Willard Dow. He had their toughness and strong sense of purpose even though he preferred a less abrupt and direct approach to people and their problems.

From the very first, Doan avoided any bruising show of authority in taking over the presidency. When the announcement of his election was prepared, he carefully arranged to have it appear that he was merely one of a three-man team who had moved into places of authority to share the duties that had been Willard Dow's.

The announcement in the company's magazine, the *Dow Diamond*, reported the reorganization in this way:

...The task of reorganization was not a pleasant one. It was carried out, however, with the full knowledge that time is of the essence in the daily affairs of men and business and that Dr. [Willard] Dow would have willed it no other way.

With these thoughts in mind, the Dow board of directors on April 5 named three men with long company service records to the top executive positions. The trio, together with the ten other directors who likewise have served many years, constitute a board which assures continuity of management for the firm's affairs.

Chosen as chairman of the board was Earl W. Bennett, who next year will complete half a century with the company. He became a vice president in 1931 and treasurer in 1934.

Named as president and chief executive officer was Leland I. Doan, a brother-in-law of Dr. Dow, who had served as vice president since 1938, secretary since 1941 and head of the company's sales organization since 1929.

Dr. Mark E. Putnam, a vice president since 1942, and long identified with Dow's production activities, became general manager.

Also named during the reorganization were two new vice presidents, Dr. A. P. Beutel, who is general manager of Dow's Texas Division at Freeport, Texas, and Russel L. Curtis, general manager of the Great Western Division with headquarters at San Francisco. Carl A. Gerstacker was elected treasurer, succeeding Mr. Bennett and Calvin A. Campbell, the firm's general counsel, was named secretary, replacing Mr. Doan....

The casual reader would have had to assume from this announcement that Lee Doan was merely one of a triumvirate chosen to direct the company's affairs. And that is the way Doan wanted it to appear. But within the inner circle there was no misunderstanding about who was boss even when Doan told his colleagues he was going to share the responsibilities of the office.

One who remembered those days of transition recalled: "A dangerous time for any company is when there is a complete change of management. Willard had been his own man. As a leader he was sometimes capricious. He would even let a young squirt like me walk in and tell him how to run the company. But he did the running. When Lee Doan came in as president, we began to discuss things for the first time as a group. Basically, the company didn't change much, but it got a little less capricious. The decisions were more orderly. We became more sensitive to economic conditions and what the competition was doing. There was more emphasis on general planning and thinking ahead. We became more customer-oriented than we had been in the past.

"It took some time to orient to the change. I guess the research people felt the change more than any others. Suddenly they had no one they could talk to. They could come to Lee, but he didn't tell them what to do next as Willard had. They could go to Willard over the heads of their superiors and he would suggest, 'Why don't you do it this way?' because he was a research man himself. Now they had no one to run to. To a lesser degree, the production people were in the same fix. They could not go to one of several key men in production and get an on-the-spot decision. The decisions had to be cleared with Mark Putnam and Mark wouldn't do anything in a hurry. It was frustrating to the wheeler-dealers. But there was more uniform treatment from Putnam. The new way of doing things may have slowed up operations in some ways when they were right, but it also slowed things that were wrong and for the long haul this was a more balanced approach to our problems.

"After his election, Lee wasn't quite certain where he stood in popularity with our people. But shortly after taking office he appeared in public for the first time at a company banquet. He told the crowd he could not be another Willard Dow, taking on all the responsibilities Willard had carried. He said he could only be Lee Doan and he didn't intend to try to change his personality. He asked the help of all those men, urging them to share the responsibilities. I don't think there was anyone present who didn't have tears in his eyes. It was an emotional moment and he swept the house. When he finished talking, they stood up and cheered him."

The policy of handing over greater responsibilities to subordinates was well timed. Dow Chemical was entering a cycle of growth in which sales would grow from $200,371,000 in fiscal 1949 to $781,434,000 in fiscal 1960; and assets in the same period would climb from $294,337,000 to $901,244,000. The business was becoming far too large for one-man control as Willard Dow had realized in his last years.

Lee Doan was as bold and aggressive as Willard Dow even though he did guide with a looser rein. In less than four years, he and his team were deep into a new $350,000,000 building program designed not only to meet the heavy demands of industry but also to help fill the urgent needs of American military services fighting in Korea. Half of the money was earmarked for the booming growth of Beutel's Texas Division where power requirements were climbing from 50,000 to 450,000 kilowatts, making this complex the second largest electric power system in the state of Texas. While Texas produced only one-tenth as many products as the old, established plant at Midland, its sixty products included such big-volume chemicals as caustic, styrene, chlorine, glycols, vinyl chloride, chlorinated hydrocarbons, and magnesium. Midland received $88,000,000 of the money with the remainder divided between other locations. These funds did not include a $13,000,000 expansion program for Dow Corning, whose silicone products were filling both military and industrial needs.

Doan followed the policy which Bennett had explained years earlier to an inquiring analyst, "We build in boom times to keep up with the demand; we build in slump times for the future; so we never stop building."

With the expansion program well underway, Doan told the stockholders: "If you were to ask me the one most fundamental factor behind our growth, I would put it down to the fact that the will to progress is a part of the personality of the Dow company.... For the long pull, we can be optimistic. Our country is in an era of inspiring scientific development far beyond anything our limited imaginations can now project."

One of Doan's early moves was to tighten control over plant production, the lack of which had begun to create serious problems. Chemicals in short supply and essential in almost all production, such as chlorine, were allocated to the geographical units to keep production balanced. The control worked through a group composed of representatives from each geographical division and from sales, with Putnam making the final decision as to who would produce what in what quantity.

In this new setup, the sales department occupied a place of importance it had never held before. Production was linked directly to the salesmen's forecasts of what they expected to sell in the months ahead. Sales estimates were made on forty major products which controlled balanced production. Helping in the control program were economic-engineering people who decided which products could be produced most economically in which plants.

Doan gave the go-ahead to his director of sales, Donald Williams, to beef up the sales organization. Williams sent recruiters to colleges and universities across the country looking for bright young men interested in a career in the chemical industry. The path from campus to selling was by no means automatic for those brought to Midland for interviews. In the 1951 recruiting campaign, as an example, interviewers talked to more than a thousand seniors. From this group, two hundred were invited to Midland for further interviews. And from this number seventy-five were given jobs. Many of them spent as much as thirty-three weeks studying plant operations and products before joining the sales force—and Dow Chemical had as much as $15,000 invested in each man.

The company's in-plant training courses were the distillation of more than thirty years of experience in fitting young men into the organization. As early as 1918 Herbert Dow had seen the need for a training course to help college graduates understand their jobs as well as the policies of the company, and to help ambitious young men without a college degree upgrade their skills.

He had turned this job over to a young high school teacher, Steve Starks, and the Starks school had become through the years Dow Chemical's own "university" and training ground for future laboratory directors, plant managers, and executives. The trainees attended classroom lectures to familiarize themselves with Dow Chemical's products, processes, and operations—and they were spread through the various departments so that they would have the counsel of older men to guide them until they could make their own way.

This system fitted snugly into the company's policy of always promoting from within its own ranks and never going outside the structure for men to fill key positions. It brought the newcomers quickly into personal contact with the top research, production, and management people.

The company's first concentrated sales campaign directed toward the consumer market put the advertising spotlight on Saran Wrap, the filmy plastic used as a household and commercial wrapping for meats, vegetables, bakery products, and other foods.

The sales campaign began early in 1953. Cincinnati, Columbus, Dayton, and Toledo were chosen as test cities. Radio and television stations broadcast Saran Wrap commercials and advertisements were placed in local newspapers. The sales of Saran Wrap jumped in all the test markets.

Encouraged by these results, Director of Sales Williams launched what was up to that time the greatest single-product promotion in the company's history. Commercial spots were purchased on three of the National Broadcasting Company's most popular television programs. Dave Garroway sold Saran Wrap on the "Today" show; Kate Smith on her "Kate Smith Hour"; and Sid Caesar and Imogene Coca on their Saturday night "Show of Shows." The Sunday magazine, *This Week*, carried a series of color advertisements into millions of homes.

The campaign was a success and established Saran Wrap as one of the leading household products in the country. It also supported Doan's conviction that Dow Chemical should move into the consumer market whenever the company had a quality product worthy of the Dow trademark.

Surprisingly, however, while pursuing an aggressive policy in production and sales within the United States and Canada in the early postwar years, Dow Chemical was slow in recognizing the opportunities in overseas trade. It was surprising because the company had a long record of doing business abroad, dating back to the early days of Herbert Dow.

The elder Dow exported bromine and bleach at the turn of the century even though these sales involved him in two trade battles that shook his small company badly. Despite these difficulties, he persisted. When his chemists and engineers succeeded in synthesizing indigo, he found a profitable market for his "Midland Blues" in China, where Dow Chemical's "chop" or trademark became well known wherever silks were being dyed. Willard Dow found a market for magnesium in Europe when few were interested in the metal in the United States. During the 1930's, the company also exported caustic soda, phenol, sodium sulfide, indigo, Epsom salts, aniline, calcium chloride, and chlorobenzene.

An export department was organized in 1936 under Manager Howard Ball to handle orders, expedite shipments, and take care of the details of overseas trade. But there was no significant effort by management to develop markets abroad. The business was largely one of taking unsolicited orders.

But World War II changed this situation drastically. The United States' chemical industry came out of the war in a strong position and with its production plant not only intact but expanded far beyond its prewar size. In contrast, the chemical industries of England and Europe had been badly battered. Many plants were gaunt wrecks. The economies of the nations were disorganized. None had developed a plastics industry on a scale to match that in the United States and the demand for plastics was growing around the world.

Pressure for Dow Chemical to move into the overseas markets did not come from the management in Midland in these years. It came from foreign manufacturers and entrepreneurs seeking licenses to use the Dow processes in rebuilding their countries' chemical industries. It also came from young salesmen who saw that Dow Chemical was overlooking an opportunity to move its surplus production into countries where many chemicals were urgently needed.

One of the most aggressive of this new young breed of businessmen—who looked at the world as their marketplace—was Dow Chemical of Canada's Zoltan Merszei. He was a dark-haired, handsome young man of Hungarian descent who joined the anti-Nazi underground in Hungary during the war. When the fighting in Europe ended, Merszei joined the sales force of export-minded Dow Chemical of Canada. Within a comparatively short time orders from Merszei's customers were pouring in from Europe and also from Latin America.

A Dow offical recalled: "Merszei was aggressive and hungry. He had good connections. It seemed to us he was swarming all over the place, finding people who had a need for our products. A real competition developed between the Toronto sales office and our people in Midland."

Another who pushed hard for export business was Clayton Shoemaker, who had come to Midland from the New York sales office. He traveled through Europe searching for outlets for surplus production and appointing well-known chemical distributors as Dow's representatives in key trade centers. By 1950, the company's exports had climbed from 5 percent of sales to the industry average of 8 percent.

Not all of Dow Chemical's older managers approved of the company becoming too deeply involved in foreign trade. But Lee Doan saw that the maverick export department had reached the point where better organization and control were necessary. In 1951, he named an export committee to coordinate foreign marketing with domestic marketing.

At this time, a combination of circumstances made foreign operations more attractive. Dow Chemical not only needed outlets for surplus chemicals but the federal government offered tax concessions to United States corporations willing to risk their capital in establishing better business and trade connections abroad. These concessions were designed to help bolster the economies of the non-Communist nations struggling to recover from World War II. The government was deeply committed to economic aid through the Marshall Plan to the rehabilitation of Eastern Europe, and to aiding underdeveloped nations in Asia and South America. Behind these commitments were the fears that unless the economies of the free nations were supported by United States dollars, their governments would fall under Communist control.

Lee Doan and his managers decided to form Dow Chemical Inter-American, Limited, responsible for all trade with Latin American countries and Dow Chemical International, Limited, responsible for the company's business in other parts of the world. Clayton Shoemaker was named president of the two subsidiaries and soon was traveling around the world organizing Dow's own international sales force. Merszei set up headquarters in Zurich as sales manager of the European operation. International offices were established in Hong Kong, Brussels, and Montevideo.

During this period, emphasis was on developing an overseas sales organization. Little serious thought was given to Dow Chemical becoming involved in production outside the North American continent. But the arrival in Midland of two visitors from Japan was to change all this.

The visitors were Kagayaki Miyazaki and Manabu Enseki, executives of Japan's Asahi Chemical Company. They were interested in joining forces with Dow Chemical in Japan to form a company for the manufacture of saran filaments which would be woven into fish nets.

Through the years, Japanese fishermen had used nets made of cotton and ramie, a plant fiber found in Asia. Since both fibers had to be imported by the Japanese, their cost created a drain of the Japanese economy. Experiments with saran filaments had convinced Enseki and Miyazaki that the synthetic would find a ready market in Japan's large fishing industry. The filament nets resisted corrosion, they were tough, and being heavier than water, they sank without weights.

Their proposition was: "We will furnish the capital. You furnish the manufacturing know-how. And the company we form will be jointly owned."

Carl Gerstacker would recall: "To tell the truth, we were sitting here during this time doing very little about foreign trade. If they beat a path to our door, we let them have it. We thought of the export business merely as a sideline and it had no real backing from management. When the two Japanese representatives made their proposition to us, we almost wished they had gone away. We didn't want to say yes and we didn't want to say no."

Lee Doan decided the Japanese's proposition was worth looking into. A Dow Chemical representative, Jack Chamberlain, was sent from Midland to investigate. At the time of his arrival, the "westernization" of Japan was well underway and the nation was making an astonishingly swift comeback from the war. Chamberlain was enthusiastic over the possibilities of a joint venture and he recommended a partnership be formed.

Agreement was reached in 1952 to form the Asahi-Dow Limited, the first of the Dow Chemical chain of partnerships abroad. It began as a reluctant venture. For a time the company made little progress. But when it began the manufacture of styrene and Styron in 1956, sales shot up dramatically and the partnership generated enthusiasm in Dow Chemical's ranks for similar joint ventures abroad.

This movement overseas as a manufacturer of chemicals was a major break with tradition. But then Lee Doan's first years as chief executive found the company involved in a good many unusual adventures. None was stranger than the chain reaction which came from Soviet Russia's first explosion of an atomic bomb, drawing Dow Chemical into the nation's nuclear defense program.

This story had its beginning in 1949 when news was flashed to the world that Soviet scientists had exploded an atomic "device." The device was an atomic bomb and its explosion ended the United States' A-bomb monopoly. President Truman's announcement of this event on September 23 added a new dimension of fear to the Cold War. Nine months later, the army of Communist North Korea drove across the 38th Parallel in a sweep to conquer the Republic of South Korea. President Truman quickly ordered General Douglas MacArthur to send American troops to the defense of South Korea. And once more the United States was engaged in a hot war.

In this international crisis, Congress authorized a stepped-up nuclear weapons program. A short time later a representative of the Atomic Energy Commission called on Lee Doan in Midland to ask the company's help in a new super-secret project involving research, development, production, and storage of nuclear weapons. There also would be responsibilities for basic research in peaceful applications of atomic energy.

The AEC had screened several companies in private before reaching a decision that Dow Chemical had the scientific and manufacturing experience required in the program. Part of this experience came from the fact that Willard Dow had been intensely interested in the post-war research into peaceful uses for atomic energy. Several Dow Chemical scientists, including John Grebe and F. H. "Heinie" Langell, had gone to the government's atomic center at Oak Ridge, Tennessee, to study possible applications of this new technology to Dow Chemical's operations. The company had organized a nuclear research laboratory and also had joined with the Detroit Edison Company in exploring the application of nuclear energy to the production of electric power. As Dow was one of the largest power users in the United States, any discovery that resulted in cheaper power would have an important bearing on the company's costs of production.

Lee Doan agreed to join with the AEC in the new project and he chose Mark Putnam to head a group of scientists and engineers to visit Los Alamos, the oldest of the nation's atomic installations, for some preliminary studies. The group received security clearance and on New

Year's Eve the group was aboard a Santa Fe train, heading across Kansas toward Los Alamos.

When Putnam returned to Midland a few days later, he called tall, scholarly "Heinie" Langell into his office and offered him the job as manager of the $45,000,000 project—which would be rated as a new division of The Dow Chemical Company. Putnam could give Langell only the sketchiest outline of what he was to manage, because of the secrecy involved. But he accepted, and began choosing his aides for key positions.

Langell was a veteran employee of Dow Chemical who in 1930 had helped build the first successful pilot plant to take bromine from the sea. He had been among those who developed the full-scale commercial plant at Kure Beach in 1933. And during World War II, he had managed the government-owned magnesium plant at Ludington, Michigan.

Langell became a member of the team chosen by the AEC to select a site for the new operation. Seven sites were considered in various parts of the country, but the team finally agreed that the place which came closest to meeting all the conditions fixed by the AEC was an area near Denver, Colorado, identified on maps as Rocky Flats.

The name was appropriate. It was a flat, rocky, lonely acreage lying between Denver and Boulder where foothills begin their climb to the towering Rocky Mountains. A railroad line ran nearby. Labor was available in Denver. Water and electricity could be obtained easily. The final decision to build at Rocky Flats was made at a secret meeting held in Denver.

Langell would recall: "It was rather funny, the extremes to which we went to keep our actions secret. But that was considered necessary at the time. Our group included representatives of the AEC, Dow Chemical, and the Austin Company, which had been chosen to do the primary architectural engineering and construction. We held our meeting in the old Olin Hotel in Denver. The hotel was in the middle of town near the capitol and was in fact an old ladies' home. But no one seemed to think it unusual for us to be meeting there."

With the site chosen, the AEC called a news conference in Denver on March 23, 1951, to announce the news.

"Are you going to make bombs?" a reporter asked.

"Not as such," the spokesman parried.

About all that the reporters got from the conference was that Dow Chemical would manage the $45,000,000 plant; two thousand construction workers would be employed at the peak of the building; there were military applications to the product; employees would work with radioactive materials; and the operation would be secret. Later announcements disclosed the materials would be plutonium and uranium.

Langell considered calling his operation the Denver Division of The Dow Chemical Company. But Davis W. Persons, AEC project engineer, suggested that "Rocky Flats Division" would be more appropriate since maps designated the area as Rocky Flats. And Persons' suggestion was chosen.

A month after the news conference in Denver, survey crews were on the ground. Construction workers soon followed and by the end of 1951 the Rocky Flats Division was operational although it was not until 1954 that it was in full swing.

Those were not easy days for the pioneers in this project. The rocky, gullied roads were so rough that automobile engines were often jarred loose from the car frames. In the winter months, winds reaching 75 miles an hour—the low limit of hurricane force—often swept down from the Rockies and whistled across the flats. Wind-driven grit scoured paint from cars, trucks, and buildings as a sandblaster would. But the work went on and Rocky Flats was on its way to becoming an important part of the government's nuclear program.

The postwar expansions put a heavy financial strain on Dow Chemical. During the lifetimes of Herbert and Willard Dow, the company had been able to finance its growth to a large extent with retained earnings. But with federal and state taxes taking larger bites from earnings during and after World War II, Lee Doan was forced to turn to external financing to pay for the building programs.

Bennett and Gerstacker in 1952 devised a financing plan to raise more than $100,000,000 in one of the largest financial transactions of its kind ever attempted by a chemical firm in the United States. It called for the sale of subordinate debentures, which were in effect a promise by Dow Chemical to pay the holders 3 percent interest a year for thirty years, at which time the notes would mature. The debentures were convertible to common stock of the company, under a schedule of conversion prices, at the option of the buyers. But being "subordinate" debentures, they stood last in line at the pay window, with all other debts having priority.

The sale of the debentures proved to be a show of confidence by buyers in the future of Dow Chemical. The notes were offered to the public through an underwriting combine headed by Smith, Barney & Company, and were sold within a matter of hours at a premium. On July 22, 1952, a check for $100,425,000 was handed over to Chairman of the Board Earl Bennett. And again there were some who remembered the day when a windblown $2 bill, found on the street in Midland, had saved Bennett from the embarrassment of having to admit that he was broke.

If there were any fears at this time that Dow Chemical was in a reckless spending mood, Lee Doan put them to rest. He told the stockholders: "...under our present tax structure there is little incentive to operate efficiently. There is, in fact, quite an incentive to operate lavishly. We can make good fellows of ourselves for 30 cents on the dollar—so we think. I contend that such thinking is fallacious, shortsighted and extremely dangerous. Furthermore, it just won't work. If we choose to spend recklessly it simply means that tax collections will fall below expectations. And if that happens we can only expect a further increase in tax rates.... In our own company we have always tried to operate economically. Today we are, if anything, redoubling our efforts in that direction. We are spending a lot of money, to be sure. But it is going for legitimate expansion and productive purposes, and we are guarding against the temptation to add frills with dollars we might theoretically withhold from the tax collector...."

The frugality which Herbert Dow had practiced and his son had encouraged had become a way of life in Dow Chemical that Lee Doan had no intention of changing. There were no frills provided for in the $100,425,000 check turned over to Bennett. If there had been, it would have shocked the entire top command. They were men schooled in a tradition of avoiding pomp and ceremony and displays of affluence—even in their private lives.

Spending for production and expansion was another matter. The era of Lee Doan was a high-spending period for Dow Chemical as the company moved in so many directions in such a short space of time.

One important decision by Doan was to build new plants, wherever possible, closer to the consumers of the plant's products. Over the years this policy would place Dow Chemical plants, installations, and laboratories in 36 states and avoid the problems and risks of too-great concentration in the older divisions.

The initial move in this direction came in 1951 when Dow Chemical moved into New England. A plant was built at Allyn's Point on the Thames River between New London and Norwich to produce styrene products for the manufacturers of housewares, toys, wall tile, refrigerator parts, television lenses, and other plastic merchandise. An 800-foot, deep-water dock was constructed so that raw materials could be shipped by water to Allyn's Point from Texas.

In this same year, construction started on a $30,000,000 plant at Madison, Illinois, for large-scale rolling of magnesium sheets. It was, in the words of Dow Chemical's magnesium expert, J. D. Hanawalt, "as significant for the magnesium industry as was the introduction of continuous rolling for the steel and aluminum industries."

Hanawalt added: "The desirability of large-scale rolling for magnesium has been discussed in the United States for some years, but it requires a large-scale volume to support a large investment, and, on the other hand, the reduced costs of a large mill are first needed to develop the volume market. It was The Dow Chemical Company which once more took the kind of step which growth of the magnesium industry requires."

The Madison plant gave Dow Chemical a close-to-the-market distribution point for shipping rolled magnesium economically to the automobile industry, airplane makers, and other fabricators. The magnesium ingots were sent by inland waterways from Texas to Madison.

While comparatively few knew anything about the fabrication of magnesium at the beginning of World War II, there were now more than thirty companies in the United States fabricating magnesium into trucks and trailers. Others had learned the techniques of using the metal in a wide variety of products, including industrial equipment and machinery. For those with a long memory, it was amusing to note that where experts in 1941 had believed United States military planes could reasonably use only 44 pounds of magnesium per plane, the long-range bombers being built during the Korean War had magnesium parts whose combined weight per plane ran from 10,000 to 30,000 pounds. And Dow Chemical had led the way in developing the technology making this possible.

Dow Chemical's subsidiary, Dowell, developed one of the more important markets for magnesium by using the metal as an electrical protector to prevent corrosion of underground tanks, steel piers, pilings, ships' hulls, water pipes, and other metal structures.

The corroding process generally resulted from electrical currents created by the bare metal reacting with chemical elements in soil and water. The flow of electricity carried away tiny particles of the metal, causing it to pit and rust. But when metal, such as a water pipe, was wired to an ingot of magnesium, the magnesium and the pipe became, in effect, the poles of a battery. The pipe became the cathode and the magnesium the anode. The electricity flowed from the more chemically active magnesium into the pipe, with the deterioration taking place in the magnesium. Thus, when tiny particles of the magnesium anode flaked off, the ingot became an expendable part of the "battery." It could be easily and cheaply replaced while the pipe itself remained undamaged.

One company found that by placing magnesium anodes along its water lines, leaks were cut by 70 percent and maintenance costs lowered as much.

From metal to plastics, Dow Chemical provided the raw materials which enabled many independent small businesses to develop throughout the country in this post-war period. This was particularly true in plastics, where, with a relatively small investment, plants could be built for molding styrene polymers into cabinets for television sets, refrigerator parts, wall tile, radio cabinets, and household wares of an endless variety and color.

One of Dow Chemical's most successful plastics was Styrofoam. This expanded white plastic, in which were trapped millions of air bubbles, was light, buoyant, water resistant, rigid, and adaptable to as many uses as the imagination could devise. One cubic foot of it weighed only 1.2 to 2 pounds and could support twenty-five times its own weight in water. It was three times as light as cork. Its multicellular structure made it useful as a nonconductor of electricity and an insulation material. It could be cut, sawed and shaped into a giant-sized toy panda, a stage setting, or a Christmas tree bauble. And it could be installed in boats, making them virtually unsinkable, or used as floating supports for boat docks.

The use of Styrofoam in boats received a boost in 1950 with the forty-third running of the motorboat Gold Cup Classic on the Detroit River. One of the entries was a speedster called Slo-Mo-Shun IV, which had been timed over a straightaway run on Seattle's Lake Washington at 160.323 miles per hour. The Slo-Mo-Shun IV had Styrofoam flotation instead of air tanks in its bow and stern, a fact noted by writers and boat designers. The craft lived up to its advance billing. It won the Gold Cup Classic and went on to capture the famed Harmsworth Trophy.

Less publicized was the Bell Telephone Company's use of Styrofoam in its system of telephone and television signal towers stretching from New York to Chicago. Atop each tower was a boxlike structure called a Delay Lens Antenna. The antenna, used both as transmitter and receiver of radio microwaves, was made of five miles of metal ribbon embedded in 500-pound blocks of foamed plastic. Styrofoam was chosen by Bell because of its light weight and its excellent electrical insulating properties.

Small businesses had been developed to weave saran monofilaments into automobile seat covers and insect screening, and to fashion saran rubber into linings for railroad tank cars carrying corrosive chemicals, greases, acids, solvents, and oils. As the number of these small firms increased, so did Dow's production.

Throughout the chemical industry, there was no growth more spectacular than that of Dow Corning. This company, which had started operations during World War II making silicone sealants for the ignition systems of airplanes, had developed more than six hundred products in a span of ten years. The most successful of its postwar consumer products was a silicone-treated tissue marketed under the trade name "Sight Savers." These tissues cleaned, polished, and protected the lenses of spectacles with so little effort that they quickly became standard items on the shelves of merchants.

Silicone products found increasing use as water repellents for leather and textiles, in heat- and weather-resistant paints, in automobile and furniture polishes, and in industry. The demand for Dow Corning products forced the company to double its size three times in ten years and then quadruple its capacity. In 1953, the company was growing at the rate of 40 percent a year as compared with the 9 percent growth of the chemical industry as a whole.

Silicone greases began to replace ordinary lubricants which could not withstand temperatures ranging from 350 to 700 degrees Fahrenheit. One oven conveyor system tested by Dow Corning experts had seventy-two hundred bearings which traveled through temperatures up to 700 degrees for ten out of every sixteen hours of its operation. Frequently the bearings froze and production had to be halted. But the use of Dow Corning 41 silicone grease eliminated the failures, reduced relubrication to once a week, and cut electric power costs by 80 percent.

In another study, experts found that motors doing heavy-duty work in an automobile parts factory burned out their windings on an average of each eight days. Each motor failure cost three hours' repair time plus $80 for the rewinding. When the motors were rewound with silicone-protected wiring at a cost of $150, they ran for six months without a halt. This meant a net savings of $8,000 for the factory in repair costs, the savings of four hundred man hours of labor, and an increase in production of forty thousand parts.

The discovery of new products and finding new uses for old products was one of the keys to Dow Chemical's growth in the 1950's. But even more important was Lee Doan's move to bring younger men into the management councils. It came at a time when the company was rapidly developing into one of the giants of the United States chemical industry and the times required a break with many customs of the past.

Doan faced up to the reality that the men who had helped Herbert and Willard Dow build the company were getting on in years and the time was nearing when age would inevitably thin their ranks. Doan began to set the stage for the transfer of power from the Old Guard to younger men.

He made his initial moves in the early 1950's. The committee-type direction of research was abolished and forty-nine-year-old Ray H. Boundy was promoted from his post as manager of the plastics department and made director of research. He had through the years contributed to the development of many of the company's most important processes and products.

Doan named thirty-seven-year-old C. B. "Ben" Branch to take over the plastics department, the fastest-growing unit in Dow Chemical. Branch had come to the company in 1937 from Cleveland's Western Reserve University and had risen to head the important Technical Service and Development Department.

In other changes, Doan chose Max Key, a twenty-four-year veteran of Dow Chemical, to manage plastics production and to be a vice president and director of Asahi-Dow Limited. Two grandsons of Herbert Dow were elected to the board of directors. One was Willard Dow's son, twenty-six-year-old Herbert Henry Dow II. The other was thirty-one-year-old Herbert Dow "Ted" Doan, a son of Lee Doan.

During World War II, Ted Doan had served for three years with the Air Force Weather Service, two of them in the South Pacific. He had returned after the war to finish his schooling at Cornell University where he was graduated in 1949 with a chemical engineering degree. After a period of student training, he went to work in the Technical Service and Development Department under Ben Branch.

It was during this period that Ted Doan and Ben Branch formed a fast friendship which was to have its influence on the future of The Dow Chemical Company.

PART FOUR *1950-1968*

Chapter Seventeen

In the aftermath of the hot war in Korea, the business boom in the United States picked up momentum. And Dow Chemical's growth was a phenomenon that intrigued the eastern financial community because the company had started in such a remote place as Midland, Michigan, and seemingly had progressed through a fierce sort of independence which took little note of what other industry leaders were doing.

A *Forbes* magazine writer arrived in Midland in the summer of 1956 to take a look at "the fourth-largest and the fastest-growing chemical colossus in the country" which was spending money at a rate that was impressive even to Wall Street.

Last month, he wrote for the September issue of his magazine, Dow was literally bursting apart at the seams with growth. In Midland, new plants were springing up like prairie flowers. In the South, at Dow's sprawling plant-sites along the Mississippi River in Louisiana and beside the Brazos River in Texas, fresh concrete and new steel seemed as commonplace as Gulf Coast sunshine. In a dozen other Dow plants scattered from Connecticut to California, old walls were coming down to allow for the restless expansion that has long been the trademark of the gentlemen from Midland.

In the decade since the War, Dow had calmly spent a whopping $700 million on new plants to manufacture its 600-odd chemical products. In the years ahead, they plan—apparently just as calmly—to shell out even more. "This coming year," says Dow's tweedy, pipe-smoking president, Lee Doan, "we will spend at least another $75 million. And it looks like we'll soon be off on another round of expansion which will overshadow anything we did before."

Even the pessimists in Wall Street these days have to agree with the optimists on a fundamental fact. That is that the money which a chemical company spends on expansion is a pretty fair bet to come pouring back in the form of lush earnings. Certainly Dow's own dynamic growth has been classic proof that this is so. On the very day that Leland Doan so blandly outlined his big future plans, he also authorized the release of Dow's annual report covering fiscal 1956 (ended May 31). It showed Dow's sales up 20 per cent to a record $565 million. It showed profits up 59 per cent to almost $60 million. But most of all it showed beyond possibility of doubt that Dow's free-handed spending is paying off. . . .

Plants were hardly "springing up like prairie flowers" nor were the millions spent as casually as it might have appeared. But the rate of expansion was impressive. The basic reason for this growth was that Lee Doan and his managers had been correct in their estimates of the nation's chemical needs in the postwar era. They had foreseen a period of industrial growth that would call for chemicals in greater and greater quantities, in an ever-widening range of uses. There was not a single one of the seventy-two major industries in the United States which did not depend to some degree on chemical products. By 1954, almost half of the chemical industry's sales were in products that had not existed ten years earlier. The chemist had become deeply involved in every facet of everyday living—food, clothing, housing, health, and transportation. By 1956 the chemical industry was pouring $275,000,000 into research, more than any other industry, and Dow Chemical was investing a greater share of earnings in research than any of its competitors.

During Lee Doan's first ten years in office, Dow Chemical broke from the ranks of medium-size companies to a rating as one of the largest manufacturers in the nation. When he took office, the company had total assets of $294,337,000 and sales of $200,371,000. At the end of ten years, the assets stood at $859,081,000 and sales at $705,442,000. An investment of $1,000 in Dow Chemical stock in 1949 was worth $5,000 in 1959.

As early as 1956, Dow Chemical was well advanced on its program to decentralize production by building plants outside the Midland and Texas Divisions. New Styrofoam plants were under construction at Pevely, Missouri, and Ironton, Ohio, and a fibers plant was going up on the James River near Williamsburg, Virginia. Near Baton Rouge, Louisiana, ground had been broken for a new complex to produce many of the basic chemicals manufactured at the Texas and Midland plants.

Looking to the future, Doan had concluded that too much concentration in Midland and Texas could lead to grave problems with water, waste disposal, depletion of resources, and labor. There were disadvantages, too, in the two main divisions becoming so big as to be cumbersome from the administrative standpoint.

Explaining the policy of plant dispersal to stockholders, Doan said: ". . . while we dislike to think of unpleasant possibilities, we cannot conscientiously ignore the very important factor of vulnerability. The concentrated, all-eggs-in-one-basket operation is vulnerable to certain hazards just as the business with a single or limited line of products is vulnerable to whims of the market.

"A major catastrophe in a concentrated installation can be not only tragic but absolutely crippling. Likewise a work stoppage, whether by means of strike or some other cause, can have extremely serious effects.

"And in these things we have also to keep in mind our dependability as a supplier. Customers who depend heavily upon us for materials essential to their own business sleep better at night when they know our production of those materials is split over two or more locations rather than concentrated in one. . . ."

The most ambitious of the new projects was the Louisiana complex—the largest venture of its kind since Willard Dow had put Dutch Beutel to building the Texas giant in 1940. Early in 1956, a team headed by Jack Stein, one of Beutel's assistants in the Texas Division, looked over possible sites in the Baton Rouge area. Stein had been one of the young men Beutel had hand-picked in Midland to help get the Texas operation underway and he had played an important part in the postwar development of the division and its production control program.

Stein's team recommended the plants be built on a 1,700-acre tract on the west bank of the Mississippi River, ten miles south of Baton Rouge and just north of the town of Plaquemine. This was plantation country and for years had been a land of sugar cane and cattle raising. But the plantations were disappearing as industries expanded along the river front, attracted by the availability of water, oil, gas, salt, sulfur, and good transportation by water, highway, and rail.

Dow Chemical purchased the 1,700 acres and later added another 1,300 acres for possible future expansion. Lee Doan named Stein as general manager of the new division and Stein picked most of his management staff from the ranks of the younger men in the Texas Division. Others came from the Midland, Western, and Rocky Flats divisions.

On a hot day in September, 1956, Dutch Beutel headed a group who came to Plaquemine for ground-breaking ceremonies. Dutch refused to use a tool so traditional as the shovel for the earth-turning. He climbed into the seat of a bulldozer, turned on the engine, and dropped the blade to cut a deep furrow in the parched grass and black soil. This act was the start of a two-year building drive in which twenty-seven hundred construction men would erect plants to produce the first of the Louisiana products—vinyl chloride, chlorine, caustic soda, ethylene, chlorinated solvents, and glycol.

Dow Chemical incorporated into the Louisiana complex the most advanced of its processes and techniques in an effort to make it a model of chemical manufacturing efficiency. But the plants were completed in 1958 in a cycle of business recession when their capacity was not needed. For a brief time Stein found himself manager of some of the world's most modern chemical plants—with nothing to produce.

Stein recalled: "As it turned out, this slack period in business was fortunate for us. We were able to capitalize on adversity. We had time to think and to plan. Midland told me that if I could find a way to operate with the few people I had, I could start production. I had kept the nucleus of the team I had chosen and we went to work. We took a hard look at our basic requirements. We found that we actually needed twenty-five to thirty fewer people than we had figured. We stripped ourselves down to where there was no fat."

The business recession didn't last long. But in this period Stein and his people evolved a unique operation: all the Dow Chemical people were salaried, but maintenance and certain services were contracted out to local firms on the basis of low bids. It was a system which Dow Chemical would adopt through its other operations on a modified scale.

The start-up of the Louisiana plants removed some of the production pressure from the Texas Division, placed Dow Chemical closer to the growing markets of the Southeastern United States, and provided back-up production as insurance against shutdowns at Midland or in Texas.

With all of the new building and expansions, however, the base of Dow Chemical's strength in the South remained in Texas where Dutch Beutel ran his operation with a degree of independence given to no other manager. The volume of chemicals which flowed from the Texas plants at Freeport and Velasco was enormous. They turned out 22 percent of all the hydrochloric acid produced in the United States. One year's production of ethylene glycol, if used entirely in automobile antifreeze, would give 15,000,000 cars and trucks protection from sub-zero temperatures. One month's production of perchlorethylene, used as a dry cleaning agent, would clean 12,000,000 men's suits. These were not only measures of the Texas Division's size but of its importance in the United States economy.

The three power plants of this division alone produced enough electricity to supply the needs of a city the size of Dallas. There were 70 miles of streets and roads inside its fences, 32 miles of railroad tracks, and 7 miles of a canal waterway for barges. The roads and waterways were traveled day after day by 520 wheeled vehicles, more than 1,800 tank cars, two tugboats, and some 40 barges either owned or leased by the company. Thousands of tons of chemicals moved to markets by seagoing tankers.

With one exception, the plants in the Freeport-Velasco complex were wholly owned by Dow Chemical. The wartime installations which had produced magnesium and styrene for the British and United States governments had been purchased by the company in postwar negotiations spread over several years. The exception was the plant producing ethylene dibromide for anti-knock gasoline, jointly owned by Dow Chemical and the Ethyl Corporation.

The men who helped Beutel build this petrochemical giant were, on the average, only thirty years old when they arrived in Texas in 1940. Now their average age was only forty-five. Their drive and vitality had contributed much to placing Dow Chemical among the world's leading chemical producers. And it was to the Texas Division that Dow Chemical turned for many of the young executives needed for new ventures such as the one in Louisiana.

Through the years, Dow Chemical had grown almost entirely from within. But in 1957 Lee Doan turned to a merger to put the company into the plastic packaging business in the United States and Europe. This was achieved through a merger with the Dobeckmun Company, one of the best-known packaging firms in the country, with headquarters in Cleveland.

Dobeckmun products were made from such raw materials as polyethylene, cellophane, saran, acetate, aluminum foil, cloth, and paper. Chemicals produced by Dow Chemical were basic in some of its products and the merger fitted into Doan's plans for moving the company toward consumer products.

The Dobeckmun Company had been founded in 1927 by Thomas Dolan, its president, and two engineers, Logan E. Becker and John Munson, to produce the first machine-made cellophane wrappers for cigars. The founders took the first syllables from their names—Do-Beck-Mun—as the name of their company.

From cellophane cigar wrappers, the company had gone on to pioneer in the design and development of flexible packages such as plastic bags, and transparent films.

Dobeckmun had three manufacturing plants in Cleveland, one at Berkeley, California, one in London, England, and one in Amsterdam, Holland. Two others, producing paper products, were the subsidiary Ben-Mont Paper Company of Bennington, Vermont, and the Adams Paper Company of Wells River, Vermont, a subsidiary of Ben-Mont.

While negotiations were underway on the merger, Doan reached a decision to put Dow Chemical into the highly competitive synthetic textile field with a fiber given the trade name "Zefran." From the days of Herbert Dow, the company had produced raw materials which could have been converted to fibers but it had made no attempt to compete with Du Pont and others in this field.

The decision to enter the textile competition was not an easy one, nor was it unanimously popular within the company. Doan and those who supported him realized they were getting a late start. But they were convinced that at last they had a fiber which would give the company a strong position in a big business that was certain to grow bigger.

Zefran was a material which could be used alone or blended easily with wool, angora, rayon, cotton, silk, or other synthetics. It had been discovered in the Dow Chemical laboratory at Pittsburg, California, where G. W. Stanton had guided the original research.

Stanton and his team had begun a search in 1949 for a luxury fiber which would meet the exacting standards of mill operators and designers. They screened literally hundreds of polymers over a period of seven years before they produced the one with all the properties for which they had been searching. The fluffy fiber was based on acrylonitrile and was called an "acrylic alloy." The first fifty pounds shipped to the Lowell Textile Institute for testing and evaluation were ceremoniously wrapped in blue ribbon and insured for $50,000.

A name for the new fiber originated unexpectedly in the Stanton household. Stanton came home one evening and announced to his family, "We need a name for our new fiber."

Stanton, his wife and daughter, Sharon, sixteen, huddled around a kitchen table trying different combinations of syllables. Sharon began toying with the word "zephyr" because it sounded so light and airy. "Why not call it Zefon?" she suggested.

Stanton sent Sharon's nomination to Midland where the new textile fibers department had turned to a computer to obtain a long list of syllables that might produce a name pleasing to the ear. With Sharon's Zefon as a starter, they arrived at Zefran.

Although the research had started in California, the development had centered in Midland, and the raw materials were produced in Texas, Doan decided the finished product would be manufactured in a plant within easy reach of eastern mills and the New York textile marketing center. For these reasons, a plant site was chosen on a bluff overlooking the James River in Virginia. The pilot plant operation in California was transferred to the new location and enlarged to produce as much as 12,000,000 pounds of Zefran a year.

The plant began production in June, 1958, and a visiting writer—unfamiliar with the processes for converting chemicals to synthetic fibers—reported with a tone of astonishment, "The production end of the plant is simply a maze of pipes, tubing, boilers and machines." And so it was. But for Dow Chemical, the James River plant was much more than just another assembly of pipes, tubes, and machines. It was a multi-million-dollar gamble that Dow Chemical could enter the textile competition as a late starter and hold its own against the best of the producers.

The growth of the plastics industry was one of the more spectacular industrial success stories of the 1950's and Dow Chemical played an aggressive role in its development. In 1940, the company was fifteenth in size in the plastics industry but in 1957 it had moved into second place behind Union Carbide. The sale of plastic products leaped from 2 percent of total sales to approximately 32 percent in this period. By 1957, the sales of plastics were greater than the total sales of all Dow Chemical products ten years earlier. The stars in Dow Chemical's products for the plastics field were styrene for the synthetic rubber industry, Styrofoam, Styron, and saran polymers for the plastics fabricators. Saran Wrap for the consumer market had been such a success that by the mid-1950's the company was moving more than five million rolls each month into the market. And in this period polyethylene was added to the plastics line.

Polyethylene was a British discovery. Chemists in the laboratories of the Imperial Chemical Industries (I.C.I.) first worked out the means for transforming ethylene gas into a solid polymer in 1933. The first pilot plant went into operation in 1938, and the plastic became an important material in Britain's war effort.

The manufacture of polyethylene in the United States was restricted under the I.C.I. patents until 1953 when court decisions forced their licensing to other United States manufacturers. Dow Chemical took advantage of this opportunity to go into the manufacture of the popular product since ethylene was one of the company's basic building materials. The process of converting ethylene to polyethylene required five basic steps. Ethylene gas, obtained from petroleum, was purified and placed under pressures up to 30,000 pounds per square inch after which a polymerization reaction took place. Unreacted materials were removed and the final product obtained. A wide range of polymers could be made to fit the customers' needs by changes in the pressures and temperatures used in the conversion process.

While strengthening its position in plastics, Dow Chemical was establishing stronger positions in other lines of chemicals. In 1954, the company became the world's second commercial producer of synthetic glycerine with construction of a Texas Division plant equipped to turn out 36,000,000 pounds a year.

For more than a century, the world's supply of glycerine was chiefly a by-product of soap making. But as soap consumers turned to synthetic detergents, the old sources of glycerine dwindled. The synthetic product had all the properties of natural glycerine and it satisfied the diverse needs of the manufacturers of such products as paint, enamel, cellophane, adhesive, paper, and cigarettes (glycerine helps tobacco retain its moistness).

The chemical solutions to industrial problems were endless, leading Dow Chemical's researchers into many strange fields. And none, perhaps, was more intriguing than the development of "chemical mining."

Early in the century, the operators of western ore mines began searching for some means other than smelting to separate metals from raw ore. Traditionally, metals had been separated from unwanted rock, earth, and other materials by the simple process of melting the metal in furnaces. The process was satisfactory in handling ores with a high metal content. But smelting alone was neither economical nor efficient with low-grade ores unless the ores were put through a concentrating process before smelting.

Several methods were found to concentrate the low-grade ores before smelting. One of the more successful was "froth flotation" in which the ore was crushed to powdery fineness and mixed with water which was agitated. Chemicals were added which, attracted to the metal-containing fine particles of the ore, floated them to the top of the tank where they could be easily removed and prepared for smelting.

Early in 1920, it was found that certain organic, sulfur-containing compounds called xanthates worked especially well in the flotation, particularly when the metals to be recovered were combined with sulfur. The flotation process has been described in this way by a Dow Chemical expert:

"The basic idea of froth flotation is the attachment of air bubbles to certain mineral particles which have been wholly or partially freed from other minerals or gangue (rock and other non-mineral substances) by crushing and grinding. This action takes place after the ore is finely ground in water.

"The air bubbles carry the wanted mineral particles to the surface leaving the unwanted materials behind. . . . Flotation sounds quite simple and in principle is, but several things must be done to make the wanted mineral particles attach themselves to the air bubbles and float.

"The ore must be ground in the presence of water to a size small enough to liberate the valuable minerals—either one from another or from adhering or enclosing gangue. This grinding is normally accomplished in a ball mill.

"The water-mineral pulp or slurry must be agitated to keep the minerals in suspension while the air bubbles are picking up the selected minerals and carrying them to the surface. The agitation also insures the maximum dispersion of air for bubble formation.

"Certain chemical collectors, frothers, and modifying agents must be added to create conditions favorable to making the chosen mineral adhere to the air bubbles and favorable to forming a stabilized froth.

"The xanthates are manufactured and used as collectors, the function of which is to promote contact between mineral particles and air bubbles by forming a thin coating over the selected minerals and thus rendering them water repellent.

"The main purpose of a frothing agent is to permit formation of finely dispersed air bubbles and a coalescent froth, above the pulp, stable enough to hold the floated mineral particles in suspension until they flow or are swept over the top of the flotation machine.

"Modifying agents perform such functions as regulating pH, depressing one mineral while allowing another to float or activating the flotation of one mineral in preference to another. . . ."

Wilhelm Hirschkind, directing research at the Great Western Electrochemical Company, saw a promising future for xanthates and he pushed research and production to aid the western mining industry. When Dow Chemical took over Great Western in 1939 this program was expanded under a Mining Technical Service centered at Pittsburg, California. Gradually, Dow Chemical became deeply involved in so-called chemical mining.

With this background, it naturally followed that Dow Chemical was greatly interested in the Atomic Energy Commission's efforts in the late 1940's to encourage uranium mining. Favorable prices for uranium-bearing ores sent prospectors, armed with geiger counters, rushing to the hills to search for deposits of the metal. The fissionable material was to be used not only in nuclear weapons, but in reactor research, industrial power development, atomic power plants for ships and submarines, radiotherapy, and for many other applications.

Among the large uranium deposits discovered in this country were those on the Continental Slope known as the Colorado Plateau, a region dotted with derelict mines left from the gold and silver boom days. Twelve big mills were built to handle the uranium ores taken from some two hundred tunnels driven into the mountains.

Milling uranium ore brought new problems. No one had any experience in milling the ore on the scale required to satisfy the government's need for the metal. The critical need was to find a means of separating the uranium from rock and other minerals quickly and efficiently.

Dow Chemical's researchers studied the problems of the Colorado mills and came up with a product called Separan 2610. It was a flocculating agent which caused uranium particles in crushed ore to join together or floc in a water solution and settle out quickly—as mud settles in a glass of water. Not only did the solids form a cake on a filter cloth, but the cake was porous and would not clog the filter.

Within a short time, almost every mill on the Colorado Plateau was using Separan 2610 to solve its separation problem, and its use spread to mills in other parts of the United States and Canada. In New Mexico, an industrial mill found Separan 2610 useful in clearing turbid river water so that it could be used in the plant's operations.

Uranium mining was only one of many unusual activities to claim the interests of Dow Chemical researchers. In a roundabout way, the researchers also became involved in a fight to save the Great Lakes fishing industry from being destroyed by the lamprey eel, a villain whose family was older than the dinosaur. The lamprey had found its way into Lake Erie by 1921, and then had spread into Lake Huron and Lake Michigan. It hatched in streams, migrated to the main bodies of water as an adult, and then returned to spawn. The larvae remained in the fresh water for six to seven years before moving into the main bodies of water as adult predators. The eel-like adult was 18 to 24 inches long and had a suction-cup mouth by which it attached itself to a fish to become a parasite. The creature gouged a hole through the fish's scales with a rough tongue and then fed on the blood and juices of its victim until the fish was lifeless.

By 1940 the lamprey was well on the way to destroying the multi-million-dollar fishing industry on the Great Lakes. From 1940 to 1950, the volume of trout taken from Lake Huron dropped from almost 4,000,000 pounds to less than 500,000 pounds while on Lake Michigan the trout catches over the same period dropped from more than 5,000,000 pounds to virtually zero. Authorities agreed that the lamprey eel, given time, would wipe out the Great Lakes trout population entirely.

Conservationists in the Canadian and United States governments and in the Great Lakes states joined forces to do battle against the lamprey. The program was taken over by an international group, the Great Lakes Fishery Commission, after 1956. Two of the leaders were Dr. James W. Moffett and Dr. Vernon C. Applegate of the United States Fish and Wildlife Service (USFWS).

Various control methods were tested and used. In the first stages, the main effort was directed at controlling the immediate threat to the lake trout. At the same time, scientists studied long-range methods for breaking the life cycle of the lamprey.

Applegate and his colleagues fashioned electro-mechanical weirs or nets to trap the lampreys on their spawning runs into tributary streams. The nets were placed in watershed streams and they proved effective in reducing the lamprey population. But this was not enough. Studies turned to chemical means of destroying the larvae in the stream beds. A search began for a chemical that would be toxic to the lamprey larvae but would not injure other fishes.

In a laboratory at Hammond Bay on Lake Huron near Rogers City, Michigan, Applegate's team tested some six thousand chemicals on lamprey larvae as well as trout and bluegill fingerlings. After almost two years of patient and frustrating work, USFWS Laboratory Director John Howell found one jar in which, he reported, "larval lampreys were dead and the trout still alive and happy." It was a beginning and the chemical compound which turned the trick was called 3-bromo-4-nitrophenol. Unfortunately, this compound was found to be almost impossible to synthesize with the required degree of purity. Also, it was expensive.

At this point, Applegate turned to the chemical industry for help. One of his letters arrived on the desk of Edwin E. Dunn of Dow Chemical's Biochemical Research Laboratory. Dunn invited Applegate to come to Midland and discuss the problem.

Within days, Dow Chemical had a team organized under research chemist Clarence L. Moyle to cooperate with the USFWS representatives. Moyle suggested that a chemical in the same family as 3-bromo-4-nitrophenol possibly would be effective and easier to produce. Nine compounds were chosen for further studies at Hammond Bay, among them a compound known as 3,4,6-trichloro-2-nitrophenol. It had been synthesized in Dow Chemical's laboratories in 1941 during a study of fungicides, but had been put on the shelf for possible future development.

The long-shot 3,4,6-trichloro-2-nitrophenol looked most promising of all the compounds in the testing stage. Within a few weeks, Dow Chemical production people in the latex-organic chemicals department had found the keys to volume production and by fall of 1957 they were able to produce the compound in a 30 percent concentration. They named it Dowlap. And now the time had come for an actual stream test to see if it killed the larvae as efficiently as it did in the laboratory.

The company's *Dow Diamond* reported the results of this test in a story written soon after the experiment was made:

A stream was picked—Little Billie's Creek near Cheboygan, Michigan.

A date was set, October 29, 1957.

And 3,4,6-trichloro-2-nitrophenol got a new name—Dowlap.

The years of labor had built up tension that was almost tangible as Moffett, Applegate, their USFWS associates and Dow representatives went to work that dreary October day along a two-mile stretch of the Little Billie's.

About 1,200 larval lampreys were confined in cages along the stream. These were the control specimens. Their reactions would be recorded hourly over a 24-hour period. If they died within the test period, the stream treatment would be considered a success. If they lived? Well, the search would start anew.

In the late afternoon, John Howell turned the valves and Dowlap was pumped into Little Billie's Creek at the rate of 30 parts to a million parts of water.

About four hours after the chemical was metered into the stream, observers at the first station downstream from the feeder noted activity among the caged control larvae. A few popped out of the mud, obviously "unhappy and uncomfortable." And as the hours wore on, more and more of the distressed larvae came out of the mud. By dawn, with nearly eight hours of treatment still scheduled, lamprey larvae native to the stream began to pile up along the banks. And as the day went on, these windrows of dead grew larger and larger and attracted gulls and sandpipers by the hungry hundreds.

At the end of the 24-hour test period, about 92 percent of the larvae in the control cages were dead. And even the living did not seem long for this world. The tension of the years broken, Moffett and Applegate almost casually pronounced the test a success. In the first press release of this first stream test of a selective chemical for lamprey control, the Great Lakes Fishery Commission said: "On the basis of preliminary evaluation the results... were very successful... indications are the final kill would top 95 percent."

The release concluded: "Further stream trials of Dowlap and other promising larvicides are scheduled in the near future. If the results of these tests substantiate preliminary stream trials findings, the chemical controls will be used in conjunction with the electric weirs. Supplementing these control methods already in use with a larvicide will hasten the day when the dread parasitic lamprey is driven from the waters of the Great Lakes and the fishery there is restored to its former productivity."

And so Dow Chemical could proudly claim a role in the battle to save the Great Lakes fishing industry.

Not the least of Doan's innovations in the 1950's was the shipment of chemicals by sea and inland waterways in tankers and barges designed and built for Dow Chemical. The first experimental shipments by tanker had begun in 1949 when the *Marine Chemist,* a converted oil tanker, was leased to haul liquid styrene to the Allyn's Point Styron plant in Connecticut.

The *Marine Chemist* proved so successful as a chemical carrier that Doan gave the go-ahead to the Shipbuilding Division of Bethlehem Steel Company to build the first tanker ever designed solely for carrying chemical cargoes.

December 10, 1953, the *Marine Dow-Chem*—551 feet long and capable of carrying 16,000 long tons of chemicals in her specially designed hold—slid down the ways at Quincy, Massachusetts. Dow Chemical was on the way to acquiring its own fleet.

Perhaps, in the hurly-burly of the 1950's, the most intriguing aspect of Dow Chemical's growth was the gradual evolution of the company from a domestic operation into an international operation. Just as Willard Dow had looked beyond Midland for opportunities (and, indeed, had been forced to do so), so did Lee Doan look beyond the borders of the United States for even wider opportunities.

The development of a "global outlook" in Dow Chemical's management was not at first a conscious effort. And in fact it grew out of events abroad rather than events at home.

First, there was a continuing demand from overseas for Dow Chemical products, services, and engineering and production know-how. The steady economic recovery of Europe was creating investment opportunities. Popular sentiment in Europe was running strongly in favor of a European trade alliance that would break down ancient barriers and stimulate the flow of goods between nations. (This sentiment was given some practical force early in 1957 when representatives of France, West Germany, Italy, Belgium, the Netherlands, and Luxembourg signed treaties creating the European Economic Community or Euromarket.)

Without any guiding foreign-trade policy, Dow Chemical by 1958 had become more and more involved in ventures abroad. Partnership plants in England were producing agricultural chemicals and plastics. Another partnership in Bombay, India, was manufacturing plastics. Still another partnership in Australia was producing styrene. Dobeckmun, the company's subsidiary, was involved in the manufacture of metallic yarns in Italy, France, England, and the Netherlands. And Asahi-Dow Limited in Japan was developing into a major supplier of plastics for that nation.

In South America, Dowell had won a strong position in servicing gas and oil wells and industrial equipment. A partnership company in Brazil was producing carbon tetrachloride, and a subsidiary in Argentina was manufacturing caustic soda and chlorine products.

Before the treaties were signed forming Euromarket, Lee Doan had agreed to a plan to establish a storage, warehousing, processing, and distribution center in Rotterdam to give better service to European customers. A subsidiary company, Nederlandsche Dow Maatschappij N.V., was formed to direct the operation which called for small plants to process Styron, magnesium alloys, glycols, and other chemicals. Specialists were to be stationed in Rotterdam to supply technical information to manufacturers and to help them with their industrial problems. From Rotterdam, products were to be delivered to customers within three to six days after an order was received.

All these ventures, from Europe to Asia to South America, had developed separately and not as the result of any organized effort on Dow Chemical's part to encourage overseas expansion. The initiative came from abroad and before Lee Doan and his people realized it fully, the company was involved in a series of operations so loosely tied together on the management level that each was virtually independent of the other.

In short, Dow Chemical in 1958 was up to its knees in foreign trade with no guiding policy. The time had come either to fish or cut bait in Europe. The younger men in the company—Carl Gerstacker, Ted Doan, Ben Branch, and Max Key among others—were pushing for Dow Chemical to make an aggressive move into foreign operations. Some of the older men maintained a "show-me" attitude and were skeptical.

While the situation was being debated, the veteran Ed Barstow, who had joined Herbert Dow in 1900 in the "bleach works" and done so much to help build the company, announced his retirement as vice president and a member of the board. At the same time, the veteran Russ Curtis stepped down from his post as board member and general manager of the Western Division.

Doan reached down into the second echelon of managers and chose Ben Branch, manager of the plastics department, and Donald Ballman, director of sales, to fill the board vacancies. Leland A. Doan, Lee Doan's elder son, succeeded Curtis as Western Division manager.

At this point in December, 1958, Dow Chemical was on the threshold of "going global."

Chapter Eighteen

The year 1958 marked the beginning of a period of broad change in The Dow Chemical Company—change which was to influence the company's policies, organization, and philosophy of doing business. It was a period involving risk and venture of a greater magnitude than any the company had experienced in all its long history.

For Lee Doan and his team of veteran managers, it was a time for the gradual shifting of controls to younger hands and a time for helping the younger men chart the course for which they had been pressing. This willingness to give the younger managers their way—once they had made a persuasive case—was in the company tradition. Herbert Dow had given such freedom to Barstow, Putnam, and Strosacker. Willard Dow and Lee Doan had operated in the same fashion in dealing with younger men and giving them their head.

Ted Doan recalled: "Once you convinced the older men your idea was good, you got their support. They gave you a remarkable degree of freedom. I remember once that Ben Branch, after a promotion, tried to get Mark Putnam to outline his specific responsibilities. Mark told him, 'I'm not going to tell you your responsibilities, I'm not going to fence you in by placing limits. You do what you must do.' That is the kind of freedom we are going to continue to give to our people."

The question of overriding importance in 1958 was whether Dow Chemical should use its energies and money to develop along domestic lines as it had done so successfully for sixty-one years, or to move strongly into overseas competition and thus become a global operation with worldwide responsibilities, opportunities, and risks. But also there were questions of where management control should be centered, how the company should be organized, and what the goals of the future should be.

Through the years, Dow Chemical's strength had been in its strategic position as a supplier of basic chemicals to other manufacturers who processed them into finished products. On this base the company had grown and prospered, climbing the ladder to rank fourth in size in the

United States chemical industry. Its researchers and engineers had developed the processes, techniques, and equipment to keep Dow Chemical out in front in supplying the basic molecular building blocks obtained from brine and petroleum.

The primary aim of Herbert Dow, Willard Dow, and Lee Doan had been to maintain this leadership in the production of basic chemicals. The guiding philosophy had been that Dow Chemical should position its strength on the basic chemicals required by United States industries and not stray too far from this base.

Younger men in the second echelon of management argued that the old base was not the secure foundation it once had been. They believed that the techniques and processes, which had long been so important in Dow Chemical's development, no longer provided the margin of advantage they once had. The oil industry, for example, was invading the chemical-making field. Others also were developing their own sources of basic chemicals. Competition in the basics was growing rapidly and the opportunities were becoming fewer. The time had come for Dow Chemical to develop a broader and more sophisticated base, to search for areas of need, and to push for products that would have a unique value rather than merely a competitive value.

Few people outside Dow Chemical's top command knew that deep and fundamental questions were being debated, or that the company was entering the most critical period of transition in its history.

As for the overseas operations, a majority of the veterans regarded them as a sideline. The foreign market was all right as a place for getting rid of surplus products, but the only truly promising market was in the United States. They questioned the idea of the company becoming too deeply involved in countries whose politics, languages, cultures, monetary controls, and ways of doing business were strange to them.

Younger men were convinced the opportunities overseas far outweighed the risks and that Dow Chemical's future lay in this direction. They came from a generation which had traveled to far places during and after World War II and they had no fears of going into strange lands to do business. In fact, they were excited by the prospect. They were eager to enter the world marketplace. They wanted to pull the fragmented overseas operations together, give them strong support from Mildand, and move aggressively into both sales and production wherever an opportunity presented itself. Among this group were Herbert Dow "Ted" Doan, manager of the chemicals department, Carl Gerstacker, the company's treasurer, and Ben Branch, manager of the plastics department.

Ted Doan would recall: "I remember that in the spring of 1958 I decided to go to Europe on business and to look over our chemical operations. Things had fallen out of bed badly here at home and I caught hell for leaving at such a bad time. But I wanted to see for myself what they were doing over there. The thing that stuck out like a sore thumb was the lack of aggressiveness and organization."

The debates came to a head when Clayton Shoemaker, who had helped pioneer Dow Chemical's postwar move into Europe, decided to retire as president of Dow Chemical International. President Doan did not lack for applicants who wanted the job—all of them young men intrigued by the opportunities they saw in foreign development.

At this point Lee Doan decided to give Ben Branch the job of reorganizing the overseas operations. To take over these responsibilities meant that Branch had to give up his post as head of the important plastics department—fastest growing of all the company's departments—and gamble with an uncertain future where the hazards could not be charted on the same graphs used at home. And a failure abroad would hardly be a recommendation for future advancement.

Branch told Doan: "The way things are now, everybody has a finger in this pot. I don't want it unless I can run it all—including sales."

To take control of all overseas sales from the sales department and hand it over to Branch called for a drastic shift in policy. But Doan, having made his decision, was ready to go all the way.

"Ben," he said, "you've got a blank check. You run the show."

Early in January, 1959, Doan announced that Branch had been appointed manager of all the company's overseas and foreign activities except those in Canada and Mexico. He was named president of Dow Chemical International. The job of running the plastics department was given to Bill Goggin.

In later years, Branch would recall: "One thing I knew when I took on this job was that if I made mistakes—and they were not too big—the company would back me up. That has been the great thing about working for Dow Chemical. You have the freedom to make mistakes.

"I remember back in 1952 when I was head of Technical Service and Development I was pushing a weed control compound called Premerge. We went to market with it after it received a good recommendation from the U. S. Department of Agriculture. We sold quite a lot of it to cotton growers in the Mississippi Delta in the spring of '52.

"One day I got a call from our man in the Delta. He said 'I don't want you to be too alarmed, but I thought you'd better know that we've got some scattered damage in the fields where Premerge was used.' Then the next day he called and said, 'You'd better get down here, Ben. We're in trouble.'

"I caught a plane to Greenville and got the story. It looked bad. At dawn, I went out to the fields to see for myself what had happened. The seedling cotton was limp in the fields, acre after acre of it. I hurried back to Greenville and called Bill Britton whose people had developed the compound. 'You had better call an Executive Committee meeting, Bill,' I told him. 'This looks bad.'

"I got back to Midland and the next morning I saw Lee Doan and told him the story. At that time I was up for a promotion to head the Plastics Department and Ray Boundy was slated to be promoted to head research. I went to the Executive Committee meeting and told my story. Someone asked, 'What will it cost us?' I said if the growers had applied all the Premerge we had sold in the area—and if the damage could be blamed on the chemical rather than a plant disease—the cost conceivably could run as high as $20,000,000.

"I was feeling pretty low after the meeting when Mark Putnan called me into his office. He said: 'This has hit you pretty hard, hasn't it?' I told him it had. 'Well,' he said, 'if there are any lessons to be learned from this, learn them. But after that, don't worry. You are doing your best for the company and this isn't going to have any adverse effect on your future.'

"The damage cost the company $250,000 but no one ever blamed me. What happened was that the Delta had had a rare combination of weather and humidity which had made the cotton seedlings susceptible to chemical injury and disease. We learned a lot from that incident—and made sure it would never be repeated. But from that time on, I also knew I had nothing to fear from making a mistake that the company could live with."

It was the knowledge that he had strong backing in Midland that gave Branch confidence to tackle Europe as he did. At any rate he gathered around him a group of young recruits who formed the nucleus of his organization. Few had any experience in business abroad. But on the other hand, they were not bound by old ties, associations, or obligations as their competitors were who were already well established in Europe.

The timing was good. Europe's economy was booming. The countries needed the chemicals and services which Dow Chemical could provide. Foreign investors were eager to help provide the cash needed for new plants and to form joint companies to operate them. Even though Dow Chemical was slow in entering the foreign field, this slowness proved to be an advantage, for Branch was not forced to conform to any previous practices.

In less than four years, Branch had Dow Chemical solidly established as one of the fastest growing American companies in Europe. Plants were operating or in the process of being built from Holland to Greece—and he had drawn plans for bringing Dow Chemical's capital investment in Europe to $200,000,000. Some of the plants were wholly owned, others were partnership associations.

Among Branch's first moves was the organization of Dow Chemical International A.G., with headquarters in Basel, Switzerland (later moved to Zurich). This was a wholly owned holding company which provided a central control over all the manufacturing and marketing subsidiaries through which Dow Chemical operated outside the United States, Canada, and Mexico. New sales offices were opened in major cities and the sales organization strengthened. In Midland, an International Traffic Department was established to handle the movement of products and supplies to points overseas.

To establish itself in the European capital markets, Dow Chemical International borrowed $14,000,000 in Swiss francs from Europeans through the sale of 4¼ percent bonds even though the money was not needed. It was a means calculated to make Dow Chemical known in the money markets and to underline the fact that the company was in Europe to stay as a member of the business community, largely manned by European personnel.

Wholly owned plants to produce Styron resins and other chemicals were built in Greece, Holland, Germany, and Italy. Partnership plants to produce plastics and chemicals were built in Spain. And this was only the beginning.

The most ambitious of all was the building of a chemical complex at Terneuzen, in Southern Holland near the Belgium border, designed primarily to supply customers in the Common Market countries. In the initial building, more than $50,000,000 was poured into the complex which, it was hoped, would become to Europe what the company's giant Texas plant had become to the United States chemical industry. Ethylene taken from the Shell Oil Company's plants at Rotterdam was converted at Terneuzen to styrene, polystyrene resin and foam, ethylene oxide, glycols, and other intermediates. From this plant came many intermediates to be processed at other company plants in Europe. And the Terneuzen operation was closely linked to Dow Chemical's storage, warehousing, shipping, and docking facilities at Rotterdam.

Within a short time Midland discovered that whenever a new plant went into operation in a foreign country, there was an almost immediate rise in exports to that country. The building of plants stimulated demand for other Dow Chemical products as manufacturers learned more about the compounds that were available and how they could be used profitably to meet the complex needs of the European community.

Gerstacker recalled: "Ben changed our whole approach to international operations. He was the kind of guy who said, 'Here I go, follow me.' And he had some strong men around him who weren't afraid to go. We went into Europe late but when we did go in, we went in strong. Ben set a pattern and it wasn't long until other companies were reorganizing along the same lines. But Dow Chemical was the most aggressive of all."

As the European operation boomed, Gerstacker and his associate, John Van Stirum, realized the way money was being handled in Europe made little sense. Dow Chemical International was dealing in an uncoordinated fashion with banks scattered throughout Europe. They would have idle money in the banks of one country while paying interest on the overdrafts in other countries. They were paying retail banking prices on all interest, fees, transfers, and collection charges. At any given time, the company might have several million dollars floating around and this annoyed the men of Midland who were not accustomed to seeing money idle.

To simplify the money problem, Gerstacker arranged to buy a 40 percent interest in a small Amsterdam bank, Bankierskantoor Mendes Gans, giving Dow Chemical a financial clearing house through which it could operate with greater efficiency and at lower cost.

At the same time, Dow Chemical's subsidiary, Dowell, strengthened its overseas position in gas and oil well services by joining in a 50-50 association with an old French firm, Schlumberger, Limited (pronounced Slumberzhay) which had a worldwide organization.

Schlumberger, Limited had been formed in 1919 by two scientist-brothers, Conrad and Marcel Schlumberger, who opened a geophysical consulting office in Paris. Their service was based on an invention designed to locate ore and mineral deposits by means of electrical measurements at the earth's surface. In later years this process was adapted to oil prospecting and was often used to provide data on rock formations without the costly mechanical coring. In time electronic logging became widely used by the oil industry around the world.

Joining forces with Schlumberger gave Dowell a complementary service to its own acidizing, cementing, and fracturing processes which had been developed to increase oil flow in oil-bearing formations. In the fracturing process, fluids containing "propping" agents, such as sand, were forced under high pressure and at high velocities into oil-bearing rock strata. The fluid acted on the layers of rock much like a strong wind separating the pages of a book, and then the sand kept the rock propped apart to permit oil to flow more easily into the well.

While these developments were underway, Lee Doan began clearing the way for an almost total management takeover by the younger men. One by one the veterans, whose experience reached back into the early days of Herbert Dow, stepped from active management into advisory positions.

Long and unbroken years of service were not regarded as anything unusual in The Dow Chemical Company—because once a man joined the company's executive ranks he rarely left seeking opportunities elsewhere. The reasons were a complex combination of pleasant living conditions, opportunities for advancement, the excitement generated by a company growing and expanding into new fields, and an informal working relationship. Over the years Dow Chemical had encouraged employees to buy stock in the company, giving them a personal stake in its future.

Early in the century, Herbert Dow had kept after his key men to buy stock. He took the attitude that a purchase of stock was a vote of confidence in the company's future. If the company prospered, the employees prospered, too, but if there were bad times, the employees should share them. Willard Dow had followed much the same policy with the result that key employees saw their personal fortunes grow as the company prospered.

In the late 1920's, Herbert Dow and his family owned some 25 percent of the company's stock. In the 1960's, his heirs and their spouses controlled 12.3 percent of the stock while 40 percent of the thirty-one thousand employees were stockholders and owned 20 percent of the stock outstanding. And most of these family and employee holdings were in the hands of Midland residents.

An almost incredible fact was that in January, 1960, almost all the key men who had joined with Herbert Dow early in the century and helped build The Dow Chemical Company into an industrial giant were still living and most of them were active in company management. The only two who had retired were Tom Griswold, Jr., the company's first engineer, and Ed Barstow, the production genius who was recognized as "the father of magnesium." Earl Bennett at eighty was a vice president and chairman of the board. Charles Strosacker, seventy-seven, was a vice president and board member. He continued to keep an eye on production as did seventy-three-year-old Mark Putnam, the executive vice president and a board member. Dutch Beutel, sixty-seven, was not only a vice president and board member but he ran the $600,000,000 Texas empire, headed the Dowell subsidiary later turned over to Carl Polk, was president of the Brazos Oil and Gas Company, and had the new Louisiana Division under his general supervision.

The shift of command actually began in 1959 when thirty-nine-year-old Robert B. Bennett was named company treasurer, stepping into the post his father, Earl Bennett, had held for so many years. Ben Branch and Donald Ballman were named vice presidents.

And then in November, 1959, came the sudden death from a heart attack of forty-seven-year-old William H. Schuette, a brilliant graduate of Case Institute of Technology who had risen rapidly to become a vice president and manager of the big Midland Division. His post was filled by thirty-four-year-old Macauley Whiting, son-in-law of the late Willard Dow. One year after the death of Schuette, the community was shocked by the death of Mark Putnam. Later in the same month, Earl Bennett stepped aside as chairman of the board and within a short time Dutch Beutel turned over the command of the Texas Division to forty-three-year-old Earle Barnes, who had helped him create the Gulf Coast giant. Other important changes came when Jim Williams took over as director of sales (later becoming manager of the plastics department). Julius Johnson joined (and later succeeded) Ray Boundy in research administration after turning over the bioproducts department to Bill Dixon.

In this shifting, Carl Gerstacker was named chairman of the board succeeding Bennett, and Ted Doan was moved from manager of the chemicals department to the post of executive vice president, succeeding Putnam.

These changes were the most sweeping that Dow Chemical had ever experienced. Not even the deaths of Herbert Dow or his son, Willard, had brought such a changing of the guard. In those two critical periods Herbert Dow and Willard had a solid team of experienced veterans to help guide the company over the shoals. They had provided much of the drive which had transformed the company from a small, isolated concern to a top-ranking business. They had helped shape the character of Dow Chemical. Each in his own way had become a legend in Midland and the story of their combined achievements was largely the story of the development of the American chemical industry from its infancy.

Each had carved out a place in the company for himself and had dominated his niche for years. They had made Dow Chemical their lives, and they had made their lives a creative adventure.

Through the years—under the leadership of Herbert Dow, Willard Dow, and Lee Doan—they had taken pride in being "different" from other companies. Some called this difference "creative discontent." Some said it was "the freedom to make mistakes." Some said it sprang from "a mania for independent thinking" nurtured in the so-called isolation of the Midwest. Whatever it was, they had been bold, strong, independent, and original in their thinking, and they had built well. It is doubtful that any other major company in the United States had such a team working together over such a long and unbroken span of years. Now this team was moving to the sidelines.

But the younger men moving up in late 1960 to take over the controls were themselves veterans. Ted Doan had been with the company eleven years, Branch twenty-three years, Gerstacker twenty-two years, Whiting twelve years, Barnes twenty years, Bob Bennett eighteen years, and Ballman twenty-five years. And yet their average age was only forty-two years.

In this shakeup, lean, intense Ted Doan emerged as the leader who, with Gerstacker and Branch, would reshape the lines of organization and point the direction the company would take in the years ahead. For two years young Doan plotted the course that would be followed and the organizational changes he believed were necessary to achieve the goals.

Ted Doan recalled: "From 1960 through 1962 I was working cautiously through our loose organization. Over the years, the real power in Dow Chemical had become centered in production, both in Midland and in Texas. The power had drifted to these centers because historically production had been the most important function—and the people who ran production were strong and able men who reached out for responsibility, men like Bill Schuette and Dutch Beutel. But the time had come to centralize this control and the veterans understood it."

For 63 years, emphasis on production had been of major importance. But as Ted Doan studied the trends, he was convinced that the production of basic chemicals no longer was the controlling key to profits and growth. As he saw it, the big-volume chemicals would remain important, but the great profits and growth in the future would come from intensified research. They would come from finding chemical solutions to such fundamental problems as housing, health, food, clothing, and water and air pollution—not merely in the United States but throughout the world.

He saw a need to return to long-range research aimed at solving vital social, economic, and industrial problems, with management willing to provide the "patient money" that would be required.

He saw Dow Chemical as a company composed of some thirty-five separate businesses ranging from pharmaceuticals to building materials; and it was necessary to group these businesses into departments in such a way that production, research, marketing, and development would be highly integrated, with products more intelligently designed to achieve an end result. And he was certain that with a better understanding between production, research, marketing, and development—and given time and money—research would continue to achieve breakthroughs opening new fields of opportunities as great as and even greater than those of the past.

In line with the emerging policy of developing more sophisticated products and becoming involved in broad problems of health, Dow Chemical in December, 1960, took over Allied Laboratories, Incorporated, one of the country's largest manufacturers and distributors of human health products. Allied Laboratories had ended its fiscal year 1959 with net sales of more than $30,000,000. Dow Chemical's common stock, selling at 75, was issued to Allied shareholders on the basis of two-thirds of a share of Dow Chemical stock for one share of Allied stock, selling at 49¾.

This merger gave Dow Chemical control of facilities which included the subsidiary Pitman-Moore laboratories in Indianapolis and Zionsville, Indiana, and Sioux Falls, South Dakota; Campana Corporation, Batavia, Illinois; Allied Laboratories, Limited, Guelph, Ontario, Canada; Pitman-Moore of Canada, Limited; Allied Laboratories International of Panama; Pitman-Moore S. p. A., Rome, Italy; and Establecimientos Francimex, S.A., Mexico City.

"We believe," President Doan said after the merger, "that the specialized research and marketing skills of Allied should blend well with Dow's efforts in exploratory chemical research and other broad research areas."

Allied brought to Dow Chemical more than six hundred products, including a long list of ethical drugs. Pitman-Moore had been one of the major manufacturers of the Salk polio vaccine and had shortly before the merger introduced a 4-in-1 vaccine, Compligen, providing one-shot protection against tetanus, diphtheria, whooping cough, and poliomyelitis. The subsidiary also had developed a complete line of animal-health pharmaceutical and biological products sold exclusively to veterinarians.

In a talk to Allied employees, welcoming them into the Dow Chemical family, Ted Doan said: "As technology becomes more widespread, the unique positions of the older members of the chemical industry, based largely on process know-how, have diminished. It will be true in the future that the successful companies must be good enough to establish unique positions in research, development and marketing so that they can charge for their products on the basis of value to the customer rather than having the price set by competition. Building new positions, each as exclusive as possible, then, is the answer to the disappearing exclusiveness of the historical chemical industry."

Young Doan disclosed in this talk, for the first time, that Dow Chemical was undergoing a "reorientation," and was in the process of adding new opportunities to the production of old-line chemicals. He concluded his talk by saying: "You can see the merger of Dow and Allied was not an unrelated event but part of a reorientation toward new growth opportunities. We realize that to be successful we have to make the maximum use of our capabilities. We went into the international business aggressively, for example, mostly because it represented an opportunity for growth in sales and profits, but also because it could provide a larger base to support our research efforts. . . . We have not only a large amount of biologically-oriented work to contribute to the Allied Division, but also the chemical synthesis people to turn up thousands of new chemicals each year, some of which may fit pharmaceutical or veterinary needs, whether or not this was their original aim. . . . Allied obviously offers us not only skill in the unique marketing methods of the pharmaceutical industry, but such things as pharmacology and clinical work, pathology, virology, and pharmaceutical product development and other areas which we of course had not developed to any extent."

As the Allied Laboratories' manufacturing, research and marketing were being consolidated with those of Dow Chemical, Lee Doan was moving to put the company in a dominant position to help municipalities and industries solve their growing problems of industrial waste, sewage disposal, and water pollution. The Industrial Service Division of Dowell, which had pioneered in the chemical cleaning of industry's boilers, equipment, and machinery, was given the status of an independent division with headquarters at Cleveland and it took over this program.

This move meshed neatly with the plans being drawn by Ted Doan to involve Dow Chemical in long-range programs dealing with the well-being of millions of people.

Early in the Administration of John F. Kennedy, Dow Chemical had begun to operate the nation's first experimental salt water conversion plant at Freeport, Texas. On June 21, 1961, Lee Doan and Dutch Beutel stood beside Mr. Kennedy at the White House as he pushed a button to dedicate the plant designed to take 1,000,000 gallons of fresh water a day from the sea. Similar ceremonies at Freeport were attended by Vice President and Mrs. Lyndon B. Johnson, Secretary of the Interior Stewart L. Udall, and Carl Gerstacker.

Dow Chemical had provided five acres of land for the experimental plant and supplied the steam and seawater feed. Through studies at this plant it was hoped that economical processes would be found to tap the sea for fresh water not only for areas of the United States but for arid countries with few fresh water resources.

No doubt Herbert Dow would have gotten a wry chuckle from these ceremonies had he lived to witness them. For he had dreamed of converting seawater to fresh water back in 1915 when he had read of a drought in California—and had been laughed at for suggesting it. Now his grandsons were seeing his old dream become a reality.

But, in a sense, most of the activities of The Dow Chemical Company in the industrial field seemed of secondary importance to what was taking place in the cluster of offices housing the company's top management in Midland. In the summer of 1962 Earl Bennett and Charles Strosacker stepped down from the powerful Executive Committee and turned over their places to Ben Branch and Donald Ballman. And then Lee Doan made his final preparations to give up the presidency.

For Lee Doan, it was the end of thirteen tumultuous years that had begun when Willard Dow died in the plane crash on the rain-soaked field in Canada. In that time he had led the company over the postwar shoals into the greatest period of growth in its history. He had poured more than $1,000,000,000 into capital improvements and expansions. He had guided the company through the first critical period of its transformation from a domestic concern into a worldwide organization with a global business outlook. He had seen the company's assets climb from $294,337,000 in 1949 to $1,055,337,000 in 1962 and sales from $200,371,000 to $890,639,000. In that same time the number of employees had increased from 14,000 to 31,000, and the number of shareholders from 19,000 to more than 100,000. He had given Dow Chemical's marketing organization a stronger position in the company.

And in his regime the company had diversified even further and its plants had been dispersed throughout the United States.

Beyond this, Lee Doan had been the bridge between the older men and the new leaders. With his quiet diplomacy he had moved the younger men into positions of control with a minimum of friction. And with this transition of management completed, he was ready to step down from the presidency.

On September 12, 1962, Lee Doan's forty-year-old son, Ted Doan, became the fifth president of The Dow Chemical Company.

Chapter Nineteen

The size of The Dow Chemical Company was both a blessing and a burden as Ted Doan stepped into the presidency of the 65-year-old company in 1962. Bigness was an asset in reducing costs, expanding quickly into promising fields, and remaining competitive in an industry where competition was growing keener year after year in the sale of basic chemicals and intermediates. The company was the world's largest and most efficient producer of chlorine and caustic soda. It ranked at the top or near the top in supplying industries with vinyl chloride, propylene oxide, glycol, phenol, synthetic glycerine, hydrochloric acid, methylene chloride, bromine, aspirin granules, magnesium, and plastic monomers and polymers. Overseas, the company was pouring money into new plants and expanding at a faster rate than any of its competitors.

But as the company had grown so had the problems of communication among management, research, production, marketing, and development. And this was the burden of bigness—this difficulty of communication which threatened to stifle individual initiative and to frustrate talent. It was a burden which young Doan was determined to overcome.

Ted Doan had no desire to play the role of the strong man calling all the signals. Indeed, he was convinced that while this form of leadership had served the company well in its earlier years, the time had come for a reorganization that would spread more of the decision-making to the middle management, leaving top executives free to make policy and long-range plans for profit growth. But before this type of organization could be fully developed, the controls had to become centered in Midland headquarters.

Doan formed a triumvirate—himself, Carl Gerstacker, and Ben Branch—to lead Dow Chemical through the reorganization and point the direction it would take in the future. He concentrated largely on planning. Gerstacker looked after finances. And Branch—promoted to the post of executive vice president—took charge of operations. The executive committee, through which Lee Doan had operated in his decision-making, became a group which reviewed the decisions of the triumvirate while the board of directors was a back-up review and advisory group.

One of Ben Branch's first moves was to launch a research program designed to improve the production processes and bring down the costs of the big-volume commodities such as styrene and phenol. Dow Chemical had always been strong on its processes and Branch was determined it would remain strong.

He pressed the division research people to step up their work on ways to improve the processes as a basic means of improving profits. And this drive worked, pushing down the costs of the company's big-base commodities and placing Dow Chemical in a stronger position to move out in other directions.

In other management shuffles, Macauley Whiting was named director of overseas operations and fifty-five-year-old Max Key was placed in charge of the big Midland Division. In the background were the veterans Lee Doan, Dutch Beutel, Earl Bennett, and Calvin Campbell to give the balance of long experience. But the younger men were now in charge.

Just as Herbert Dow, Willard Dow, and Lee Doan had avoided drafting a rigid organization chart, so did Ted Doan. He believed that rigid, military-like lines of command were too confining for individual initiative and that group decisions were imperative. He had the enormous task of breaking down the old organization and reshaping it to the new plan.

The old organization had developed around the company's divisions and in time these divisions—particularly in Texas and Midland—had become empires within an empire. They competed with each other for plants and projects. Each had its own research laboratories and each pursued its own independent research. Each had its own development, design, and construction services. And each contributed its share to jealousies between partisan groups. The divisions had become more or less isolated from direct management control.

An example of inter-division friction arose in 1943 when the Texas Division built a carbon tetrachloride plant, using a process that had been developed by the Western Division. The plant failed to produce at its rated capacity. Beutel put Earle Barnes to work seeking the trouble and after a time Barnes was certain there was some element in the plant feed acting as an inhibitor to the production of carbon tetrachloride. However, the Texas Division had no research laboratory at that time because Willard Dow had decreed the research would be centered in Midland and California.

A team of chemists came from the California division to study the Texas problem and reported the trouble was not caused by an inhibitor, but was the result of the plant being "under-engineered." The only remedy would be to rebuild the plant.

Beutel's hackles rose over the slur against his division's engineering, and Barnes challenged the report of the visiting firemen. His tests indicated that a trace of ammonia in the Freeport water was the guilty agent. When ammonia-free seawater was used instead of the Freeport water, the plant began to produce at capacity.

After this incident, Beutel was determined to have his own research facilities and not to be dependent either on Midland or the Western Division. Secretly, he had Barnes organize a research center, covering up the costs with a bit of bookkeeping sleight-of-hand. When this became known in Midland, there was an uproar. But Beutel insisted he had to have his own research center for developing new products and processes.

It all ended with a high-level meeting in Pittsburg in February, 1947, with Charles Strosacker and Ray Boundy acting as referees. Beutel won his battle but not without some bruised feelings.

Gerstacker would recall another incident: "I remember soon after World War II, I was trying to be the company's production control man. Willard showed me reports he had received from Beutel, asking for an expansion, and Willard didn't know what it all meant. He wanted to set up some method by which he could check on Texas production and he asked me to do it. I went to Texas and Dutch damned near threw me out of his office—and probably should have. A young upstart was meddling in his affairs. Maybe he thought I'd go away and not bother him after the blow-up. But I didn't. I had my jaw set and we had a battle. Then we worked out a way to report production satisfactorily."

Doan's primary concern in those first years was to install the organization plan he had developed before he became president: the dividing of Dow Chemical into product departments with teams organized in each department to develop and promote the various business groupings.

In this structure, the major departments were chemicals, plastics, metal products, bioproducts, packaging, and consumer products, each headed by a manager who reported directly to Branch. Each department manager had a staff of managers who headed business teams responsible for a certain group of products. These teams brought together men from marketing, research, production, and development. Linked to the business teams and reporting to them were product teams responsible for the management of certain specified products. The system also made it possible for teams to be organized for special projects and products.

In its total effect, the reorganization was the breaking down of Dow Chemical into relatively small, manageable businesses in which performances at all levels could be checked, problems identified, and goals fixed with a degree of cooperation that had been possible only in the earliest days of the company.

"These businesses," Branch explained to an employee group, "are designed to be as close as we can come to a small business with the flexibility and maneuverability of a small business, and with all of the strength in depth of a big company."

The system was not one suddenly imposed on the company. Actually it had begun to develop in the late 1940's with the organization of a plastics department under Ray Boundy. Then in 1956 Ted Doan had set up the chemicals department. It was from this base that Doan set out to reorganize the entire company and establish new relationships between product departments, research, production, business teams, and product teams. It was a breaking down of old walls, the broadening of contacts between departments, and the opening of opportunities for men who had the desire and ability to grasp more responsibility.

Distribution, which had been the responsibility of the different production divisions, was linked to marketing and purchasing and placed under the direction of Vice President Don Ballman. And in 1965, the company's manufacturing centers were placed under effective centralized control for the first time when fifty-seven-year-old Max Key was made director of manufacturing, engineering and maintenance. The management of the Midland Division went to Harold Bosscher.

Explaining the company's reorganization to a group of European business men, Gerstacker said: "We believe in something you might for want of a better word call 'democracy.' We operate largely on the basis of group decisions and with a surprising amount of overlapping of duties and responsibilities. We are in many respects the opposite of a military organization with its carefully defined lines and bounds of authority.

"We believe that this loose, freedom-oriented organization gives our people the very maximum chance to use their initiative, to develop their initiative, to develop their ideas and their abilities, and to make their maximum contribution.

"Linked with this we have an unwritten law that we promote wherever possible from within the organization. We don't hire executives; we develop them."

To another group, Ben Branch said: "Where top management act as long-range leaders of change, middle management will increasingly act as managers of change. They will have new, broader charters to run day-to-day operations. In fact, they will take over many of top management's jobs of today, leaving the top men free to carry out broader responsibility."

One of the new departments to emerge from this reorganization was the Government Affairs Department. For many years Dow Chemical had supplied products, technical services and research facilities to federal agencies. But this business had grown with no one person responsible for its development.

Dutch Beutel took over the task of organizing and managing the new department. And he set out in his usual hard-charging manner to place Dow Chemical in a stronger position to bid on contracts in the government's programs of defense, nuclear development, oceanography, waste and water treating, pollution control, and space exploration.

But as a result of fulfilling a contract obligation to the United States government, The Dow Chemical Company became—in 1966—the target of perhaps the most abusive attack ever launched against an American business firm. The attack was part of a nationwide anti-war campaign whose primary aim was to force American withdrawal from Vietnam where United States military forces were fighting to prevent a Communist conquest of South Vietnam.

The United States' involvement in Vietnam—reaching back through the Administrations of President Truman, President Eisenhower, President Kennedy, and President Johnson—had distressed millions of Americans of all political shades. And this distress grew as the fighting became more intense and claimed more American lives.

It was by no means a "popular" war. But the debate over the American role in South Vietnam and the most effective way to obtain peace often degenerated into violent actions by a minority.

For many years the government had bought products from Dow Chemical ranging from measles vaccine to magnesium. But it was the Air Force's use of one product as an offensive and defensive weapon in Vietnam which made the company a target for attack.

The product was napalm, a jelly-like, inflammable substance packed into canisters and dropped by planes on observed or suspected enemy targets in the jungle fighting. Napalm bombs had become one of the important weapons used to support American troops in certain combat situations. At times, troops threatened with being overrun by the enemy had called for napalm strikes on their own positions. More than once these supporting strikes had saved the units from annihilation.

Such a time came in June, 1966, when the 1st Brigade of the 101st Airborne drove into the mountains of the Kon Tum Province along the border of Laos and Cambodia. The battle that developed was described in this manner in the Associated Press' annual roundup of important news events:

The engagement was noteworthy for an exploit involving Captain William S. Carpenter, Jr., known to sports fans as the "lonesome end" of West Point football teams 15 years earlier. Carpenter's company, on outpost duty, was attacked by a battalion of North Vietnamese and badly mauled in close-quarter fighting. At one point, the Reds were so sure of victory that their buglers sounded taps for the beleaguered Americans. In the emergency, Carpenter called for an air strike on his own position, aiming "to take a few of them with us." The strike, with bombs and napalm, broke the Communist assault, enabled what was left of the trapped unit to hook up with another company in a defense perimeter; later, the survivors were removed by helicopter.

Napalm was not a new weapon. It was invented in 1942 by scientists from Harvard University and the Army Chemical Warfare Service for flamethrowers. During World War I, both the Germans and the Allies had used flamethrowers which hurled burning gasoline. But the gasoline was not very effective because it burned too quickly.

The napalm of World War II was a combination of coconut oil, oleic acid and naphthenic acid (the word "napalm" derived from naphthenic). These compounds formed a powder which was mixed with gasoline to produce a gel of any desired consistency. The mixture was used by the Marines in their flamethrowers as they attacked Japanese entrenched in caves, holes, and bunkers on Guadalcanal and other Pacific islands. It was used in infantry assaults on German positions in Europe and in Allied bombings of enemy positions. It was a weapon also in the Korean war.

By 1965, the Air Force had developed a new formula for napalm. It called for 25 percent benzene, 25 percent gasoline, and 50 percent polystyrene, the latter a plastic material manufactured by Dow Chemical and others. The Air Force contracted with Dow Chemical to supply part of its needs, and this was done at a plant at Torrance,

California, which employed less than a dozen workers. In terms of dollars, the contract was a small one in the range of $5,000,000 in 1966, or about one-fourth of one percent of the company's total sales. The profit involved was of little material significance.

As the United States stepped up its war effort in 1966, opposition to the war increased. Anti-war groups began taking to the streets in increasing numbers to stage protests. Pickets carried signs labeling President Johnson, Secretary of State Dean Rusk, and Secretary of Defense Robert MacNamara as "murderers." The debate over Vietnam often degenerated into violence, abusive name-calling, attempts to interfere with or evade the draft, and charges that American pilots were ruthlessly killing Vietnamese civilians with napalm. But those who demonstrated against the use of napalm to defend American troops curiously found no reason to protest the Communist Viet Cong's deliberate campaign of murder and terrorism waged against South Vietnamese civilians.

On Saturday, May 28, 1966, more than one hundred pickets paraded at Dow Chemical's plant at Torrance, protesting the making of napalm. On the same day, a noisy group of some seventy-five persons picketed the offices of the company in New York's Rockefeller Center. Among the organizations represented was the United States Committee to Aid the National Liberation Front (the NLF was the political front of the Viet Cong). One picket carried an NLF flag. They chanted "Napalm burns babies, "Dow makes money," and "Nazi ovens in '44, napalm in '66."

Newspapers carried stories of the picketing and television cameras brought pictures of the protesting groups to television sets throughout the country. Almost immediately leaders of the anti-war movement centered their abuse on The Dow Chemical Company from among all the many companies in the United States supplying war materials to the armed forces. Napalm had become the emotion-rousing symbol in the movement whose primary aim was to force the United States to withdraw from Vietnam.

In the early demonstrations, Dow Chemical issued a formal statement saying in part: "Our position on the manufacture of napalm is that we are a supplier of goods to the Defense Department and not a policymaker. We do not and should not try to decide military strategy or policy.

"Simple good citizenship requires that we supply our government and our military with those goods which they feel they need whenever we have the technology and capability and have been chosen by the government as a supplier.

"We will do our best, as we always have, to try to produce what our Defense Department and our soldiers need in any war situation. Purely aside from our duty to do this, we will feel deeply gratified if what we are able to provide helps to protect our fighting men or to speed the day when the fighting will end."

The anti-Dow Chemical campaign was picked up by anti-war groups on university campuses across the country. Dow's recruiters were harrassed as they tried to carry on job interviews with students. Demonstrations erupted on the campuses at Harvard, Princeton, University of California, Wisconsin, Minnesota, and many others. At Madison, Wisconsin, university officials were forced to call in police to break up a demonstration.

At Princeton, President Robert F. Goheen defended the right of all company recruiters to visit the campus and interview graduate students. He rejected student demands that they be barred.

Dr. Goheen was a veteran of combat with the First Cavalry Division in World War II. He told the students: "I probably have a somewhat different view of napalm than you do, because I remember vividly how it helped save the lives of many of my friends in the hills east of Manila in 1945 and on other occasions as well." He went on to say: "When representatives of companies come to the campus to recruit, they provide Princeton students with opportunities they might not otherwise have to gain information and make their own judgments and choices about future careers. We could only deny students such opportunities when to fail to do so was demonstrably injurious to the university, to the country, or to both."

At times, the anti-Dow Chemical campaign in some university newspapers became grossly irresponsible. Such was the case when a Dow Chemical recruiter, Glenn Allen, visited the campus of the University of California at Santa Barbara in January, 1967, to interview students. Anti-war demonstrators tried to halt the interviews, carrying signs which bore such slogans as "Burn, Baby, Burn," and "Help Dow Burn People."

A student newspaper, *El Gaucho,* burst forth with a banner headline: " 'Yes, We Burn Babies,' Dow Rep Boasts to Picket."

Three days later, a small item appeared in *El Gaucho* reading:

RETRACTION—*El Gaucho* erred in its reporting of Dow Chemical's appearance on campus last Thursday.

Apparently an impersonator, pretending to be the representative from Dow, made the statements concerning the burning of babies that was reported in Monday's *El Gaucho.*

Our reporter took the word of several demonstrators who heard the impersonator make those statements.

Dow's true representative, Glenn Allen, informed us that it is against the company's policy to talk to demonstrators, and he never went outside the building.

El Gaucho would like to apologize to Dow Chemical and Allen for misrepresenting his statements, and we would like to retract those statements falsely attributed to Allen in Monday's paper.

It is doubtful that all those who saw Monday's blaring headline, and believed it, also noted Thursday's apology.

Alkis Mangriotis, a senior at UCSB, wrote to the editor of *El Gaucho*:

"I am addressing this letter to the people who picketed The Dow Chemical Co. It was an idiotic and childish demonstration of anti-Vietnam sentiment. Dow makes chemicals of various kinds: fertilizers, plastics, and napalm among many others. These products can be used in profitable or in destructive ways. I think that it is obvious that Dow does not bomb Vietnam, but the Air Force, the government, we. We are carrying out the war, not that company, nor any other. They produce what we ask them to produce. If we don't like the bombing, let us change the government policies. If they picket Dow they should also picket Standard Oil, U. S. Steel, IBM among hundreds of others because they probably provide the fuel, the construction material, and the guidance of the bombers. Besides, The Dow Chemical Co. was recruiting research chemists, not necessarily napalm producers. I hope that picketing students would think more clearly before they stand for hours accomplishing nothing."

But it was the active, vocal minority who captured the headlines.

Protestors distributed pictures of babies allegedly burned by napalm and played on the theme which implied that thousands of innocent civilians were victims of napalm burns.

One of the first on-the-spot surveys seeking the truth or falsity of such claims was made in early 1967 by Dr. Howard A. Rusk, medical editor of *The New York Times*.

Dr. Rusk's report from Saigon said in part:

For the last week this writer has been on an intensive tour of 20 Vietnamese civilian hospitals from the 17th Parallel in the North to the Gulf of Siam in the South.

The facilities visited ranged from an isolated dispensary serving the Montagnards in the highlands to large provincial civilian hospitals in the hottest combat areas.

To many Americans, Vietnam is a distant and devastated country filled with children who have been burned by American napalm bombs.

This picture simply is not true.

The very nature of the fighting in Vietnam has made civilian casualties inevitable.

From the beginning of the struggle, the Viet Cong have continuously used terror tactics against civilians.

As the military activities have become intensified the Viet Cong have deliberately wiped out villages and mined busy roads.

More and more civilians have been inadvertently caught in the crossfire despite the very stringent precautions taken by the United States and Allied forces.

Not even partial statistics on the number of civilian casualties were available until last November when the first nationwide hospital survey was held.

Monthly surveys since indicate that, nationwide, approximately 15 per cent of all hospital admissions are war casualties. The remaining 85 per cent are for disease and accidents.

Certainly there are burned children and adults in Vietnam.

This writer personally saw every burn case in the 20 hospitals he visited. Among them was not a single case of burns due to napalm and but two from phosphorus shells.

There have been cases of severe burns from napalm but the numbers are not large in comparison to burns due to accidents.

Of the scores of American physicians queried many had not seen a single case of burns due to napalm and others had seen but a single case. For every case of burns resulting from war there are scores of cases of burns resulting from gasoline.

Because of inflation the cost of fuel for cooking is very high. As a result, many Vietnamese farmers and villagers pilfer or buy stolen gasoline. They are inexperienced in its use and try to use it like kerosene. The results are tragic. . . .

During the summer of 1966, a team of distinguished physicians, appointed by President Johnson, made a survey of South Vietnamese civilian war casualties and the hospital facilities available to give them medical care. The team was headed by Dr. F. J. L. Blasingame, executive vice president of the American Medical Association.

The team's report to President Johnson said in part:

"Prior to leaving the United States, the team was aware of exceptional public interest in the number and type of civilian burn cases in Vietnam.

"Throughout our visit, individual team members paid particular attention to burns. The cases were relatively limited in number in relation to other injuries and illnesses, and we saw no justification for the undue emphasis which had been placed by the press upon civilian burns caused by napalm.

"A greater number of burns appeared to be caused by the careless use of gasoline in stoves which were not intended for gasoline. Probably most of the burns occurred from this source."

For those seeking the facts, these reports by trained observers on the scene should have laid to rest the claims of widespread burnings by napalm. But the campaign against Dow Chemical continued.

For months the Administration in Washington merely observed the attacks on Dow Chemical, issuing no comment. But in 1967 Secretary of Defense Robert MacNamara wrote to Ted Doan saying in part:

"The implication that napalm is used indiscriminately in Vietnam is not true. General Earle G. Wheeler, Chairman of the Joint Chiefs of Staff, has said publicly that napalm is a military necessity. It answers a specific military need in certain combat situations peculiar to the type of warfare practiced by the Viet Cong.

"General Wheeler has also pointed out that the precautions we take against injury by this weapon to noncombatants are as painstaking as we can make them without hamstringing our military operations. By contrast, the Viet Cong has repeatedly carried on terror and murder campaigns directed against innocent civilians. . . .

"There are also charges that your company is a war profiteer, charges made by persons ignorant of the purchasing procedures of the Department of Defense and of your company's role as a defense supplier. As you well know, our contracting procedures insure that there can be no profiteering. . . .

"The protestors who attempted to interfere with recruiting efforts by any company as a form of protest against either a military weapon or the war in Vietnam were misdirecting their efforts. These are matters of military policy and foreign policy over which private industry has no control. Along with you, we deplore the isolated instances where demonstrations have gone beyond mere protest to the point of interfering with the rights of students to discuss employment opportunities with any prospective employer in whom they may be interested.

"Your employees and stockholders should be aware that your company is performing a service for our armed forces—a service that plays a vital role in protecting our fighting men."

Mixed with the letters of protest written to the company were letters of support, many of them from fighting men in Vietnam. A winner of the Medal of Honor wrote, "War and killing are not at all pleasing to anyone. The infantry in Vietnam fights to win and stay alive. We need and are thankful for napalm." An enlisted man wrote, "The war would not end if companies such as you suddenly refused to manufacture napalm and other military supplies." Another: "The effectiveness of napalm in saving U. S. lives is overwhelming."

The letters of support were welcome, but the harassment and abuse and sometimes obscene charges, and the efforts to cripple Dow Chemical in the marketplace, weighed heavily on Ted Doan and those around him, as well as on thousands of company employees and stockholders. The board of directors discussed the possibility of withdrawing from napalm production. But a great deal more was involved than a simple decision to drop a relatively small contract with the government. There was the matter of a company's right to deny weapons to American troops fighting for their country and their lives on a foreign battlefield.

The decision of the board was that Dow Chemical had no choice other than to continue fulfilling its contract. In discussing the problem in an article written for the *Wall Street Journal* in December, 1967, Ted Doan said in part:

"Why do we produce napalm? In simplest form, we produce it because we feel that our company should produce those items which our fighting men need in time of war when we have the ability to do so.

"A quarter of a century ago this answer would have satisfied just about everyone who asked this question. Today, however, it doesn't. Today we find ourselves accused of being immoral because we produce this product for use in what some people consider an unjust war. We're told that to make a weapon because you're asked to do so by your government puts you in precisely the same position as the German industrialists who pleaded at the Nuremberg trials that they were 'only following orders.'

"And these are just a few of the milder charges in a barrage of protests that has included picketing of some of our plants and sales offices, boycotts against our products, thousands of letters of protest to the company and to individuals within the company, and, most publicized of all, organized demonstrations on campuses across the nation which have ranged from peaceful protest to violent and physical obstruction of Dow job interviews.

"The central issue, of course, is the war in Vietnam. This is not a popular war. No one likes war, least of all the men who have the dirty and dangerous and heart-breaking job of having to fight it. All of the debate in the world about how we got there or how we get out is proper and right in its place, but it doesn't change the fact that we are there nor the fact that our men are there and need weapons to defend themselves.

"...what of the argument that we are no different from the German industrialists who 'just followed orders'? We reject the validity of comparing our present form of government with Hitler's Nazi Germany. In our mind our Government is still representative of and responsive to the will of the people.

"Further, we as a company have made a moral judgment on the long-range goals of our Government and we support these. We may not agree as individuals with every decision of every military or Governmental leader but we regard these leaders as men trying honestly and relentlessly to find the best possible solutions to very, very complex international problems. As long as we so regard them, we would find it impossible not to support them. This is not saying as the critics imply that we will follow blindly and without fail no matter where our Government leads us. While I think it highly improbable under our form of government, should despotic leaders attempt to lead our nation away from its historic national purposes, we would cease to support the Government. But I can foresee this happening only if through resort to anarchy we prevent the functioning of democratic processes.

"Our critics ask if we are willing to stand judgment for our choice to support our Government if history should prove this wrong. Our answer is yes. . . .

"Basically the debate over Vietnam, as long as it remains peaceful and honest debate, is a healthy thing. And many of the questions being asked are pertinent questions which business must ask itself. Business should and must be willing to discuss some of these questions with the campus and intellectual community which has raised them—discuss them not in the emotional atmosphere of demonstrations and confrontations but under conditions which will allow a true dialogue.

"Equally important, however, is the challenge to Dow and the business world to focus attention and action on an issue far more vital than Vietnam. That issue is peace itself, the lasting peace that man has sought throughout history. Such lasting peace can be achieved only when we find solutions to such basic world problems as hunger and disease and lack of economic opportunity.

"These are things that Dow is working on right now—things on which we spend vastly more time and money and effort than we spend on the production of napalm. We intend to continue making napalm because we feel that so long as the United States is sending men to war, it is unthinkable that we would not supply the materials they need. But we also intend to continue to direct our talents and efforts toward that better tomorrow for all mankind that can build lasting peace. . . .

"We firmly believe that the young men and women truly concerned about doing something to build a better world rather than just talking about it are in the vast majority. We intend to make every effort to convince them that the business world offers one of the best opportunities to do that job effectively."

The campaign had no apparent short-term adverse effect either on Dow Chemical's sales or its recruiting. But the nightmarish nature of the sensational charges tended to obscure the contributions which the company had made and was making to the health and well-being of people, to industrial research, and to the discovery of new and useful products.

Among these was the discovery of a vaccine, Lirugen, that immunized children against common measles and its often crippling or fatal effects. This discovery was made in Dow Chemical's Pitman-Moore laboratories by Anton Schwarz.

After a period of careful testing, the vaccine was used on a large scale for the first time when a measles epidemic threatened in California's Los Angeles County in early 1966. More than 100,000 injections of the one-shot vaccine were given to children over a ten-day period. Within three weeks, the reported cases peaked at 540 and then steadily dropped. Dr. Benjamin A. Kogan of the Los Angeles County Health Department, said, "This is the first time in a quarter of a century that the weekly incidence of measles—having once exceeded 500 cases a week—has dropped below 300 a week this early."

The program was considered so successful that county officials recommended an immunization program on a year-round basis. And when reports of the Los Angeles success reached other parts of the country, similar programs were organized. The United States government's Communicable Disease Center contracted for one million doses of Lirugen for use in its measles eradication program across the nation. And the Government Agency for International Development (AID) chose Lirugen in its program to inoculate more than twenty-four million children in fifteen West African countries.

Among other important products to come from the company's laboratories were a rabies vaccine and an effective, nonexplosive anaesthetic. Also, scientists and engineers at Dow Corning were deeply involved in research to help the medical profession solve many of its problems. A popular move had been the organization of an Aid to Medical Research Center where the medical profession could obtain technical assistance without charge in developing new medical tools from silicone products.

In 1940, silicones had been little more than a curiosity. But in twenty years Dow Corning scientists had made them the base of a fast-growing business. The uses for silicones seemed endless. Silicone rubber and wiring had been incorporated into pacemaker heart units (the small, battery-powered, transistoerized mechanisms implanted in patients to keep their hearts beating regularly by means of electrical impulses). Silicone materials were used in heart-lung machines. Silicone products were used by plastic surgeons in restoring the natural appearance of a woman's breast or a damaged ear. They were used in fashioning artificial human organs, in bandages, in the treatment of burns, and in scores of other ways.

In the nation's space program, silicone products found heavy use as sealants, greases, adhesives, electrical insulation, and heat shields. Their resistance to aging, to heat and to cold, and to chemical action gave space scientists and engineers materials peculiarly adaptable to the program. When Astronaut Edward H. White II made his famous twenty-one-minute "stroll in space" in 1965, the 27-foot hose which supplied his oxygen was made of Dow Corning's Silastic silicone rubber.

Among new products exciting to Ted Doan was a new family of chemical polymers, with the trademark Pusher, which held the promise of greatly increasing oil recovery in fields throughout the world. This was the sort of chemical development which fitted into his long-range program of finding chemical solutions to major problems.

The Pusher program began when scientists and engineers began experimenting in 1956 with chemicals that would alter the viscosity of water and in effect thicken it so that when the water was forced down into an oil field, it would act as a "pusher" to shove the oil from sand, rock, and crevices into the well. In one of the Brazos Oil and Gas Company fields in Kansas, the Pusher process recovered 350 barrels per acre-foot from an area which normally would have yielded only 150 barrels per acre-foot had the old water-flooding technique been used. It was the hope of Doan and others in Dow Chemical that the Pusher process would become a major factor in oil recovery around the world.

Another new product was a liquid fuel gas, trademarked MAPP, which quickly became a competitor of acetylene and propane gas. It combined the high heating qualities of acetylene with the safety of propane. The combination was achieved by rearranging the hydrocarbon molecular structures of acetylene and propane. This resulted in a new gas called "stabilized methylacetylene," the basic ingredient of MAPP. The new gas was quickly accepted by industry, among the first users being the Buick Division of General Motors in Flint, Michigan, which used MAPP to flame-harden automobile parts.

Dow Chemical marked up another achievement in 1963 by building the first commercial installation to employ atomic energy as a catalyst in a production process. In this process, cobalt-60 was used as a catalyst to produce ethyl bromide, important in the production of solvents, fumigants, refrigerants, and a number of pharmaceutical compounds.

The process resulted from more than seven years of research. The reaction vessel—about the size of a 30-gallon hot water tank—was buried in concrete. Raw materials were piped through the underground reactor and exposed to the radiation energy emitted by rods containing small slugs of cobalt-60; a chemical reaction resulted to produce ethyl bromide which flowed from the reactor uncontaminated by the rays. It was a pioneering effort which Midland scientists hoped would lead them to other chemical processes using atomic energy.

So much has happened so fast in Dow Chemical in the 1960's that not even company employees have been able to keep track of all the changes. The company organized its own worldwide engineering and construction service. The development of the textile business was made the responsibility of Dow Badische, an associated company. The company moved strongly into the international pharmaceutical field by acquiring controlling interests in Italy's large pharmaceutical group, Ledoga, and in LIFE, the largest pharmaceutical house in Ecuador.

But nothing, perhaps, was more significant than the overseas developments. While Ted Doan was reshaping the domestic organization, Macauley Whiting, President of Dow Chemical International, was taking a hard look at the overseas operations where growth was even faster than it was at home. In 1952, Dow Chemical's sales from foreign exports and manufacturing were only 6 percent of total sales. But by 1965 the foreign sales were 16 percent of total sales (25 percent with Canada included). If the indicators were accurate, the foreign growth would continue to out-distance domestic growth for years to come.

One of the major problems was that the foreign and domestic operations had become increasingly interdependent and yet their management was only loosely tied together. Whiting was convinced the foreign operations would have to be integrated with management in Midland. As matters stood, Dow Chemical was no longer a large domestic producer with sideline interests abroad. Its interests had become global and management had to be organized on that basis.

To achieve better coordination, Whiting proposed the foreign operations be divided into four areas—Europe-Africa, with headquarters in Zurich; Latin America, with headquarters at Coral Gables, Florida; the Pacific, to be run from Hong Kong; and Canada, where Dow Chemical of Canada had long been well established. Each area would have a manager with almost total control over his own production and sales; each manager, eventually, would have funtional departments similar to the corporate departments. Through these managers, exports, sales, and production around the world would be closely linked with Midland.

Whiting's plan was adopted and put into effect in early 1966 as Dow Chemical was pushing a new round of expansions overseas and doubling its investment in the $100,000,000 complex at Terneuzen, Holland. Additions at Terneuzen included a large naphtha cracking plant to produce ethylene and other olefins, a plant for low-density polyethylene, and a number of derivatives.

As the overseas business grew in volume and complexity, Ted Doan, Carl Gerstacker, and Ben Branch agreed that a more sophisticated approach was needed in the European banking operations. The result was the formation in 1965 of a wholly owned bank in Zurich, Switzerland, with paid-in capital of $18,000,000. The bank did not do business with the Swiss public or accept deposits and make loans to Dow Chemical. Its main purpose was to make medium- and long-term loans to the company's European customers in a market where money usually was tight. The bank proved an instant success—and in its first six months turned a profit of $287,643.

During the years of Ted Doan's presidency, Dow Chemical truly has become a global operation. They have been years of constant change, innovation, growth and considerable tumult. In 1964, Dow Chemical broke the billion-dollar mark in sales and joined the relatively small group of American businesses ever to achieve that peak. From 1962 to 1967, sales increased from $890,639,000 to more than $1,138,300,000. In that period, profits rose 80 percent averaging an increase of about 12 percent a year. And all this came during the most sweeping reorganization in the history of the company.

The Dow Chemical Company had traveled a long road to reach this point. In 1907, Herbert Dow was struggling through a money panic and fighting to keep his small chemical company from bankruptcy. Sixty years later his grandson was chief executive of the same company. But its plants were spread around the world. It had assets of about $2,000,000,000. And it ranked as the fourth largest chemical company in the United States.

What are the secrets of this achievement?

Ted Doan sat in his office late one summer afternoon and pondered the question. Finally he said:

"It all comes down to people. We've had the good fortune to have men who were outstanding and independent thinkers, and they were models for others. They were strong men who believed in themselves and in the company. Sometimes you wonder where the Strosackers and Boundys and Barstows and Bennetts and Beutels of the future will come from. But we have them. They're out there. Men like Branch and Gerstacker and others like them. And they make the future look good."

Conclusion

Interstate Highway 75 runs north from Detroit some 100 miles into Lower Michigan's Saginaw Valley. Midland-bound motorists leave I-75 at Bay City on the edge of Lake Huron and veer westward on Highway US-10. After swinging onto the Midland turnoff they pass the brightly colored towers and minarets of The Dow Chemical Company sprawled over a huge tract alongside the Tittabawassee River. Beyond these is the business district of the town. And still further along are uncommonly attractive homes, gardens, parks, tree-shaded streets, schools, golf courses, churches, and all the outward signs of a community that is prospering.

It is difficult for the stranger to realize that this modern town of some 30,000 people (the average age is twenty-four) was, three-quarters of a century ago, a forlorn village sitting in a dreary countryside that had been stripped of its timber and abandoned by the loggers. Honky-tonk saloons dominated the main street. The dirt roads leading from town wandered away into nowhere and, it seemed, so did the future of the town and its people.

The contrast between the old Midland and the new Midland is startling. And no one can stay long in the town without becoming aware that the change was brought about by Herbert Dow and his young dream that he could take bromine from the brine with electricity. This is the legend with which Midland lives, like the stories of the Indians who once roamed the forests of towering white pines.

Midland is an interesting town, only partly because it is the headquarters of a chemical company that is out-ranked in size only by Du Pont, Union Carbide, and Monsanto. Perhaps its real attraction is that there are more brains, talent, and varied personalities among its inhabitants than are normally found in a place of its size.

On this score, an observer once said: "We have more Ph.D's per square acre than you'll find most anywhere else. These fellows tend to marry women with virulently high IQ's. Wives around here prepare breakfast and then a paper on the latest trend in economics before going to art class."

It is not unusual on any one day at the Midland Country Club—the company's favorite place for entertaining visitors—to hear conversations in Japanese, French, Spanish, German, or Italian. The visitors come from all over the world to confer, to dicker, and to study, with the result that Midland is about as isolated from the current of international affairs as the United Nations.

Because strange languages are not unusual, one group of neighborhood youngsters thought it not strange that a dog on their block could speak French quite fluently.

This came to light when Mrs. B., the Brittany-born wife of a Dow Chemical employee, began conducting French classes in her home for the children of neighbors. It was her habit at home to converse only in French with her husband—and to fuss, scold, command, and otherwise communicate with her dog in her native tongue. The dog understood his French-speaking mistress quite well, often growling in his throat and muttering as dogs will.

Mrs. B. was unaware that her young students had taken such an interest in her dog until they appeared at her door one morning before school with a petition.

"Mrs. B.," the spokesman said, "can we take your dog to school with us?"

Mrs. B. was surprised. "Now why would you want my dog in school?"

"Well," the youngster said, "we want to show him to our class. He's the only dog in town who speaks French."

Chamber of Commerce statistics show that Midland residents are the graduates of some 500 American and 30 foreign universities. As high as 92 percent of the registered voters can be expected to turn up at the polls on election day. The town has 40 churches. Eighty-five percent of the families own their own homes. Some 1,200 acres are in parks and more than 500 acres in a city forest. Midland supports its own symphony orchestra, the Midland Art Association, and the Little Theatre Guild. The 1,000-member Sportsmen's Club operates its own lodge and has a 120-acre tract with bait-casting ponds and target-shooting areas. A modern, 225-bed, nonprofit community hospital was built and equipped through fund-raising drives. The public library is one of the most heavily used in the state. The 1,500,000-cubic-foot Community Center provides facilities for instruction and entertainment ranging from ballet to bowling. Northwood Institute, a coeducational institution located on a 200-acre tract in the city, offers two-year degrees in liberal arts, advertising, automotive marketing, banking and finance, business management, journalism, retailing and marketing, and secretarial science. In addition to the Institute and the public schools, the town has two Catholic and one Lutheran elementary school and a Catholic girls' high school. Nearby are Delta College, a two-year community college, Alma College, Saginaw Valley College and Central Michigan University. Not so far distant are the University of Michigan and Michigan State University.

Midland is a town with a large percentage of high-income families because the company employs so many scientists, engineers, managers, and skilled workers. Through the years many employees invested in the company's stock and saw its value multiply. Those who bought 100 shares of stock at 40½ in 1923—exercised all stock rights and retained all stock dividends—have seen the investment grow to 16,446 shares of stock which, on January 15, 1968, were worth $1,414,356. Stock that was purchased in 1945 for $1,000 was worth more than $8,600 in 1967.

Curiously, in an age of growing absentee ownership, those who built Dow Chemical and made their fortunes in the building remained in Midland as did most of the sons and daughters and grandchildren. They involved themselves in the community affairs and "Dow money" was given generously to education, churches, recreation centers, and cultural projects. The menfolk almost invariably knew from boyhood that their careers would be somewhere with The Dow Chemical Company.

Among the "old families" in Midland are the Bakers and Curries and Crisseys and Balls, and Reinharts and Siases, and Towsleys, and Harts. They were farming the land and managing small businesses when Herbert Dow arrived in 1890. Then came the Bennetts, Barstows, and Doans. Families intermarried to link the town closer to the company, both socially and economically. Inevitably, with this cross-linking of families, and as sons followed in the steps of fathers, there was talk of nepotism.

An oldtimer said; "Sure, we know if a choice has to be made there is always a point in favor of the house. But they work so damned hard at their jobs and get such results that nobody can say they didn't deserve it. But it's no big problem. The company is growing in so many directions there are opportunities all over the place."

The management of Dow Chemical is sensitive to any suggestion that Midland is a "company town" because the phrase carries the implication that the company presides with feudal benevolence over the affairs of the people. To an outsider, it seems that this sensitivity often leads to a self-conscious effort to avoid linking the name of the company with the name of the town.

There is some doubt that the company could dictate to the townspeople even if it tried. Willard Dow found this to be true on one occasion in the late 1930's when a CIO union group asked permission to hold a meeting in the Community Center, largely financed by "Dow money" and gifts by Ed Barstow.

Dow voiced his objections to the governing board of the Center (some of them Dow Chemical employees) and was promptly overruled on the grounds that the Center was open to any group of citizens wanting it for reasonable cause.

"I guess the board was right," Willard said later. "There's too much attention paid to the Dows in this town as it is."

But the Dow imprint is on Midland and noticeably so in the distinctive architecture of many of the homes, churches, and community buildings designed by Alden Dow, the rebel son of Herbert who didn't go into the chemical business. The unconventional structures—showing the influence of the master, Frank Lloyd Wright, on the pupil, Alden Dow—are among the showplaces of the town.

Ed Barstow and Charles Strosacker were among those who grew up with Dow Chemical, became wealthy, and used generous shares of their money to help charitable causes and promote community services. But the largest contributions through the years have come from The Herbert H. and Grace A. Dow Foundation. The nonprofit foundation was established in 1936 by Mrs. Herbert Dow "in memory of her late and revered husband, Dr. Herbert H. Dow, and in token and esteem of the mutual friendship which has always existed between the members of the Dow family and the citizens of the City of Midland."

At this time 100 shares of Dow Chemical stock were deposited in a trust. Other gifts were made by Mrs. Dow in later years, and then at her death in 1953 the Foundation received a bequest of 150,000 shares. From this fund, large sums have been poured into worthwhile causes.

The Foundation provided funds for the Grace A. Dow Memorial Library, a modern, 70,000-square-foot building designed by Alden Dow as the nucleus of a cultural center. It was completed in 1955 and in 1967 its shelves held more than 120,000 books and they were increasing at the rate of 500 a month. Donations were made to the building funds of hospitals, schools, and churches and to charitable organizations, the Little Theatre Guild, the Midland Art Association, Interlochen Arts Academy, an addition to the courthouse, property for a municipal golf course, a science building at Kalamazoo College, and the installation of a closed-circuit television system at the University of Michigan Medical School. These were but a few of the Foundation's gifts.

Not many are left in Midland who knew Herbert Dow in his young days. One who did is eighty-seven-year-old Earl Bennett. He still has an office at Dow Chemical's Headquarters building. Almost every weekday, weather permitting, he arrives to read his mail, check company reports, and chat with those who drop in for advice or to reminisce.

"My memory is not so good," he says with a twinkle. "I used to be able to remember things that hadn't even happened."

And then he amazes the visitor with his storehouse of remembered lore. He remembers how much bromine sold for in 1903 and how cold the wind was that day in 1907 when he found on the street the $2 which saved him from the embarrassment of admitting he couldn't buy a loaf of bread. He remembers the price wars with the British and Germans and how Tom Griswold, Jr., built chlorine cells from secondhand lumber and old nails. He remembers his first trip to Wall Street and how big the city seemed to a small-town boy. He chuckles over the time he visited Europe and was mistaken for royalty because he signed the hotel register, "Earl Bennett—Midland." They called him the "Earl of Midland." There isn't much he doesn't remember about The Dow Chemical Company and he is the last of the old, old guard who saw it all happen.

Dutch Beutel remembers a lot of the story, too, although he came to Midland several years after Bennett. At seventy-four, he maintains a pace that would wear out men half his age, directing the big Government Affairs Department and holding membership on the executive committee and the board of directors.

Lee Doan is another who saw much of the building. He continues as a board member, chairman of the executive committee, and a member of the finance committee. His office is only a few paces down the hall from that of his son Ted.

Among the scientists who contributed so much to the discovery of new products and new processes, William R. Collings, seventy-four, is still active as honorary chairman of the Dow Corning Corporation and advisor to Chairman Shailer Bass, with whom he worked in pioneering a silicones industry.

At Dow Chemical of Canada, Limited, in nearby Sarnia, N. R. Crawford had turned over the presidency to L. D. Smithers. They had built Dow Canada into one of the company's strongest links with the help of such men as John Smart, Paul Scott, and B. A. Howard.

Most of the others who played leading roles in the building of Dow Chemical are dead—Griswold, Barstow, Strosacker, Britton, Veazey, and Hale.

Don Gibb, who helped introduce plastics to the American scene as Dow Chemical's first manager of plastics sales, sat in his lakeside cottage in Upper Michigan one day and talked of the men with whom he had worked before his retirement.

"Looking back," he said, "you realize what strong men they were and how much talent they had. But they weren't on a lofty plateau above you. They got down in the dirt with you when there was a job to be done.

"I remember as a young man I bought a furnace for my house and it just about broke me to buy it. Dutch Beutel was head of the pipe shop at the time with all he could handle at the plant. But one morning he turned up at my house in overalls and installed the furnace in my basement. He said he wanted to be sure the job was done right—but the truth was he knew I was about broke.

"They weren't men who were always easy to work with. Working with Strosacker was a little like being on the same team with Ty Cobb. There were times you hated his guts, but you never wanted to see him playing for another team and you were a better man for having been on the same team with him.

"One time Dutch bawled out two of his men who hadn't done their job the way he thought it should have been done. As he turned to leave them, he growled; 'And when I'm gone I don't want you saying, 'I'm glad to get rid of that old +$%—&'()*!' One of the men said, 'Why, Dutch, I've never heard anybody call you old.' "

Not many of the people and few of the old landmarks remain from the early days of Herbert Dow. One of the last landmarks is the rambling old house out on West Main Street which Dow built just before the turn of the century. It was called a "mansion" in those days, but it really is only a large, comfortable frame house with a mid-Victorian dignity about it. A caretaker keeps it much as it was when Mrs. Dow died.

The gardens around the house—a place of beauty that was created out of a virtual wilderness—draw hundreds of sightseers each year.

Beyond the house and gardens is the orchard where Dow experimented with his first agricultural chemicals and to which he retreated when he wanted to leave behind the affairs of business. The gnarled trees produced a bountiful harvest of apples each fall for many, many years but they are coming down to make way for the new Midland Center for the Arts building.

From his dream grew the old house and the gardens and the orchard. From it also came a modern little city... ways to take chemical treasures from the sea... a company that had ventured forth from Midland to girdle the globe.

All this, and more, from the dream of a man they called "Crazy Dow."

Index

Acetic anhydride, 91
Adams Paper Company, 234
Agency for International Development (AID), 271
Aid to Medical Research Center, 272
Air pollution, chloroform plant, 57
Airplanes: Herbert Dow on future of, 90
  magnesium in, 6, 85, 90, 100, 121, 136, 147-149, 163, 169, 171, 176-177, 226
  silicones in, 192, 228
  World War II, 160-161, 163, 169, 171, 176-177, 192
  Wright brothers, 55
Ak-Bulak, Russia, eclipse observation, 150-151
Allen, Glenn, Dow Chemical recruiter, 265-266
Allen, William, chemist in sales force, 135-136
Allied Laboratories, Incorporated, merged with Dow Chemical, 254-255
Allied Laboratories International, 254
Allied Laboratories, Limited, 254
Allyn's Point, Connecticut, Dow plant, 225
Aluminum Company of America (Alcoa), 180, 182
  magnesium, early use, 99
American Business World, 128
American Magnesium Corporation (AMC), 99, 101
  and I. G. Frabenindustrie, Magnesium Development Corporation, 136-137
  magnesium manufacture stopped, 121
  patent rights, 120-121

Ammonia in water, 260
Ammonia plants, bombing of, 196
Amsterdam, Bankierskantoon Mendes Gans, 250
Anilin oil, 87
Aniline: dyes, 16-17
  as gasoline additive, 104
Applegate, Vernon C., of Great Lakes Fishery Commission, 240, 241
Argentina, Dow subsidiary, 243
Arnold, Thurman, Attorney General, 167, 168
Arsenic in oil-well treatment, 130
Asahi Chemical Company, 221
Asahi-Dow Limited, 221, 229, 243
Aspirin, 87, 91, 202
Atomic bomb, Russian, 222
Atomic Energy Commission, 222-223, 238
Atomic energy research, 222-224, 273
Austin Company, 159-160, 223
Australia, Dow partnership plant, 243
Automobiles: Ford Model T, 77-78, 103, 121
  Herbert Dow's first, 75
  magnesium in, suggested uses, 101
  in 1900, 49-50
  in 1924, 103-104
  self-starter, 103

Babson, Roger, 123
Bakelite, 97
Baker, W. L., store in Midland, 3, 4
Ball, Howard, manager of export department, 219
Ballman, Donald, 6, 202, 203, 253
  on board of directors, 244
  vice president, 252, 261

Barnes, Earle B., 253
  research on competing companies suggested, 204
  Texas Division, general manager, 252, 259-260
Barstow, E. O., 6, 8, 73, 75, 84, 85, 111, 118, 126, 127, 245, 279, 281
  on board of directors, 124, 201
  bromine from sea, project, 128, 129
  chloroform odor control, 57
  first job with Dow Chemical, 53
  magnesium from sea, 149
  magnesium production, 85-86, 99-101, 166
  Midland Community Center sponsored, 85
  research and development, 68, 81, 96, 143
  retirement, 243, 251
  Texas plant development, 171
Baruch, Bernard, 90, 185
Basic Magnesium, Incorporated, 170, 177
Bass, Shailer, 192, 280
Baton Rouge, Dow plant (see Louisiana Division)
Bay City, Michigan, Dow plant, 176
Bell Telephone Company, Styrofoam used, 227
Ben-Mont Paper Company, 234
Bennett, Earl Willard, 6, 9, 51, 58, 75, 84, 85, 94, 126, 127, 139, 259
  assistant treasurer, 123
  on board of directors, 124, 201, 215
  director of Dow Chemical of Canada, 189
  financing: debenture sales, 224-225
  postwar expansion, 208
  first job with Dow Chemical, 51-52
  magnesium monopoly charge, 167
  memories, 280
  New York banking houses visited, 151
  panic of 1907 described, 64-65
  resignation, 252, 256
  in styrene research, 145-146
  treasurer, 124
  vice president, 215, 251
Bennett, Robert B., son of Earl Bennett, 252, 253
Benz, Karl, 18
Berle, Adolf A., quoted, 129
Bernstorff, Count Johann Heinrich von, 82, 88, 89
Beutel, A. P. ("Dutch"), 6, 94-95, 253, 256, 259, 280, 281
  assistant general manager, 131
  on board of directors, 210, 252
  bromine from sea, plant construction, 137-138
  in Dow Well Service (Dowell), 131
  Government Affairs Department, management, 262
  iodine plant study, 131-133
  Louisiana ground-breaking ceremony, 232
  magnesium production problems, 165-166
  phenol production process, 98
  pipelines, 94-95, 108
  Texas Division, general manager, 201, 208, 233, 252, 260
  Texas plant development, 161, 171-174
  Texas scouting trip, 154-155, 158-159
  vice president, 215, 252
  waste disposal problem, 154
  Willard Dow's relationship with, 209
Beutel, Mrs. A. P., 94-95, 137
Blasingame, Dr. F. J. L., survey of Vietnam casualties, 267
Blue, Robert, 166
Boats, Styrofoam in, 227
Bombay, Dow partnership plant, 243
Bonus March, 1932, 129-130
Boron, magnesium production problem, 166
Bosscher, Harold, in Midland Division, 261
Boundy, Ray H., 6, 131, 248, 252, 260, 261
  bromine from sea, project, 118

Index

director of research, 229
research and development, 143, 145, 205
synthetic rubber program, 186
Bragg, Sir William, quoted, 143-144
Branch, Ben, 6, 13, 229, 243, 245, 253, 261, 262, 274
  on board of directors, 244
  executive vice president, 258-259
  foreign operations, development, 246-247, 249-250
  president of Dow Chemical International, 247
  vice president, 252
Branson, Carl A., 138, 162
Brazil, Dow partnership plant, 243
Brazos Oil and Gas Company, 208, 252, 272
Brine: chemical contents, 34
  Michigan deposits, 1, 7-8, 28
  in oil wells, 20
  products extracted from, 1, 2, 7, 20-21
    (See also Bromine; Chlorine)
  salt from, 20-21
  wells, sulfuric acid treatment, 130
Britain (see Great Britain)
Britton, Edgar C., 6, 95-96, 281
  phenol production process, 97-98
  research and development, 143
  silicone research, 191
Bromides, 53, 68
  German monopoly (see Deutsche Bromkonvention)
  in World War I, 81
Bromine: extraction from brine, 2, 20-22
  blowing-out process, 21-24
  electrolysis, 22-24, 29
  gasoline additives from, 6, 104-105
  production expanded, 94
  from sea, 105-109, 118-119, 128-129, 137-139
Buna-N synthetic rubber, 170
Buna-S (GRS) synthetic rubber, 170, 184, 186, 187
Burbank, Luther, 61
Burdick, E. C., chemist, 85

Bureau of Aeronautics, 148
Burow, Albert, 28, 29
Burow, Julius, 28
Butadiene, 7, 12, 170, 184, 186

Calcium chloride, 76, 87
Campana Corporation, 254
Campbell, Calvin, 208, 259
  in airplane accident, 212-213
  on board of directors, 210
  secretary, 215
Campbell, Mrs. Calvin, 212-213
Canada: Dow Chemical operations, 206-208
  synthetic rubber program, 188-189
Canadian Synthetic Rubber, 188
Canton Chemical Company, 22-23
Carbon tetrachloride, 74-75, 91, 259
  chloroform synthesis from, 56, 81
Carpenter, R. R. M., vice president of du Pont, 118
Carpenter, Captain William S., 263
Case School of Applied Science, 16-17, 20, 37
  honorary degree for Herbert Dow, 114
  research for Dow Chemical, 72
Caustic soda, 91, 158, 258
  in phenol process, 97, 98
Cellulose, wood distillation as source, 144-145
Chamberlain, Jack, Japanese sales investigation, 221
Chemical Engineering Award, 171
Chemical industries; advances in, 78-79, 140-141, 147, 200, 231
  in World War I, 80-81
  in World War II, 195-196
Chemical mining, 237-238
Chile, iodine monopoly, 7, 104, 122, 133, 156
China, dyes sold in, 219
Chlorbenzol in phenol production, 97
Chlorine, 258
  evaporation process, 76
  extraction from brine, 33-35, 37, 40
  in phenol process, 98

products, 76, 91, 153, 158
Chlorine bleach, 3-4, 34, 35, 40, 53
  British competition (see United Alkali)
  electrochemical manufacture, 43, 47
  Great Western Power Company, 152-153
  production discontinued, 75
Chlorine cells, improvement, 67-68, 71, 75-76
Chloroform, 91
  synthesis from carbon tetrachloride, 56, 81
Churchill, Winston, 163, 212
Cleveland Cliffs Iron Company, 144-145
Cliffs Dow Chemical Company, 145, 156
Coalwell, Norris, 138
Collings, William R., 6, 85, 143, 280
  in Corning Glass–Dow Chemical partnership, 192
  silicone research, 191
Communicable Disease Center, 271
Compligen vaccine, 254
Cone, Lee H., chemist, 82
Convers, A. E.: chairman of board of directors, 91, 110, 117
  letters from Herbert Dow, 60, 81, 83
  president of Dow Chemical, 43, 46, 83
  on price war with Deutsche Bromkonvention, 61
Coolidge, Calvin, President, 116, 134
Cooper, H. S., in Midland Chemical Company, 32, 33, 39, 40
Corning Glass Works, Dow Chemical partnership, 191, 192, 217, 228
Corpus Christi, Texas, 158-159
Cote, Elzie, tribute to Herbert Dow, 125
Cottringer, Paul, 98
Crawford, N. R. (Russ), 162

president of Sarnia plant, 207, 280
Crider, J. S., 117, 123
  on board of directors, 201
  letter from Herbert Dow, 107
Currie, G. A., Congressman, 90
Curtis, Russell: on board of directors, 210
  in Great Western Division, 201
  retirement, 243
  vice president, 215
Curtiss, Frank A., letter from Herbert Dow, 42

DC4 (Dow Corning 4), silicone product, 192, 193
Defense Plant Corporation, 169, 171, 173, 176
Department of Justice, magnesium monopoly charge, 167, 168
Depression: of 1907 (see Panic of 1907)
  of 1920s, 93–94, 126
  of 1930s, 12, 123–124, 126, 129–130, 133–134
Detroit Edison Company, atomic energy research, 222
Deutsche Bromkonvention:
  Herbert Dow confers with, 69–71
  price war with Dow Chemical, 6, 55–56, 59–61, 66–71
Dewey, Bradley, Rubber Director, letter to Willard Dow, 198
Diamond Magnesium Company, 169
Diphenyloxide, 99
Dixon, Bill, 252
Doan, Herbert Dow (Ted), 243, 245–247, 261, 273–275
  on board of directors, 229
  executive vice president, 252
  on napalm, 269–271
  organization policy, 253–255, 258–259
  president of Dow Chemical, 13, 257, 258, 274
Doan, Leland A., son of Leland I. Doan, 244
Doan, Leland I. (Lee), 105, 256,

259, 280
  on board of directors, 201
  director of Dow Chemical of
    Canada, 189
  management policy, 215–216,
    229
  plant dispersal policy, 231–232
  president of Dow Chemical, 12,
    214–216
  resignation, 12, 256–257
  sales director, 124, 135, 202, 204
  sales philosophy, 203
  spending policy, 225
Doan, Mrs. Leland I. (Ruth Dow),
    12, 36, 124, 137
  childhood, 42, 66
Dobeckmun Company, 243
  merger with Dow Chemical, 234
Dominion Rubber Company, 188
Dow, Alden, son of Herbert Dow, 66
  as architect, 115, 173
  on board of directors, 201
  Camp Chemical, Velasco housing,
    173
  Lake Jackson, near Velasco, 174–
    175
  Midland architecture, 279
Dow, Helen, daughter of Herbert
    Dow (see Hale, Mrs. William J.)
Dow, Helen, sister of Herbert Dow
    (see Griswold, Mrs. Thomas, Jr.)
Dow, Herbert Henry, 1–11, 14, 25
  argument, love of, 102
  birth, 19
  Canton Chemical Company, 21–23
  at Case School of Applied Science,
    16–17, 20
  death, 6, 11, 125
  Dow Chemical Company: board
    of directors, disagreement with,
    109–111
    incorporation, 43–44
    president and general manager,
      election, 90–91
    sale to syndicate, offer rejected,
      83–85
  Dow Process Company, 37–43
  electrochemical manufacture,
    statement on, 42–43
  engineers, use of, 160
  in England, 67, 69–71
  fiftieth anniversary recalls, 199
  in Germany, 66
  home in Midland, 46, 281
  honorary degree, 114
  horticulture, interest in, 57, 67
  in Japan, 110, 113
  landscape gardening, interest in, 57,
    110
  magnesium, interest in, 89–90, 170
  in management: criticism of, 72–
    74
    early years, 8–9, 57–59
    ideas on, 111–112
  marriage, 4, 30–32
  Midland, Michigan: courthouse,
    113–114
    housing for employees, 85
    landscape gardening, 113
    Library, 85
    plant, building design, 44
  Midland Chemical Company, 24,
    28–40, 51
  new products and methods, search
    for, 72–73, 96
  office, new, request for, 83
  Perkin Medal Award, 124–125
  spending habits, 83
  in War Industries Board, 90
Dow, Mrs. Herbert Henry (Grace
    Ball), 42, 59, 66, 102, 109, 134
  foundation established by, 279
  marriage, 4, 30–32
Dow, Herbert Henry, II, son of
    Willard Dow, 212, 229
Dow, Herbert H. and Grace A.,
    Foundation, 279–280
Dow, Joseph, father of Herbert Dow,
    19, 45
Dow, Margaret, daughter of Herbert
    Dow, 66
Dow, Ruth (See Doan, Mrs. Leland
    I.)
Dow, Willard Henry, 6, 10–12, 86,
    96, 105, 279
  assistant general manager, 115

birth, 40
childhood, 42, 66
death, 12, 212–213
Dow Chemical of Canada,
  president and director, 189
  expansion, attitude toward, 152
  on German ammonia plants, 196
  magnesium monopoly and
    conspiracy charges, 167–169,
    178–183
  management responsibilities, 200–
    202, 210–212, 216
  on postwar development, 197–198,
    210
  president of Dow Chemical, 11,
    126–127
  research, attitude toward, 146–147
  sales, attitude toward, 202, 204
  on Texas plants; 163–164
Dow, Mrs. Willard Henry, 212–213
Dow Badische, 273
Dow Chemical Company: Allied
  Laboratories, Incorporated,
  merger with, 254–255
  Chemical Engineering Award, 171
  chronology, periods, 11–13
  Corning Glass Works, partnership
    with, 191, 192, 217, 228
  debenture sales, 224–225
  Dobeckmun Company, merger
    with, 234
  du Pont offers to buy controlling
    interest, 117–118
  early staff members, 5–6, 8
  employees (see Employees)
  Ethyl Corporation, joint operations,
    128, 138, 147, 234
  expansion program: 1901, 53–54
    1935–1938, 143, 157–158
    1945–1949, 199, 206–208
    1950s, 216–217
  fiftieth anniversary, 199–200
  foreign operations, 12, 219–222,
    242–243, 246–251, 273–274
  formation of, 2-3, 11, 43-44
  Goodyear Tire and Rubber Company, joint operation, 170, 185
  growth: 1897-1947, 199-200
    1930s, 142-143, 155-156
    1949-1962, 216, 230-231, 256
    1960s, 274
  incorporation transferred to Delaware, 208
  library, 95
  magnesium monopoly and conspiracy charges, 167-169, 178-183
  management, 8-9, 12-13, 127, 200-202, 210-212, 215-216, 229, 245, 251-253
  Midland Chemical Company
    merged with, 51
  organization structure, 258-262
  plants decentralized, 225-226, 231
  products: 1910, 74-75
    1916, 87
    1929, 117
    1947, 205-206
    1962, 258
  research (see Research and development)
  sale to syndicate, offer rejected, 83-85
  sales department, 202-205, 217-218
  stock: employee purchases, 112, 251
    family ownership, 251
    listed with New York Stock Exchange, 152, 156
  trademark, 92
  training courses, 85, 218
  World War II awards, 198
Dow Chemical Inter-American, Limited, 220
Dow Chemical International A. G., 249
Dow Chemical International, Limited, 220, 247
Dow Chemical of Canada, Limited, 189, 191, 206-207, 220, 274, 280
Dow Corning, 191, 192, 217, 228, 272
Dow Diamond, 164, 165, 194, 214–215, 241–242
Dow Process Company, 37–40
  merged with Midland Chemical

Company, 41–43
  payment of stock to partners, 46–47
Dowell, Incorporated (Dow Well Service), 131, 143, 155, 252
  fracture, use of, 154
  Industrial Service Division, 255
  magnesium, use of, 226
  Schlumberger, Limited, associated with, 250–251
Dowicides, 99
Dowlap, 241
Dowmetal, 99
  eclipse observation equipment, 150
Dowtherm, 99
Dreisbach, Robert, 97
  styrene research, 145–146
Dressel, G. F., 138, 139, 171
Drugs and health products, 254–255, 271
Dunn, Edwin E., in lamprey eradication, 240
Du Pont de Nemours, E. I., and Company: dyes, 82
  experiment on bromine from sea, 108
  offer to buy controlling interest in Dow Chemical, 117–118
  synthetic rubber, 184
Dyes, 81–82
  aniline, 16–17
  Chinese use of, 219
  German monopoly, 6, 17, 81–82

Eastman Kodak Company, bromides for, 68
Eclipse observation equipment, magnesium, 149–151
Edison, Thomas A., 17
Electricity in White House, 23
Electrolysis: bromine extraction, 22–24, 28
  chlorine process, 43, 47
  magnesium production, 86
Elektron, German name of magnesium, 100
Employees: in Depression of 1930s, 133–134
  fiftieth anniversary summary, 199
  housing, Midland, 85
  number of: in 1938, 156
    in 1962, 256
  profit–sharing plan, 53
  stock purchases, 112, 251
  strike, 209–210
  training courses, 85, 218
England (see Great Britain)
Enseki, Manabu, 221
Epsom salts, 76, 91
Establecimientos Francimex, S. A., 254
Ethocel, 144, 145, 193
Ethyl bromide, atomic energy in production, 273
Ethyl Corporation, 11, 107, 119
  joint operations with Dow Chemical, 128, 138, 147, 234
Ethylene, 158
  Dutch plant using, 249
  mustard gas from, 91
  polyethylene from, 236
Ethylene dibromide, 158, 234
  as gasoline additive, 104–105, 107, 118, 127
  General Motors purchase, 106
  production increased, 108, 147
Ethylene dichloride, 158, 186
Ethylene glycol, 158, 207, 233
Euromarket (European Economic Community), 242
Explosions, 35, 45, 47

Fay, Jesse B., letter to Herbert Dow, 57–58
Ferric bromide, 31
Ferric chloride, 74
Firestone Tire and Rubber Company in Canada, 188
Forbes Magazine, 230
Ford Edsel, 212
Ford, Henry, 5, 77–78, 103, 211–212 wages raised, 77–78
Ford Model T, 77–78, 103, 121
Ford Motor Company: magnesium production, 170
  management problems, 211–212

290   The Dow Story

Francis Ferdinand, Archduke, assassinated, 79–80
Frasch, Herman, theory on oil–well treatment, 130
Freeport, Texas, 158–159
  Dow plant, 160–164, 169, 209, 233
  salt water conversion plant, 256
  styrene production, 186
Froth flotation, 237–238
Fungicides, 99

Gardiner, Ewart L., article in Midland Sun, 114
Gas from oil wells, 155
Gasoline: additives, 104–105
  anti–knock, 6, 11, 103–105, 108, 147, 158
  prejudice against, 107–108
General Motors Corporation, 103, 104
  bromine from Dow Chemical, 105–106
  Frigidaire Division, 195
Germany: bromide manufacture (see Deutsche Bromkonvention)
  chemical industries, 16–17, 81
  Dow operations in, 249
  dye monopoly, 6, 17, 81–82
  magnesium production, 100–101
  scientists, 16–17
Gerstacker, Carl, 6, 13, 211, 221, 224, 243, 246, 253, 256, 274
  on board of directors, 211, 252
  in foreign operations, 250
  reorganization explained, 261–262
  treasurer, 215, 258
Gibb, Don, 139, 281
Glesner, Leo, 138, 162
Glycerine, synthetic, 237
Goggin, Bill, 247
Goheen, Robert F., president of Princeton, 265
Gold from sea, rumors of, 139, 140
Gold bromide, 53
Goodrich Rubber Company in Canada, 188
Goodyear Dow Corporation, 170
Goodyear Tire and Rubber Company:
  in Canada, 188
  Dow Chemical operations with, 170, 185
Government Affairs Department, 262
Graves, James C.: in Dow Chemical, 45, 47, 59, 60
  in Midland Chemical Company, 35, 40
Great Britain: alkali combine (see United Alkali)
  Dow partnership plants, 243
  magnesium ordered in World War II, 162, 169
Great Lakes Fishery Commission, 240, 241
Great Western Electrochemical Company, 152–153, 238
  Dow Chemical acquires, 153–154
Grebe, John J., 6
  atomic energy research, 222
  bromine from sea, research, 118
  iodine process, 133
  oil–well treatment, 130, 131
  research and development, 143, 145, 146
Greece, Dow plants in, 249
Green, Colonel E. H. R., 5, 142
Green, Hetty, 3–4
  Dow stock bought by, 5, 142
Greene, George W., 171
Greene, Leo, 166
Griswold, Nelson: on board of directors, 211
  in Cliffs Dow Chemical Company, 145
  Texas plant development, 161–162, 171, 172
Griswold, Thomas, Jr., 6, 8, 44–45, 47, 53, 68, 75, 84–87, 94–95, 160, 281
  retirement, 251
Griswold, Mrs. Thomas, Jr. (Helen Dow), 44
GRS (see Buna–S)
Haber, Fritz, scientist, 153
Hackenberg, H. E., secretary: in England, 69–71
  sale of company to syndicate

favored, 83–84
Hacking, John, in Sarnia plant, 190
Hale, William J., 6, 95, 281
  phenol production process, 97–98
  research laboratory organized, 95
Hale, Mrs. William J. (Helen Dow), 95
  childhood, 36, 42, 66
Hanawalt, J. C., on magnesium rolling, 226
Harding, Warren Gamaliel, President, 93, 116
Harlow, Ivan, 132
  bromine from sea, research, 118, 119, 128
  Texas plant development, 171
Harr, A. R., 117
Harrison, Benjamin, President, 23
Heath, S. B., 171
Heath, Ted: iodine process, 133
  research and development, 143
Helman, B. E.: in Midland Chemical Company, 31–35, 39–41
  sells interest to Dow, 46
Hens, experiment with, 18
Hirschkind, Wilhelm, chemist, 6, 153–154, 238
Hitler, Adolf, 157, 160, 172
Hock, Clarence, 164
Holland (see Netherlands)
Honore, Paul, artist, 114
Hoover, Herbert, President, 130, 134
Howard, B. A., 280
Howe, B. W., in Midland Chemical Company, 29–31
Howe, C. D., Canadian Minister of Munitions and Supply, 188
Howell, John, in lamprey eradication, 240, 241
Hulbert, W. L., in Midland Chemical Company, 29–31
Hull, Cordell, quoted, 161, 183
Hunter, Ralph M., 166, 171
Hyde, J. Franklin, silicone research, 191
Hydrochloric acid, 233
Hydrogen: from chlorine process, 76

from phenol process, 98

I. G. Farbenindustrie: agreement with Dow Chemical rumored, 182
  and American Magnesium Corporation, Magnesium Development Corporation, 136–137
  magnesium, competition with Dow Chemical, 120
Imperial Chemical Industries, 236
Incubators, 18–19
Indigo, synthetic, 81–82, 89, 219
Industrial Workers of the World (IWW), 93
Insecticides, 74, 91, 99
International Minerals and Chemical Corporation, 169
International Traffic Department, 249
  (See also Dow Chemical Company, foreign operations)
Iodine: blowing-out process, 133
  Chilean monopoly, 7, 104, 122, 133, 156
  as gasoline additive, 104
  Io–Dow Chemical Company, 133, 143, 156
  Jones Chemical Company, 122, 131–132
  Long Beach plant, 132–133
  from oil-field brine, 122
  silver process, 132–133
Io–Dow Chemical Company, 133, 143, 156
Ironton, Ohio, Dow plant, 231
Iroquois Cement Company, 65
Italy, Dow operations in, 249, 273

Jacobsohn, Herman, of Deutsche Bromkonvention, 55–56, 59, 71
James River, Dow plant, 231, 235–236
Japan: Dow sales in, 221
  magnesium sold to, 183
Johnson, Julius, in research administration, 252
Johnson, Lyndon B., President, 256,

264, 267
Jones, C. W., 131–133
  iodine process, 122
Jones Chemical Company, 122, 131–132
  as Io–Dow Chemical Company, 133
  in Long Beach, 132–133

Kennedy, John F., President, 256
Kettering, Charles F., interviews with Herbert Dow, 103–107
Key, Max, 243, 261
  in Midland Division, 259
  vice president and director of Asahi–Dow Limited, 229
Kipping, F. S., silicone named by, 191
Knickerbocker Trust Company, 63
Kogan, Dr. Benjamin S., on Lirugen, 271
Korean war, 216, 222, 226
Kure Beach, North Carolina: bromine from sea water, 119, 128
  bromine plant, 138, 140, 147, 200, 223
  production costs, 154

Lake Jackson, Texas, 174–175
Lampreys, eradication, 239–242
Langell, F. H., atomic energy research, 222–224
Ledoga, Italian pharmaceutical group, 273
Lehman Brothers, 151
Lessing, Lawrence P., quoted, 78
LIFE, Ecuadorian pharmaceutical firm, 273
Lincoln, Abraham, 112
Linville, J. A., in Canton Chemical Company, 22
Lirugen vaccine, 271
Long Beach, California, iodine plant, 132–133
Los Alamos, New Mexico, 222–223
Los Angeles: styrene plant, 186
  water shortage, 112–113
Louisiana Division, 252

Plaquemine plant, 231, 232
Lowry, Fred, general plant superintendent, 95
Ludington, Michigan, Dow plant, 176, 223
Lusk, Fred, in iodine plant, 132–133

Mabery, Charles F., 17
MacArthur, General Douglas, 130, 222
McDade, Louisiana, Jones Chemical Company, 122
McGranahan, George M., 161, 171, 172
McGregor, Rob Roy, silicone research, 191
McKinley, William, President, 49
MacLaughlin, E. R., 171
MacNamara, Robert, Secretary of Defense, 264, 268
Madison, Illinois, magnesium plant, 226
Magnesium, 6, 11, 85–86, 89–90, 96, 136–137
  in airplanes, 6, 85, 90, 100, 121, 136, 147–149, 163, 169, 171, 176–177, 226
  aluminum alloys, 99–101
  American Magnesium Company patent rights, 120–121
  casting, 101, 136, 177
  Dowmetal, trade name, 99
  eclipse observation equipment, 149–151
  flares, 91
  foreign sales, 147
  Freeport plant, 164–166, 169
  German production, 100–101
  Herbert Dow's interest in, 89–90, 170
  I. G. Farbenindustrie competition, 120
  incendiary bombs, 169, 171
  manganese alloys, 101
  monopoly and conspiracy charges, 167–169, 178–183
  postwar decline, 209
  production expanded, 121–122, 147–148

production problems, 165–166
production process improved, 99–101
rolling, 226
from sea, 149, 154–155, 158, 164–165, 171
uses, 226–227
suggested, 101
in World War II, 6, 149, 162, 163, 169–172, 176–183
Magnesium chloride, 76, 164
Magnesium Development Corporation, 136–137, 180
Magnesium hydrate (milk of magnesia), 164
Mallinckrodt Chemical Works, 59
MAPP gas, 272–273
Marquette, Michigan, Cliffs Dow Chemical Company, 145
Marysville, Michigan, Dow plant, 176
Massachusetts Institute of Technology, 212
Mathieson Alkali Works, 170
Mencken, H. L., quoted, 116
Menzel, Donald H., astrophysicist, 149–151
Merszei, Zoltan, in export sales, 220
Michelson, Albert, 17
Michigan: brine deposits, 1, 7–8, 28
lumbering industry, 26–27
Midgley, Thomas, Jr.: anti–knock gasoline investigated, 104–106
bromine from sea investigated, 119
interviews with Herbert Dow, 103–107
letter to Willard Dow, 105–106
Midland, Michigan, 1, 10, 24, 27
Community Center, 85
courthouse, 113–114
Dow plant: fiftieth anniversary summary, 199–200
first buildings, 44
in 1890, 25–28
Herbert H. and Grace A. Dow Foundation, gifts, 279–280
housing for Dow employees, 85
landscape gardening, 113
Library, 85, 279

in 1900, 51
in 1926, 114
in 1960s, 276–281
Midland Chemical Company, 24, 28–40
merged with Dow Chemical, 51
merged with Dow Process Company, 41–43
new organizations, 56, 73–74, 81
Midland Division, interdivisional relationships, 259–260
Miller, Jacob, in Canton Chemical Company, 22
Mine Workers Union, 209
Minger, F. R., 171
Mining: chemical, 237–238
uranium, 238–239
Mining Technical Service, 238
Mittnacht, Arthur, 139
Miyazaki, Kagayaki, 221
Moffett, James W., of Great Lakes Fishery Commission, 240, 241
Monochlorbenzene, 87
Monochlorbenzol, 91
Morgan, John Pierpont, 64, 93, 123, 129
Morley, Edward, 17, 72
Morrison, William, electric automobile, 50
Moyle, Clarence L., in lamprey eradication, 240
Mustard gas, 91

Napalm, 263-264
Dow Chemical statements on, 264-265, 269-271
protests against, 262-271
National Aniline, 82
National Broadcasting Company, Saran Wrap advertising, 218
National Defense Advisory Council, 184
Navarre, Ohio, Dow Process Company, 38-39
Nederlandsche Dow Maatschappij, 243
Neoprene, 184
Netherlands, Dow operations in,

294 The Dow Story

243, 249, 250
New York Herald-Tribune on Dow
　　Chemical wartime production,
　　181
New York Stock Exchange, Dow
　　Chemical stock, 152, 156
Nicholson, John R., Canadian
　　Deputy Comptroller of Supplies,
　　188, 189
Nieuwland, Rev. Julius A.,
　　synthetic rubber research, 184

Office of Price Administration, 169,
　　170
Ohman, M. F., iodine process, 133
Oil wells: brine in, 20
　gas from, 155
　Pusher in, 272
　in Sarnia, 189
　sulfuric acid treatment, 7, 130
Ontario Nickel Company, 65
Orthophenylphenol, 98-99
Osborn, J. H., 54, 59
　on birth of Willard Dow, 40-41
　in Dow Chemical, 43
　in Dow Process Company, 37, 38
　letter from Herbert Dow, 72
　in merger of Midland Chemical
　　Company and Dow Process
　　Company, 41-42
　　in Midland Chemical Company,
　　　24, 28-31
Osmun, Roy, bromine from sea
　　investigated, 119, 128

Palmer, A. Mitchell, Attorney
　　General, 93
Panic of 1907, 63-65
Paraphenylphenol, 98-99
Pardee, James T., 117, 126, 211
　in Dow Chemical, 43
　in Dow Process Company, 37-39,
　　41
　letters from Herbert Dow, 74, 110
Paris, Rupert, sales manager, 59, 60
Patrick, J. C., Thiokol discovered,
　　186
Payne, H. L., letter from Herbert
　　Dow, 112-113
Pearl Harbor, Japanese attack, 171
Perchlorethylene, 233
Perkin, William H., aniline dye
　　discovered, 16, 124-125
Perkin Medal Award, 124-125
Permanente Metals Corporation, 170
Persons, Davis W., AEC engineer,
　　224
Pevely, Missouri, Dow plant, 231
Phenol, 11, 89-91, 96-97, 259
　by-products, 98-99
　production process, 97-98
Picric acid, 89, 91
Pierce, James, styrene research, 146
Pitman-Moore, 254, 271
Pitman-Moore of Canada, Limited,
　　254
Pitman-Moore S. p. A., 254
Plaquemine (see Louisiana Division)
Plastics, 7, 143-144, 193-195, 203,
　　227-228, 234, 236
Poffenberger, Noland, 130
Polk, Carl, 252
Polyethylene, 236
Polymer Corporation Limited, 188,
　　207
Polystyrene, 144, 146
Post, Charles, in formation of Dow
　　Chemical, 41-43, 46
Potassium bromide, 31, 68
Premerge, damage from, 247-248
Princeton University, protest
　　against napalm, 265
Profit-sharing plan, 53
Proximity Manufacturing Company,
　　82
Pure Oil Company, 130
Pusher polymers, 272
Putnam, Mark E., 6, 81, 96, 127,
　　216, 217, 245, 248
　atomic energy research, 222-223
　on board of directors, 201, 252
　coordination of geographical
　　divisions, 202
　death, 252
　director of Dow Chemical of
　　Canada, 189

executive vice president, 252
phenol production process, 98
research and development, 143
vice president and general manager, 215

Quayle, William O.: chloroform synthesis, 56, 57
in Midland Chemical Company, 73-74
Quinlan, Robert, 130

Reconstruction Finance Corporation, 170
Regina Sublima music box, 48
Regnault, Henri Victor, chemist, 194
Remson, Ira, quoted, 16
Research and development, 68, 72, 94-96, 140, 146-147, 259
atomic energy, 222-224, 273
chemical mining, 237-238
in Depression, 127, 135
fiftieth anniversary summary, 205
General Research Group, 202, 205
laboratories, 143, 205
lamprey eradication, 239-242
styrene, 145-146, 259
Richards, L. J., 171
Rockefeller, John D., Sr., 64, 93
Rocky Flats, Colorado, 223
Rocky Flats Division, 224
Roosevelt, Franklin Delano, President, 134-135, 170
in preparedness program, 160-161
in synthetic rubber program, 184, 185
Rotterdam, Dow subsidiary company, 243, 249
Rubber, in World War II, 172, 183-185
Rubber, synthetic: early experiments, 72
Goodyear Dow Corporation, 170
in World War II, 7, 12, 183-191
Rubber Reserve Company, 184, 185
Rusk, Dean Secretary of State, 264

Rusk, Dr. Howard A., report on Vietnam casualties, 266
Russia: atomic bomb, 222
eclipse observation, 150-151

St. Clair Processing Corporation, 188
Salicylic acid, 87
Salk polio vaccine, 254
Salt (see Sodium chloride)
Sanford, Charles, Sarnia project manager, 190
Sanford, Ross, 130
Saran, 193-195, 228, 236
Japanese sales, 221
Saran Wrap, 194, 218, 236
Sarnia, Ontario: Dow plants, 207-208
oil wells, 189
synthetic rubber plant, 186, 188-191, 206-207
Schlumberger, Limited, Dowell associated with, 250-251
Schuette, William H., 252, 253
Schwarz, Anton, Lirugen discovered, 271
Scott, Paul, 280
Sea: bromine from, 105-109, 118-119, 128-129, 137-139
fresh water conversion: Freeport plant, 256
Herbert Dow's idea, 112-113
magnesium from, 149, 154-155, 158, 164-165, 171
products from, 6, 12, 158
Separan 2610, 239
Shell Oil Company, 249
Sherbrook, Harland, 138, 161
Shigley, C. M., 162, 171, 172
Ships (see Tankers)
Shoemaker, Clayton: in export sales, 220
president of Dow Chemical International, retirement, 247
Short, Charles, 138
Sight Savers, 228
Silicones, 191, 228, 272

in airplanes, 192, 228
  lubricants, 228
  in spacecraft, 272
  surgical use, 272
  in World War II, 192-193
Silver iodide process, 132-133
Smart, John, 280
Smith, Albert W., 20, 34, 72-74, 109, 120
  chloroform synthesis, 56
  in Dow Chemical, 43, 110-111
  electrochemical manufacture, explanation of, 42
  on indigo production, 82
  mustard gas process, 91
Smith, Herman, 138
Smith, Joseph P., in Canton Chemical Company, 22
Smith, Barney & Company, 151, 224
Smithers, LeRoy D., 162
  general manager of Sarnia plant, 207
  president of Sarnia plant, 280
Sodium chloride, 76
  from brine, 20-21
  phenyl process by-product, 98
Solvay Process Company, 36
Spacecraft, silicones in, 272
Spain, Dow operations in, 249
Staley, Cady, 38, 43
Standard Oil Company, tetraethyl lead poisoning in laboratory, 108
Stanton, G. W., Zefran developed, 235
Starks, Stephen, director of training courses, 218
Staudinger, H., chemist, 194
Stein, J. R.: Louisiana operations, general manager, 232-233
  in Texas Division, 162, 171
Stock market crash, 1929, 123-124
Stockwell, John E., 17
Stoesser, Sylvia, styrene research, 146
Strike at Midland, 209-210
Strosacker, Charles, 6, 68, 73, 75, 81, 84, 85, 96, 104-105, 126, 127, 245, 260, 279, 281
  on board of directors, 124, 252
  director, Dow Chemical of Canada, 189
  phenol production process, 97
  research and development, 143, 145
  resignation, 256
  vice president, 252
Styraloy, 146
Styrene, 7, 12, 144, 170, 193, 236
  Allyn's Point plant, 225
  Canadian production, 207
  Japanese production, 221
  research on, 145-146, 259
  synthetic rubber, 184-186
Styrofoam, 195, 227, 236
  in boats, 227
Styron, 146, 193, 195, 236
  Japanese production, 221
  Sarnia plant, 207
Sulfuric acid, oil-well treatment, 130
Sullivan, Eugene C.: in Corning Glass—Dow Chemical partnership, 192
  silicone research, 191
Synthetic rubber (see Rubber, synthetic)

Taft, William Howard, President, 74
Tankers: Marine Chemist, 242
  Marine Dow-Chem, 242
Teal, Frank, barber, 42, 102
Terneuzen, Netherlands, Dow plant, 249, 274
Tesla, Nicola, 17
Tetraethyl lead: as gasoline additive, 104
  poisoning from, 108
Texas, search for sites, 154-155, 158-159
Texas Company, 119
Texas Division, 201, 233-234
  expansion, 208-209, 216-217
  glycerine plant, 237
  interdivisional relationships, 259-

260
(See also Freeport; Velasco)
Thiokol, 186, 187, 202
Thiokol Corporation, 186
3-bromo-4-nitrophenol, 240
3, 4, 6-trichloro-2-nitrophenol, 240-241
Tiffin, Edward, Surveyor General, 26
Time on Dow Chemical wartime production, 182-183
Tonow, Paul, landscape architect, 113
Torrance, California, napalm plant, 263-264
Tripp, Charles, oil well in Sarnia, 189
Truman, Harry S., President, 177, 222
Truman Committee, 177, 178, 180, 186
Tuttle, Bloodgood, architect, 113-114

Udall, Stewart L., Secretary of the Interior, 256
United Alkali, British bleach combine, 6, 40, 51
  Herbert Dow visits, 67
  price war with Dow Chemical, 54-55
University of California, Santa Barbara, protest against napalm, 265-266
Uranium mining, 238-239

Vaccines, 254, 271
Van Stirum, John, 250
VC Plastic, 194
Veazey, W. R., 6, 85, 86, 96, 111, 281
  on board of directors, 201
  research and development, 143, 205
  Texas plant development, 171
Velasco, Texas: Camp Chemical, 172, 174
  Dow plant, 171-174, 176, 208, 233

Lake Jackson, 174-175
styrene plant, 186
Thiokol plant, 187
Vietnam war, 262
  napalm, protests against, 262-271
Vinylidene chloride, 158

War Production Board, 170, 185, 186
  letter to Willard Dow, 198
Ward, Louis E., 171
  chlorine process improved, 75
Warrick, Earl L., silicone research, 191
Waste disposal, 154, 255
Water pollution, 154, 255
Weed control compound, damage from, 247-248
Wheeler, General Earle G., 268
White, Edward H., II, astronaut, 272
Whiting, Macauley, 253
  director of overseas operations, 259, 273-274
  vice president and manager of Midland Division, 252
Wiles, Charles, 166
Wilhelm II, Kaiser, 50, 88
Williams, Donald, sales director, 217, 218
Williams, James Miller, oil wells in Sarnia, 189
Williams, Jim, sales director, 252
Williamsburg, Virginia (see James River)
Wilson, Woodrow, President, 88-90
Wintergreen, oil of, 87
Wood distillation, 145
World War I, 11, 79-80, 87-89, 92
  chemical industries in, 80-81
World War II, 12, 157, 160-163, 171, 172, 196-198
  airplanes, 160-161, 163, 169, 171, 176-177, 192
  chemical industries in, 195-196
  magnesium, 6, 149, 162, 163, 169-172, 176-183
  plants in safe areas, 175-176
  silicones, 192-193

synthetic rubber, 7, 12, 183-191
U.S. preparations, 160-161
Wright, Frank Lloyd, 115, 173, 279
Wright, Orville and Wilbur, 55

Xanthates, 153, 237-238

Zefran, 235
Zimmerman, Arthur, German
　Foreign Secretary, 88
Zinc chloride, 74
Zurich, bank, 274